D0777066

Making a Friend in Youth

Robert L. Selman and Lynn Hickey Schultz

MAKING A FRIEND IN YOUTH

Developmental Theory and Pair Therapy

The University of Chicago Press
Chicago and London

Robert L. Selman is associate professor of education and psychiatry at Harvard University and director of the Manville School of the Judge Baker Children's Center in Boston. He is the author of *The Growth of Interpersonal Understanding* as well as many articles on child development.
Lynn Hickey Schultz is research fellow in psychiatry at the Massachusetts Mental Health Center of the Harvard Medical School. She is the coauthor (with E. G. Pitcher) of *Boys and Girls at Play*.

The University of Chicago Press, Chicago 60637
The University of Chicago Press, Ltd., London
© 1990 by The University of Chicago
All rights reserved. Published 1990
Printed in the United States of America

99 98 97 96 95 94 93 92 91 90   54321

Library of Congress Cataloging-in-Publication Data

Selman, Robert L.
    Making a friend in youth : developmental theory and pair therapy /
  Robert L. Selman and Lynn Hickey Schultz.
       p.   cm.
    Includes bibliographical references.
    ISBN 0-226-74790-5 (alk. paper)
    1. Pair therapy.   2. Childhood friendship.   3. Friendship in
  adolescence.   4. Child development.   I. Schultz, Lynn Hickey.
  II. Title.
    [DNLM: 1. Child Development.   2. Child Psychology.
  3. Interpersonal Relations—in infancy & childhood.
  4. Psychological Theory.   5. Psychotherapy, Group—methods.   WS
  105.5.I5 S468m]
  RJ505.P33S45 1990
  618.92'89152—dc20
  DNLM/DLC
  for Library of Congress   89-20362
                                                                  CIP

⊗ The paper used in this publication meets the minimum
requirements of the American National Standard for
Information Sciences—Permanence of Paper for Printed
Library Materials, ANSI Z39.48–1984.

Contents

DA

Preface

This book tells a story—perhaps I should say more precisely, a history—of the theoretical, clinical, and research efforts made during the 1980s by members of the Group for the Study of Interpersonal Development to construct a therapeutic approach based on developmental principles. The ideas and activities we describe in this book began about ten years ago with an attempt to help children and adolescents, isolated by their own all-too-familiar patterns of aggression or withdrawal, to understand what it means to become and be a better friend. In this preface, I would like to tell you a little about the history of the project itself, and in that way acknowledge the important contributions members of our group, as well as colleagues, have made to both its emergence and its current shape.

This book is about the child's growing capacity for making and keeping friends, the capacity within the self and in mutual collaboration with a partner as a member of a pair. What do I mean by the phrase "mutual collaboration," and how do youngsters who by their nature and experience are troubled and friendless come to act in ways that begin to approach that level of capability? What are the steps they need to take along that path? These are the themes of this work.

It is hard to pinpoint the precise moment of conception of this line of work, but the gestation period of this book has been about nine years in length. Clearly it has progenitors described in my earlier work, *The Growth of Interpersonal Understanding.* But with the completion of that earlier phase of research, the members of our group, many being both clinical practitioners and researchers, were faced with a puzzling, if not disturbing, situation. In that earlier work I had proposed a model, reviewed rather briefly in chapter 1, for describing the development of children's understanding of interpersonal relationships, such as the nature of friendship or of peer relationships. I described how the ontogenesis of these conceptions, specifically their form, could be viewed as a function of developmental changes in the capacity of individuals to coordinate social perspectives. But what might the relationship be between interpersonal understanding and interpersonal development, where the latter is more broadly construed to include both actual behavior and ongoing personal relationships? What good was a theoretical formulation of the development of the understanding of friendship if it could not contribute to the theory and practice of interpersonal development, particularly with respect to the facilitation of growth in the capacity for interpersonal relationships, for making friends, in children with problems in this area?

For almost two decades, our group, now called the Group for the Study of Interpersonal Development, has called two institutions home: the Manville School of Boston's Judge Baker Children's Center and the Laboratory of Human Development of the Harvard Graduate School of Education. It is this shared community that has enabled us to undertake this effort, and to which I refer when in this book the term "our" is used. We have been fortunate over these past years to have a setting (I do not like the term laboratory when describing practical work with children, but I suppose it is truly a living laboratory) in which to do our clinical and empirical work. The Manville School's educational and day treatment program has afforded our joint clinical-research team the opportunity to interact with children who despite generally adequate cognitive functioning have interpersonal problems of such severity that they require a special milieu for educational, emotional, and social development to take place.

The ideas which underlie the work reported in this book were born in the late 1970s, when my colleague Steven Brion-Meisels and I received support from what was then the Office of Special Education of the United States Department of Education to develop an interpersonal decision-making curriculum for early adolescents with the kinds of interpersonal difficulties endured by Manville students—severe problems getting along with peers in school and the neighborhood, with teachers at school, and with parents at home. We divided into two teams. Steven's team took on the work of curriculum development and I led a team of researchers-evaluators whose job it was to devise a way to evaluate the effectiveness of the methods designed to help these students get along with others. This was our opportunity to shift our developmental focus from interpersonal thought to interpersonal action, and we did so by focusing on the ways children negotiated conflict.

Of course, when I locate the beginning of this project at around 1979–80, I do not mean to imply the work began in a vacuum. As I noted earlier, we have been fortunate to be able to live and work in two homes—Manville School, a home of service and child psychotherapy training, and Harvard University, a home of theory and research. Drawing on some basic research begun in the latter locale several years earlier by doctoral student Carolyn Stone and me and funded by the Foundation for Child Development, then under the able leadership of President Bert Brim, we began to look at interpersonal interaction from our developmental point of view. In her doctoral dissertation, Carolyn began the "ground-breaking" work of describing what actual strategies for interpersonal negotiation might look like in children when viewed from the theoretical purview of the development of the coordination of social perspectives. But back then both the basic normative developmental descriptive work (with Carolyn) and the applied work (with Steven) focused on children in peer groups, six or seven students at once, and we found the social interaction too fast and furious for us to understand clearly the developmental aspects of the interpersonal behavior of either the individuals or the group. We decided that to understand interpersonal behavior from a developmental point of view, as well as to facilitate change in social abilities, we had to start with a more basic unit, the pair.

Thus, in the fall of 1979, Russ Lyman, then a counselor in the Manville School and now a practicing clinician, and I opened the "friendship pair therapy" clinic in our school. Joined by Amy Demorest, we began to work simultaneously on both our developmental research on interpersonal growth and on the principles and practice of pair therapy treatment with children and early adolescents. Over the past decade many people have come through that ongoing joint clinical-research program. In my mind certain people deserve special mention. Steven Shirk, Catalina Arboleda, Keith Yeates, and Debbie Russo all came through the Judge Baker Children's Center clinical child psychology internship training program. Each not only did the clinical work of the pair therapist, but also contributed to the scientific work of the clinical-developmental research. Pauly Hahn, the Manville School's director of clinical services during those years, with now forty years of service to the Judge Baker center as an individual psychotherapist, dared to be trained as a pair therapist. Through her participation our knowledge of the therapeutic process has been significantly deepened.

A major force in moving this work forward and providing the resources to pull the ideas and work of this book together began in July 1986, when I received joint support from the William T. Grant Foundation (Robert Haggerty, president) and the Spencer Foundation (Lawrence Cremin, president) to study ways to adapt pair therapy to a less clinical (therapeutic), more normative (preventive) context, the public school. Keith Yeates has been my co-investigator in that enterprise, and although the story of that project is yet to be completed or completely told, both foundations' support has helped the pair therapy project as well.

As I noted earlier, the Manville School is the place where most of the clinical work in this book has been done. Manville is not simply a laboratory for research. It is a living, breathing school, with all the feelings and stress that living social organizations embody, and maybe a little more. Day to day, David Gilmore, the principal, and Hanna Savransky, the educational coordinator, have run the school with vision, patience, and integrity. They have nurtured an institution healthy enough for research to happen, if not to flourish. Pauly Hahn and Mira Levitt, the current clinical director, have constantly watched over our students and have provided clinical insights into our work. Nancy Jacobs, who has bridged school (now as intake coordinator) and research (now as research coordinator) with me for twenty years, deserves special recognition for her many contributions. Manville's parent institution, the Judge Baker Children's Center, directed with care by Stan Walzer, and by Julius Richmond before him, has been equally supportive. Ronald Burd, now the president of the Devereux Foundation and a good friend, was also a source of support as interim director during the transition years at the center. No less important has been the commitment of the Judge Baker's Board of Trustees, who have worked mightily to help maintain resources for research on an equal footing with those for service and clinical training.

Across the river, the faculty and students in the Laboratory of Human Development at Harvard's Graduate School of Education have played equally essential roles in the progress of this work. Conversations, opportunities for shared teaching, and the deeply insightful atmosphere of inquiry at this teaching and research institution have provided a challenging and supportive context that encourages us to strive to think deeply, as well as to communicate ideas freely, clearly, and vigorously. My recent doctoral students there, including Michael Krupa, Lynn Schultz, Sigrun Adalbjarnardottir, Jeff Beedy, and Len Fleischer, have each done empirical work critical to the ideas expressed in this book.

Colleagues elsewhere, for example, Bill Beardslee at Boston's Children's Hospital Department of Psychiatry, Jim Youniss at Catholic University, Ned Mueller at Boston University, Elice Forman at Northwestern, and Bill Damon at Brown University, have all done work, talked with me, or provided critiques in ways that have influenced the course and flow of this book.

I am profoundly and deeply saddened that this book will never be read or reacted to by my mentor, longtime friend, and colleague, Lawrence Kohlberg, who was a professor at Harvard from 1968 until his tragic death in 1987. I would have liked Larry to have seen his lasting influence on this work as well as to have the work benefit from his insight.

Many of the chapters in this book have involved the participation of the Group for the Study of Interpersonal Development at one or another level, and I would like to use this opportunity to acknowledge their contributions specifically. Chapter 1 serves to set the historical stage for this work. It reviews our earlier work on interpersonal understanding and frames the way we look at the relation between interpersonal thought and action.

Chapter 2 was initially drafted with the assistance of Amy Demorest some five or six years ago. It describes the general features of our developmental model describing strategies for interpersonal negotiation as well as an early method we used for the observation and "diagnosis" of various strategies. The current version draws heavily on an article written by Lynn Schultz and me, "Children's strategies for interpersonal negotiation with peers: An interpretive/empirical approach to the study of social development," which appeared in a volume edited by Thomas J. Berndt and Gary W. Ladd, *Peer Relationships in Child Development* (New York: John Wiley & Son, 1989).

Chapter 3 details the specific features of this model, with examples drawn from everyday life. Amy Demorest and I originally culled the vignettes reported in this chapter from observations made by early project members, and wrote about some of them in a chapter called "Putting thoughts and feelings into perspective: A developmental view on how children deal with interpersonal disequilibrium." That chapter appeared in a book edited by David Bearison and Herb Zimilies, *Thinking and Emotions: Developmental Perspectives* (Hillsdale, N.J.: Lawrence Erlbaum, 1985). Chapter 4 draws upon some recent work done in collaboration with Catalina Arboleda and Keith Yeates on the observation of clinical pairs and with Michelle Glidden, who, working on our current project, reviewed our videotapes of public school children's dyadic interaction in a search for instances of shared experience between them.

Chapters 5–7 reflect the current state of the art of pair therapy practice and technique. It is difficult to specify with great accuracy the many contributions to these ideas over the years of every trainee who was supervised or every staff member who tried out this approach. Certainly Russ Lyman and Steven Shirk in the early years of the project did much to shape the basic nature of the treatment. And even as I write, new ideas about treatment are emerging from the work of current pair therapists in training.

I can be more specific about the contributions of members of our group in chapters 8–10. Chapter 8 owes much on the clinical side to Pauly Hahn and on the research side to Catalina Arboleda, who co-authored with me a preliminary version of the research reported there published in the 1985 volume of the *McClean Hospital Journal*, "Pair therapy with troubled early adolescents: Implications for practice and research." Chapter 9 is based on an integration of two recent papers, each of which discusses a different aspect of the same case. The first, "Fostering intimacy and autonomy," I wrote for the tenth anniversary issue of a series edited by William Damon, *New Directions in Child Development: Today and Tomorrow* (San Francisco: Jossey-Bass, 1989). The other first appeared as "The development of close relationships," in *Entering the Circle: Hermeneutic Investigation in Psychology* (Albany, N.Y.: SUNY Press, 1989) edited by Martin Packer and Richard Addison, and was co-authored by Lynn Schultz, Brina Caplin, Katherine Schantz, and myself. As doctoral students at the Harvard Graduate School of Education and as psychology trainees at the Manville School, Brina and Kathy demonstrated the value of an integration of clinical and research training.

Chapter 10 is also built upon a foundation of earlier research, an analysis undertaken by Keith Yeates and me and initially written about in a chapter entitled "The social regulation of intimacy and autonomy in early adolescence." This chapter appeared in a book edited by William Kurtines and Jack Gewirtz called *Moral Development through Social Interaction* (New York: John Wiley & Son, 1987).

The last section of the book returns to our initial theoretical question: that of the relation of interpersonal thought to action. But we now address this problem at a different, and hopefully deeper, level of understanding. Chapter 11 deals with the basic question of why it is so difficult to put our best interpersonal understanding of ourselves, others, and our relationships into practice. If we know what makes a good friend, why can't we be a good friend? Mira Levitt, an important colleague and good friend, played a significant part in shaping the ideas presented in our response. The ideas of this chapter, particularly our perspective on the connection between object relations theory and the gap between thought and action, were elaborated by empirical and theoretical work undertaken by Lynn Schultz.

And chapter 12 brings this volume of our story to a close, or more precisely, our history up to the present. It articulates some ideas our research has led us to propose for future study, ideas about what we believe our research suggests are the basic mechanisms of psychosocial development. It addresses directly why we think that the forms of change that we try to obtain and which we advocate are ethically compelling as well as scientifically valid.

As the senior author of this book and director and principal investigator of the ten-year project it describes, I would like to say a few words about Lynn Schultz's contribution. Although Lynn's participation did not begin until halfway through this project, our interactions over the last several years, in her transition from student to colleague, including both the contribution of new ideas into the ongoing analysis as well as shared writing of all the chapters in the final draft, dictate that she share authorship with me. With her significant and deeply substantive contribution to every chapter, this book is a much more worthy piece.

Critically important to the success of the project and this book have been the support and collaboration of the members of my family. My parents show a continuing interest in my work and my sons, Matthew and Jesse, are a continuing source of energy and inspiration. In fact some of the ideas and research described in chapter 9 came from long hours playing the computer game Wizardry with them. Indeed, if you ask him, Matt Selman will tell you that much of the theory of this book derives from a conversation we had during a car ride one winter night in 1981, when at the age of nine he articulated four types (levels, if you will permit me) of strategies to deal with a close friend who had not yet returned a borrowed book to him.

Finally, there is the intense and most meaningful collaboration of my wife, Anne. A talented and busy professional in her own right, she overhauled and edited the earliest most difficult drafts of this book, a labor of great love and skill without which I am quite sure this book would never have been completed. But even more, she has given me unstinting support and unwavering en-

PART ONE

The Development of Intimacy and Autonomy

CHAPTER ONE

From Interpersonal Thought to Action: A Developmental View

Arnie, thirteen, claims to need no friends. At school, he often sits in a corner by himself during classes; at lunch, he usually chooses to eat alone; and as he walks down corridors, his eyes are cast down, his vision turned inward. His "interpersonal" life is filled not with friends but with fictional characters from the science fiction and horror comics and books he carries everywhere. Half kidding and half serious, he is preoccupied with his need to be able to "stand alone," to protect himself from these characters, and he is obsessed with his own extreme and primitive sense of autonomy ("I don't need to rely on nobody"). But this espoused autonomy is often belied by his intense and sudden anger when a peer he likes joking with is a few minutes late for a meeting or when a teacher he depends on does not give him the attention he demands. Often Arnie appears sad and lonely, his affect and action constricted and depressed.

Arnie's schoolmate Mitchell is also thirteen and friendless but not for lack of effort. Mitchell would desperately like to have a friend but has never seemed to have learned how to go about making or keeping one. Mitchell literally throws himself on his classmates, trying (too hard) to be included in their interactions, but seldom if ever succeeding. Part of the problem is that the strategies he uses to try to make friends are more like those of someone half his age. He giggles uncontrollably, does not focus his attention on the social scene, and often misreads the subtleties and nuances of his peer's intentions, actions, and feelings. He tattles one day and expects the victim to be his friend the next. When even slightly rebuffed, he reacts with epithets and curses, only to expect forgetfulness if not forgiveness. Desperate for an early adolescent form of intimacy, Mitchell, like Arnie, is confused and lonely.

This book offers a way to look at, understand, and facilitate growth in children's interpersonal relationships. It tells two sto-

3

ries, one about normal interpersonal development, particularly development toward the capacity for mutual collaboration as achieved through processes of intimacy and autonomy. But more directly and specifically, it describes interpersonal development in pair therapy, a context in which socially inept children can move along the road toward, if not ultimately achieve, the capacity to use mutual collaborative methods when dealing with others in close dyadic relationships.

Mitchell and Arnie are in pair therapy together. Pair therapy is a program of clinical intervention and developmental research and assessment for children with emotional and interpersonal difficulties. Its aim is to help troubled children like Arnie and Mitchell, who have poor or virtually no peer relationships, develop the capacity to establish and maintain close friendships. Since the pair therapy project began more than ten years ago at the Manville School of the Judge Baker Children's Center in Boston, approximately fifty pairs of preadolescents and early adolescents have participated in the treatment.

The term "pair therapy" may be somewhat misleading because a triad is involved in the treatment. Two children and a pair therapist meet regularly together, typically once a week for about an hour. The adult therapist plays a crucial role, facilitating and mediating the pair's social interactions and providing the two with a "third-person" perspective on their interactions and relationship.

Pair therapists foster psychosocial and personality development by encouraging the pair to do things together and then to reflect on the degree of success and level of maturity of "how we did." In promoting the pair's mutually rewarding social interactions as well as each individual's insight about the role of the self and the other in the interaction, the treatment provides what the influential psychiatrist and interpersonal theorist, Harry Stack Sullivan (1953), described as an opportunity for "consensual validation," a process of social communication that serves to restructure the children's immature interpersonal functioning. The therapist uses the actual social relationship between the pair to facilitate their psychosocial and emotional growth by helping them develop more mature ways of sharing experience and negotiating the inevitable conflicts that arise as they choose and implement activities during sessions, thus providing the children with a corrective interpersonal experience.

But pair therapy is more than simply a program of clinical intervention—it is also a research project designed to study developmental processes. The therapy is used as a vehicle to characterize the developmental and dynamic qualities of close friendships, which is the general goal of our developmental research. More specifically our goal is to study the therapeutic process of pair therapy. We examine the ongoing social interaction between the three participants, the therapist and the pair, to elucidate development in the construction of the relationship between the two children. Clinical, research, and the theoretical perspectives mutually enhance each other in this work. The clinical practice provides social interaction data in a context designed to facilitate a natural process of change, thus enabling the research activity to address basic questions of social and personality development. In turn, developmental theory honed in the research provides a road map of what constitutes progress (or regress) in the form and function of peer relationships as they develop during pair therapy.

We need to say something at the outset about the formal evaluation, or lack thereof, of our pair therapy approach. It is to a degree frustrating to be unable to report a wealth of "hard data" on the effectiveness of a program of treatment on which we have worked for a decade. However, the cold truth is we cannot, and there are two basic reasons for this. One is largely a function of the context in which we have done our work, and the other is a function of the priorities we have consciously set within the work itself. To work in a comprehensive educational and therapeutic environment, like Manville, does not easily allow for implementation of experimental designs used in the rigorous and controlled comparisons of treatments. Although throughout our efforts we have continuously asked for informational feedback, written reports on our cases, presented them at progress conferences, and informally followed the pairs, we have done only one pilot evaluation study. It did demonstrate some behavioral and cognitive change in a group of pairs across one year of pair therapy (Lyman and Selman, 1985), yet even that must be considered inconclusive. But equally constraining as the context is our own feeling that the project has been an evolving one, and that we must first direct our energies toward understanding the nature of developmental change before attempting to measure or evaluate it.

Although the children with whom we work have emotional and interpersonal difficulties severe enough to qualify for a host of traditional psychiatric diagnoses, our orientation does not rely primarily on conventional diagnostic categories or look specifically for syndromes, even though they may receive this kind of assessment in the course of other aspects of their program at the school. The theoretical underpinnings of the therapeutic perspectives and techniques of pair therapy assessment and intervention are essentially *developmental* in nature. We describe communicative and psychosocial functioning (and malfunctioning) in developmental terms. But what *kinds* of development does pair therapy try to foster? What, specifically, are our developmental terms?

The Development of Interpersonal Understanding

The developmental theory underlying our research and therapeutic work began with a focus on social cognition and its development in the context of close and meaningful relationships, from early childhood through adolescence. The central unifying thread, or spine, as it were, of social-cognitive development, as we have conceptualized it, is the developing ability to differentiate and coordinate the social perspectives of self and others, both cognitively and emotionally. We call this ability "social perspective coordination" and define it as the child's capacity to differentiate and integrate the self's and other's points of view through an understanding of the relation between the thoughts, feelings, and wishes of each person (Selman, 1980).

Both the clinical assessment and intervention techniques of pair therapy are based to a large degree upon the core social-cognitive ability to coordinate social perspectives. Although our present research has shifted from an earlier focus on interpersonal thought to the study of interpersonal action, we nevertheless still rely on the levels of social perspective coordination to assess children's developmental status. When we look at their behaviors, decisions, or speech acts, we attend to how they understand the nature of the self and of relations between the self and others, both in general and in more specific, of-the-moment interactions. We particularly emphasize how these general and more context-specific understandings change with increasing interpersonal maturity. Other approaches to developing social relations, such as cognitive-behavioral (e.g., Dodge, 1980) or psychodynamic perspectives (e.g., Blatt, 1974; Vaillant, 1977), have increasingly informed our ideas about threats to healthy interpersonal development. However, we believe that the social-cognitive component of social development is a uniquely powerful organizing and explanatory force for describing, diagnosing, and treating ills or missteps in children's social and emotional growth.

Developmental levels in the coordination of social perspectives and their application to how children come to achieve their interpersonal understanding were formulated, described, and documented in our earlier research, summarized in *The Growth of Interpersonal Understanding* (Selman, 1980). This book traced the intellectual history and theoretical antecedents of our developmental model, from the social philosophies of James Mark Baldwin (1902) and George Herbert Mead (1934), through the developmental psychology approaches of Jean Piaget (1965) and Heinz Werner (1948) to more recent social psychological applications of Lawrence Kohlberg (1969) and his associates.

The social-cognitive levels of social perspective coordination integrate Mead's (1934) view that role-taking is a fundamental process in the socialization of the self with the Piagetian structural-developmental tradition's focus on the organization and emergence of forms of knowing. Framed in the structural-developmental tradition of Piaget and Kohlberg, each new level of social perspective coordination is viewed as a fundamental reconceptualization of what the growing individual understands to be the core psychological and social qualities of persons and relationships. These levels are a way to characterize how the growing child makes sense of his or her observations and experiences of interacting with others. There is a "logic" to each of these levels and their sequence. The order of their emergence seems—empirically as well as theoretically—to be the path all children take. However we cannot be certain that everyone attains the higher levels, nor do we believe that everyone progresses through the sequence at the same pace.

A key early step along this logical path of social development comes when children begin to discover (or make) the distinction between intentional and unintentional acts. This form of understanding precedes their ability to understand that people have the capacity for entertaining multiple intentions simultaneously. In further steps, children must make the discovery that the self and others can have different feelings about some jointly perceived event before they can understand that two persons (self and other) can simultaneously be thinking about their own and the other's differing perspectives about a situation or each other. That is, one must be able to differentiate perspectives before one can integrate them. These kinds of continuing "marvelous discoveries" or intellectual breakthroughs on the part of the child cannot be "taught" in a conventional sense, by simply being "told to them." These steps of progressive sequential discovery toward the mature coordination of social perspectives are naturally generated differentiations and integrations based upon the *meaning* children make of their own personal experiences and social interactions.

Although the social perspective coordination levels are viewed as real phenomena (as ways of social thinking) rather than hypothetical constructs, they are only "real" when they operate upon specific social content (e.g., interpersonal understanding of behavior) in a specific social context (e.g., in hypothetical reflection or real-life actions). Thus, the levels of social perspective coordination provide a "deep structure" with which to evaluate various contents of thought and action, such as conceptions of friendship or ways of relating, but cannot be "seen" apart from the specific content (Selman, 1976).

In the earlier (1980) volume that serves as a foundation for this one, it was proposed that the nature of children's developing interpersonal conceptions, specifically of friendships with peers and relationships with parents, could be more deeply understood and made more meaningful if viewed through the lens of their developing capacity to coordinate social perspectives. Most relevant to our research on pair therapy is the interpersonal understanding domain of friendship. It seems important to understand what children like Mitchell and Arnie look for in friendship and why friends are important to them before we can begin to help them most effectively.

Arnie and Mitchell had no friends, yet they did have ideas about friendship as well as experience interacting with peers. If you were to ask Mitchell what makes a good friend, he would reply seriously, "You have to do things for the other person if you want him to like you, do what he wants if you want him to be a good friend." In contrast, Arnie would say in a "ha ha" tone, "*You* might think a good friend is somebody you understand and trust, but really the best friend does your every bidding, he would do everything for you like a robot, even destroy the world if you asked." Both Arnie's and Mitchell's espoused conceptions of friendship are one-way, focused on only one person at a time and on only that person's subjective perspective in the social relationship, a level, as we shall see, well below the norm for early adolescents.

However, there are several differences in these two conceptions. Most obvious, the boys have opposite orientations to the self and other, Arnie's being a one-sided "you give, I take; you do what *I* want" attitude, and Mitchell's an equally lopsided "I give, you take; I do what *you* want" orientation. Moreover, despite Arnie's unilateral stance, his sarcastic tone and opening clause ("*You* might think a good friend is somebody you understand and trust") suggest that on some level he "knows" that friendship can be more than one-way assistance even if he does not "feel" safe or confident enough to functionally apply his more sophisticated sense of reciprocity, even in the calmness of a reflective interview. Both boys are indeed friendless and express a relatively low "working" developmental understanding of friendship, but whereas Mitchell is confused and naive, Arnie is cynical and defensive.

In our earlier work on the development of interpersonal understanding, we found that although almost all the children referred to the clinic school that Arnie and Mitchell attend had problems making or keeping friends, some children in the school had levels of interpersonal understanding comparable to (or even above) their "better adjusted" peers on a reflective interview probing different domains of interpersonal relations (Selman, 1980). And although on average these children's conceptions lagged behind those of better adjusted children, often by the time they reached adolescence, they "caught up," at least in their conceptions, if not their behavior (Gurucharri, Phelps, and Selman, 1984). Although this may have been a function of the special therapeutic treatment they received, it may also have been related to other complex aspects of the relation between interpersonal thought and action that provide a focus for this book.

Furthermore, many of the other clinical cases, like Arnie, had lower levels of interpersonal understanding *on average* but were comparable to matched public school peers on the level of their highest expressed thoughts. This suggests that even in a reflective interview, troubled children are particularly vulnerable to regression and function inconsistently, with their higher capabilities accompanied by lower level and more profound oscillations.

But before we can understand the relationship between the level of perspective coordination in the understanding of friendship and the unbefriending behavior of isolated and troubled children like Arnie and Mitchell, we must first ask what friendship means for normally developing children. What are the functions of friends, the forms in which friendships are established, and the challenges to their continuity for all children as they get older?

Levels of Friendship Understanding and Perspective Coordination

Both a typical four-year-old and a typical fifteen-year-old, when asked what makes two people good friends, are each as likely as the other to respond spontaneously, "If they are close to each other." These words ("being close") can look and sound the same and still mean different things—that is, have different "conceptual structures" and meaning. A critical feature of the reflective interview methodology of our earlier developmental research is an essential probing beneath the surface responses children give to questions about their espoused friendship beliefs to more fully understand their meaning, a meaning that is strongly, although of course not completely, influenced by developmental factors.

When further questioned, the fifteen-year-old would most likely respond "Being close means have a friend who shares the same values as you, and you can share with them things you wouldn't share with anyone else, personal things." In contrast, the five-year-old would probably respond, "Someone who lives close to you." To the typical adolescent, closeness in friendship suggests a sense of psychological mutuality, to the young child, physical proximity. This does not mean that only the older child is necessarily capable of intimate or close friendships and the younger is not, but only that the less mature and less experienced child construes the experience of closeness and intimacy in friendship differently than the more "grown up" one does.

Thus, the assumption of our research and clinical assessment is that the "deep structure" of the levels of perspective coordination can be used to analyze more fully the developmental aspects of the meaning children make of the core issues that define their social relationships. With respect to friendship, we have explored children's understanding of issues of trust and reciprocity, closeness, jealousy, conflict and its resolution, and formation and dissolution of the friendship. The developmental changes in the meaning of these issues will become clearer as we describe the analysis of friendship conceptions through the sequence of perspective coordination levels.

The levels begin at "0" and end at "4," a classification system meant to suggest four qualitative shifts in interpersonal understanding across the age range from preschool to adolescence. But as Jane Loevinger (1976) has pointed out in her comprehensive book, *Ego Development*, in any developmental system of analysis, the initial (first) level and the final (last) level are most difficult to capture in a definitive or denotative way, for each faces an undescribed border. Certainly that is the case here. We hope the reader will not interpret our Level 0 to mean that we believe that nothing comes before this level of interpersonal development. Indeed theoretical observers and empirical researchers such as Stern (1985), Trevarthan (1980), Mueller and Lucas (1975), to name a few, have clearly articulated the progress made by infants and toddlers in interpersonal development not only with caregivers, but also with peers. And Flavell's recent work with his colleagues (e.g., 1981) has carefully articulated the positive aspects of perspective taking that is within the competency of children much younger than we interview and observe. Our Level 0 then is meant to describe the transition process through which the young child progresses beyond a "sense of self and other" (Stern, 1985) to a capacity for *self-reflective* awareness of self and other.

The following descriptions of levels in friendship understanding also provide an opportunity to describe the core social perspective coordination levels upon which our current developmental model of interpersonal thought and action is based.

Level 0—Egocentric Understanding of Friendship. In the younger child's Level 0 thinking, friendly actions are often equated with (not clearly differentiated from) either physical characteristics or capabilities rather than psychological intentions. One four-year-old told us he trusted his friend because "if I give him my toy, he won't break it." When questioned further, instead of focusing on his friend's sense of responsibility, he noted, "He isn't strong enough." Considerations of jealousy and exclusion at this level also emphasize physical aspects. One four-year-old assured us, "The new girl can't join in the play because the two old friends are already playing and there is no more room." As adults, we might interpret the child to be saying, "I don't want the new girl to intrude," and indeed, this may be the feeling being expressed, but we think that in the young child's mind psychological intrusion is in some way confused or conflated with physical overproximity.

Level 0 Social Perspective Coordination. Behind these egocentric understandings of friendship is the least differentiated level (0) of social perspective coordination. Young children (roughly about ages three to six) cannot clearly differentiate physical and psychological characteristics of persons. Although they are becoming aware that both feelings and thoughts can be observed and recognized as experiences of the self, they often still confuse what is subjective/psychological with what is objective/physical. This leads them to tend to confuse the relation between observable actions and internal feelings and the distinction between intentional and unintentional behavior. To the extent that they are beginning to clearly differentiate between self and others, it is largely in terms of physical, objective entities, not as psychological, subjective agents. There is little clear-cut recognition that the self and another may interpret a jointly observed social situation differently. Concomitantly, more often than not, there is an automatic reduction of differences in the perspectives of self and other to differences in mere perception.

Level 1—Unilateral Understanding of Friendship. Using one-way social perspective coordination to conceptualize friendship, children begin to realize that feelings and intentions—not just actions—keep friends together or divide them. But what limits thinking at this level is the unilateral concern with the subjective experience of only one party to the relationship. As one seven-year old reported, "You trust a friend if he does [an action] what you want [a feeling or intention]." At this level, children still tend to construe that a friend who is not invited to a party would be unhappy basically because of being denied what he or she wanted to do (to go), not because of being upset at being rejected by another person, an idea that requires taking a "second person" perspective. Although "rejected" may indeed be how the friend actually feels, if he or she cannot easily conceptualize the perspective of the significant other making a choice between the self and someone else—a reciprocal or "Level 2" coordination—then he or she cannot readily put thoughts and feelings together in a way that enables an understanding of feelings of being rejected in the way more mature thinkers do. Thus, the response is not necessarily defensive, as it might be if espoused by an older individual who "knows better."

Level 1 Social Perspective Coordination. At Level 1 (usually emerging and consolidating between about five to nine years of age), the key conceptual advance in social perspective coordination is the clearer differentiation in the child's mind between physical actions (behaviors) and psychological characteristics (thoughts, feelings, and intentions) of others. As a result, intentional and unintentional actions are differentiated and a new form or level of understanding is generated—that each person has a unique, subjective, covert psychological life. However, at this level the subjective states of others are still thought to be legible by the simple perceptual reading of their surface actions ("if he smiles, he must be happy"). This unilateral way of thinking lacks a sense of "reciprocal perspectives."

Level 2—Reciprocal Understanding of Friendship. By using reciprocal social perspective coordination, conceptions of trust, jealousy, and rejection in a friendship can encompass an understanding of the feelings and intentions of both parties. "Trusting a friend," one nine-year-old observed, "means if you want to do things for him, he will want to do things for you." Similarly, youngsters who reason at Level 2 are coming to understand painful issues such as jealousy between friends to mean the excluded child has feelings of being intentionally left out by the other.

Level 2 Social Perspective Coordination. The key conceptual advance in perspective coordination at Level 2 (usually constructed between ages seven and twelve) is the growing child's ability to mentally step outside himself or herself to take a self-reflective or "second-person" perspective on his or her own thoughts and actions. When children attain this ability they also realize that others can do so as well. People's thought and feeling states are seen as potentially multiple. For example, it becomes understood that one can be both curious and frightened about some event. (However, these subjective reactions are often still usually seen as quasi-physical groupings of mutually isolated and sequential or weighted aspects, for example, first curious, and then a little bit scared.) Both the self and others are thereby understood to be capable of taking (choosing) actions they may not even want (intend) to do. Persons are understood to have a dual, layered social orientation: there is one's visible appearance and then there is the "truer," below the surface, hidden reality that only the self can know.

A new form of understanding of social reciprocity is the hallmark of Level 2 perspective coordination. It is an understanding not just of the reciprocity of actions, but the reciprocity of thoughts, feelings, and intentions between persons. The (usually by now preadolescent) child can more readily put himself or herself in another's shoes and realize the other will be able to do the same. At level 2 the child also recognizes how the duality of outer appearance and inner reality implies that people can purposefully deceive others about their inner states when interacting socially. This is understood to place limits on the accurate reading of another's inner perspective.

Level 3—Mutual Understanding of Friendship. At Level 3, mutual commitment within a relationship, rather than simple two-way reciprocity or détente between parties, is the major organizing principle around which children think about issues in friendship. At this collaborative level individuals feel that both trust and jealousy are related to the bond of commitment between friends, often seen as an exclusive bond that takes time to forge and does not easily allow for intrusion by others. As we will see, the emergence of this level of understanding roughly corresponds to that period of preadolescence or early adolescence when young persons often form powerful attachments with one particular friend (chumships, in the words of Harry Stack Sullivan). A twelve-year-old noted, "Trust is everything in friendship. You tell each other things that you don't tell anyone else, how you really feel about personal things. It takes a long time to make a close friend, so you really feel bad if you find out that he is trying to make other close friends behind your back."

Level 3 Social Perspective Coordination. By early adolescence (the beginning conceptions may emerge as early as age eight to ten but are usually more completely formulated no earlier than age fifteen), the critical conceptual advance is toward an ability to take a truly "third-person" perspective, to step outside not only one's own immediate perspective, but outside both the self and other's perspectives, viewing them as a system, a totality. The result is that children can now see themselves as both actors and objects, simultaneously acting and reflecting upon the effects of actions taken on themselves.

The third-person perspective of Level 3 permits more than simply taking of another's perspective on the self. At Level 2, the logic of reciprocal perspectives—the chaining back and forth of perspectives—becomes apparent to the child, but not necessarily its full implications. At level 3, the limitations, and ultimate futility, of attempts to understand interactions on the basis of the simple reciprocity model alone are now recognized. The third-person perspective of this level allows the adolescent to step outside an interpersonal interaction or relationship abstractly and to mutually coordinate and consider the perspectives and interactions of self and other(s). When individuals use this level of understanding they can begin to see the logic of coordination of reciprocal perspectives and hence establish a basis for the belief that satisfaction, security, understanding, and resolution must be mutual and coordinated to be genuine and effective. Interpersonal relationships are viewed as ongoing systems in which the self and others' thoughts and experiences are mutually shared.

Level 4—Interdependent Understanding of Friendship. Many adolescents will pass through a period of conceiving of friendship as intense exclusivity (at Level 3), then move to a new level of understanding of how friends could be mutually close and intimate yet still grant each other a certain degree of autonomy and independence (Level 4). "If you are really close friends and trust each other, you can't hold on to everything. You gotta let go of each other once in a while," advised one astute seventeen-year-old subject in our earlier studies. "Give each other a chance to breathe."

Level 4 Social Perspective Coordination. Two new notions are characteristic of Level 4 social perspective coordination. First, there emerges an understanding that to the extent that actions,

thoughts, motives, or feelings are psychologically determined, they need not necessarily be self-reflectively perceived. It is now better understood that there are complicated and dynamic interactions within and between persons that cannot always or easily be comprehended introspectively by the "observing ego" (a "Level 3" capacity). Thus, individuals achieving this level generate a conception or notion of the unconscious in individuals, whether or not it is so named. Persons are thereby seen to be capable of doing things not that they "don't want" to do, as at Level 2, but that they "don't completely understand why they do or don't want" to do.

Second, the individual now conceptualizes subjective perspectives of persons toward each other (mutuality) as existing not only on the plane of common and overt expectations or awareness, but also simultaneously at deeper, more symbolic levels of communication. For example, there is an understanding that in long-standing and committed relationships, interpersonal interactions take on an interpretive meaning, particularly in relation to the history of the relationship, even if these meanings are not apparent to the actors, let alone to observers of the immediate interaction who do not have historical perspective on the relationship. A kind of quick glance or a single word can have a deeply shared meaning that "goes without saying," or beyond the information given.

Because the work reported in this book focuses on the psychosocial development and treatment of children and early adolescents, it makes much use of the concept of the "third-person perspective." This capacity, which normatively emerges by the end of this age period, provides a kind of developmental target or goal, a point on a metaphorical map of social development toward which we aim. Yet we certainly do not wish to imply that treatment is incomplete and should continue until this capacity is formed and used productively. As you will see in our clinical case material, much work and effort is necessary to foster movement from any level to the next, particularly when fighting the defensive forces of psychopathology. Any movement, whether from levels 0 to 1, levels 1 to 2, or levels 2 to 3, is a valued and long-term therapeutic goal.

On the other hand we do not wish to imply that there is no further interpersonal (social-cognitive) development beyond Level 3. On rare occasions we sometimes do see further progress during adolescence, both in social-cognitive and interpersonal development, even in troubled children. Although this further development of social cognition will not be a primary focus in the remaining chapters of this book, we have described friendship understanding and perspective coordination at Level 4 because we believe that it is nevertheless valuable for you to understand how we believe social perspectives are coordinated in older adolescents and adults.

We hope that this set of descriptions suggests the way children's developing interpersonal understanding is hierarchically organized, forming an increasingly comprehensive set of insights. As children gain higher levels of interpersonal understanding, they do not simply discard lower levels, they transform them. A child newly capable of understanding that jealousy in a close friendship can occur because of feeling rejected by another person does not forget that one may be covetous of a friend's physical capabilities or material possessions. However, children who have attained this higher level of understanding will likely find physical, material envy to be more peripheral or secondary, and even if they have these feelings, they will be more able to put them in perspective. In fact it is a natural part of development to differentiate *envy*, feelings regarding others' possessions, from *jealousy*, feelings regarding others' feelings of affection.

Conversely, the developmental differentiation of envy and jealousy does not imply that children with lower-level (less differentiated) understanding will not actually feel jealous if a valued playmate rejects them for another. It does suggest, though, that the younger or less mature child does not naturally differentiate a psychological experience of personal rejection from its physical or material terms, which he or she can comprehend and articulate much more readily. Ultimately, it is not that feelings are constant and conceptual sophistication changes our understanding of them, but that with development there is a continuing differentiation and integration of both thought and emotion.

From Interpersonal Understanding to Interpersonal Action

The use of levels of social perspective coordination can be a powerful tool with which to analyze how the developing child understands and gives meaning to interpersonal relationships. As such, it also serves as a guide to development more broadly defined. But the work of treating children like Arnie and Mitchell who are friendless by dint of their own immaturity or the lack of proper social supports can not just rest on the plane of their level of interpersonal knowledge alone, it must move to the plane of their interactive social behavior and actual interpersonal relationships.

Movement toward higher levels of social perspective coordination in the ability to understand friendships in less egocentric and unilateral ways is an important and necessary condition for children's interpersonal growth, but it is not a sufficient one. In order to help children develop socially we must facilitate processes that also allow them to act in a friendly manner (behavioral development) and consistently be a good friend (personality development).

Although we attempted to tie each level in the coordination of social perspectives to the concrete example of friendship understanding in the previous section, the descriptions of the levels were still quite formal and abstract. Quite reasonably, you might ask how they are operationalized in everyday thinking, feeling, and acting. As presented above, each developmental level in the coordination of social perspectives is a basic form of social understanding that has implications for the way many different kinds of social processes and functions are organized. But, in addition to conceptualizing each level in the above way (ontogenetically as a new capability), we can also think of each level as a theoretical tool for observers to use as a way to analyze and give a deeper meaning to other, closely related aspects of social thought *and* behavior.

An example drawn from a commonplace family interaction is perhaps the best way to introduce what we mean by how the capacity to coordinate social perspectives is applied in *action* (as opposed to reflective understanding). This material will provide a frame of reference for a more formal description of the levels of action through which we believe children and adolescents progress, presented in following chapters.

Three out of five members of a family are sitting in the living room watching television: the mother, the father, and their seven-year-old son. The son's younger sister, who is three, walks in, goes directly to the TV set, and, without speaking to or looking at anyone, switches the channel to her favorite show. Neither parent seems visibly upset. The father merely gets up, changes the channel back, and explains calmly but firmly to the daughter that she must consider the others who are watching (one of many times this socialization process will occur). Although the daughter may react with some distress, the parents remain fairly imperturbable. Interestingly, her brother's reaction is not so benign. Visibly upset, he yells in a loud and angry voice, "Turn that back!" He seems to see his sister's actions as far from cute or inevitable, but as annoying and unfair, and maybe even aimed at him.

Now consider another version of the same family scene, this time with a slight change in the cast. The same trio is again watching television. This time, it is the thirteen-year-old older brother who walks in and does what appears to be exactly what we described his little sister doing. His parents' reactions are different, more powerful, and more equivocal. Now it is the father who gets angry, appearing to find the behavior rude, inappropriate, and thoughtless. The mother, on the other hand, seems to feel (in this case, more accurately) that her son's intent was less hostile and more complex, that he was aware of the rudeness and was only trying to get a rise out of his family members before returning to the original channel. Again, the seven-year-old reacts differently from his parents. In fact, he seems less perturbed, and certainly less agitated than when his sister did "the same thing," reacting with limited annoyance, clear acceptance, and even something close to amusement or enthusiasm.

Most of us will quickly identify all kinds of social-emotional-family dynamics content in these interactions. Maybe the little sister is spoiled, and the parents are fondest of her, as their last child, and have special rules for her. Maybe the middle brother is suffering raging sibling rivalry, dating from her birth and subsequent feelings of being displaced. The young teenager is perhaps going through a period of mild rebellion and provocative testing of his autonomy, which succeeds in, among other things, dividing his parents, eliciting indulgent and protective responses from his mother and confrontative, even competitive, responses from his father. And we can imagine that the middle son might well be coping with (or defending against) rivalrous feelings towards his older brother by identifying with him and idolizing him.

All these explanations notwithstanding, there is a fundamental process to all this that is very much a matter of common sense and common knowledge, though rarely reflected upon in our experience. This more fundamental process—social perspective coordination—underlies in varying degrees each family member's behavior. As commonplace as these interactions might be, and as little as they surprise us when we witness them, on a careful second glance they are profoundly revealing. We tend to take little note, unless our consciousness is raised, of how differently all three members of the original viewing trio respond to the same surface action on the part of the youngest and oldest siblings. Yet when a small child does something that we would normally characterize as at best "thoughtless," adults tend to tolerate if not ignore it. "She's only three," we say. "She doesn't understand." The common sense of development in social cognition (here, social perspective coordination) is part of the fabric of what we all know. "She is too young [a developmental assessment] to under-stand [of cognitive ability] how she is affecting other people [which is social in nature]." This is an unreflected-upon part of common cultural knowledge. Rare, and frowned upon, would be the adult who becomes over severe or outraged with this child, as abusive parents sometimes do. We will assert repeatedly in this work that disturbances in the acquisition and application of this social knowledge have profound effects on social development.

Our example illuminates social development even further when we examine the actors' reactions one by one. The little sister may not clearly think about or even really reflectively know, much less acknowledge to herself, that other people have different perspec-tives and needs in a complex social interaction like this one. This is true on a perceptual level (we are all familiar with the three-year-old speaking on the phone who points out something in the room to her listener) as well as a psychological one. If the seven-year-old had done what his siblings had done, we would be likely to attribute it to defiance or willful ignoring of others for some reason, because we assume that at his age, he knows better. We recognize that he has achieved at least some more differentiated understanding that per-spectives can differ. When the older teenage brother does it, we not only assume that he knows better, but that in fact it is likely that he is playing some much more complicated "perspective game," based on our belief that he is capable of doing a great deal of internal rep-resentation—and manipulation—of the possible reactions among various separate selves ("If I barge in and turn the station, they will know that I am acting impulsively 'just' to get them aggravated"). None of this is news. As normally functioning adults, we have a pretty clear intuitive, working, experiential sense of what kind of understanding of other people's perspectives we can expect indi-viduals to possess at various ages.

We have considered the *actions* typical of the social-cognitive abilities of people at various stages of social development, but what about their *reactions*? What kind of developmentalists are we at different ages in observing others? The parents clearly have a strong sense of what they can expect their children to under-stand about others' separateness and needs at different ages. Both easily accept that their daughter does not fully understand the social effects of her actions, and just gently point her in the right direction, assuming that in time and with training she will "get it"—that is, attain this understanding. (Note the natural way in which the terms "get it," "thoughtless," "thoughtful," and "know better" emerge in our discussion. They are certainly a part of the lexicon of the natural social-cognitive developmentalist in us all.)

The parents' reactions to their older son's behavior are much more complicated. They both clearly expect more thoughtful behavior from him, based on their belief that he will not only possess a more sophisticated understanding of others' needs and perspectives, but also apply it more generously and considerately than he has. Because this child is older, their understanding of his understanding leads them to make more complex and differing interpretations of his behavior, based on the more complex social thought they attribute to him, using their own sophisticated reasoning. The mother exemplifies this more, in her guess that her son is being in some fashion deliberately provocative but not hostile. The father, who is upset and angry, makes a less differentiated interpretation, rising to the bait, as it were, not seeing the distinction between good-natured kidding and disrespect, and attempting at some level to blow his son down. In the face of strong emotion, we might conclude he does not apply his highest level of understanding, his capacity to take a "third-person" perspective on the family scene, particularly with regard to his older son.

What of the other reactor, the seven-year-old? He reveals that although he may be more advanced than his sister, he is not yet a very sophisticated or complete developmentalist. He "doesn't understand" how she could ignore the rest of the family—he wouldn't. Even more, he "doesn't understand" how his parents could put up with it so calmly, especially when he knows perfectly well that the same behavior would not get the same reaction if *he* were to perform it. This seven-year-old is beginning to know that other people's perspectives and needs are distinct and potentially different from his own and has learned that it is often a good idea to try to accommodate to those other selves' needs in some way, if for no other reason than to get his own needs met. But he does not seem to clearly understand that his sister does not know all this, and that she cannot be expected to at her age. Note that his way of dealing with her involves a direct attempt to change *her* behavior ("Turn that back"), rather than her perception of things, let alone his own viewing habits.

What do we make of his reaction to his big brother? He sees that big brother is not obeying the social rules of consideration either, but his initial flash of annoyance toward his brother is not expressed as it was in the case of his sister. The younger son lacks the developmental norms of his parents, and in fact applies his own rules to his brother as he does to his sister: if I gotta do it, so do you. But something else in the relationship's unique history causes his annoyance to be subsumed. Perhaps it is admiration for the brother, or a sense of the relative distribution of power between the two of them, or whatever. Like his father, he applies his own level of understanding differently under the influence of differentiated emotional forces. The form that his way of dealing with the potential conflict takes this time, in contrast to his attitude and style of acting toward his younger sister, involves a change of his own behavior, from an annoyed dictatorial reaction to a relatively supportive and perhaps even subservient one.

This example, we hope, conveys a bit of what we mean by social cognition in action and how we are all developmentalists with regard to these abilities. We "know," speaking roughly, that even children who are "doing OK" start off life by being unable to identify and acknowledge, much less understand and consider, other people's viewpoints. And we "know" that ultimately they will be able to do all this.

Many things obviously contribute to growth in an individual's ability and willingness to behave thoughtfully, maturely, and effectively in interactions with others. But we believe that a particularly critical prerequisite for this growth is the ability to understand others' views and coordinate them with one's own. This is what we mean by social cognition: conceptualizing social relations in terms of the viewpoints of the self and others. It is our assumption that what goes on between and among people will be affected by and depend to a degree on the level of sophistication of these crucial social abilities.

Thus, the three-year-old changes the channel of the TV because she either does not consider the perspectives of the other viewers or she naively assumes they will want to see what she wants to see (or both). The seven-year-old is becoming more aware that his sister's viewing interests actually may be different from his own. But he is not yet clearly aware that she is not aware of the differing perspectives. He has (or takes) what we call a Level 1 first person perspective, rather than his younger sister's Level 0 egocentric perspective. Clearly, the thirteen-year-old in our example has achieved at least a reciprocal or second person perspective (Level 2) if his intentions are to act as if he does not consider the other viewers' perspectives, all the while explicitly doing so. We assume that both parents in the earlier vignette are capable of collaborative and mutual (Level 3) perspective coordination. What is less clear is whether each is using it, and if so, just how. The mother seems to be able to stand more easily outside the family system; her perspective has distance, a third-person orientation. The father, in contrast, though probably capable in other circumstances, seems to be caught up in the dynamics, and thereby seems to have less a sense of distance or perspective.

Although the developmental levels of social perspective coordination are clearly relevant to the foregoing family interaction, we are left with the question of how *behavior* can be understood from a developmental point of view when two people with different social-cognitive competence on the surface appear to act the "same" way (like the three-year-old daughter and thirteen-year-old son) and when two people with similar social-cognitive capacity can react so differently (the mother and father).

An implicit goal of our earlier work on the development of perspective coordination in interpersonal thought was to gain an understanding of the *functional* role of social-cognitive development in social behavior in the real world, such as the living room world of the family above. Our current "real world" is the pair therapy room of the clinic school where we treat socially and psychologically troubled children, all of whom have a track record of interpersonal difficulties with peers and adults alike. Thus, although understanding the development of social thought was the figure of the earlier work, an interest in the relation between interpersonal thought and action provided the ground. In our current research, whose goal is to describe how the developmental maturity of interpersonal thought helps to give meaning and structure to observable social behaviors, figure and ground are reversed in the explicit study of interpersonal action.

Our earlier work on interpersonal understanding rested firmly in the Piagetian tradition in its focus on the relation of expressed thought to underlying cognitive structures, its emphasis on the developmental level rather than the particular content of thought and on patterns of thinking rather than emotions or behavior, and its interest in satisfying the essential stage criteria of structured wholeness, invariant sequence, and universality. Yet even when measuring interpersonal understanding in strict Piagetian fashion, issues of the relation of thought to action begin to emerge.

The reflective interview, based in Piaget's *méthode clinique* is the primary measurement technique for formal stage descriptive analysis in most structural-developmental research (Damon, 1977; Turiel, 1982), including the study of interpersonal understanding. This approach is considered to yield more a measure of competence than performance, tapping social cognition under optimal conditions of content (for example, thinking about a hypothetical situation) and of context (in a calm and private one-to-one dialogue). Although this "unnatural" content and context render it only marginally relevant to the conditions under which most people normally *use* or *develop* their social-cognitive abilities (Jaquette, 1980), even within studies employing reflective interviews the distinction between competence and performance is relative. There is varying performance even under reflective interview conditions when, for example, reasoning about different social relationships.

It makes common sense that *how* we think about social behavior is influenced by *what* we think about and *where* we think about it. Evidence (e.g., Jaquette, 1980; Walker, de Vries, and Trevethan, 1987) suggests that fluctuations in the developmental level of social reasoning increase as the content of reasoning moves from hypothetical to real-life content (e.g., from somebody else's problem to one's own) and the context in which the reasoning is elicited moves from individual reflective interviews to more naturalistic settings (e.g., real-life problem-solving discussions). That is, reasoning performance relative to competence fluctuates more the closer we are to action itself, which is real-life *and* naturalistic, when noncognitive factors have more potential to depress social performance by constraining the ability to use one's full social-cognitive capacities. Adequate interpersonal understanding is necessary but not sufficient for mature or adequate social behavior, which is an expression of feelings and motives as well as thoughts.

Reasoning in a naturalistic context about real-life content (e.g., a classroom discussion about social problems students experience with their peers) is as close to action as one can get within the Piagetian paradigm. Yet a methodology that necessarily relies on reflective verbal reasoning alone to assess social problem-solving behavior does not help us assess the developmental maturity of the family members' interactions described earlier in any obvious way. Social actions represent the application of unverbalized, usually unreflective if not unconscious, processes that do not always reflect highest competence level. We cannot stop the action and probe the actor's reflection about his or her actions when observing natural ongoing social behavior, which would be necessary to evaluate that behavior within the Piagetian paradigm.

As our work progressed we increasingly found that to understand the relation between inferred or underlying social-cognitive processes and directly observable actions, it was necessary to assess social interaction itself developmentally. This book is about our developmental model of thought *and* action, both based on levels in the coordination of social perspectives.

Social perspective coordination seems rather conspicuous in the earlier family vignette even though the actors were not reasoning about their behavior because the interaction focused on important autonomy issues for the younger brother as well as the younger sister and older brother, on *interpersonal negotiation* in which the actors were in conflict. Negotiation occurs by definition when people's perspectives differ and therefore it is probably easiest to infer from these interactions the extent to which perspectives are or are not coordinated. Thus, we began our study of interpersonal action with a focus on the social regulation process of interpersonal negotiation. Our developmental model of interpersonal negotiation strategies (Selman, 1981; Selman and Demorest, 1984; Selman and Schultz, 1988), which has been developed and applied largely in the study of pair therapy, is described in chapters 2 and 3.

Although conflict is inherent in the pair therapy context, as it is in all interpersonal relationships, and the development of more mature strategies for interpersonal negotiation helps facilitate growth in the pair's relationship, pair therapy also, as we shall see, enables closeness and connection between the two children. To study this aspect of interpersonal development we have expanded our developmental model to include a second social regulative process, the intimacy process of shared experience (Selman, 1989; Selman and Yeates, 1987). The analysis of shared experience is described in chapter 4.

What enables us to code social behaviors, both processes of autonomy and intimacy, using the developmental heuristic of social perspective coordination levels is a reliance on Wernerian orthogenetic rather than Piagetian ontogenetic principles. Heinz Werner's (1948, 1957) comparative principle of orthogenesis characterizes development broadly—wherever it occurs (i.e., whether in molar processes such as ontogeny or pathogenesis or in a more molecular process of development within a single interaction or relationship known as microgenesis)—as a regulative process proceeding from a state of global undifferentiation to a state of differentiation and hierarchical integration. The orthogenetic principle thus includes not only the structural-development (Piagetian) principles that describe forms of social-cognitive development, but also other developmental processes that can illuminate the context-dependent dynamics of interpersonal action by taking into account its interrelated emotional and cognitive components.

The Relation between Interpersonal Thought and Action: The Role of Psychodynamic Processes

If one follows Werner, rather than Piaget, fluctuations in the developmental level of social actions across contexts may reflect a flexible, socially competent adaptation to particular contexts of social interaction, or they may reflect contextually overdetermined rather than socially determined actions. In some contexts lower level (less complex) actions may be more adaptive than those suggested by one's highest competence (thought) level. For example, the mother in the family described above might "impulsively" grab or unilaterally order rather than try to persuade her three-year-old daughter if she runs into the road in front of ongoing traffic. However, all persons sometimes act (i.e., negotiate) less maturely than they are capable when more mature action is appropriate—in those contexts that "bring out one's worst." In this sense we can regard "gaps" between developmental levels of thought and action (temporary regressions in action) to be manifestations of the "psychopathology of everyday life," when unreflective (unconscious) processes may override reflective abilities. Moreover, large and chronic gaps between thought and action levels define some forms of actual psychopathology.

The immature behavior of the father when provoked by his older son in the family interaction described earlier is an example of an everyday gap between thought and action. Something in the particular history of the father-son relationship—perhaps even the father's relationship with his own father—seemed to influence the meaning the father made of his son's action, which in turn may have precipitated his angry overreaction.

In contrast, Arnie's consistently unfriendly behavior is an example of a more pathological kind of gap. As we suggested earlier, Arnie seemed to have the capacity for reciprocal (Level 2) perspective coordination, but acted in a lower-level way in all his peer relations, often barricading himself behind a wall of books. Mitchell's social behavior was equally immature, but he showed a profile of low action and low thought instead of a gap. His unilateral (Level 1) actions when he *tried* to make friends (giving peers gifts and expecting them to thereby be his friend) reflected an equally low-level interpersonal understanding (that "a best friend is somebody you *must* do things for").

In chapter 11 we will explore the idea that both thought/action gaps and "across-the-board" low-level interpersonal development in part may be linked to deficits in intrapsychic development. Specifically, we use the psychodynamic processes—object representation and mechanisms of defense—to understand the relation between development in interpersonal thought and action. Both these intrapsychic processes have the potential to either promote or interfere with the application of social-cognitive competence in interpersonal development, with object representation processes affecting the negotiator's unconscious thought (i.e., social representational) processes, and defense mechanisms operating unconsciously in the action taken (Schultz and Selman, 1989).

Are the troubled children like Arnie and Mitchell whom we treat with pair therapy merely developmentally delayed in their interpersonal and intrapsychic functioning or are they different? Like the field of developmental psychopathology as a whole, which integrates developmental psychology's assumption of essential continuity in functioning with the traditional assumption of clinical psychiatry that there is discontinuity between illness and normality (cf. Rutter and Garmezy, 1983), we observe both connections *and* lack of connections between normal and pathological functioning. When we consider a single developmental line of these troubled children's psychological functioning, such as that of interpersonal understanding, we assume the children fall on a developmental continuum with their better functioning peers and thus are delayed. But psychological development, as Werner points out, proceeds along multiple developmental lines, and to the extent that these children's profiles differ across a number of psychological domains—or to the extent that their problems have a biological rather than a psychogenic basis—then we consider them to be "different"—that is, pathological.

Despite the fact that we consider psychosocially troubled children to be to some extent "the same" and to some extent "different" than their better adjusted peers, we do not try to "cure" them, in the sense of repairing what is broken. Rather our goal is to foster their developmental progress. Our developmental approach to interpersonal thought and action provides a special developmental map to guide the therapeutic process of pair therapy. As we shall see in chapters 5 through 7, although the session-to-session (proximal) goal of pair therapy is to provide a corrective interpersonal experience for the pair, the long-term goal is movement through developmental levels toward a capacity for mutuality and collaborative actions. These experiences are facilitated and coordinated by the adult therapist and driven by the natural desires of the members of the pair, as with all children, to experience closeness and intimacy as well as separateness and autonomy with a friend. This develops *felt understanding*, the synchrony of thought and action, competence and performance, affect and cognition, and intimacy and autonomy.

Toward Collaboration: The Function of Intimacy and Autonomy Processes

The capacity for collaboration in our developmental model, like maturing friendship understandings, is conceptualized to be based upon the developing ability to coordinate the social interaction between the self and significant others from a third person perspective, to go beyond simply taking the second person point of view required for mere cooperation. Ordinarily, as we have suggested, this transition is constructed in preadolescence or early adolescence. Mutual collaboration, as the expression or application in action of the capacity to reflectively experience the interaction between self and others, is akin to what Anna Freud (1936), in speaking about self-reflection in *The Ego and the Mechanisms of Defense*, termed in a somewhat different theoretical context, the development of the "observing ego."

Mutual collaboration with and for each other over time as a reflective method of relating can be recognized in the way a person interacts with another (communicating and resolving differences), demonstrating in both words and deeds, in thoughts and feelings, a respect for self and other. Although the reflective capacity for mutual collaboration normally begins to develop in early or middle adolescence, we believe its use and refinement in establishing and maintaining relationships thereafter constitute a lifelong process. Accordingly, it continues to broaden, deepen, and be transformed as a function of the developmental tasks and contextual challenges of social interactions encountered across one's lifetime.

But what kinds of social interactions are essential for social and interpersonal development in the way we have just described it? We believe that intimacy and autonomy, the two types of social regulation processes that we study with our developmental model of interpersonal action, represent two basic and complementary kinds of social processes that the individual must experience, be guided to and through, and learn to manage. Intimacy processes foster closeness and connectivity between the self and the other; autonomy processes foster clear boundaries delineating the needs of self and other as separate and distinct, albeit related. From our perspective on the nature of personality development, mutual collaboration is based on the development of both the capacity for intimacy, sharing, and community (self-other integration) and the capacity for autonomy, agency, and the sense of selfhood (self-other differentiation).

Intimacy and autonomy processes are operationalized in our constructs of shared experience and interpersonal negotiation strategies, respectively. As suggested in Table 1, these processes do not represent static phenomena, but rather psychological processes that function throughout life, from infancy to old age. Instead of simply achieved (have/don't have) products or properties within an individual, they are aspects of the self's actions in ongoing relationships with others. Infants as well as young adults achieve a form of intimacy with parents, even if infants do not fully understand the basis of their own or their parents' feelings toward them (Stern, 1985; White, Speisman, and Costos, 1983). Both toddlers and adolescents struggle with parents for a type of autonomy, even if toddlers cannot function as independently (Erikson, 1963). Preschoolers as well as preadolescents have meaningful and deep attachments with peers, even if younger children, as we have noted, define their friendships in superficial, nonpsychological terms (Brenner and Mueller, 1982; Gottman, 1983). All intact individuals in social relationships continually seek to establish and maintain both a sense of intimacy and a sense of autonomy with the significant other persons in their lives. But *how* they do it is the developmental question of interest.

Our constructs of intimacy and autonomy are related to but not identical with those of other theorists. In the domain of moral development, for example, Carol Gilligan (1982) has distinguished two "voices" or modes of thinking about relationships: a morality of responsibility and care, emphasizing connection with others, and a morality of rights and justice, emphasizing separation and individuality. Sidney Blatt and Shula Shichman (1983) have similarly identified two configurations of personality based on a dichotomy of the self's concern with interpersonal relationships versus concern for individual identity. They theorize that the developmental lines toward higher forms of intimacy and autonomy normally develop as a complex dialectical process. Accordingly, various forms

Table 1

Intimacy Function (Sharing Experience)	Core Developmental Levels in Capacity to Coordinate Social Perspectives	Autonomy Function (Negotiating Interpersonal Conflict)
Shared experience through collaborative empathic reflective processes	Mutual Third-Person Level (3)	Negotiation through collaborative strategies oriented toward integrating needs of self and other
Shared experience through joint reflection on similar perceptions or experiences	Reciprocal Reflective Level (2)	Negotiation through cooperative strategies in a persuasive or deferential orientation
Shared experience through expressive enthusiasm without concern for reciprocity	Unilateral One-Way Level (1)	Negotiation through one-way commands/orders or through automatic obedience strategies
Shared experience through unreflective (contagious) imitation	Egocentric Impulsive Level (0)	Negotiation through unreflective physical strategies (impulsive fight or flight)

(Left axis: Development)

of psychopathology are considered distortions of both lines but are more blatantly manifest in one or the other. Kohlberg (1973), whose "morality of justice" Gilligan criticizes as one-sided, actually believed, like Blatt and Shichman, that interpersonal maturity represents an integration of the developmental lines of intimacy and autonomy. These themes are also present in contemporary research on adolescent development within the family. Catherine Cooper and Harold Grotevant (Grotevant and Cooper, 1986) have found that a continuing interplay between individuality and connectedness in the ongoing mutual regulation of family relationships is an important indicator of adolescents' individual and relational well-being.

We shall see in chapter 4 that the capacity for intimacy is defined in our work as the ability to share experiences with another person, congruent with Sullivan's emphasis on the developmental power of consensual validation. We define the capacity for autonomy as the ability to understand, coordinate, and negotiate one's own needs with the needs of another person, particularly when they potentially, or actually, conflict. This definition of autonomy may appear idiosyncratic when compared with Erikson's (1968) emphasis on identity, yet it is similar to that of Piaget in *The Moral Judgment of the Child* and in keeping with our emphasis on personality development in the context of developing close relationships.

If each of these two social regulation processes is developing adequately, both separately and together, children entering adolescence can begin to use a third-person perspective to foster a collaborative attitude as well as mutually collaborative methods of sharing experience and negotiating with the significant other people in their lives. But what does "developing adequately" mean in concrete and observable terms, and what do distortions of these processes (fixations, regressions, extreme oscillations) actually look like? It is at this level of specificity that theory usually falters or collapses. In a modest way we have attempted to use the context of pair therapy to pick up some of the slack, to study the development of levels of interpersonal negotiation (autonomy) and shared experience (intimacy) by trying to foster their growth.

With troubled children and adolescents, these capacities seem to be best fostered in therapeutic contexts that encourage actual social interaction *and* its interpretation. In this view effective therapeutic interventions must create environments conducive to the development of advancing forms of intimacy and autonomy. Pair therapy is just such a context, one where socially immature, but cognitively capable, youngsters can take the often shaky first steps in this direction, putting their most competent level of interpersonal understanding into action in an emotionally meaningful constructive context.

Given our research interest in the cognitive, affective, motivational, and dynamic factors underlying both the normative development toward collaborative *behavior* and the barriers that hinder its development and use, systematic studies are very difficult. It is hard to observe individuals in dynamic interaction with significant others as intensively and over as long a period as is necessary to derive general principles of interactions. The pair therapy project has allowed us to study relatively long-term interpersonal interactions by providing a context in which we can examine and report on intensive developing relationships, which we will do in chapters 8 to 10. As we hope to demonstrate, pair therapy with children and adolescents is an exceptionally rich setting for research on the processes of interpersonal development and therapeutic change.

Conclusion: Does Thought Lead Action or Action Lead Thought?

In this chapter we have described the arena and antecedents of our work, laid out levels in the coordination of social perspectives, and described how they underlie interpersonal *understanding*, particularly of friendship. These are the cornerstones of our study of interpersonal *conduct*.

But in looking at the relation between interpersonal thought and interpersonal interactions and relationships, the seeds of paradox have already been planted. In essence, there are two models for their relation. One model assumes that the level of interpersonal understanding develops through the process of making sense of actual interaction. We can see "evidence" for this point of view by comparing the age range Sullivan theorizes that the collaborative process emerges in actual *interaction*, usually as early as eight or nine, and the age range at which we observe collaborative *thinking* and mutual reflection to be something young people can articulate, usually not earlier than ages 12 or 13 and often quite a bit later (Selman, Beardslee, Schultz, Krupa, and Podorefsky, 1986). Such theorizing, if supported by research, would clearly indicate that levels of interpersonal development emerge first in the structures of social interaction and only sometime later find their way into an individual's consciousness and reflective understanding.

At first glance, the second model appears to posit the converse: that level of interpersonal *understanding* provides the upper limit of what developmental level of *conduct* may be used, the sine qua non. Thus, according to this view, level of interpersonal understanding is an enabling and requisite factor in the use of a particular level of conduct but is no guarantee.

These two views appear to conflict, but we feel that they are reconcilable and in fact complementary. Reconciliation becomes possible when we consider a theory of interpersonal understanding and conduct mediated by core levels in the coordination of social perspectives as a central operation. The first model—action (or experience) preceding thought (or concepts)—is applicable to the process of the construction of new knowledge, specifically interpersonal understanding. The second model (level of thought preceding and allowing for action) is applicable to the state of affairs of interpersonal knowledge *in use* (e.g., in interpersonal negotiation and shared experience), once the individual has already achieved a level of interpersonal understanding, and is attempting to *consolidate* that understanding with subsequent experiences in regulating interpersonal relationships.

The first model suggests that interpersonal understanding develops through the individual's making meaning of the experiences of dealing with others—that is, through making sense of the rules of conduct that guide social regulation processes such as interpersonal negotiation and shared experience. This model speaks to the mechanism, whether we call it disequilibration and reequilibration or use other language, by which action and experience inform the growth and development of social cognition. The second model says that the higher the level of interpersonal cognition held by the individual, the more sophisticated and the greater the possible number of behavioral strategies the individual will have available for subsequent interaction. Once a level of interpersonal understanding has already been constructed, this level will allow for a range of strategies, but will not determine which strategy from the repertoire is chosen. This is analogous to the developing piano prodigy whose finger size, as it grows, enables certain greater virtuosity of performance, but does not insure it. Thus we can think of the relation between knowledge and conduct as two-way: the first model speaks to how understanding comes about (through interactive experience), and the second to how it is used once established (subject to the vagaries of emotional and motivational forces in particular social situations).

We believe that *both* these models operate during the therapeutic process of pair therapy to produce change. In setting the stage for the growth of intimacy and autonomy processes in the pair's social interactions and relationship, the pair therapist facilitates the growth of both interpersonal thought (social perspective coordination) and action (its application in negotiation and shared experience). The core levels of social perspective coordination are the mediating central operation for growth in social thought and action, providing us with excellent tools for understanding, describing, and intervening in the day-to-day functioning of both domains. According to our model, interpersonal maturity (as differentiated from chronological maturity) is the continued advancement and synchrony of interpersonal understanding and action levels through development. By facilitating both the negotiations of conflicts and the sharing of experience between two troubled children in what is probably the most supportive peer social context they experience, the therapy encourages growth both at the cutting edge of their social competence (their interpersonal thought) and actual social behavior, and in the consolidation of their ability to apply their higher, already acquired levels of interpersonal understanding in their action.

In our model, we have identified two forms of interpersonal immaturity: the premature fixation of both understanding and action, and the use of lower-level strategies by individuals who "know better," and who thus exhibit a discrepancy between how they can think and how they act. When either a pattern of relatively low-level understanding and low-level action exists or a gap between level of interpersonal understanding and action is consistent and chronic, clinically we must ask whether and how to intervene to raise the understanding and action levels or close the gap. It is probably the latter task of closing the gap—helping children apply what they "know" but do not "feel"—that is more salient in our treatment. There is a developmental ceiling that clearly and obviously limits the level of interpersonal relating for younger children, but this competence level is less often *the* constraining factor in the production of higher-level behavior by troubled children, older adolescents, or adults. Which kind of interventions are effective in these situations is the kind of question our clinical research addresses.

The heart of this book presents three pair therapy cases in detail, showing, we hope, concretely *how*—not that—the treatment works, using the theoretical model honed in the clinical research to inform the course of the therapeutic process. At that point we will share with you a fuller story of Arnie and Mitchell, the two friendless boys described at different points in this introduction.

Our analysis of actual pair therapy cases using the theoretical model of interpersonal negotiation strategies and shared experience suggests that the nature of the social interaction in pair therapy, guided by the therapist's role, changes not only with different phases that we have identified in the therapy (described in chapter 6), but, more importantly, with the developmental levels of the two children. The pairs of children in the three cases are each operating at different levels of interpersonal negotiation and shared experience. Hence their stories depict different developmental transitions during the course of the pair therapy (shifts from Level 0 to 1, 1 to 2, and 2 to 3, respectively).

To fully understand the pair therapy process, including the therapist's role in producing change, the reader must understand our

CHAPTER TWO

Children's Strategies for Interpersonal Negotiation with Peers

Two Ways to Get Along: Interpretive Descriptions

In the early afternoon, six-year-old Jeremy phones his friend Brian from down the block, asking him to come over to play. Brian and Jeremy have known each other for a year and a half, since they started all-day kindergarten together. Here is how their play begins:

When Brian arrives at Jeremy's house, he quickly bursts through the door, throws off his coat, barely stopping to hang it up on an empty coat hook in the downstairs hall, and charges up the stairs with Jeremy in quick pursuit. They head straight for his room. In the middle of the floor stands one of Jeremy's newest acquisitions, a latter-day "boys' dollhouse" recently handed down to him by his older brother, called the "Star Wars Death Star Space Station," modeled after the space station in the movie "Star Wars." This highly visible toy is the immediate object of Brian's attention, and he heads directly for it.

As he does, Brian says, "Now, let's play a little bit here," referring to the space station model. His tone is firm and commanding. He quickly moves to the model, sits on the floor and begins to work the trash compactor, turning the knob that moves the wall in and out. At almost exactly the same time Brian makes his move, perhaps a moment later, Jeremy, anticipating Brian's move, yells out in a somewhat urgent tone, "I'm doing the trash compactor, Brian!" Jeremy then reaches for the compactor knob as he speaks, but his hand arrives at the knob a moment after his friend's. Jeremy's look is questioning, both uncertain and concerned. Brian says with a slight scowl, "You've already played with this, but it's new to me." His tone is more forceful than Jeremy's, perhaps strengthened by the force of his argument, but it does not communicate anger. As Brian says this, he visibly tightens his grip on the compactor knob. Jeremy appears to sit back on his heels for a moment, then draws back his outstretched arm.

Jeremy makes no active challenge to Brian's assertion and claim, but shows his discontent by withdrawing from the joint involvement, moving away to the other side of the room. There he rummages through a cardboard box of Star Wars figures, and he pulls out a few of the plastic characters from the movie to play with. He carries a few of them to the floor and fiddles with them somewhat absently with a slight frown. Several seconds later he says aloud, "Okay, but next time I get to choose first!" Jeremy's statement is uttered in a matter-of-fact tone of voice; he apparently assumes it will be accepted with the same force of logic by Brian as Brian's statement was accepted by him. In any event, for whatever reason, Jeremy does not even turn around to check Brian's reaction. Indeed, Brian does take Jeremy's last, "equalizer" remark in silence.

After playing on the space station with Jeremy for several more minutes, Brian withdraws to a different area of the room. He starts to explore some science material, and then comes across a shoebox labeled "Creepy Crawlies." These are miscellaneous rubber toy insects and monsters that Jeremy has collected from gumball-like machines at the local supermarket:

> "I want to try all the finger ones," announces Brian, referring to those that are attached to rings and can be worn on fingers. He picks the box off the shelf and flips it over to let the entire contents spill onto the floor. Excitedly, he then starts rummaging through the pile to find the finger ones, discarding to all points of the room those that do not fit this criterion. As the rummaging continues, Brian gets more stimulated and he throws the discarded vermin more widely and further across the room. "Look, I've got all the animals on my fingers!" he finally exclaims. Jeremy, who has been watching Brian occasionally from his place at the space station, says with real authority, "You've got to pick them all up. That's the rule here." His remark is made matter-of-factly rather than with anger. This rule to which Jeremy makes reference is one he has heard many times from his parents, but one he himself usually follows only after threat of some consequence. But as Jeremy did before, Brian now calms down noticeably, and starts to pick up the strewn articles with an easy compliance. Jeremy watches Brian for a time and then offers the Star Wars characters, saying, "You can use these if you want. It's okay with me."

When Brian has finished collecting the creepy crawlies, he joins Jeremy once again at the space station. Jeremy has added some superhero figures to the arena, and both boys return to a shared fantasy play of good and bad characters in combat with one another. Their play is interactive, animated, with much talking and laughter, yet structured and organized. They pursue this fantasy play for about fifteen more minutes, until they get hungry. Jeremy, being a good host, asks Brian if he wants something to eat. When Brian answers affirmatively, Jeremy shouts down the stairs to ask his mother for a snack. This is the first time either one of the boys has addressed an adult since Brian's arrival over half an hour before.

Before considering how we interpret this play session, let's look at another example of peer interaction in which the feeling of the interchange is quite different. The second interaction is between two children who both have a history of problematic and unskilled interpersonal functioning. Once we have a comparative feeling of these two instances of peer interaction, and an intuition of their relative social maturity, we will outline a set of criteria within a developmental framework for looking at the adequacy of social interactions in general.

The setting in which we find two nine-year-old girls is quite different, the small private day school for children with emotional problems where we conduct pair therapy. The two girls are meeting in a room designed to approximate, as much as possible in an institutional setting, the same feeling of safety and supply as Jeremy's room, although it is not expected to duplicate it. Nevertheless, it is a room that is familiar to both girls. They have been meeting there regularly, once a week for one and one-half years, with a pair therapist. The adult therapist who usually meets with them for their hour together notes that the last several sessions have gone particularly smoothly, and asks the girls whether they would like to be alone to play; one of the goals of pair therapy is to foster each dyad's capacity to function without the need for complete adult regulation or direct assistance. Because they both indicate they would like to be alone, the therapist withdraws to an observation room behind a one-way mirror looking directly into the pair therapy room where she is available if needed. The pair begins like this:

> Immediately after the therapist has left the room, Tania calls out, "Is there a model? Where's a model for me?" It is not obvious to whom she is directing this inquiry, and her tone is demanding, but has a half kidding quality to it.

Janine responds, her voice typically sharp and clipped: "You want to make a model, you can make it out of clay." There is a tough-luck and unsupportive quality to this response. "Take your shoes off, Tania," she barks with a wry, disapproving look. Janine kicks off her own shoes somewhat vehemently and defiantly.

Tania has begun to work with some clay, and Janine joins her at the table. Janine remains standing as she picks up some clay and continues to talk about her shoes. "If this was my room, I would just kick them across the room. I don't care who knows. I just kick them as hard as I can. Everything. Pillows too, everything is a mess." Janine is speaking with bravura and smiles in a "so there!" way. Tania stands up to reach across the table and grab half of the still unclaimed clay. She takes no more and no less than half, and sits back down to model her growing piece. She has focused on her clay throughout Janine's soliloquy, but occasional glances toward Janine suggest that she has been monitoring Janine's activity. Janine suspiciously eyes Tania's movement toward the unclaimed clay. She appears to contemplate a reaction, some kind of objection, but remains silent. Tania then declares, "Don't talk about yourself. My room's a pigsty." This is said in a manner that suggests a competition has begun. Janine seems willing to enter into the competition. "You know what? I have clothes hanging on my wall right now. That's why my mother threw my toys out." (In a recent session Janine had reported in an "I don't care" manner that her mother had recently thrown away all her toys because she had refused to pick up her room at home.) Janine ends her claim with a giggly, somewhat artificial and forced laugh. In fact, Janine's mother reported that Janine was furious around the toy incident.

"My cat almost jumped out of the window today," she states almost as an afterthought, also in an "I don't care" tone. She continues to fiddle absently with her clay. "Mine almost went out when I was going to my cab," offers Tania. Janine says, "My cab almost left because the cat almost fell out of the window." Tania cackles appreciatively at this. "My mother grabbed it by the tail," Janine says giggling, "and pulled it back in like it was a fishing rod." She sits down now and begins to work with the clay more constructively. After a pause Janine says, "She's a fat one, my cab driver." It feels like the girls are competing to "out-naughty" one another in a battle of malevolence.

The girls' interaction continues in a kind of power struggle between them that never gets resolved. Tania becomes frustrated, bored, restless, and agitated in turn while playing with the clay, and asks Janine to play puppets with her. Janine is belligerent but eventually picks up a puppet as if she is doing Tania a big favor. They order each other around, arguing about the puppet show, then about a doll bed, which Janine claims as her own:

Tania says with exasperation, "So, it's your damn bed. I don't care! Now I'm the reporter. Have you seen a huge green monster?" "No!" says Janine, wound up with excitement. "Say 'yes'!" asserts Tania. Janine says, "YES!" very loudly. Then she begins to make monster noises, and Tania screams loudly in response, hopping up and down. Janine changes her monster noises into screams now, and both girls stand with their eyes closed trying to outscream each other. Of course this mayhem succeeds in bringing the therapist into the room.

Tania immediately runs over to pull on the adult's arm, saying, "We want to do a play for you. You sit here. C'mon," she says, leading her to a chair. Janine mopes and eyes Tania as the latter is being forceful in getting the adult's attention. Tania runs back to the stage after seating the adult, and she picks up a lion puppet. "C'mon, Janine, let's do a play," she says. She places her lion puppet on the stage to growl at Janine, saying, "I'm going to eat you." Janine then whines a bit frantically, "I need a lion too," her voice rising rapidly in pitch. Janine starts to look through the puppet box, pulling puppets out and dropping them all over the floor.

Tania starts moving impatiently, and she pulls at Janine's sleeve saying "C'mon, this lion of mine isn't in the show anymore," as if Janine shouldn't need one either then. However, Janine jerks her arm away, and snaps back, "If you have an animal, then I have to have one too." She pulls out a very large puppet. "You can't have that one!" declares Tania. Janine asserts, "Yes, I can too!" Tania responds with a rising voice, "I'm not using mine. It'll just stay on the stage. I'm not using it!" She sounds almost frantic, but Janine ignores her. Finally Tania throws her lion puppet on the floor and angrily says, "You can take your stupid pet." Janine glares at Tania, and then at the puppet at her feet. She returns her glare toward Tania, who stands with a frown, her arms folded and hip stuck out. "I don't want the damn puppet," seethes Janine, and she bolts out of the room before anyone can stop her.

The duration of this whole interaction, from its optimistic start to its disastrous termination, was twelve minutes.

An Interpretive/Empirical Approach to
Studying Social Regulation between Peers

Pair therapists strive to develop children's ability to regulate their peer interactions without constant adult support, something that seems to come naturally to Jeremy and Brian. When children in pair therapy give evidence of gaining the capacity to use adaptive forms of these social regulations in their interactions with each other under therapeutic supervision, usually after many months or even several years of pair therapy, the therapist slowly withdraws, occasionally even leaving the therapy room (while continuing to monitor the pair from an adjoining observation room). As the brief report from the case of Janine and Tania demonstrates, members of the pair usually show signs of regression to less functional behavior during those sessions when the therapist first withdraws. But the goal of this form of treatment is that, with time and continued therapeutic work, the two children will be able to recover and learn to use the higher-level social skills attained with the therapist's guidance when they are alone together.

Pair therapists hold the relationship together when the pair cannot. In this case, the stress of the new situation (being alone without the therapist) upset the balance of Janine and Tania's newly developing social skills, but Janine's impulsive retreat was only a temporary break in their relationship. She did come back into the room (of her own accord), and the therapist discussed what happened with the girls, reflecting on the interaction and repairing the relationship by opening up communication with and between them. This continuity in the pair's relationship—the assurance that the pair will keep meeting together whatever may happen in a particular session—provides the children with a novel and unaccustomed connection with a peer. (Of course, the pair therapy could be ended if the therapist decides that the interaction between a pair is so conflictual that the peer relationship is destructive rather than therapeutic.)

The work of the pair therapist is guided by an assessment of the pair's level of social maturity. This "developmental diagnosis" relies on our theoretical model of interpersonal negotiation strategies and shared experience, based on social perspective coordination levels. The social regulation processes that enable close interpersonal relationships between peers to develop are a target of treatment in pair therapy and the object of study of descriptive research.

The two dyads in the foregoing examples of peer interaction provide a dramatic contrast in how to get along: the relationship between the two boys in the home setting grows and stabilizes as we watch, that of the two girls in the clinical setting falls apart completely. These differences in tone and outcome are striking, yet it is nevertheless difficult to describe the dynamics of the interactions in a way that illuminates how close peer relationships develop or fail to develop in quantitative or causal terms.

For this reason, among others, a number of researchers in developmental psychology and the philosophy of social science have recently advocated the use of hermeneutic methods, which examine the structure, organization, and intelligibility of human action in meaningful rather than formal or causal terms (e.g., Gergen, 1985; Packer, 1985; Scarr, 1985). In contrast to traditional positivist approaches to knowledge that aim to elucidate *objective* elements of social action and interchange by analyzing either abstract systems of relations or mechanistic systems of forces and causes, both of which end up decontextualizing—and therefore distorting—behavior, the interpretive approach highlights the importance of a particular context in understanding the *meaning* more than the explanation or cause of social behavior.

This interpretive attitude and focus on personal meaning in longitudinal-historical context is also articulated in clinical theory. Psychoanalysts in the narrative tradition, who reject Freud's metapsychology of natural-science forces, energies, and mechanisms, view persons as agents who construct situations (e.g., Schafer, 1983; Modell, 1984). In this view social action is uninterpretable out of context and agents define situations over time in ways that imply what they do in them. Furthermore, specific actions are "overdetermined" or have multiple meanings, both conscious and unconscious, and so can be described only selectively and meaningfully, not inclusively and objectively, by agent and observer alike.

The recognition of the intimate relationship between the meaning of an action and the specific contexts in which it takes place, and the consequent view that these contexts are psychosocial-historical constructions rather than objective phenomena, is integral to our approach. In our efforts to understand social regulation processes in children's peer interactions, we have used a method that we label the "interpretive/empirical case study" approach. Our method consists of an integration of traditional observational ("empirical") methodology and intensive, longitudinal study of pairs of children in therapy using hermeneutic ("interpretive") analysis. This interpretive/empirical approach powerfully informs us, we believe, about why Jeremy and Brian got along, and why Janine and Tania did not.

But if behavior has multiple interpretations, what meaning do we seek in these relationships? Gergen and Gergen (1982) argue that the choice of meaning in explanations of human behavior cannot be established only empirically but rather also must be based on one's values. In this view, the narrative interpretation one chooses is not simply a matter of objective truth but of one's sense of valuation. Our quest for developmental meaning in observations of children's peer interactions is closely related to the goals of our clinical practice: we value mutuality and collaboration, and the aim of pair therapy is to help children generate ways to relate to others more reciprocally and collaboratively, and less impulsively and unilaterally.

The therapeutic goal of fostering collaboration in children's peer relations gets translated into explanations of behavior and clinical interpretations that are very different from—but not necessarily contradictory to—the therapeutic goal and value of explicating insight for the individual child, as in psychodynamically oriented individual therapy. For example, in evaluating the social interaction between Tania and Janine, we would give a semantic and pragmatic explanation of the social regulation processes that are failing (they cannot share or take turns), whereas from the perspective of individual interpretive treatment, a thematic explanation could be made instead (each feels needy and depleted and so acts greedily). A content-based inner/dynamic interpretation of the interaction when the two girls are discussing their cats could be that they are "really" (also) speaking about themselves: they feel trapped, mistreated, and uncared for by their mothers and wish for escape. A more form-based outer/interactional interpretation of the same interchange is that in their search for intimacy/connectedness the girls are colluding in each other's low-level, disorganized, and impulsive expressiveness, and thus fail to regulate one another. These themes and forms of social interaction eventually must be woven together to tell a complete and meaningful story of the interaction.

Strategies for Interpersonal Negotiation: A Descriptive Tool for the Analysis of Dyadic Peer Interaction

The children in the two opening vignettes exhibit similar kinds of feelings of the sort that are inevitable in close and meaningful relationships at all ages. On the positive connection side, for both pairs of children there are instances of sharing experiences and fantasy play. On the conflictual side, both interactions contain feelings of frustration, possessiveness, competition, and anger.

However, we find the two narratives also suggest significant differences in the ability of the peers to regulate their social interaction without adult support. Jeremy and Brian's fantasy play together with the miniature "Star Wars" figure (although not described in detail) represents an age-appropriate form of shared experience important for the development of the capacity for connectivity and mutuality. There appear to be opportunities for shared experience in the interaction between Janine and Tania as well, but for reasons that are not apparent or easy to fathom, this potential is realized only with an extremely low-level, primitive form of sharing, with disastrous effects on their interaction. Tania and Janine appear to have difficulty connecting with each other, much less maintaining that connection, so we witness very little shared experience in their play together. However, both dyads engage in lots of negotiation, the part of the model on which we will focus in this chapter and the next.

Brian and Jeremy use many orders and commands in trying to subtly negotiate their relative power and control. Yet their interaction progresses as if with checks and balances, as they flexibly respond to each other's needs and intents. They appear to have a number of alternative negotiation strategies and tools for internal and external control that allow their interaction to continue to progress through rough spots back to more balanced states (e.g., Jeremy's "backing off" to restore both his own and the dyad's equilibrium). Our overall impression is that they are able to monitor internal disequilibrium with flexibility, complement each other's asserted wishes, and maintain interpersonal equilibrium. This is clearly not the case with Janine and Tania. The girls' internal modulation of needs and wishes appears to be very erratic, and their personal and interpersonal equilibrium are altogether destroyed within twelve minutes.

Can the differences in the quality of individual and mutual control in these two sets of peer social interactions be sharpened in a developmental light? The interpersonal negotiation strategies model allows us to compare, at both a molar level of the general form of the ongoing interaction and a molecular level of specific sequences of strategies in particular contexts, the form and function of each pair's conflictual interactions. In the following sections, we will describe the interpersonal negotiation strategies model and a three-step procedure used to apply the model to actual social interaction. The balance between the positivist (or "objective") and the interpretive (or "subjective") aspects of our model shifts at each of three analytic steps leading from recorded social interaction (e.g. from videotape records) to an interpretive story of interpersonal negotiation and social regulation. New layers of meaning are brought to bear at each step by superimposing interpretive molar information onto the molecular behaviors. To do this, we use information successively from different levels of analysis: first, from the *behavioral* interaction to identify contexts for interpersonal negotiation, then from the *psychological* context to "diagnose" the actual negotiation strategies used (analogous to, but not synonomous with, "coding"), and then from the *psychosocial-historical* context to interpret the meaning of the diagnosed strategies.

Selecting Interactions Defined as Contexts for Interpersonal Negotiation Based on Behavioral Clues

The first task in interpreting social regulation processes with the construct of interpersonal negotiation strategies is to identify negotiation behaviors, or "contexts for interpersonal negotiation," in the ongoing stream of peer interaction. Interpersonal negotiation strategies are the methods by which one person tries to meet personal needs and goals in interaction, and often in conflict, with another person to whom he or she has some degree of positive ongoing attachment. Two criteria define what we call a context for interpersonal negotiation.

First, the interaction must take place in the context of an *ongoing relationship* in which each person cares beyond the moment about the "significant other." Social relationships differ from social behavior per se in several ways important for the process of interpersonal negotiation. Relationships involve the complex influences of interactions on interactions and so have emergent properties not present in component interactions (cf. Hinde, 1979; Sroufe and Fleeson, 1986). In particular, because relationships exist over time, their cognitive/affective psychological aspects transcend their overt behavioral ones. Interactions within relationships are affected by the history of the dyad as well as the complex relational histories of each person. Therefore, ongoing relationships with personal meaning for each social partner are contexts in which mutual expectations are often disrupted and conflicting motives can be easily aroused. They are also contexts in which caring and investment can powerfully motivate actors to attempt to achieve interpersonal equilibrium.

Second, the relationship must be in momentary *disequilibrium*. This disequilibrium is manifest in both observable outer behavior and inferred inner thoughts and feelings. Interpersonal and internal disequilibrium arise simultaneously from the dyadic context of the interaction—not from within one individual or the other—as aspects of the situation (including each person's actions) interact with aspects of each person's internal state. *Interpersonal disequilibrium* is overt, even if subtle, behavioral opposition and subsequent mutual effect. For example, when Brian reaches for the trash compactor, Jeremy resists, reaching for the trash compactor himself and calling out "I'm doing the trash compactor." Then Brian persists forcefully, asserting, "You've already played with this, but it's new to me." Complementing this behavioral disharmony is *internal disequilibrium* or inner conflict over wanting one's own needs met, yet at the same time caring about the other person. In the trash compactor example, Brian is driven by his strong desire to operate the attractive toy, but his resistance to Jeremy's response also reflects internal disequilibrium (although he probably was not fully aware of it): he relinquished his claim (from which we may infer that his friend counted with him) but he was discontent (reflecting his own unmet desire to play with it), withdrawing from close interaction as a way, perhaps, to focus on his own internal state before reestablishing close contact.

In identifying contexts for interpersonal negotiation, we use behavioral criteria to define relationships in disequilibrium. Note, however, that negotiation is a more inclusive concept than the traditional notion of social conflict. The behavioral resistance in overt social conflicts also defines contexts for interpersonal negotiation. But in some more subtle negotiations the potential conflict does not become overt, because no direct resistance is met. If, for example, Jeremy had wanted to play with the trash compactor but did not say so or indicate his desire some other way, it would still have been a context for negotiation, but it would have been much more difficult to identify as such because the interpersonal disequilibrium would have been less visible. In such cases, subtle affective cues to inner disequilibrium (i.e., expressions, tones, etc.) are used to identify the interaction as a context for negotiation. Thus, interpersonal negotiation involves potential as well as overt conflict, and very subtle behavioral clues are used to identify contexts in which resistance is not manifest overtly because actors suppress their own desire for the sake of interpersonal harmony, with consequent (but often almost invisible) internal disequilibrium.

Strategies of different levels and orientations are often employed within one negotiation context as the interaction unfolds and each person's behavior is colored by that of his or her partner (as is the case with the opening gambit of Jeremy and Brian's play). Therefore, when our goal is to understand the process of negotiation in a specific context for negotiation, we examine the sequence of molecular behaviors. However, it is also useful to examine molar patterns, and therefore contexts for negotiation are not always parsed up into molecular units but are often summed across interactions or relationships. For example, although it was not the case with either of the dyads in our examples, a pattern of dominance often gets established early, quickly, and almost unnoticeably in a particular interaction or relationship. In these cases the repeated interactional patterns can be summarized on a more molar level.

In addition, clinical work needs models that are usable at a molar level as a tool for summarizing the multiple and complex interactions that occur across time in a clinical context (e.g., during an hour of pair therapy, or across several sessions). This summarizing across interactions allows clinical observers to communicate in a common language about their impressions of how the processes of treatment are progressing, as well as how the capacities of the individuals are developing. Thus, we choose contexts for negotiation at molar as well as molecular levels of analysis, depending on our immediate research or clinical purpose. This flexibility permits both microanalytic analyses of the process of negotiation in specific sequence of dyadic interaction and macroanalytic analyses of more general patterns of an individual's negotiation within and across particular contexts.

Diagnosing Interpersonal Negotiation Strategies in Two Psychological Dimensions: Developmental Level and Interpersonal Orientation

The interpersonal negotiation strategies model provides not only a useful net for catching negotiations as they float down the stream of social interactions in middle childhood and early adolescence, but also a taxonomy for categorizing them into meaningful and useful classes. In the second step of our interpretive/empirical analytic procedure, we diverge from traditional observational research in using psychological instead of behavioral criteria, and thus we "diagnose" rather than "code" the social behaviors.

Instead of using traditional criteria of morphological or functional equivalence to code social interaction, we use developmental criteria based on a heuristic derived from structural-developmental theory. This cognitive-developmental construct is the coordination of social perspectives, which was introduced in the first chapter. The perspective coordination model provides a developmental framework for organizing forms of interpersonal behavior, including interpersonal negotiation (and shared experience), as well as forms of interpersonal understanding (e.g., friendship concepts). Although the identification of developmental levels of social perspective coordination in interpersonal understanding in our earlier work reflects a positivist and rationalist notion of social-cognitive competence, our use of these levels in studying conduct—in the social regulation processes of interpersonal negotiation strategies and shared experience—takes on a more hermeneutic flavor. This is because in moving beyond the developmental description of the *social-cognitive capacity* to coordinate perspectives when thinking about the social world, trying to understand the child's *social behavior* (in both its molecular and molar forms) in a meaningful way from a developmental perspective, we are guided by a social interaction contextual metaphor (based on Wernerian orthogenesis) instead of an individual competence-based metaphor (based on Piagetian principles).

The "developmental diagnosis" is made by evaluating the internal disequilibrium that is inferred from the observed behavioral cues that had initially signalled the context for interpersonal negotiation. Observed social action (i.e., the behavioral disharmony that signals interpersonal disequilibrium) is not by itself interpretable developmentally—that is, in terms of the ability to differentiate and integrate the social perspectives of self and other. The developmental diagnosis of overt manifestations of social conflict requires analysis of latent dimensions of the inner disequilibrium—namely, the ways in which and the degree to which the actor in dealing with the experience of disequilibrium appears to understand and coordinate the thoughts, feelings, and motives of both self and other.

The interpersonal negotiation strategies model assumes that the coordination of social perspectives is intrinsic to the process of balancing personal and interpersonal needs in ongoing relationships and that mature negotiation is based on the increasing ability to coordinate (i.e., differentiate and integrate) the perspectives of self and other. The four developmental levels of interpersonal negotiation (refer back to Table 1) reflect different levels of sophistication in perspective coordination.

Strategies classified as Level 0 are primitive and physical, impulsive fight or flight, often but not always driven by "out of control" feelings like rage or panic. They reflect no perspective taken on the negotiation—that is, a lack of reflection on or coordination of the perspectives of self and other in the consideration of a particular social problem.

Level 1 strategies reflect a "one-way" or "unilateral" perspective. At this level, although it is recognized that the perspectives of self and other may differ in the particular situation and that the parties must interact to resolve the conflict, the strategies are not coordinated—that is, based on the simultaneous consideration of the two perspectives. These often power-oriented negotiations include one-way commands and orders or, conversely, simple and unchallenging accommodations (giving in) to the perceived needs and demands of the other person.

Strategies at Level 2 are psychologically based reciprocal exchanges that coordinate the perspectives of both self and other in the ability to reflect upon the negotiation from a second person perspective. It is understood at this level that both self and other are planful and self-reflective, and that the thoughts, feelings, and actions of each influence those of the other. Level 2 strategies include psychological trades and exchanges, verbal persuasion or deference, convincing others, making deals, and other forms of self-interested cooperation. The self may go first at Level 2, but not control completely. Conversely, the self may defer to the other but not yield totally.

Collaborative (Level 3) strategies represent a consideration of the need for an integration of the interests of self and other so that the negotiation is viewed from a third-person perspective. These strategies involve compromise, dialogue, process analysis, and the development of a shared goal of mutual understanding. There is an understanding that concern for the relationship's continuity over time is a necessary consideration for the adequate and optimal solution of any immediate problem.

But how does one make the plunge from observed social interaction to these deeper, more inferential diagnoses of levels, each of which represents a uniquely shaped conceptual lens through which self is viewed and understood in relation to other *at the moment of the action?* Meaningful developmental diagnosis of the ways actors actually deal with themselves and others to simultaneously balance inner and interpersonal feelings of disequilibrium requires considerable inference about psychological dimensions underlying the observed actions. In evaluating the developmental maturity of conduct, it becomes necessary to study how individuals put emotions as well as cognitions into perspective in ongoing social interaction. Internal motives and feelings, as well as external factors, evoke, inhibit, or otherwise mediate the extent to which individuals actually use their optimal perspective-taking ability as interpersonal conflicts evolve out of particular social contexts. In contrast to the traditional coding of children's peer interactions, in which molecular behaviors are usually coded in a "context-free" way by matching each behavior to an item in a behavioral taxonomy that is also more or less molecular ("physical aggression" or "hit"), we use contextual cues to translate the molecular negotiation behaviors into the four molar developmental categories of physical impulsivity, unilateral control, reflective reciprocity and mutual collaboration.

The INS diagnosing process assesses more than surface behavior and words to capture the deeper meaning of an interpersonal negotiation in a relatively objective way. The force and style of actions and the tone and volume of phrases are noted in our attempt to assess the cognitions, feelings, and intentions that underlie the observed behavior. Reports of facial expressions (e.g., a "wry disapproving look") and tone of voice (e.g., "threatening tone") reflect interpretations of underlying feeling and intent. Some inferences of feeling and tone are made explicitly from behavior (e.g., "Apparently recovered from his losing skirmish to get first choice, Jeremy stands up to join Brian"). Different impressions of tone and intent make for very different interpretations of negotiation strategies, and this kind of "subjective" information is crucial for translating the observed social conflict interactions into the molar levels of interpersonal negotiation.

The INS model provides four tools for the observer to organize the subjective, psychological information that needs to be considered to accurately diagnose the negotiation behaviors. These tools-of-inference are in the form of operationalized psychological components inherent in all negotiative acts. Three of the components together represent the developmental dimension of an interpersonal negotiation strategy: (1) a cognitive *construal of self and other* or interpersonal understanding component (the construal of the perspective of self in relation to the perspective of other that operates at the moment in the particular interactive context); (2) an *affective disequilibrium* component (the way the individual perceives and attempts to control emotional disequilibrium arising in that interpersonal context); and (3) a *primary interpersonal purpose* component (the dominant intention or purpose of the actor in that context).

The fourth tool for diagnosing conflictual interactions is the *interpersonal orientation* component of negotiation, which is used to identify the way control is asserted rather than the form of the control. This personalitylike dimension addresses upon whom the actor predominantly acts in attempting to deal with disequilibrium within the self and between the self and other. It classifies social action into one of three modes of control: in the *other-transforming* mode, the individual primarily attempts to change the thoughts, feelings, or actions of the other; in the *self-transforming* mode, the actor predominantly works on changing his or her own thoughts, feelings, or actions to mesh, or at least not conflict, with the perceived needs of the other. The *collaborative* mode, integrally connected with the higher developmental levels, integrates self-transforming and other-transforming actions.

With respect to interpersonal orientation, at the lower developmental levels where the social perspectives of self and other are either undifferentiated (Level 0) or differentiated but unintegrated (Level 1), each strategy is isolated, rigid, and polarized, at one extreme or the other of a behavioral continuum ranging from physically withdrawing self-transforming strategies to aggressive other-transforming strategies. With developmental maturity, interpersonal orientation becomes more integrated and equilibrated between the two orientations, first either becoming assertively ordering or submissively obedient (Level 1), then either persuasive or deferential (Level 2), and finally collaborative (Level 3). Collaborative actions synthesize differentiated conceptions and perceptions of self and other, and represent a mixture of accommodation and assertion, entailing simultaneous attempts to change self and other. Table 2 illustrates this dependent relation between developmental level and interpersonal orientation.

Although all the components are intertwined in conduct, it is useful to separate them in order to explicate how complex social conflicts are reduced to our four deceptively simplistic levels of interpersonal negotiation. These theoretical tools facilitate the inferential process of "diagnosing" the developmental maturity of interpersonal negotiation (itself in great part characterized by the degree to which actors are able to accurately infer their partners' inner, subjective experience). However, the four components do not represent a traditional scoring system but rather guides for

Table 2

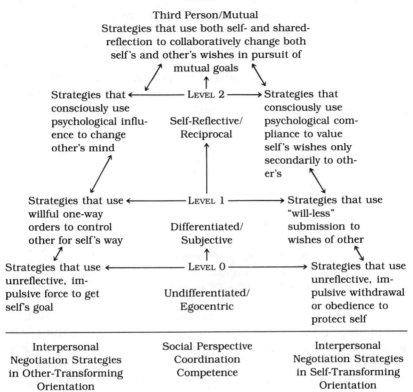

LEVEL 3

Third Person/Mutual
Strategies that use both self- and shared-
reflection to collaboratively change both
self's and other's wishes in pursuit of
mutual goals

Strategies that ←———— LEVEL 2 ———→ Strategies that
consciously use   consciously use
psychological influ-   Self-Reflective/   psychological com-
ence to change   Reciprocal   pliance to value
other's mind   self's wishes only
                                            secondarily to oth-
                                            er's

Strategies that use ←———— LEVEL 1 ———→ Strategies that use
willful one-way   "will-less"
orders to control   Differentiated/   submission to
other for self's way   Subjective   wishes of other

Strategies that use ←———— LEVEL 0 ———→ Strategies that use
unreflective, im-   unreflective, impulsive force to get   Undifferentiated/   pulsive withdrawal
self's goal   Egocentric   or obedience to
                                            protect self

Interpersonal Negotiation Strategies in Other-Transforming Orientation	Social Perspective Coordination Competence	Interpersonal Negotiation Strategies in Self-Transforming Orientation

making a clinical judgment of development level and interpersonal orientation for a negotiation strategy or series of strategies. The developmental level of a particular strategy is diagnosed by asking a series of questions for each component, which are presented in the next chapter. Because of the logically and psychologically linked nature of the levels across the four components, the responses to these questions converge to define a certain gestalt or tone of a particular negotiation, and the reliability of any particular coding judgment using our model does not depend upon how reliably one can code a particular component (e.g., intent).

Thus, the questions for each component generate inferences from which we seek converging evidence for our judgments of developmental level and style. We use these questions to make the developmental diagnosis either as individual observers or, as in pair therapy research, through consensus among observers and therapists. These tools of inference guide the diagnosing of discrete, molecular behaviors in microanalyses of particular peer interactions in our roles as researchers and the evaluation of more molar patterns of repeated behavior (e.g., across pair therapy sessions) in our roles as clinical interventionists. For example, when Janine states to Tania, "You want to make a model, you make it out of clay," we report that her voice is sharp and clipped. Thus we infer a more irritable, angry feeling, a more bossy and controlling intent, and a more competitive perception of the other person than if the exact words were said in the warm, supportive tone of a suggestion. Indeed, there is a striking difference in the overall tone of the boys' and the girls' interactions that implies very different personal meanings in the interactions of the two dyads, even for negotiations diagnosed at the same level and orientation (e.g., Level 1 other-transforming orders).

Interpreting Interpersonal Negotiations: Placing Diagnosed Strategies in the Psychosocial-Historical Context

The third step of our analytic procedure—interpreting the diagnosed strategies—places them in the larger social matrix of the relationship. Although the settings and goals of the interactions of Brian and Jeremy and those of Tania and Janine are admittedly different in critical ways, the interactions share an important feature from the point of view of a developmental model of interpersonal negotiation. Much of the interaction in both episodes is in the form of orders, sometimes accompanied by impulsive physical behavior. The children often appear to act with a construal of the interaction as a battle of wills, and with the intent of attaining the self's goals alone, not caring—or at least not caring much—about the wants of the other. According to the developmental scheme just presented, these negotiations would fall at Level 1 in an other-transforming orientation. Both pairs of children appear to use many unilateral, assertively ordering strategies, yet this way of interacting seems more successfully used by the boys at home than by the girls in the clinic setting. Why does the interaction of the girls go badly and end with what amounts to a total breakdown of interaction, when the predominant use of orders worked so well for the boys?

Negotiation behaviors at the same developmental level and interpersonal orientation have different personal and developmental meanings depending on their context. The act of "diagnosing" negotiation strategies gives them *developmental* meaning, but the *functional* meaning of a negotiation strategy is inherently contextual. To interpret the meaning of a negotiation strategy in terms of its adaptive function in regulating the interaction, we must examine its place in the larger social context—that is, in the context of the ongoing relationship. Relevant kinds of analysis for evaluating contextual meaning include assessments of the individual (each person's personality style and interpersonal understanding competence level), the dyad (the past history of the relationship and the sequence of events in the present interaction), and the system (each person's relationship history with significant others, which socializes specific relational patterns and group norms).

The two opening narratives provide such a striking contrast in social regulation that we can make a rather rich and illuminating (though incomplete) interpretive description of the different dynamics of the peer interactions by examining only one of the aforementioned relevant factors: the sequence of negotiations occurring in these particular sessions. The sequential unfolding of social interaction is the focus of many traditional quantitative analyses of social interaction, but our analysis is more qualitative and contextual.

We have noted that during their play period the boys negotiated with many orders and commands, frequently in a one-way or unilateral manner that did not call on forms of reciprocity or compromise. Brian commanded Jeremy to yield the trash compactor. Later, with a firm, "Jeremy!" he insisted that his friend calm down. Jeremy ordered Brian to allow "C3PO" to stay on the space station. At another time he asserted that Brian has "got to" pick up the strewn creepy crawlies. An adult who views commands as only a negative aspect of social interaction might come away from this interaction thinking it uncooperative and hence unsociable if not unsuccessful, yet the boys seemed to accept each other's commands relatively easily and naturally. Jeremy and Brian were able to use each other's orders as a means or source of external control, alternately regulating each other.

The boy's use of (Level 1) orders and commands often constituted the application of a strategy one level higher than the impulsive behavior of the peer, and it was often offered—and accepted—as a source of control for maintaining self-regulation in the context of the interaction. This regulation often was given in the form of orders (Level 1) addressed to a child who was hinting toward expressive behavior characterized by (Level 0) impulsivity. For example, when Jeremy became almost frenzied in his play with the space station model, finally throwing some model pieces out of the compactor with a shriek, Brian said firmly and angrily, "Jeremy!" Although he was becoming very involved in the fantasy play, and his excitement and agitation were not derived from interaction directly with Brian, Jeremy had started slipping toward a wild expression of aggressive impulses. However, he was able to control these impulses when Brian's firm tone indicated that the equilibrium of their play was in jeopardy. Thus when Brian became disequilibrated (upset) by Jeremy's impulsive expressiveness, their interaction shifted from connection-oriented shared experience to negotiation. Brian's Level 1, other-transforming communication in response to his own discomfort served as a cue to Jeremy to take self-transforming actions to bring himself back into control, and he was able to so with a little help from his friend.

Later these reciprocal roles were reversed. When Brian began to "lose control," scattering the creepy crawlies to the four corners of the room with aroused inner excitement, Jeremy told Brian that he had to follow the rule of cleaning up after himself. Again the expressive interaction turned into negotiation; Jeremy's Level 1, other-transforming strategy, made as a one-way order, served as an external force for Brian, which he was then able to use for self-regulation. He calmed down and reordered the crawlies.

Not only were the (Level 1) orders offered to a child who was regressing toward (Level 0) impulsivity, in other exchanges the claim with a call to fairness and reciprocity (Level 2) was offered after Level 1 or 0 demands were tried, as in the first negotiation about the use of the trash compactor. Further, the strategies Jeremy and Brian used as declarations and assertions of the need for the other's self-control were not only often one level above the level where the more disequilibrated child appeared to be functioning, the child who was being "regulated" was able to accept these strategies as "fair" in the sense that he recognized the strategies as more adequate ways of dealing with disequilibrium. Although upset, Jeremy was able to "listen to reason" when Brian claimed that he (Brian) should get to play with the compactor first. In turn Brian was able to tacitly accept that Jeremy should have first pick next time. Thus, each child was responsive to later controls for regulating the self's behavior and maintaining fairness. It is also interesting to note that Brian's Level 2 statement also was followed by a classic Level 2, self-transforming strategy and statement from

Jeremy—"OK, but next time I get to choose first." Higher (Level 2) strategies seemed to beget higher level strategies in this pair.

With Janine and Tania, however, the orders and grabbing came at a level that was equal to or lower than the level of the other's behavior, and they were competitive and potentially destructive to the relationship, rather than supportive and regulating of it. When either of these two children put forth an assertion of will in Level 1 form, the other matched her, will to will, in a confrontative way. In the very first exchange Tania yelled out with a harsh demandingness, "Where's a model for me?" (Level 1). Janine's response was an irritated, barked order: "You want to make a model, you can make it out of clay" (Level 1). Later as they were planning the puppet show, Tania asserted, "Quick, get on that side, on that side!" Rather than accepting Tania's direction, Janine countered in a Level 1 fashion, "No, don't do that. Do it there." Later, in their interaction around the puppet, Tania declared with building frustration, "You can't have that one!" "Yes, I can!" Janine growled back. Whereas Brian and Jeremy were able and willing to accept each other's Level 1 or Level 2 assertions of will and postpone or compromise their own needs with self-transforming actions matched in level, Janine and Tania each pulled tighter on the ends of the negotiation rope held between them. When one tugged with Level 1 other-transforming strategies, the other tugged back forcefully *in kind,* as if unwilling to lose even an inch of what they must have as theirs.

Furthermore, each girl reinforced and accentuated the regressive (Level 0) impulsivity of the other, rather than serving as a source of external regulation and control. When either started to lose control, and her impulses began to dictate her actions, the other would collude and join with these chaotic feelings, actually dropping in level, instead of curbing them with helpful, higher-level strategies. First, the girls seemed to compete in an attempt to "out-naughty" one another as they talked with increasingly disorganized thoughts about messy rooms and cats escaping or being tortured. On the heels of this "discussion" Tania screamed, "What should I make?!" expressing frustration and helplessness about her work with clay. Janine's response reflected this helplessness as she screamed back wildly, "Nothing!" Later Janine threw clay at Tania in an impulsive way, and Tania's response was to screech with surprise. Compare this to Brian's controlling glare at Jeremy when he started to throw materials frantically: Brian's glare served to calm Jeremy down, but surely a screech does not have this effect. As the play evolved, Janine's monster noises led into a screaming competition between the girls. And finally when Tania furiously threw the lion puppet at Janine's feet, spitting out, "You can take your stupid pet," Janine's response was an impulsive (Level 0) physical exit from the scene. Thus, both girls lacked the ability to regulate each other's primitive expressiveness. Each got caught up in the partner's loss of control instead of switching the expressive interaction into a negotiative mode with helpful, chaos-curbing orders, as the boys did.

Our model points out that low-level strategies demonstrate less of an ability to integrate other-transforming and self-transforming orientations within one context for negotiation. Generally speaking, peer interactions at the lower levels can remain mutually satisfying (i.e., the relationship can continue) only if the children can shift from one orientation to the other across different situations during the course of a play session. Brian and Jeremy were able to take turns acting in other-transforming and self-transforming ways. Brian ordered that he have first shot at the trash compactor, trying to make Jeremy change his wants or actions toward using the compactor; Jeremy, however reluctantly, withdrew his pursuit of the compactor. Later Jeremy insisted that Brian not take the "C3PO" from its initial place, and Brian agreed.

Janine and Tania, on the other hand, showed a stubborn unwillingness to take any self-transforming action. Both girls were rigidly locked into strategies of only one interpersonal orientation, each battling to make the other change for the self. For whatever reason, such a switch probably would have felt to both like too much loss of control; such flexible behavior was too unfamiliar for them.

When Tania tried to engage Janine in a game of checkers or play puppets (perhaps because she felt more competent at these activities than at clay modelling), Janine refused to budge from her own interests (perhaps because she felt more secure working with clay). Through the negotiation for working with clay versus puppets, there was no true sense of compromise, even when surface statements or actions took the form of compromise. After Janine adamantly rejected Tania's overture, barking "No! I'm doing a clay bunny!," Tania called upon a principle of apparent reciprocity. She said, "I did your stupid clay for you." The form of her words had the superficial appearance of Level 2, calling for a fair exchange, and implying that each should accommodate (self-transform) by spending time doing what the other wanted. However, the tone of Tania's statement conveyed unmasked anger, such that the feeling was not one of mutual sympathy but one of embattled challenge. Tania even undercut her own accommodation (of doing the clay) by calling it "stupid," thus attacking the value of the activity and of Janine's interests. Therefore, although the actual words called for compromise and a transforming of the self's interests, the tone offered an angry battle cry from an unchanging and entrenched self.

Likewise, Janine's apparent compromise to join Tania at this point was really a compromise only if viewed at the level of gross motoric behavior (she *did* walk over to the puppet corner), but not if other relevant cues are taken into consideration. The "style" or "tone" of her movement to join Tania was replete with resistance, as she forcefully hurled her work onto the table and clomped stiffly across the room. At the same time she commanded, "Let me finish this," in a tone that seemed to tell Tania to "bug off." In Janine's response, then, we see angry rejection at the same time that she joined Tania's puppet play: Janine strongly undercut her manifest self-transforming action with not-so-latent other-transforming tones and words.

We might conjecture that if either child had carried through consonantly with her self-transforming surface actions, interpersonal equilibrium might have been restored. What if Tania's call to mutual accommodation had been offered with sympathy? What if Janine had joined the puppet play with temporary willingness rather than violent resistance, or had asked to finish the clay in a compromising tone? The girls might not have wound themselves into such distress and disequilibrium. Instead, by the time Janine joined the puppet play, she felt resentful at giving up her own wants, and Tania felt resentful of Janine's rejection. In consequence, both girls tried to order each other and refused to be self-transforming, and both internal and interpersonal affective disequilibrium escalated until Janine finally bolted from the room.

It is important to note, especially following an example such as this session with Janine and Tania, that other-transforming strategy use, in and of itself, is not inherently "bad" or maladaptive. For Brian and Jeremy it presented no problems. That the rigidity and lack of alternatives and flexibility are the problem is brought home by observing that children whose maladaptive social behavior is passive and extremely withdrawn experience equally severe difficulties in their peer interactions in or out of pair therapy because of being self-transforming.

The microanalysis of Brian and Jeremy's play shows that both had the capacity to provide regulation to, and accept regulation from, each other. Orders abounded in their interaction, but they were not responded to in kind. In contrast, the responses given by Janine and Tania were matched in level and orientation, and seemed to escalate the power struggle or loss of control, whereas Brian and Jeremy gave complementary responses that ultimately checked any escalation. The boys' responses were complementary in level and orientation, and, furthermore, their flexible use of different levels and orientations was cued to the context, that is, to their perception of the other's construal, affect, and intentions. They generally responded to orders from the other either with an accepting self-transforming strategy (presumably when they felt their partner's command was a reasonable suggestion) or with a higher Level 2 other-transforming persuasion (when the other's Level 1 behavior was not found reasonable). Moreover, they also used orders when they perceived the other was "losing it" (losing control with impulsivity and lack of perspective). Their orders, despite being "only" Level 1, were offered and accepted as helpful controls, intended for managing behavior or maintaining fairness in the interaction. The boys' orders resulted in successful maintenance of the interaction rather than in the kind of unyielding competition that Tania and Janine engaged in, which was potentially destructive of the interaction and ultimately, if left unsupervised, of the relationship.

To fill out the interpretation of our direct observations of these two peer interactions, we also need to use information about the children's personalities, their past histories as individuals, and the past history of their particular relationship. For example, if we knew that Brian was much more bossy and controlling at his own home than when at a friend's, this would tell us something about his general interpersonal orientation beyond what we were able to see in one observation. Or, if we knew that Janine usually had a sharp gruff tone in her dealings with most significant others, we would be appropriately wary of attributing to her current behavior a specific anger at Tania or at something that had just happened. Instead it would suggest that generally speaking she construes relationships between the self and other(s) in terms of battles for control of objects, as well as control of other's actions, and she sees these battles requiring orders, threats, and commands, rather than persuasions or collaborations.

One of the most informative contextual factors for interpreting the developmental meaning of peer interactions, and function and dysfunction therein, is a comparison between the children's expected capacity to understand interpersonal relationships and the extent to which they apply that understanding in their social interactions—that is, the relationship between their levels of interpersonal thought and action. The (Level 1) ordering strategies are typical and age-appropriate for children of Jeremy and Brian's age, and are acceptable forms of interaction to them. At six years of age a child may be expected to have developed a reflective awareness of differences in perspective at a concrete level of individual likes and dislikes, needs and wants. The boys' Level 1 interpersonal understanding was developed to such an extent that they could apply that understanding consistently across situations. Moreover, occasionally Brian and Jeremy used higher, Level 2 negotiations, reflecting their ability to try out the cutting edge of their competence, a level of perspective coordination that was beginning to develop but was not yet integrated. Thus, Brian and Jeremy's modal Level 1 negotiation strategies and occasional Level 2 strategies were matched to their expected level of social-cognitive competence; there was a congruence for both these children between their age-typical level of understanding and their performance.

The girls, however, were older than Brian and Jeremy—nine rather than six. With these added years we expect to see Janine and Tania use a greater repertoire of strategies in negotiations with peers, reflecting a higher level of interpersonal understanding. We expect the nine-year-olds not only to have acquired a higher level of interpersonal understanding, but also to use that functional understanding of reciprocity in more challenging forms of interpersonal relationships with peers. It is not possible to determine from the narrative we presented whether the two girls had achieved the reciprocal level of social perspective coordination, but (knowing their previous interactions and personal histories) we know that the girls did have this Level 2 competence because they demonstrated reciprocal interpersonal understanding in less personally threatening contexts. Another indication that their competence was at Level 2 was their use of the hollow Level 2 statements we described earlier, those whose surface, apparently reciprocal, meaning ("I did your stupid clay for you") is belied by their angry tone.

In the twelve minutes of their interaction, Tania and Janine *not once* displayed what should be a well-established level of negotiation by this age (i.e., Level 2), much less "cutting edge" strategies at Level 3. This discrepancy—the developmental gap—between their actual ways of relating (predominantly at levels 1 and 0) and their normatively expected capacity of understanding relationships (at Level 2 with perhaps some hints of Level 3) is striking. Chronologically, Tania and Janine no longer inhabited a predominantly unilateral (Level 1) social world. Orders are not enough anymore once reciprocal (Level 2) understanding becomes the norm. Children's "required" roles evolve as they grow up, and the life tasks of nine-year-olds differ from those of six-year-olds: preadolescence brings tasks that require greater reciprocity of thought and action than those of the juvenile period of middle childhood. Therefore, each girl may have wanted and expected reciprocity and sensitivity to her needs, but neither received this from, or offered this to, the other in actual negotiation.

In essence, reciprocal control of affect seems to be one thing friends are for at any age or level. But the reason that the control and mutual regulation worked for the boys yet not for the girls goes beyond this. The six-year-old boys had something else going for them: a long-standing set of positive shared experiences together, a connection on which to base their mutual social regulations. Moreover, the opportunity for shared experience and expressive emotional behavior—which for six-year-olds often centers around fantasy play—continued in this session. Tania and Janine did not get along well enough to be able to begin to play together—their toys (e.g., the puppets) became weapons in their embattled relationship instead of props for the shared experience of fantasy play.

In interpreting specific interpersonal negotiations or series of negotiations we rely heavily on information about the history of the present ongoing relationship. How, for example, do we interpret the lack of reciprocal (Level 2) negotiation in Tania and Janine's play? Because we do know that the girls had used reciprocity in their dealings previously (i.e., when the therapist had stayed with them), we interpret these particular twelve minutes as a temporary regression in the service of ultimate progression instead of as a hopeless and complete disaster.

Our interpretation is enriched further by considering the dyad's past individual emotional/relational histories, a kind of analysis that goes beyond the meaning-description that we more often engage in to a kind of explanation-description. The girls did not cue themselves to the context of the ongoing peer relationship the way the boys did, probably because they brought too much emotional "baggage" to the interaction from their past relationships. The girls did not expect reciprocity from each other because most likely neither had gotten their needs met with positive emotional responsiveness in their past or present primary relationships. Their negative, distorted construal of the other in all close relationships led them to act in a predeterminedly rejecting way, without taking into account the nature of the details and cues of the particular context and the identity of the other. In contrast, although the boys' responses to each other were also shaped by their idiosyncratic past relational histories, they were open to meet the reciprocal regulation requirements in the ongoing context of their relationship to the extent that their developmental level of social perspective coordination allowed.

It seems that strategies at the leading edge of children's age-appropriate repertoire, such as the reciprocal persuasions of Jeremy and Brian, provide the optimal challenge for growth in a peer relationship. In contrast, the age-inappropriate fixation of the troubled girls in the new context of this particular session at a unilateral level (orders) were not adequate to regulate their interaction. Instead, they seemed to create a context conducive to social chaos, in which both girls degenerated to extremely low-level behavior.

In addition, we believe that the kind of alternation of orientation in the play of Brian and Jeremy, in which the boys were complementary in their responses but alternately got their own way and gave in to the other, is optimal for social development. It may be common, though, to observe complementarity in orientation in which one child is consistently other-transforming and the other child always self-transforms. This rigid, defensive configuration may function for the time-being (at least the dominant/ subordinate pattern maintains the relationship) but generally does not seem to be a fertile context for social growth. In contrast, the patterning of orientation in Tania and Janine's interaction— rigidly other-transforming at the same developmental level—destroyed the interaction and probably would have destroyed the relationship itself if the larger context were not that of pair therapy, in which the adult therapist has an opportunity to mediate the impasse.

CHAPTER THREE

Theory in Action: Evidence from Observations

This chapter illustrates the second of the analytic steps of our interpretive/empirical approach to social interaction, the developmental diagnosis of interpersonal negotiation strategies. Often, in their quest for correlates, continuities, and causes of behavior, research psychologists are loath to do the basic developmental-descriptive work that serves as the foundation for their analyses. Here we take the time to present the kinds of questions we must ask ourselves *as* we observe social interaction to make an assessment of interpersonal negotiation strategies from a developmental point of view. Following this discourse on our "developmental attitude" toward the data, are a series of examples of children's and young adolescents' actual negotiation strategies.

The latter analysis is of everyday exchanges that are commonplace and concrete, and at the same time open to interpretation. Remember, it should be neither expected nor predicted that an individual will necessarily negotiate consistently at any one level or orientation across all relationships or contexts. The negotiation orientations and levels are essentially cartographic descriptions of negotiation behaviors in the context of live interactions. In this sense, momentary or historical interpersonal contexts are as important a set of factors in the level and orientation of the strategy used as is the level of social-cognitive and behavioral competence the individual has attained. Thus, although individuals may have a disposition to function within a particular orientation or at a particular level, negotiation strategies are not simply internal competence achievements. They are live-action phenomena—states not traits—influenced by the great complexities of social cognition in action.

Furthermore, the use of a given strategy is rarely the isolated choice of an individual participant. Instead, the level and orientation of strategies used by one person have a strong influence upon the level and orientation of the strategies used by the other. A person can bring another down to his or her level, and conversely one person can raise another up (within the constraints of that other individual's ontogenetic capacity). In other words, because the model is not solely focused on ontogenesis, the emergence of new strategies in an *individual's* repertoire (which is the thrust of this chapter), it can account for the sequences of strategies, both within and between persons, that occur during specific social interactions or within the development of specific social relationships.

It is important to recognize that within developmental constraints people's strategies are variable across contexts, and the model provides a way to categorize these *strategies*, not to classify the *individual* himself or herself—for example, as a "Level 2" or a "self-transforming" person. Persons are not "Level 1" or "other-transforming," but active negotiators whose strategic choices are affected by factors as wide ranging as their social-cognitive competence, the behavior of the others in a negotiation, and as transient and diverse as what they had for breakfast, whether they had breakfast, or what the weather is like.

Additionally, although it may be tempting to characterize people who use predominantly other-transforming strategies as aggressive or dominant, and to characterize those who use many self-transforming strategies as submissive or passive, this equation of an orientation use with a personality type is somewhat risky and dangerous for a number of reasons. First, many of the distinctive features of strategies within any given developmental level hold true for both orientations—for example, at Level 0 both other- and self-transforming strategies are impulsive. Furthermore, the strategies within a single developmental level and the same orientation can be different enough behaviorally to represent different character or personality styles.

For example, at Level 1, the individual who constantly uses threats of force (an other-transforming strategy) is likely to be seen (depending on age, culture, and other critical factors) as bossy or hostile, whereas the person who uses another strategy of the same level and orientation—e.g., criticizing the other's skills to rationalize pursuit of the self's interests or activities—is likely to be viewed as arrogant or conceited (once again, factoring in key contextual issues). Both strategies are at the same orientation and level, yet each are characteristic of different personality styles. Therefore, before trying to characterize personality dimensions, we should look at people in various contexts. Depending on a person's variability in levels, orientations, and strategy types (and the degree of variability may itself reflect something of the individual's personality), it may be necessary to examine varyingly large numbers of that individual's strategies before acquiring the sense of consistency connoted by the term "personality."

Any strategy, regardless of its developmental level or orientation, represents an attempt to exercise some kind of control over (i.e., an attempt to resolve) feelings of disequilibrium. The polarity of self-transforming versus other-transforming strategies decreases with developmental maturity because the perspectives of self and other are themselves brought into conjunction in the management of control, which is a constant element in all negotiation. But the model stresses that a collaborative orientation is not simply some *midpoint* or compromise between two orientations or poles, but the increasing *integration* of the two orientations at a qualitatively differentiated level of development. It is not until one is capable of the higher level strategies, with which one can more easily share control rather than totally grab for it or yield it, that one is actually more in control, instead of being either out of control of overcontrolling.

It is no more or less adaptive per se to use an other-transforming than a self-transforming orientation, or a high-level or low-level strategy. Adaptation, as a criterion, is based on functional considerations, on how well the individual's strategies "fit" with those of the others with whom he or she interacts. The descriptions of strategies at lower developmental levels, although they may connote undesirable behavior from an adult's standpoint, reflect structures that are part of the process of normal development, and therefore are age-appropriate for young children. It is only when these forms of interaction rigidify and represent the limits of response of older individuals who should "know better" that there is cause for some concern.

Even for older persons, low-level strategies may in fact be appropriate, in the sense of being functional, in certain contexts for negotiation. Whereas in the domain of reflective interpersonal *understanding*, higher levels are expected and preferable, in that they signify greater conceptual competence and greater insight into the nature of persons in relationship to one another, in the domain of interpersonal negotiation strategies it is not always the case that higher is better. When behavioral scientists use the term "better," they are not necessarily making value judgments. Developmentalists using structural models usually take "better" to mean greater complexity (usually cognitive complexity), higher-level mental processes, or greater behavioral differentiation and hierarchical integration. Those using primarily functional models often use the term "better" contextually to mean more adaptive, a better fit into some ecological niche. In this functional sense, various levels and orientations of negotiation strategies may be more or less optimal or adaptive in various contexts. In a context requiring mutuality (for example, an ongoing close personal friendship), higher-level strategies are preferable because they show consideration for the feelings and cares of both self and other, and for the growth and development of the relationship itself. However, in a context in which the issues are genuinely urgent short-term goals, higher-level strategies may be less appropriate (meaning less functional) than those of lower levels, which attend to immediate goals. The qualities that characterize lower-level strategies, such as immediate reactivity to a situation, may make them the strategies of choice in such contexts, regardless of the conceptual maturity of the user.

Given these provisos and qualifications, of course, this model does make partial claims about the generalizability or consistency of what we consider to be interpersonally mature conduct, both from a developmental and an adaptive standpoint. It implies that certain social interactions and competencies are shared by individuals functioning at the higher levels, and that these are better in terms of being more adequate for the complexities inherent in mature interpersonal relationships. For a strategy to be structurally or developmentally classified at higher levels requires evidence of an observing self, of the capacity to perceive and understand the complexity of others' feelings with compassion, and, equally important, to perceive and understand the nature of feelings within the self and synthesize these conceptions and perceptions in action. Certainly, over time this is also likely to prove more functionally adaptive as well.

Coding Questions for Developmental Diagnoses of Interpersonal Negotiation Strategies

As mentioned in chapter 2, the developmental level of an interpersonal negotiation strategy is diagnosed through converging evidence from the three components of the strategy that represent its developmental dimension (construal of self and other, affective disequilibrium, and primary purpose). Here are the questions we ask about these three components and interpersonal orientation for each strategy in order to make a diagnosis (that is, in more conventional terms, in order to "code" the strategy). For now, we will refer back to the social interactions described in that chapter to help concretize this interpretive process, but the rest of the chapter will expand greatly on these examples.

How Is Construal of Self and Other Classified by Level? The first question we ask is, How does the actor appear to construe the psychological nature of the self and other in the context of the negotiation? This cognitive component defines the nature and capacities of the actors involved, as understood at that moment:

> Does the actor appear to construe one or both actors as objects, as objective barriers to each other's quest for a goal, without appearing to consider the self or other as having subjective interests within the context of the negotiation? Does the actor ignore the significant other as having no vested interest or claim whatsoever in the context? If so, then the construal is classified as *Level 0*. For example, when Janine bolts from the pair therapy room, she totally ignores Tania's internal state and appears to consider her as only a block to obtaining her own powerfully felt, but largely uncomprehended, needs.

> Does the actor appear to construe the other as a separate individual with interests and desires that are viewed as necessarily in direct competition with those of the self for a scarce or limited resource so that only one individual can achieve his or her goal? If so, then the construal would be classified as *Level 1*. Jeremy's construal of Brian as in competition for the space station represents both self and other as having separate wills and purposes, but each individual's motives are seen in an "either-or," "mine versus yours" light.

> Does the actor seem to suggest that each party can consider the other's perspective, at least enough to speak to one another's concerns? Is there a sense that the disequilibrium may be due to conflicting feelings within the self or between self and other? If so, then the construal would be classified as *Level 2*. Brian's subsequent attempt to provide a reason why he should play with the space station shows his recognition that it is possible to change Jeremy's thoughts and feelings through (self-interested) communication.

> Does the actor seem to recognize that both parties include, as part of their deliberations and as part of their self-interest in the negotiation, the interest of the other as well as the interest of the relationship as it is represented in the specific negotiation under consideration? If so,

then the construal would be classified as *Level 3*. None of
the children in the chapter 2 examples exhibit this level of
construal because the cognitive capacity to reflect
simultaneously on the self, other, and the relationship—
and to appreciate the needs of all three as well as the
mutual effect within the dyad—does not normally develop
until adolescence.

What Is the Actor's Purpose in the Context for Negotiation? The
primary interpersonal purpose component of a strategy is the dominant goal-oriented motivation of the behavior, motivation in the
sense of what the person thinks is his or her reason for attempting
to achieve some goal or to deal with the goal achievement of another. Similar to the view of some action theorists, motivation or
purpose is used in our developmental analysis as the "forward pull"
of a to-be-achieved goal on current conduct rather than as the
"from-behind-push" of unconscious motivation to explain conduct
(e.g., Eckensberger and Meacham, 1984). We use the term "primary intent" because we appreciate that at successive developmental levels, new intents are added while old intents may still be
relevant, albeit no longer primary. Immediate goals tend to focus
on the allocation of goods, social services, or attention, but longer-
term relationship-oriented goals are inherent—though often unat-
tended to—in contexts for negotiation, which involve achieving
subjective as well as objective desires (e.g., affection as well as good
fortune):

> Is the primary purpose to achieve a self-defined goal,
> without any consideration of the goals or purposes or
> interest of the other parties involved? Is the actor
> pursuing immediate physical goals? If so, then the
> primary purpose would be classified as *Level 0*. Janine's
> enraged bolt from the pair therapy room was motivated by
> her own immediate need to escape a situation she could
> not control any other way, without reflection on what effect
> her furious action would have on her in the future, or how
> her pursued goals, which were undifferentiated from her
> action, related to Tania's goals.
>
> Is the primary purpose to establish a position of sole
> power and control in the interaction—be it for self or
> other—so as to be the one to decide who goes first, gets
> what, or keeps what, who wins or yields control to the
> other? If so, then the primary purpose is classified at
> *Level 1*. When Jeremy announces "I'm doing the trash
> compactor," he is attempting to establish his goals at the
> expense of, and distinct from, those of Brian. He calls it

out as if, since his words will race past Brian and reach the compactor before Brian's hand reaches it, his own claim for the compactor should be respected. This suggests that Jeremy is aware that Brian's perspective differs from his own, and that he must state his claim and his justification to Brian to give it social validity and negotiable force.

Is the primary purpose to "make a pact" satisfactory to each party? Is this agreement, however, thought to be achieved either by changing the other to accommodate that person's perspective to the self's or by changing the self's perspective to fit with that of the other instead of by mutual accommodation? If so, then the primary purpose would be classified as *Level 2*. When Brian explains, "You've already played with this, but it's new to me," he is trying to establish his own goals as more primary and to deemphasize Jeremy's goals by psychological manipulation. He plays up to Jeremy's thoughts to influence his wishes—and ultimately his actions. He does not try to rest merely on a unilateral and physical "I got here first so it's mine" claim. Instead he feels the need to provide a rationale for his claim. (However, regardless of his level of justification, we do not expect that Brian would be willing to lighten up his firm grip on the compactor knob.)

Is the primary purpose to have both parties achieve a sense of collaboration, a sense that each person has individual interests as well as mutual interests and that some balance needs to be achieved? Is the goal seen to be to resolve conflicts in contexts for negotiation that maintain the balance of the relationship by striving for long-term as well as short-term goals while trying to achieve the particulars? If so, then the primary purpose would be classified as *Level 3*. Again, none of the children in our chapter 2 examples have attained the capacity to use shared reflection to pursue mutual goals with the understanding that mutuality of outcome and communication in its pursuit are as important as the particular outcome with regard to their initial goal in an interpersonal negotiation.

How are Perception and Control of Affective Disequilibrium Classified by Level? The affective component of an interpersonal negotiation strategy attends to the way the person perceives and attempts to control internal emotional disequilibrium arising in a context for interpersonal negotiation. Three aspects of affective disequilibrium are qualitatively distinct at each developmental level. Two of these aspects represent the perception of the upset— its *cause* (how the disequilibrium came about) and its *locus* (where the bad or painful feelings reside). The third aspect of affective disequilibrium we consider is *the way it is dealt with* in the attempt to return to a balanced or calm psychological state:

Does the negotiation context appear to generate in the person a diffuse, global, and undifferentiated sense of cause and locus? Does the person appear to experience the disequilibrated feelings as all-encompassing and out of the self's control such that relief must come from some external source of control or authority? If so, then the affective perception and control would be classified as *Level 0*. When Janine bolts from the room, ending her interaction with Tania, she makes no conscious attempt to control her enraged, angry feelings through planned action. She cannot deal with these "out of control" feelings. Instead, her feelings control and literally propel her.

Does the person seem to perceive feelings as distinct but *objective* elemental phenomena that can only be changed or soothed if the self's perceived goal is achieved, but in no other way (I will feel badly until I get what I say I want)? Does the actor appear to believe that internal feelings can only be changed through changes in factors external to the self (nonintrapsychic factors)? If so, then the affective perception and control would be classified as *Level 1*. When Jeremy makes his one-way challenge to Brian's claim on the trash compactor, his tone is urgent and concerned, yet his look is questioning and uncertain. His emotional state appears distinct from his action, yet the feelings are transitory, and he seeks relief from them by trying to change Brian's actions instead of acting directly on his own feelings.

Are the feelings being experienced understood to be subjectively as well as objectively caused? Are they recognized to be due to conflicts within the self (I want that toy, but I also want you to play with me)? Are disequilibrated feelings dealt with by trying to push them out, down, or inside the subjective self? If so, then the affective perception and control would be classified as *Level 2*. Brian reacts to Jeremy's challenge to his claim to the trash compactor with a tone that is explaining, yet delivered with force and a slight scowl. The combination of reasonableness and force suggests that he recognizes the conflict between his personal and interpersonal needs (getting what he wants, yet not alienating Jeremy) as well as the conflict between his immediate goals and those of Jeremy.

Are disequilibrated feelings experienced as painful but workable—that is, changeable through actions the self can take? Are disequilibrated feelings located in a historical context, viewed as being related to past events, experiences, and relationships, as well as being mutable through future actions? Are feelings managed or controlled through a process of "working through," including the expression of feelings or communication and clarification of feelings with a significant other who may be party to their cause? If so, then the affective perception and control would be classified as *Level 3*. The children in our previous examples are too young to have achieved the capacity to discriminate the variety of feelings within self and between self and other inherent in a particular context for negotiation, to view their place in the broader historical context of the self and the relationship, and to slowly and reciprocally work to integrate the feelings into the relationship through internal and shared reflection.

How Is Interpersonal Orientation Classified? Although in practice a person never acts solely upon the self or upon the other, nor are actions solely derived from within the self independent of the complexity of the interactions between self and the other, it still remains useful to look upon actions directed primarily toward the changing of the self or the changing of the other, or, at the higher levels, the changing of both. This social action dimension of the model represents an attempt to begin to redefine some classic dichotomies in personality theory within a unified development framework—dichotomies such as passive and aggressive, introverted and extroverted, or acting-out and withdrawn.

The INS model suggests that neither a self-transforming nor an other-transforming strategy is necessarily less or more mature or pathological. Rather it is the rigidity, or lack of differentiation, at the lower levels in contexts where higher-level functioning is both expected and adaptive that determines the degree to which there is normality or pathology, maturity or immaturity. It is often the case, particularly at the lower developmental levels of negotiation, that it is much easier to diagnose orientation than level. Thus, one can use orientation to help determine level:

Does the actor use unreflective physical force to make absolute and impulsive demands or to totally reject or ignore the validity of the other person's needs? If so, then the orientation would be classified as *other-transforming at Level 0*. Janine's angry bolt from the pair therapy room is an example of such an impulsive and total rejection of the other person in a context for negotiation. Or does the actor show impulsive withdrawal or total capitulation (i.e., unreflective and automatic compliance with and acceptance of the wishes of the other person)? If so, then the interpersonal orientation would be classified as *self-transforming at Level 0*. If Janine had run from the pair therapy in helpless panic instead of rejecting rage, it would reflect such an unreflective and total withdrawal from her conflict with Tania.

Is the actor observed to be commanding, ordering, bullying in interactions with others, perhaps even using the threat of force to attempt to change the other's actions so that the self's unilaterally defined goals will be achieved? If so, the interpersonal orientation would be classified as *other-transforming at Level 1*. Jeremy's announcement that he was doing the trash compactor was delivered with such a commanding, ordering tone. Or does the actor appear to take actions that are submissively obedient to the other—that is, consciously putting the other in a position of control and the self in a weaker or submissive position, quick to withdraw the legitimacy of his or her own recognized will or interest in the arena of negotiation? If so, the interpersonal orientation would be classified as *self-transforming at Level 1*. Brian's compliance with Jeremy's order to pick up the "creepy crawlies" reflected his obedient submission to Jeremy's will.

Does the actor appear to attempt to use psychological influence (e.g., manipulation) or persuasive tactics in order to change the other person's perceived wishes, views, or feelings so that they match, and thus facilitate, the achievement of the self's wishes? If so, the interpersonal orientation would be classified as *other-transforming at Level 2*. Brian's forceful but reasonable response to Jeremy's challenge to his control of the trash compactor was assertive and persuasive, but he accommodated Jeremy's perspective to the extent that he put psychological effort and energy into the process of influence, recognizing the existence if not the full legitimacy of Jeremy's perspective, rather than simply using physical force or the threat thereof. Or does the actor appear to be compliant to the other's wishes, not by negotiating away all the self's interests as at the lower self-transforming levels, but by putting them second, or "on hold," in order to keep the relation with and liking of the other person a high priority? If so, the interpersonal orientation would be classified as *self-transforming at Level 2*. Jeremy's deferential response to Brian's persistent but reasoned claim to the trash compactor ("Okay, but next time I get to choose first") relinquished his immediate claim but made it clear that his own desires, though deferred, were still recognized and valued.

Does the actor appear to try to strike a balance between meeting the self's felt needs and meeting the expressed needs of the other? If so, the interpersonal orientation would be classified as *collaborative* (Level 3). There are no examples of a collaborative orientation in the two opening narratives of chapter 2 because, as we have mentioned, these children have not acquired the capacity for mutual coordination of perspectives (Level 3) necessary to integrate self-transforming and other-transforming actions into more equilibrated action in Level 3 negotiation. Interpersonal negotiations at this level are more likely to lead to mutually satisfying outcomes because of the balancing of the perspective of self with that of other, or self-agency and assertion with relatedness and accommodation.

Examples of Actual Negotiation Strategies

The examples below are organized by level of negotiation. The sections for Levels 0 to 2 divide naturally into two parts, one for each orientation, and the Levels 3 and 4 section deals in one part with the emerging collaborative orientation. Table 3 provides a sampling of prototypical strategies. We touch upon many of these, some in relatively great detail and others quite lightly, to describe the nature of the strategies' underlying structure by analyzing the components that define their characters. That is, we try to illustrate how the form of the actor's construal of self and other, primary purpose, and perception and control of affective disequilibrium help us assign the strategies to their respective developmental levels, as distinct from levels above or below.

The examples in the last chapter differ from the case examples in this chapter. With Jeremy and Brian and Tania and Janine we had some information not only about the immediate interaction but

Table 3
Some Prototypical Interpersonal Strategies Coded at Developmental
Levels 0–3 in Each Orientation

Other-transforming Orientation	Self-transforming Orientation
LEVEL 0	
A. Forcefully blots out other's expressed wish B. Unprovoked impulsive grabbing C. Absolute repulsion of other	A. Takes impulsive flight B. Uses automatic affective withdrawal C. Responds with robotlike obedience
LEVEL 1	
A. Uses one-way threats to achieve self's goals B. Makes threats of force C. Criticizes other's skills as a rationale for self's activity	A. Makes weak initiatives with ready withdrawal B. Acts victimized C. Appeals to source of perceived power from a position of helplessness
LEVEL 2	
A. Uses "friendly" persuasion B. Seeks allies for support of self's ideas C. Goal-seeking through impressing others with self's talents, knowledge, etc.	A. Asserts self's feelings and thoughts as valuable but secondary B. Follows but offers input into other's lead C. Uses self's feelings of inadequacies as a tool for interpersonal negotiation
LEVEL 3	
A. Anticipates and integrates possible feelings of others about self's negotiation B. Balances focus on relations with focus on self's concrete goal	

also about the physical context and social relational contexts, the distinct personalities of each child, and to a slight degree their personal histories. Any interpretation of both the developmental and adaptive nature of a negotiation is likely to be more valid when it draws on such information.

The examples in this chapter are limited to accounts of the interchange itself at the moment, without dealing in much detail with the broader social environment or psychological context, a knowledge of the children's personalities, their personal histories, or their relationships to one another over time. This is because the following examples are chosen to convey *prototypical* strategies, commonly used by an individual, to illustrate the model. They are used to give substantive form to the abstract structure of the model's levels and orientation. Because the examples are illustrations rather than assessments, we worry less about accuracy in the complete interpretation of these examples, and thus less about having the richer information that would be necessary in the developmental diagnosis and contextual interpretation of ongoing processes of interpersonal negotiation, as in clinical settings.

These examples are also meant to demonstrate that on the one hand behaviors may look similar (to be in the same orientation means to have the same "surface manifestations") and yet be at different developmental levels, and conversely, that behaviors may at first glance appear quite disparate (be in different orientations) and be at the same developmental level. This, among other things, explains the necessity for structural analysis of the underlying organization of interactions. In addition, every strategy presented in this chapter could be interpreted differently in a functional sense if it were considered in a markedly different context than the "normative" context that we imply in these descriptions. Consider, for example, the Level 0 strategy of *Taking Impulsive Flight*—that is, leaving the scene of an interpersonal negotiation context without communicating when faced with some perceived resistance from a significant other. This behavior could be interpreted as more functional if taken under severe duress rather than under relatively benign conditions. From a structural perspective, it would be diagnosed at a higher level if it were *consciously* chosen as the best alternative given the circumstances, if, for example, the actor considered that the particular other party was impossible to reach, or that time out to simmer down was needed. Thus, the following examples are offered with this proviso: all other things being normal, this would be a prototypical strategy of this level and orientation, according to our interpretation of the developmental components.

As to the "normativeness" of the examples, most of them are presented as they would develop ontogenetically in the individual with age. In other words, examples are chosen from age-typical groups—that is, children who are acting with age-appropriate strategies, strategies that typically are constructed and implemented during the given age period. We do not include in this chapter examples of the "regressive" use of low-level strategies used by individuals who "know better." Nor do we show the "socially immature" use of low-level strategies by older, perhaps clinically disturbed, children.

Our sources of data for this chapter have been varied and diverse, systematic and accidental, detailed and fleeting. Our primary sources have been:

1. Systematic observations of interactions in natural settings—that is, playgroups, preschools, schools, overnight and day camps, homes, clubs, over a period of nine years. Most of the analyses were based upon narrative descriptions; where possible, videotaped observations were used for analysis. Most of the vignettes in the following sections rely upon data from these sources.

2. Formal and controlled naturalistic (as opposed to laboratory) observational studies. Two such studies have been completed. The first (Selman, Schorin, Stone, and Phelps, 1983) observed the social interactions of four groups of public-school girls, ages eight to eleven, who interacted in after-school activity groups once a week for an hour and a half over the course of twelve weeks. Narratives by observers and videotape recordings were used. The second (Selman and Demorest, 1984) involved only two subjects, two nine-year-old boys, who met regularly for two years in pair therapy with an adult therapist, and whose interactions were unobtrusively observed by two researchers trained to identify contexts for interpersonal negotiation and to classify the strategies used by the children.

3. Systematic and ongoing observations of over fifty pairs of interpersonally troubled children and young adolescents, in the age range of eight to sixteen, who have been participants in the pair therapy project. Several pilot studies on both the clinical (Selman and Arboleda, 1986) and research (Lyman and Selman, 1985) aspects of this project have been undertaken.

4. Unobtrusive observation of small groups (six to eight students in a group) of early adolescents with social and emotional difficulties who participated in either classroom discussions (Selman, Lavin, and Brion-Meisels, 1982) or twice-weekly adolescent issues seminars (Brion-Meisels and Selman, 1984) across the span of the school year.

5. A series of interview studies with children aged seven to twelve (Abrahami, Selman, and Stone, 1981; Adalbjarnardottir and Selman, 1989) and eleven to nineteen (Selman et al., 1986) designed to examine how youngsters across this age range think about the processes of interpersonal negotiation and the resolution of interpersonal dilemmas when they are not directly involved in the negotiation process, and how their thinking relates to fami-

ly mental health and their own behavior (Beardslee, Schultz, and Selman, 1987). These studies allows us to probe for the underlying processes of thought that youngsters growing up can bring to common, everyday situations involving negotiations with significant others.

It would be as inaccurate to suggest that the examples that follow were selected to conform to an already prefitted and fully-formed model as it would to claim that the model itself was developed directly from observations of social interaction uninformed by previous theoretical presuppositions. The process was interactive. Admittedly the core assumptions, spelled out in chapters 1 and 2, were constantly in the observers' eyes as, and even before, data were formally gathered. However, the observed actions and interactions sometimes verified the theory, sometimes invalidated it, but were always an abrasive to the possible oversimplification of a priori theorizing. Each observation and analysis forced us to demonstrate how and why that interaction, and the observed strategies within it, could be considered to be one level rather than another, one or another orientation, or sufficiently informative to support any valid categorization at all. Examples presented challenges to model building, and hence reshaped the model.

Level 0: Negotiation for Egocentric Goals by Unreflective, Impulsive, Physical Actions
The Other-transforming Orientation at Level 0

Other-transforming strategies at Level 0, like self-transforming strategies, are largely physicalistic, impulsive, and unreflective. The purpose is simply to achieve the self's perceived goals, without reflection on the possible impact of one's own actions on the individuals involved. Neither the feelings nor the intentions of the other are consciously acknowledged or considered. A two-year-old child is newly exercising this type of strategy when in response to her mother, who is shaking her head back and forth no to the child's request for a piece of candy at the supermarket, the child takes the mother's head in her own hands and moves it up and down yes. The child's strategy suggests, as one possibility, a belief that a change in the mother's surface physical actions (the direction of her head) is all that is required to change the mother's decision—and yield the child the much sought-after candy. Or alternatively, it might suggest that in the child's repertoire, there is a direct connection between the direction of head shaking and goal achievement. Up-down means "I get it"; side to side means "I don't." This delightfully primitive strategy, undertaken without rancor, indicates a lack of differentiation between action and intention, between inner choice and outer signification, which is characteristic of Level 0. By changing the mother's physical actions, the child either expects to concomitantly change her intent or fails to acknowledge intent, much less view it as separate from or relevant to her own goal-seeking activity.

Three types of Level 0 strategies (as noted in Table 3) have been seen regularly in our observational forays. We will provide an example and analysis of the first, *Forcefully Blocking Out the Other's Expressed Wish,* and then discuss one other briefly. This first strategy reflects pursuit of the self's goal by a direct sensory drowning out (denial) of the expression of the other's conflicting wishes. The aphorism "What I don't know (meaning here don't perceive, am not aware of) won't hurt me" is literally translated into "won't affect me." If the significant other's wishes cannot be registered, then, for all intents and purposes, they do not exist:

> Carol, age five, and Alice, age six, are playing at Carol's house with a record player. Carol wants to play "Old MacDonald," but Alice wants to hear a different song. As Alice starts to say why she should have her turn to choose, Carol yells, "Quiet!" As Alice tries to continue speaking, Carol's volume escalates and she screams systematically, "Shut up! Shut up! Shut up!" until finally she stands, exhaustedly yelling into Alice's face, drowning out her words. As she does this she puts on "Old MacDonald" and begins to listen to it, without a glance at Alice, as if, by dint of sheer effort, the issue has been settled satisfactorily.

Characteristic of Level 0 strategies in general, Carol's conduct acts to completely cut off the possibility of further negotiations. She uses vocal force to prohibit Alice from communicating her claim, as if this would be equivalent to Alice's having no claim. To the extent that Alice's wishes conflict with her own, Carol appears to construe Alice and her wishes as one, and as a barrier to her own wishes. Emotionally, Carol appears to be overwhelmed for the moment of the disequilibrium by distress from perceived jeopardy to her immediate wants. This distress is directly and impulsively expressed in action. It also appears to be fleeting, associated with only the impediment to her goal, rather than to be lingering, as if it related to some way Alice treated her. Her act is an immediate pursuit of her own goal, without reflective consideration of her own or Alice's purposes or of the effect of her goal pursuit on herself, Alice, or their relationship.

This "out of perception/out of contention" type of strategy can be distinguished from a similar-appearing Level 1 strategy in which the child attempts to "shout down" another in a competitive way. In that case the shouting has a combative purpose and reflects an awareness of the distinctness of the other person's needs and a wish to overcome them.

A closely related strategy is *Unreflective Impulsive Grabbing.* Often in preschools we observe a child who has been playing with a particular toy put it aside, only to grab it immediately from a newcomer who had entered the first child's "play sphere" and, without prior knowledge of the first child's earlier interest in the toy, begun to play with it. The first child acts as if his or her prior interest in the toy is sufficient to justify his or her (re)possession of it. How the child deals with his or her feelings—that is, whether or not he or she grabs—in large part seems to be determined by his or her own perception of the relative power of the two parties. Other-transforming strategies can be reactive to others as well as initiating, as our first example was. One common instance that we call *Absolute Denial and Rejection of the Other* is simply to ignore the active strategies of the other. For instance, a child who reacts to a request to finish playing and come to dinner by completely ignoring the request, as if it did not exist, is using a strategy of this kind.

The Self-transforming Orientation at Level 0

When experiencing conflict with another, the person acting at Level 0, using self-transforming strategies, has limited choices: (a) bodily removal of the self from the social environment and physical space where the disequilibrium is occurring; (b) removal of the self from any sensory or perceptual relationship with the other person involved; or (c) giving in thoughtlessly to the other, operating as if the self had no psychological awareness or agency of its own. As in any Level 0 strategy, disequilibrium is dealt with by attempting to end the interchange in which conflict is experienced, rather than by working through the conflict by interactive dealings with the other. In the self-transforming orientation the other is experienced as an overwhelming force that the self must either flee from or be engulfed by.

Responding with Robotlike Obedience is an extreme behavior in which the individual acts as if he or she were literally under the spell or will of a significant other. The self's will and feelings are not integrated into the individual's interactive plan. Instead the other's perceived wishes are unreflectively followed, with no working differentiation between the perceived wishes of other and self:

> Five-year old Vicky is playing with two older children during a school recess. The three girls are involved in a game of tag. Vicky is "it." As the game begins, Vicky runs after one of the older girls, Carrie. As Carrie is approached, she stops running, turns directly toward Vicky and commands, "Don't tag me, go get Susan." Vicky, stopping in her tracks, even as Carrie is within range, wheels and begins to run toward Susan. When she approaches her, Susan says in a giggly order, "No, don't get me, get Carrie." Once again, obediently, Vicky stops and reverses, running after Carrie. The two older girls manipulate Vicky this way for several minutes. Never does Vicky disobey an order, although her expression gradually changes from a smile to a puzzled and worried look. Even when she begins to tire, Vicky continues to act like a yoyo on a string or a frisbee in the hands of the two older girls.

Vicky's actions suggest that, in this instance, she construes both her older playmates as having total control over her and herself as relatively powerless. Her primary intent appears to be to remain a part of the game, itself rigid and somewhat unilateral. The change in her facial expression from a smile to a frown suggests some distress, but she deals with this internal disequilibrium by denying her own feelings and complying with the older girls' wishes. The interpersonal disequilibrium between her wanting to achieve some success at the game of tag and the desire of the other girls to "pull her string" is resolved by her total submission to their whims. Vicky may not act this way all the time; she may function in a totally opposite orientation when she plays with younger children, or more passive peers. But such disparate orientations are common at this low developmental level of conduct. If she had acted as she did to please her admired elders instead of thoughtlessly and without design, the strategy would still be self-transforming but would be classified at Level 1.

A second common strategy type classified as Level 0 self-transforming is *Taking Impulsive Flight*. With this strategy, as its name implies, the child reacts to the disequilibrium caused by conflicting wants by taking impulsive, uncontrolled flight away from the field of social interaction. By leaving the conflict behind, it no longer exists for the child. The child is not necessarily fearful or enraged; the predominant affective quality here is one of impulsivity (as in lack of reflection between affect felt and action taken), and the key action is fleeing, leaving behind all possible interactions with other, as if this will "work" and no other negotiative options were available. The distinction between this form of flight and the flight associated with higher levels is that at Level 0 the leaving is truly impulsive and without consideration of its effect on the other, the self, or the relationship, rather than, for example, at Level 1, where the strategy is intended to affect or control the other.

The third strategy, *Automatic Affective Withdrawal*, is in some ways more extreme than either of the first two and is more likely to be seen in interpersonally troubled and fragile children. Here the self deals with interpersonal conflict by becoming both intentionless and affectless, acting in ways that are often described as catatonic. This paralyzed, blanking-out behavior is a direct expression of the experience of feeling overwhelmed by the force of the significant other, regardless of the actual force that other applies. It is self-transforming in that it clears the way for the other to pursue whatever course of action is desired. The self stays in the physical space, but is by no means there psychologically.

Level 1: Negotiation for Control by One-way "Will-driven" Power
The Other-transforming Orientation at Level 1

Other-transforming strategies at this level involve implicit reference to power and control in the establishment of one-way resolutions of interpersonal disequilibrium. To the extent that the self's and other's wills are viewed as distinct, interpersonal issues are construed in terms of who is to control whom. Under the stress of interpersonal disequilibrium, fairness is not differentiated from feelings, so that to a child functioning at this level, failure to get what she or he wants is equated with (or undifferentiated from) being treated "unfairly."

The primary strategy we will focus on as an example of this level and orientation is labeled *One-way Threats or Bribes of Power or Affection*. This strategy reflects the individual's attempts to use relationship-oriented resources of power and control to get his or her way. This typically includes simple threats of withdrawal of affection ("I won't be your friend anymore, unless . . .") or bribes of affection ("I'll like you if . . .") or "plain old" bribes ("If you come over now, I'll give you some of my ice cream"). The goal of the bribe, however, is not to change the other's feelings but to change his or her behavior. Interestingly enough, often what really seems to be at stake, although this may not be clearly perceived by the participants, is getting one's own way at the expense of the other's, rather than actually acquiring the goods or services under consideration:

> Liz and Cindy, two eight-year-olds, walk over to a table
> with drawing materials on it. As Liz sits down, Cindy
> casually picks up a purple pen from the table to draw with.
> Liz says she would like to use the purple pen to finish a
> picture she started earlier. Cindy says she really wants to
> use the pen and will give it to Liz when she is done.
>   Liz seems unhappy with this arrangement, and tells
> Cindy she should pass the pen on if she is really a good
> friend. "You want me to be your friend, don't you," she
> adds. A number of other strategies are used as the
> discussion continues, until finally Cindy says, "Okay, go
> ahead and take the dumb old purple pen." Liz responds,
> "Oh, never mind. I don't need it."

This example illustrates the Level 1 "battle of wills." Liz uses withdrawal of her friendship as a lightly veiled threat. And in the end, we sense that the issue here is her having her own way, although it may not be clear to Liz herself that this is what she wants. When Cindy rejects the "dumb old pen," Liz no longer wants it as much. Earlier, Liz attempts to take advantage of (her perception of) Cindy's desire for her friendship. Her negotiation with Cindy is "one-way" in the sense that it does not leave room for any input from Cindy—Cindy must conform or lose Liz's affection. Liz appears to view her own affective disequilibrium as a function of Cindy's not doing what she wants, rather than as a function of her own need to control the interaction. We sense this from her lack of real satisfaction when in the end she gets her chosen pen. The strategy is transforming of the other at Level 1 rather than Level 2 because it represents Liz's attempt to influence and change Cindy's behavior (but not her interests) in order to achieve her own ends. Interestingly, technically, Liz is expressing the willingness to focus on her own intentions (implicitly, I'll stay your friend), but only contingent on Cindy's changing hers. This is an advance over the absolute nature of Level 0 strategies.

We also distinguish this strategy from a Level 0 strategy because of its reflective quality and the mediation of intent. At Level 0, strategies are impulsive, lacking any reflection on the intentions of self or other. If she were functioning at Level 0, Liz would not threaten to withdraw her friendship. She would act out her feelings of frustration directly and impulsively—for example, making a quick exit to take away her friendship by removing physical proximity or a quick grab to get herself the pen. In the present example, Liz has more control of her feelings and of how her behavior will affect Cindy than would be true in Level 0 strategies. She uses her awareness of her own efficacy, her potential effect on Cindy, to create a strategy that from an adult's perspective appears coercive, but from a child's perspective is viewed less pejoratively. The strategy is not Level 2, however, because although it acknowledges that Cindy has a will and interests of her own, it does not give any credit to those interests by allowing Cindy's desires to have any influence on the final outcome or by attempting to change her desires. This strategy is one-way (Liz will dictate what Cindy will do), whereas Level 2 negotiations embody some reciprocity in considering the other's wishes, although (if other-transforming) still pursuing the self's. At Level 2, Liz would try to convince Cindy to change her mind to be in line with Liz's own, rather than to try to simply control or overpower her.

Other strategies characteristic of this level and orientation include *One-way Threats of Force* and *Ordering Others with Criticism as a Rationale*. Five minutes on any playground filled with preschoolers or early gradeschoolers will reveal many examples of the latter. As two children run across the grass toward the one remaining swing, one yells out to her peer who is running faster, "I get the swing first! I can swing higher than you." A child walking onto the field wants to be pitcher, and he says to the boy holding the ball, with all the force of what appears to be good sense to him, "Gimme the ball—I'm the best pitcher." Two children line up to hit the first pitch, and one orders, "I'm up first." All of these strategies are one-way orders, with the only attempt at explanation, justification, or trying to convince the other being the one-way focus on the self's comparative skill, power, or efficacy, rather than an appeal to fairness or turn-taking.

The Self-transforming Orientation at Level 1

Level 1 self-transforming strategies show movement away from the Level 0 absolute giving up of the self's goals in favor of those expressed by the other. There is an increasing yet still tentative acknowledgment of the validity of one's own psychological will and wants, yet the experience of disequilibrium is still dealt with by reducing or giving up one's own wants if that will remove the conflict. In other words, the self's need to find a sense of control and equilibrium is achieved by submitting to the other, who is perceived as stronger or in some way more powerful. If the other can control the self, then at least the self feels in (some) control.

In the use of *Weak Initiative with Ready Withdrawal*, the self tentatively takes the initiative to make a suggestion but is ready to give in or give up quickly if this suggestion is perceived to be rejected. The rejection of the suggestion is personalized and therefore not well differentiated from an overall rejection of the self. Giving in quickly resolves the disequilibrium. A limitation of Level 1 self-transforming strategies is an inability to place another person's specific reactions to one's own specific suggestions into the larger context of the other's immediate interests, which may legitimately differ from one's own. Therefore feelings of relative insecurity in the given interaction guide the actor's approach:

> Ted, age seven, is working on an airplane model as he sits on the floor. Peter, also seven, walks slowly toward Ted and leans down to ask in a quiet voice, "Ted, please may you have a checkers game with me?" Ted is still bent over his model as he responds, matter-of-factly, "I'm doing a model right now. You can watch me doing it." Ted continues working with his head down, not paying attention to Peter, and Peter stands for a moment staring at Ted with a blank expression. Peter then slowly drops to sit next to Ted, his head and gaze bent toward the floor, and the corners of his mouth turned down in a slight frown. He says quietly, "Okay, if you don't want to play with me, I'll just wait."

We can see by the words "please may you" that Peter's initiation of a request already is quite weak. He appears to anticipate a strong willful directive by Ted, and his total compliance by sitting and watching reinforce this view. Thus, although the "will" of both self and other are clearly recognized as distinct by Peter, he perceives their relation to rest upon the power of one will (here Ted's) over another (here his own), rather than upon equal credit for each. His purpose in dealing with the disequilibrium, as it is in other-transforming strategies, is to establish a stable balance of power and control, through one "will" having all the force. Peter appreciates the distinction of inner wishes and external acts, yet he appears to see the reason for his choice of how to deal with his inner disequilibrium as the external force of Ted's refusing to play with him. That is, he does not deal with his feelings internally, but rather through the external action of submitting to Ted's perceived power. Peter is self-transforming here because he readily gives in to Ted's desires. However, note that there is some advance toward more balance in orientation than at Level 0: Peter does initially put forth his own wants, and he clearly distinguishes his wants from Ted's.

A self-transforming strategy at Level 0 would be not to attempt any initiative at all, because the self's wants and acts would be seen as totally determined by the acts of the other. This Level 1 strategy also is distinct from a Level 2 strategy, however, for at Level 2 Peter would give more credit to his own wishes. Resolution of the disequilibrium raised by differing wants would not entail only one person's having his way at Level 2. Instead, Peter might suggest a trade to Ted, such as "If you spend the next ten minutes finishing your model, then let's spend ten minutes playing checkers, okay?"

Yielding to Source of Power to Gain Protection or Liking refers to a set of activities whereby the individual consciously and reflectively puts himself or herself in a subordinate position in order to give the dynamics of the relationship an unambiguous definition. The other then becomes a protector, it is hoped, and the other's perceived power may indeed serve the self in some way. *Indirect Asking* as a Level 1 form of negotiation involves an expression of the self's wishes in an indirect way so that they can be easily ignored by the other, and not taken as disruptive. Indirect asking is employed in order to protect the self from the other's anticipated or assumed battling resistance:

> Tricia, age six, is building a car with a whole set of wheels available. Paula also has a car to play with, but it has only two wheels. Paula walks over to show Tricia her car. She rolls her two-wheeled car down the ramp next to Tricia, as if trying to get her attention. Paula then says aloud, as if to the air only, "What I need is two more wheels." Tricia makes no response. Paula slowly rolls her two-wheeled car away from where Tricia is, and then rolls it back again. As she returns she says toward Tricia, but not directly to her, "If only I had back wheels." When there is again no response by Tricia to Paula's indirect request, Paula withdraws to the other side of the room and begins to read a book.

Here, Paula's indirect overtures have avoided for her the responsibility for initiating a negotiation, but the only goal she fulfills is that of avoiding conflict.

Level 2: Negotiation for Influence by Conscious Reciprocal Psychological Persuasion

The Other-transforming Orientation at Level 2

If, at Level 0, other-transforming strategies aim to control others' actions, and at Level 1 to control their wills, then at Level 2 they attempt to control others' interests and intentions. Persuasion, manipulation, and influence-peddling are all strategies used at Level 2 to attempt to convince the other to change his or her thoughts or feelings, so they will be in line with those of the self. It is important to stress that Level 2 strategies are not simply the use of more sophisticated techniques to attain the same ends. With development, and with the implementation of higher-level strategies, comes a shift in purpose and goal. There is a significant difference between, at Level 2, wanting the other to *agree* with the self and, at Level 1, coercing the other to *go along* with the self.

Level 2 other-transforming strategies are actions taken on another who is construed as potentially receptive and reasonable. Yet if the self anticipates an unwillingness on the other's part to go along, more subtle or deceptive means may be used to meet the self's defined wishes. This readiness reflects the fact that at Level 2 the self's goals are still more important than the process used to achieve these goals and than how the self's interests affect the mutuality of the relationship. It is not until Level 3 that strategies are designed to arrive at mutual solutions to which both parties can fully agree. Here is an example of a strategy we call *Friendly Persuasion:*

> Eddie, age ten, wants to go sledding, and he asks Jim, also ten, to go with him. Jim is wearing a new pair of pants that he does not want to get wet, and he is not sure whether he wants to go sledding. Eddie smiles endearingly at Jim and says, "Come on, Jim, you're such a good sledder and it's so much fun to go with you. You're so good at sledding you won't even get your pants wet." Actually, Eddie knows that Jim is not a particularly good sledder, but he wants Jim's company.

Here we can see that Eddie pursues his goal to go sledding with Jim by trying to manipulate Jim's ambivalent feelings so that he will want to go sledding too. He recognizes that Jim's feelings, thoughts, or motives can be changed through flattery or manipulation. Thus in this strategy both self and other are construed as capable of making decisions based on reflection, and multiple desires within the self and other are recognized. Eddie deals with his emotional or inner disequilibrium by controlling his immediate wishes to go sledding, postponing gratification until he can arrange a shift of Jim's wishes to be in line with his own. The strategy is other-transforming because Eddie is trying to change Jim's wants and subsequent actions so that his own goals will be met. Note, however, that there is a greater representation of the opposite orientation than at lower levels. This is reflected in the openness of his communication to feedback and exchange. In contrast, at Level 1 Eddie might say, "You can use my new sled if you come" (a blatant bribe, aimed only at getting his own way), and at Level 3, he might respond with, "If we head home right now, you could borrow my old snow pants, and we'll still have time to sled for almost an hour."

We call a second Level 2 other-transforming strategy *Seeking Allies for Support of Own Ideas*, the seeking of allies who are like-minded with the self to help convince the significant other to join in "their" way of seeing things. A third strategy is called *Guilt-tripping*, and consists of a reference by the other-transformer to his or her past actions and good intentions toward the other, followed by a call for the other to reciprocate. For instance, eleven-year-old Sandy is over at her friend Kate's house. Kate wants to play Parchesi, but Sandy wants to watch television. They don't have time to do both. Sandy works to solve the conflict by saying, "Come on, Kate, lots of times I've done stuff because you wanted to. I think it's your turn to do what I want." Although turn-taking is a common process of social regulation across the developmental spectrum, the rationale in this particular form invokes the generality, "I've done stuff for you," exemplifying Sandy's good intentions, and her use of the past favor to convince Kate to want to put aside her own self-interest in order to reciprocate.

The Self-transforming Orientation at Level 2

Higher levels of interpersonal negotiation entail an increasing movement toward a balance between the self- and other-transforming orientations. The Level 2 self-transforming orientation is reflected in the self's increasing sense of control of his or her own feelings and an increasing capacity to tolerate the discomfort and disequilibrium of anxiety due to interpersonal uncertainty. Correspondingly, the other is viewed not as only overwhelming or controlling, as at earlier levels, but as also (more) open to suggestion and discussion. There is a greater willingness, at this level, to act on the self's capacity for efficacy and agency, for taking an active role in determining the course of social interaction in a negotiation context. There is a greater willingness to assert and articulate one's own wishes and ideas so that they will be considered in the process of negotiation, even if transforming the self turns out to be the final outcome.

However, although the self's wishes are now willingly aired for consideration, they are still ultimately made secondary to the perceived wishes of the other. The emotional stability of the self is still protected by yielding to the needs of the other rather than by moving to a new level of equilibrium based on balancing the needs of both the self and the other. Still, by comparison with those at lower levels, Level 2 strategies in the self-transforming orientation evidence a greater trust in the "dealing capacity" of both persons. The self is more willing to expose personal weaknesses and to express a wish that may meet with a negative reaction if not full rejection. Likewise, the self is able to perceive accurately when the other's request is not an absolute order or intimidation, but an assertion to which the self can react with some opportunity for consideration and freedom of opinion.

As a case in point, we will look at an instance of a strategy we call *Asserts Own Feelings But as Secondary*. With this strategy, the individual asserts the credibility and value of his or her own wants or thoughts while still placing them in a secondary position to the other's. The individual still ultimately attempts to achieve equilibrium by appeasing the other, but there is a building trust in the potential of a balanced resolution of interpersonal disequilibrium:

> Joey and Mark, both nine, are sharing a soda from a can. Joey says that he wants to drink the first half, and then Mark can finish the second. After a moment of apparent thought, Mark nods. When Joey has finished his half, he drops the soda can onto the table, saying "Here, Mark," and leaves to work on his drawing. Mark picks up the can and steadily downs most of the rest of the soda. Soon after, Joey returns to the table, picks up the can, and peers inside. Finding almost no soda left, he begins to berate Mark. "What do you think you're doing pigging all the soda? Half of it's supposed to be mine!" Mark appears taken aback, and he only slowly fumbles out, "You can have that, but you said you were done!" Joey denies it and continues forcefully, "You owe me another soda now." Mark shakes his head slowly and says with quiet firmness, "You gave it to me, Joey. Next time I'll make sure you're really done before I start it."

In this example, although Mark ultimately self-transforms by not insisting that the small amount of soda remaining is really his, he shows a willingness to stand up for his own views when he perceives himself as being unfairly treated. This indicates a trust that although the self and another person may have differing thoughts, feelings, or motives, each is potentially capable of reflection, self-restraint, and compromise. Mark seems able to recognize that his experienced disequilibrium results from a conflict between personal and interpersonal wants. He does not want to be controlled, yet he does not want to offend Joey; he wants his views to be respected, yet he wants to keep Joey's acceptance and friendship. He deals with this disequilibrium by prioritizing feelings internally (putting his desire for respect equal to his fear of rejection) and by ordering the feelings of self and other by external action (saying that he will abide by a deal in which his short-term wants follow after Joey's). Mark's purpose in this case is to use self-reflection and self-control to establish equilibrium through fairness rather than controlling force. On the whole, this strategy is self-transforming but not completely so: Mark complies in relinquishing the remaining soda, but attempts to influence future dealings. Certainly, he shows relatively less changing of himself in the face of Joey's accusations and orders than he might have at lower levels—he does not buy him a new soda.

At Level 1, a self-transforming strategy in this case would be to submit to Joey's interpretation of the situation, in effect agreeing that he should have saved Joey more soda (in the face of Joey's greater power). If Mark, on the other hand, were acting at Level 3, he would come up with a more equilibrated balance between his and Mark's wants and thoughts. Mark would be able to articulate that he feels Joey is making an unjust claim—perhaps to say that he understands that Joey may really want more soda but Mark does not owe it to Joey, because he fulfilled their original agreement.

Level 3: Negotiation for Collaborative, Mutually Satisfactory Ends by Reflective Communication of Thoughts and Feelings

Strategies at Level 3 attempt to balance actions taken on the self and actions taken on others to restore inner and interpersonal equilibrium, thus establishing a collaborative orientation. At this level, strategies deal as much with reflections on one's own and the other's feelings about the particular relationship or negotiation as with individual actions toward overt goals. Strategies classified at this level are employed with an anticipation of the possible feelings of the other toward one's own intended negotiation, as well as an expectation of how one will react to the actions of the other. Consider the following vignette:

> Two "best friends," Kathy and Sally, are working on their own puppet show for a big extra-credit project for their seventh grade art class. They have never actually made puppets before. They have decided that Kathy is in charge of making the puppets, but she is having a difficult time. She is making hand puppets out of cloth, and she becomes increasingly frustrated as she tries to glue the first puppet's arms closed at the seams. She asks Sally to help her by holding one arm. The glue keeps smearing and will not hold. Kathy, increasingly frustrated, says, "Hold it still or it'll never dry!"
>
> Sally, clearly now affected by Kathy's frustration, looks somewhat stung by her short-tempered remark. "Look, Kathy," she says in an even tone, "I think you ought to try staples." Kathy responds, in utter frustration, "If you're so smart, *you* make the puppets." But she then immediately adds, "Oh, I'm sorry, Sally. What am I thinking? I just asked *you* to help *me!*" Kathy looks directly at her friend with an open, somewhat apologetic expression and adds, "I feel so aggravated, I just lost it." Kathy's questioning look is answered by a pause, and then a smile from Sally. "That's OK, Kath. Remember when I did it to you yesterday? About being late?" Kathy smiles, and then Sally continues, "I could have been cooler about it, too, I guess. I've never actually made them either, but don't you think staples *would* work better?" The girls wash their hands, locate a stapler, and continue their work, now more successfully, while gossiping about teachers and classmates.

In this example, both girls falter initially, but come out solidly Level 3 in their negotiation. Their initial emotional disequilibrium stems from Kathy's ineffective techniques, which cause her, and probably Sally too, to feel frustrated. Quickly, however, the source of the disequilibrium becomes dual and interpersonal: Kathy's snapping at Sally and Sally's implicit criticism of Kathy. Each quickly recognizes and finds ways to acknowledge the effects of her own behavior on the other's feelings. "Oh, I'm sorry . . . I just lost it." "I could have been cooler about it, too, I guess."

Furthermore, they put the problem in the context of their relationship, rather than focusing exclusively on the immediate issue of particular techniques or frustrations. "What am I thinking? I just asked *you* to help *me!*" "That's OK. Remember when I did it to you yesterday?" Facial expressions and tones of voice are also a part of the communication, reinforcing the importance each places on the strength of the long-term relationship and *each* person's feelings than on immediate actions vis-á-vis the puppets, even though both are quite concerned with the success of the project. Self-other construal, perception and control of affect, and primary intent all focus on a balancing of both actors' needs and an acknowledgment that this balancing is of primary importance to both. (This, incidentally, also illustrates Sullivan's concepts of security needs in the intense preadolescent chumship. There is a strong sense communicated by both girls that their closeness and ability to continue to be sensitive to it are of primary importance.)

Interestingly, both girls begin with what look like other-transforming strategies. "Hold it still or it'll never dry!" "I think you're going to have to try staples." But each immediately reflects and switches to more self-transforming stances. "Oh, I'm sorry, Sally. What am I thinking?" "That's OK. Remember when . . ." etc. Then Sally, in a way that is sensitive to Kathy's needs, shifts again to an other-transforming tack. "Don't you think staples would work better?" What might be seen as flexible shifting from self- to other-transforming orientations (or the reverse) *within a specific context for negotiation* (somewhat different from say Jeremy and Brian's shifting back and forth *across contexts* in the last chapter), is characteristic of mutual collaborative Level 3 negotiations. It also raises a couple of other interesting points.

First, although the initial forays are other-transforming and not Level 3, the later statements and actions are self-transforming and are Level 3. This should not mislead one into thinking that other-transforming negotiations are lower level than self-transforming ones. Here, it is simply the case that the self-transforming, accommodating remarks and reactions were appropriate to establishing a collaborative solution. Sometimes, as a later example illustrates, other-transforming negotiations are also appropriate to initiating a collaborative orientation. Level 3 negotiations often take the form of a sequence of strategies at both other-transforming and self-transforming orientations that balance out on a molar level to constitute a collaborative orientation.

Second, when we do make other- and self-transforming attributions at this level, each orientation resembles the other more, and so they are harder to distinguish than they are at earlier levels. A case could even be made that Sally's final suggestion about stapling may not really be other-transforming at all, but simply an open, collaborative initiative.

A comparable Level 2 strategy in this situation might be to place less value on the feelings of the other and the open process of communication for mutual influence that lead to a solution that fulfills the needs of both parties. Rather, Sally might just try to persuade Kathy to accept her idea, perhaps by saying, "You know, I've made puppets before and I can tell you it'll be a lot easier for you if you staple them."

As children grow older, the focus of their interpersonal negotiations changes, from a singular focus on toys and games to relationships themselves, from who gets what and when to who likes whom and how people treat each other. It is probably not a coincidence that the (Level 3) capacity for mutual collaboration emerges and begins to consolidate at about the time that most adolescents are turning their attention to the often extremely intense and public disequilibrium engendered by powerful boy-girl and peer-group needs and pressures, pressures arising from within the self and throughout the culture.

Although they may be harder to observe, the contexts in which interpersonal negotiation take place and are ongoing multiply greatly during this period. At the least, the term "negotiation" now takes on its more commonplace meaning. Negotiations go on actively with peers, with teachers, with employers (for some), with parents, and, perhaps for the first time, with members of the opposite sex—around topics such as dating, having strong feelings for someone, going steady, and the like. The length and complexity of these negotiations may increase greatly, and the core nature of the negotiations often shifts. Although many of them still may be oriented to activities (who does what and who gets to choose) and concrete products (who has what), perhaps just as often the negotiations are focused on or around feelings and relationships themselves (who likes and is "going with" whom, how much they are liked, and whose feelings have been ignored or hurt). The following vignette exemplifies the functional utility of Level 3 strategies in these newly emerging contexts:

> Marian, age sixteen, is talking on the phone with her boyfriend of five months, Eddie, also sixteen. She has a sensitive and important message to communicate to him, and she has been preparing herself for this interaction for some time. It is a message she feels will most likely put their relationship into conflict: she feels she wants to go

with other boys, not steadily with Eddie, and she believes that Eddie wishes them to remain dating exclusively one another. "Eddie, I think we have a problem, and if we do I need to talk seriously with you about it. I still want to go out with you, but I want to go out with other guys, too." Eddie objects, as Marian expected he would, and the dialogue continues for some time. During the course of the conversation, Marian tries to explain why she feels as she does.

Finally Marian says, "Look, Eddie, if you want, I'll try it your way a little longer, but if I still feel the same way, I want you to try it mine. But then if we can't agree, I think we'll have to talk again, and we'll both have to decide for ourselves what we want. See, I just don't think it would be fair to either of us if I didn't tell you this now, and I hope you'll tell me how you're feeling as we go along. I hope you'll tell me if you don't think this is working out."

There are several indications that Marian is functioning in this negotiation in a way that we would classify as Level 3. First, what may not come across on paper is the feeling state she is in, and the sense of her power and autonomy in relation to Eddie's. Although Marian agrees after some discussion to try it Eddie's way a little bit longer, she makes this decision from a position of independence, and not as a "you first, me second" type decision that might be typical of Level 2. She is willing to try, given the circumstances, but as an equal who assumes that Eddie will feel better or at least treated more fairly and honestly if she raises the issue now, and expresses her concern for his feelings. (Also, although she feels relatively autonomous, she is not dictating a solution, but attempting to weigh and consider Eddie's feelings in an ongoing way.)

Second, Marian couches the problem as a shared one, "We have a problem," at the same time she seems to realize that certain decisions are hers alone to make (reflecting a high-level consciousness of autonomy and intimacy needs, incidentally). In addition, she couches the possible consequences in terms of their long-term relationship and how each feels about the other, not simply in terms of one or the other of them "winning." In sum, she seems to respect both Eddie and herself, and hopes that Eddie will be able to communicate to her how he feels as they explore this unfamiliar territory.

Missing from this vignette are two things. First, it does not report Eddie's statements, feelings, and reactions; these will obviously affect the level and effectiveness of Marian's strategy.

Second, we see Marian presenting to Eddie her ideal conceptualization of the issues: identifying the problem as mutual, reflecting on her feelings and sharing them with Eddie, looking at the long-term implications of the decision and the negotiation process itself. Once she is off the phone, given that this is an issue where deep feelings are involved, things may not go quite so smoothly. Her sensitive and mature Level 3 approach, which is in some ways other-transforming but open-ended and not rigid, may not be met with equal perspective by Eddie, and she may not "stay on track" herself.

Communication is far from perfect, and the complexities of real-life contexts serve to muddy the clear waters of idealized levels. Nevertheless, in an individual's negotiation with another, one can look for the core assumptions, and if they include a sense of collaboration, a view to mutual agreement, a belief in the communication of inner reflections, and a concern with the long-term implications of decisions for the relationship, these factors differentiate Level 3 negotiations from those at lower levels.

There is also the question of whether Level 3 strategizing can resolve even later, often more intimate interpersonal negotiations. If it cannot, can this new collaborative orientation be said to be truly integrative of earlier, more polarized, orientations, or will further integrations be expected at Level 4?

Toward Level 4: Negotiation for Intimacy in a Relationship through Interpenetrating, In-depth Understanding

We do not have a collection of observed Level 4 strategies that is comparable to what we have for the other levels. This is both because we have not yet studied Level 4 to any large extent, and because the behavior and negotiations that best utilize this level are often private and usually highly personal in nature. Level 1 strategies are appropriately used to learn the tasks of childhood, to share materials in the immediate context of play activity. As the task becomes learning to achieve a balance of interests between the participants in shared activities, particularly games, Level 2 strategies come to the fore. When the task is to maintain mutual coordination over the rough course of the inevitably conflict-generating events of close and sometimes closed personal friendships, Level 3 negotiations will be needed. Many of the tasks of early adolescence among peers are appropriately viewed as tasks of this form of mutuality, the establishment and maintenance of satisfactory relationships with peers. This requires of the individual the ability to share common interests, to resolve differences, to trust and be trusted, and to reveal vulnerabilities.

The forms of negotiation characterized as Level 4 emerge from the need to cope with the powerful emotions and doubts that can be generated when people attempt to share their deepest and most uncertain experiences with one another, and to relate to each other in the context of major commitment in intense and intimate relationships, marriage being the prototypical but by no means the only case. By intimacy, we do not simply mean sexual intimacy, but rather the many "places" of long-standing relationships where, by choice, individuals make personal commitments to one another.

The establishment and maintenance of the capacity for a mutually reflective form of intimacy, rather than a mutuality of interests, involves more subtle and complicated skills, skills needed for truly long-term coexistence. In particular it requires a flexibility of relating between self and other within the process of a relationship, to be at times supportive of, dependent upon, or equal to each other.

In this connection, another interesting speculation about Levels 3 and 4 has occurred to us. We have suggested that at Level 3 there is a coming together of orientations such that there is the establishment of a collaborative orientation characterized by a lack of distinction between orientations, by flexibly switching orientations, or by combining and integrating orientations. That is, the impression is given that strategies at Level 3 are fully balanced, or equilibrated, with respect to whether actions are directed toward the self's or toward the other's perspective and concern. But there is a set of negotiation strategies associated with Level 4 as well. Therefore it follows that these strategies should be more advanced, more differentiated and integrated. Thus, we speculate that complete integration is not achieved until Level 4 (or beyond), that at Level 3 the orientations do not yet come together fully.

We believe that as we delineate strategies at Level 4, those that appeared balanced and equilibrated at Level 3 will be found not to be completely so, in ways not heretofore considered. At Level 3 the balanced transformation of self and other involves mutual transformation in the sense that each person is considered to have the capacity to change; it involves mutual transformation within one person's construction of the situation as that person considers both parties. However, it may be that at Level 4, when the issue of negotiation is an in-depth interpersonal intimacy, equilibrated transformation of self and other involves mutual and simultaneous change in shared thoughts or feelings. That is, transformation is simultaneously and mutually carried out on the conduct of individuals negotiating together, rather than being carried out within one person's consideration of a negotiation strategy.

Another intriguing possibility, which probably has a different kind of validity, is that individuals in a long-lasting intimate relationship need to be able consciously to call upon both self- and other-transforming orientations. It is in this sense that the integration of orientation at Level 3 may once again be differentiated to a certain extent at Level 4. Although we can speculate on this topic, it takes us toward adult development, which is beyond the reach of our data and focus. Therefore, although we have tried to make the point that the collaborative process of Level 3 does not necessarily represent an endpoint, neither a final nor an optimal level of interpersonal development, it nevertheless will serve us well as a goal toward which to aim in the study of interpersonal development through adolescence, at least through its early phase.

The use of our three analytic steps—identifying contexts for negotiation, coding or diagnosing their level and orientation, and interpreting those actions in context—is a powerful, subtle, and inclusive way to sort, structure, and give meaning to social interactions. Seeing what and how interpersonal relationships work (the meaning of "work" of course being affected by our values) is a first descriptive/diagnostic phase, albeit a significant and time-intensive one. The second phase is to continue to explore application of the model to see whether and how it can help us to "fix" what does not work.

Essentially, the interpersonal negotiation strategy model can be construed as a model of how, with development, the individual maintains a feeling of control and reaches resolution when needs conflict in close dyadic and interpersonal situations. This emphasis on control, and emotional equilibrium, however, is not limited to one developmental level; it is at the heart of all negotiation strategies. And the validity of this negotiation model is both clinical and empirical. Clinically, we want to see how useful the model is in an approach designed to help troubled youngsters feel more in control as they relearn (or learn) to develop close interpersonal relationships with a peer. Empirically, we want to see whether reliable approaches can be developed to operationalize the model and to test the validity of some of its claims.

Forms of Shared Experience

A Shared Experience in Pair Therapy

Norman and Andrew, both age nine, have been in pair therapy once a week for almost an entire year. The year's process and progress traversed three distinct periods. During the first period, which lasted about six weeks, there was much social comparison and competition between the two boys. Their subtle or not-so-subtle testing of each other's skills, sizing each other up, and vying for dominance and control provided many contexts for interpersonal negotiation. Andrew, with better athletic ability and greater persistence, appeared to gain ascendancy. Once the initial ambiguity about power relations was settled through various battles over topics such as which activity would be chosen, who would go first, and who had cheated or not, the pair was able to move into a second period of relationship.

In this second period, the two boys focused less on concerns about direct power and control, and more on each member asking the other, "What can you do for me?" During this phase, the boys appeared to form an alliance of sorts and—significantly—selected games they could play against the therapist. In particular, they repeatedly chose to play, during their sessions, a tag game called Cat and Rat.

In this game, the therapist was designated as the cat and the two boys as the rats. The goal of the game is for either or both of the rats to cross from one goal line to the opposite one without being tagged by the cat, who roams the field between. The definition of winning was left up to the two boys, so that it could be individual—each boy could consider himself a winner if he made it across the field—or it could be shared, construed by each as both boys eluding the dangerous cat and crossing the opposite goal line, often together. In this second period of their pair therapy, the boys played the game together with their therapist, but in an individualistic mode, with each boy working independently to avoid the cat, or even using the

96

other boy as a decoy for his own success, regardless of what happened to him.

Eventually, after about eight weeks of playing this way, the two boys, who had become very skilled at it and now understood the range of potential strategies involved, spontaneously began to play in a more collaborative fashion. In this third period of their pair therapy, they began to take cooperative actions to make sure that they both evaded the cat: not crossing the goal line until each was sure the other would also make it across, shouting verbal warnings to each other whenever one appeared to be trapped, making spontaneous attempts to try to lure the cat away from the other rat when he appeared to be in danger of being trapped in a corner, and shouting pleas for assistance from one rat to the other, none of which they had employed during the previous phase of the playing of the game. The boys also made statements such as, "I'm sure glad you saved me from getting caught," or symbolic gestures such as handshakes and other mutually understood nonverbal expressions of success and togetherness.

Perhaps most striking of all, following the "defeat" of the cat at the hands of both rats, the two would cross the goal line and make victory signs to each other accompanied by deep and unselfconscious laughter. This shared laughter, the shared feeling of joy and success through cooperative actions, here against a common "enemy," stands out as a powerful form of bonding and social regulation that these two children, and others like them, seem to have such a difficult time finding or constructing for themselves elsewhere.

From Interpersonal Negotiation to Shared Experience

The story of Andrew and Norman suggests that the establishment of autonomy and agency on the one hand and intimacy and sharing on the other were significant organizing themes in the development of their relationship. The two themes attained ascendancy in a specific order in their relationship within pairs, with concerns and themes of autonomy (in the form of "negotiation") preceding themes of intimacy. Moreover, the intimacy theme emerged only after the establishment of a "common ground" or "home base activity"—that is, a shared activity in which both participants clearly understood the guidelines and explicit rules, and in which each felt very comfortable and at least minimally competent. Finally, in this account the hallmark of intimacy seemed to be a mutually acknowledged commingling of affect. We believe that this may be the most important therapeutic component that makes a dyad such a powerful, magnetic, sought-after, and passionate force, not only for these children, but in most people's lives.

The pair therapy process with children unused to playing well with others usually, though not always, seems to move from an initial focus on the social regulation processes of autonomy (developing strategies for interpersonal negotiation) to subsequent emphasis on the regulations of intimacy and connection (the development of shared experience). During the initial phases of pair therapy, social regulations in which power and autonomy are negotiated often occupy the center stage. But once some balance (or imbalance) of power is established in the pair (and if the treatment process is going well), these processes become less obvious, less salient, less dominant "figures," and more ever-present, still powerful, yet less obvious "grounds" upon which the second class of social regulation processes—namely, those that bring the partners closer together as a pair—become more prominent, and begin to do their work.

This book is following the same developmental course as our program of research and Norman and Andrew's pair therapy, from themes of autonomy to those of intimacy, from a focus on negotiation to one on shared experience. Our research, and this book thus far, has spent less time constructing an account of the kinds of shared experiences that support growth in the developing capacity for intimacy than that of the negotiation processes that support growth in autonomy. To redress this imbalance we are currently beginning to build a theoretical account of the connection-oriented processes of social regulation and the role of shared experience in social development. The reader will find that the practice of pair therapy reported in this book is more heavily weighted toward negotiation than shared experience, but this is more for historical reasons than for theoretical or even practical reasons. Negotiation plays a particularly salient role in the section on practical therapeutic techniques (chapters 5 to 7), but the complementary and equally powerful role of shared experience in the therapeutic process of pair therapy is conspicuous in the case studies that follow (chapters 8 to 10).

Because the pair therapy project was begun to help children with poor peer relationships become more adept at getting along, it was the fights, disagreements, and conflicts the pairs were getting into that caught our eye and called for our clinical attention.

Interactions involving negotiation rather than shared experience were the natural "way in" when treating these children in pairs—they generally did not have "intimate" interactions with friends but invariably did have fights with their peers.

The intensive focus of our initial years of theoretical, empirical, and clinical work on the autonomy-related processes of interpersonal negotiation somewhat obscured the complementary difficulties these children were having in establishing and maintaining a sense of closeness with peers. Once our attention was refocused in this direction, it seemed possible, indeed likely, that the difficulty and discomfort the pairs had in achieving a sense of closeness or intimacy may have actually played a role in generating many of the conflicts (contexts for the negotiations) they resolved so inadequately with their truncated and immature repertoires of interpersonal strategies, just as poor negotiating clearly interfered with their closeness.

In refining our techniques for helping these children improve their negotiation and conflict-resolution skills, we observed that the closeness and intimacy they came to demonstrate with one another in this therapeutic context—one made safe, sound, dependable, and continuous by the pair therapist—was a major factor in encouraging them to venture to try new and unfamiliar (higher-level) negotiation strategies. We also realized that, without particularly noticing it at the time, we had been facilitating their shared experiences just as much as their negotiations all along.

Shared Experience in the Three Cs: Chumship, Consensual Validation, and Collaboration

Earlier we alluded to the importance of the work of Harry Stack Sullivan for our theory and practice. With our turn toward processes of intimacy, his work comes to the fore again. In his model of interpersonal dynamics, Sullivan (1953), the psychiatrist whose theoretical interests link him with our work through a long line of social psychologists and social philosophers (James Mark Baldwin, 1902; Charles H. Cooley, 1902; George Herbert Mead, 1934), provides us with an account of the role of shared experience in interpersonal and personality development. For Sullivan, personality development is not merely age-descriptive, and it does not evolve by virtue of individual development, but only in continuing and ongoing interactions between and among people. Thus, he called his personality theory a theory of interpersonal relationships, and he viewed the mechanism of personality development as a product of shared experience. He made a point of distinguishing personality in this sense from individuality.

Most theories of personality development attempt to either account for variations in personality configuration or focus on what dynamic and psychological influences generate pathological adult personality structures. Sullivan, in contrast, asserts that the study of personality development is not what is different among individuals but what is similar. Sullivan adopted a developmental perspective and attempted to define what interpersonal dynamics are necessary for the growth of a healthy personality. Simply put, he considered interpersonal maturity to be the increasing capacity for relatedness to others.

For Sullivan, personality maturity depends upon the context of the interpersonal system within which the individual functions, and is achieved and maintained through a system of relatively enduring modes of relating. The incentives for growth of interpersonal maturity relate to the reciprocal exchanges between the growing person and the people—the "significant others"—upon whom he or she is dependent for the functional requirements of *satisfactions* (largely biological needs) and *securities* (predominantly social in their origin).

Each Sullivanian stage in the sequence of personality development is as important as the last or the next for the growth of interpersonal competence in the interactions between self and significant others. In infancy the intimacy of the interaction between parent and child does not develop on a conceptual or reflective level of understanding, but rather is spread through a process of emotional *contagion*, whether positive or negative. The task of Sullivan's next childhood (preschool) stage is to learn to modify behavior because of the inevitable need for a process of *accommodation* to the personality of others. In so doing the child begins to learn the rudiments of compromise and competition, to learn that one cannot easily obtain satisfactions or securities on an all-or-none basis.

The urgent need for peers with whom to share experience appears in the juvenile period—probably the period we would now include as early elementary grades (roughly kindergarten through second grade). Peer interaction at this stage of interpersonal development is based on the security need for interaction with individuals on the same level, who have similar activities, interests, and attitudes toward authority figures. In this sense there is a new tendency toward peer *cooperation*, both toward accommodation to peers (as well as adults) and toward the beginning of social self-regulation. But this cooperative process remains, in Sullivan's terms, relatively egocentric. For children in this period of development, it is merely the price they discover they must pay for access to satisfaction and security through people who are still viewed chiefly as sources of either gratification or frustration.

As the child's personality develops, securities, the meeting of social needs, become increasingly more important than satisfactions, the meeting of biological needs. From Sullivan's perspective, a major shift occurs in the preadolescent and early adolescent years when peers are experienced as important as, or more important than, parents as significant others who meet satisfaction and security needs. Preadolescence, roughly defined as about ages eight to twelve, is the period during which the capacity for *collaboration*, as distinct from cooperation, can develop.

According to Sullivan, the prime interpersonal mechanism for this is the acquisition of a close friend, one whose importance begins to approximate the preadolescent's importance to self. This achievement, which Sullivan calls "chumship," marks the emergence of the capacity for mutual love, not necessarily in a sexual sense, but in the sense that the satisfaction and security of another person becomes as significant to oneself as one's own. Whether or not it is only through a single close friendship or through friendship generally that the process develops, the acquisition of this sense of collaboration, or what Sullivan called "the quiet miracle of preadolescence," marks a major ("continental") divide in the climb toward interpersonal maturity. Those who do not experience or negotiate this transition successfully, continue to view other people only as sources of gratification or frustration. Those who do are ready to deal with, manage, or (in our language) negotiate the interpersonal challenges of adolescence and adulthood, including feelings of lust and the security and satisfaction of intimacy and sexual love.

Within Sullivan's framework, interpersonal maturity, as a stage of personality growth, is an open-ended phase rather than the attainment of a final formally defined stage, a way of being rather than a place to be. According to our reading of Sullivan, it is marked by the capacity to collaborate in as broad an arena as possible, and is conspicuous by virtue of the minimal manifestation of the urge to either dominate others or remain dependent upon and subordinate to them. As when reading Piaget's description of cognitive maturity, we picture an individual capable of mobile equilibrium, here in the interpersonal sphere. With respect to Werner's developmental theory, it corresponds to a capacity for flexibility (rather than lability) and stability (rather than rigidity).

Although constrained by individual biological and intellectual capacities, the processes of emotional contagion, accommodation/competition, cooperation, and collaboration are interpersonal—and developmental—in their emergence. Sullivan believed that all persons, with the exception of those seriously biologically or intellectually impaired, have the capacity to develop collaborative activity, but whether or not they implement this process depends on the quality of their experiences with others, in particular, "significant others." Much of the clinical and research activity described in this book is based upon the hypothesis that successful negotiation of the dyadic relationship (i.e., chumship), the foundations of which are so importantly established in each of the earlier stages of development, leads to the capacity for enduring relationships throughout life, relationships in which there is collaborative mutuality between equals.

Finally, Sullivan stressed that communicative competence was critical for mature interpersonal behavior. His own clinical experience led him to believe that people's difficulties in using language as a tool for meaningful communication of thoughts and feelings interfered with the adequate establishment of useful interpersonal relationships and sharing of meaningful experience. It is at the juvenile period, he stressed, that the individual needs to further develop language as a tool for communication in order to move away from this natural phase of egocentricity. As this tool is refined in the course of the natural "give and take" of social intercourse, further key growth takes place in the process of consensual validation, or the sharing of similar interpretations of experience, a growth that begins in infancy and continues to adulthood. These mutually validated interpretations at each stage are not necessarily accurate (in fact, they may be wildly inaccurate from a third person's perspective), but they are shared.

Not only language, but also other channels of communication must develop for the process of consensual validation to ripen and mature, yet Sullivan viewed language as most important to this process. Through consensual validation, the individual gives up immature forms of autonomy and gains great richness in the sharing of experience, the growth of interpersonal understanding, and the benefits of others' experiences. Shared meaning, rather than egocentric meaning, makes durable interpersonal relationships possible. An integrated personality must be able to enter into this process, a fact most clearly revealed when the interpersonal process breaks down. This is why, Sullivan believed, and we concur, that many of our clearest insights into the processes of interpersonal relationships come from the data of psychopathological forms of interpersonal relationships.

The key connection between Sullivan's corpus of theory and the clinical, research, and theoretical work reported here revolves around the "three Cs": collaboration, chumship, and consensual validation. We believe that consensual validation, as part of the normal developmental processes of social regulation, makes and is made possible in large part by processes of social-cognitive development. It is generated in close to its recognizable adult form during preadolescence, the major developing character or structure of which is the capacity for collaboration, the action equivalent, in our terms, of the social-cognitive capacity for mutual or third person coordination of perspectives, as both understood and felt by the individuals involved. This develops commonly, though not necessarily, in a dyadic process, via the intense feelings generated in chumship. Once formed, it takes years of experience to be forged into a consolidated and generalized means of dealing with other people.

It is these higher level processes that tend to be lacking in troubled and friendless children's repertoire and experience. In many ways, the clinical work in this book can be viewed as a test of certain of the key ideas Sullivan put forth—in particular how chumship, or an intense paired relationship with a peer of relatively equal status—can help individuals achieve the capacity for collaborative relationships through the growth of reliable and meaningful communication and consensual validation in shared experience. Sullivan's theory of interpersonal development provides us with a rationale not only for the structure of pair therapy (to the extent that the pair's relationship grows into a "chumship"), but also for the importance of studying the role of shared experience in that growth.

Sharing of Experience versus "Shared Experience" Interactions

Pair therapy is a unique context for the sharing of experience, given its triadic structure and self-constructed agenda, in which the pair's interests and inclinations, in interaction with the therapist's guidance and suggestions, steer the activities and hence the social interaction during the sessions. This sharing of experience in the triad serves three distinctive functions for the two children.

First and foremost, it is a context in which the pair can have fun and share positive experiences together (with the therapist), learning how to feel comfortable with unaccustomed levels of intimacy. Second, it is a supportive setting for the pair to learn to get along and constructively resolve their inevitable conflicts. Third, the treatment provides the pair with a place to help each other experience and work through pain, in learning to share and reflect on, rather than act out, negative feelings brought into or generated in the sessions.

Sullivan's notion of shared experience encompasses the whole range of interpersonal experiences in pair therapy sessions, including what we have identified as contexts for interpersonal negotiation. Sullivan, however, seldom directly addresses the role of interpersonal conflict in personality and social development, although it is implicit in such Sullivanian processes as accommodation and competition. In explicitly distinguishing interactions involving conflict from those that do not, we thereby also highlight interactions involving interpersonal harmony. Thus we have identified a social regulation process complementary to interpersonal negotiation in which affect and meaning are shared in a particularly intense way. We have termed this type of interaction "shared experience" and consider it distinct from the Sullivanian "sharing of experience," which includes all social interactions within an ongoing interpersonal relationship.

"Shared experiences," in our strict sense of the term, are identified, regardless of form, in those instances in which the pair verbally or behaviorally expresses the *feeling*, perhaps even more than the clear *understanding*, that "We are in this together." Although forms of shared experience involve cognitive, affective, and behavioral aspects in varying distributions, we believe that the most powerful constant across all these forms may be the sharing of similar affect. The shared affect may include a range of feelings, from sadness to joy, from indignation to understanding, or from anger to humor. One of the most cohesive expressions of feeling that contributes to the long-term regulation of a pair may be shared laughter, accompanied by the many strong positive feelings that are generally associated with it, as we saw in the pair therapy of Norman and Andrew.

Shared experience has some different qualities than interpersonal negotiation. Both are interactive, in the sense that the strategies of one person can be undertaken only in relation to another's and in most cases are closely dependent upon those taken by the other. However, in negotiation the actions are still largely of the individual and are identified and classified as such. Shared experience, in contrast, is a more *transactive* phenomenon in which each partner makes a contribution to a process that enlarges the experience for both. The whole (the dyad's experience) is greater than the sum of the parts (each individual's experience). In participating together, each gains an extra validation of the self, through the other, beyond that possible when the same activity is experienced alone. The actors experience an "interpenetration" of established boundaries in the shared experience, and they feel "connected" in a way they do not in other types of interactions, particularly negotiations.

Despite these differences between the intimacy and autonomy processes of shared experience and negotiation, we view them as falling along a single continuum of social interaction. Shared experience, at the opposite end of the continuum of social regulation from negotiation, is characterized by expressive instead of negotiative behavior, and by harmony and the absence of both inner and interpersonal conflict. In interpersonal negotiation the actors' perspectives conflict; in shared experience they are coordinated. Most of everyday social interaction falls in the middle of the continuum, as neither purely expressive nor purely negotiative. Indeed, many of the more primitive episodes of shared experience have a contestlike, and hence negotiative as well as shared, feel to them, and we believe that both processes always function in tandem in an ongoing relationship, even when one process seems to dominate.

Shared Experience: Developmental Levels and Interpersonal Orientations

The processes emphasized in successive phases of Sullivanian personality development—contagion, accommodation/competition, cooperation, and collaboration—helped shape our thinking about the developmental meaning of the different sorts of shared experience episodes we identified in our videotapes of pair therapy sessions. Yet we found we needed more formal developmental principles to code ("developmentally diagnose") these shared experiences than Sullivan provides. Once again we turned to Werner's theory of orthogenesis (development defined as movement toward greater differentiation and hierarchical integration). In so doing, we have ordered examples of shared experience into forms ranging from the primitive, global, and undifferentiated to the psychologically complex and hierarchically integrated and differentiated.

As when developing the analysis of interpersonal negotiation strategies by level, we relied upon our earlier work on levels in the coordination of social perspectives as an analytic tool to generate the following four tentative levels (or forms) of shared experience. To see how the shared experience levels relate to the corresponding negotiation and perspective coordination levels, refer back to Table 1.

Our pair therapy tapes suggested that at the most primitive level (0), what seems to be shared (more literally "spread" in an unreflective way) is one child's impulsive and motoric activity. The experience often starts with one actor's impulsive expressiveness and appears to be transmitted to the other through a (Level 0) *process of contagion*, rather than by any clear awareness. For example, two very immature boys, Korey and David, both age nine, developed an often repeated form of sensorimotor imitation in the course of their pair therapy together. If Korey reached for a drink, David did the same; if David bounced a ball or crossed his legs, Korey automatically did so too. Neither seemed aware of the imitation, but each appeared soothed by it. This kind of activity is often poorly regulated, so that an outside agent is often needed to control the expression of the common action should it become overstimulating.

At a higher level (1), children appear to "share" actions more consciously. But usually this occurs in a somewhat paradoxical way: one actor "commands" the other to participate, not necessarily or only through orders or dictates but rather through a kind of expressive enthusiasm. And the other takes pleasure in following (accommodating). Often this *unilateral* form of shared experience—a term meant to capture its paradoxical nature—is seen in fantasy or role-play situations in which turns were taken at being in control (although one partner usually determined the switching of roles). For example, Kenny (age nine) and Peter (age eight) played a fantasy game (of Kenny's design) in which each had a chance to exert "laser power" over the will and behavior of the other. *Both* clearly shared the fact that *both* children participated, a sign of Level 1 perspective coordination.

In contrast, shared experiences at the next level (2) involves *reciprocal reflection* on the experience of actions. In other words, the accent falls on reflecting *with* another who has had the same or a similar (in-common) experience. Both children participate equally, but the focus of the experience is on each self's own satisfaction, without a strong or clear investment in the meaning of the sharing for the other. In-common sharing and acknowledging of common concerns with a friend, resulting in reassurance or comfort, is a vivid example. Another kind of shared experience common at this level, though less dramatic, is one in which each member of the pair is intent on gaining consensual validation on the meaning of the actions, attitudes, or personality of a third party (e.g., a teacher the participants share or a peer with whom each interacts). For example, Jane (age twelve) asked Karen (also 12), "Do you like Harriet?" in a tone that conveyed that Jane clearly did not. Karen read the meaning correctly and the two went on to gossip merrily about Harriet's weaker features.

A more mutually collaborative form of reflective shared experience consists of communications in which the other person's concerns are felt to be as significant as one's own. At this level (3), rarely glimpsed in our pair therapy cases, each participant clearly regards the other as part of a mutually experienced "we." For example, as we describe in chapter 10, Donna (age fourteen) and Brenda (age thirteen), shared their anxiety in moving from junior high school to senior high school next year. They discussed why each of them would miss their favorite teacher, experiencing each other's feelings and listening to the other empathically. Finally, each added how glad she was that she would have the other for company and support in this transition.

Can shared experience, as a social regulation process complementary to interpersonal negotiation, be characterized not only by developmental level, but also by interpersonal orientation? We believe it can. Although the affect in shared experience is harmonious rather than conflictual, at each of its first three levels one of the participants is more of a leader and the other is more of a follower—that is, as in interpersonal negotiation, one participant usually is dominant (if not specifically other-transforming) and the other is self-transforming to the extent that he or she "goes along," in the sense of showing a willingness to participate in the actions or ideas introduced by the more expressive member.

At the most primitive level (0), one participant acts and the other imitates, as Korey and David were doing above. At level 1, one participant expresses and controls an interest and the other hangs on, perhaps even sometimes worried about not being part or being left out of the experience. In the previous example of unilateral shared experience, although Kenny and Peter alternated as controller and controllee, Kenny, who was generally other-transforming in the pair's negotiations, always determined when the switch occurred. However, Peter's experience of being in control of the laser power sometimes, even if he was not in control of when, was a rare and positive experience of wielding and sharing power for him.

At the reciprocal level (2) one participant brings up ideas and themes and the other adds on and elaborates them. In the Level 2 example above, Jane's assertiveness (other-transformingness) derived from her initiation of the tone and topic, and Karen's self-transformingness from her "taking up the conversational ball," but both participated relatively equally in the subsequent gossiping. Like interpersonal negotiation, at the highest collaborative level (3) of shared experience, there is an integration of, and hence a balance between, the two interpersonal orientations. In Brenda and Donna's empathic and mutual sharing of deep concerns above, there was a simultaneous assertion of the self's needs and accommodation to (in the sense of a "taking in" of) the other's needs.

Normative Examples of Shared Experience

In keeping with our belief in the importance of monitoring the interplay between normality and pathology in the study of interpersonal development, we have begun to study shared experience in normative settings as well as pair therapy. As part of a larger research project (Selman and Glidden, 1987; Yeates and Selman, 1989), we developed a social problem-solving intervention in the public schools similar in structure to pair therapy (i.e., two children working with an adult, called the "trainer"). This intervention, designed as an educational experience for children in grades three to five, was shorter (only ten weeks) and more structured than pair therapy. However, in addition to formal instruction in our model of interpersonal negotiation, these sessions included a free-play portion somewhat similar to that in pair therapy sessions. Following are some examples of shared experience gleaned from the free play of these elementary school children.

Level 0. Two fifth-grade girls, both age ten, had been at a slumber party the night before and were in a silly mood in their fourth session. Their contagious foolishness and hilarity is a model instance of Level 0 shared experience:

> Connie, off-camera at the moment, fakes a loud hiccup.
> She is the more dominant one generally as well as in this

interaction. Margo imitates Connie with equally loud feigned hiccups, accompanied by gales of laughter from Connie. Margo, giggling and looking at Connie, shifts to making loud and indescribable hoarse sounds. Connie, again in the dominant role, comes into view, making a face that has a rather grotesque effect because she is using both hands to stretch the skin around her eyes. Margo, again following, remarks "Oh, it's easy" and makes the same face, as Connie laughs. Margo gets up and comes right up to the camera to give us a close-up of her contorted face with tongue stuck out and inner eyelids exposed, while Connie laughs hilariously in the background. As Margo withdraws, Connie comes forward, bringing her similarly wild-eyed "face" up to the camera lens amid Margo's boisterous laughter.

Level 1. In their first two sessions, Katy and Denia unanimously chose a Barbie doll set to play with from the four choices they were offered. During the second session the two third-graders (age eight) engaged in the following discussion about the Barbie equipment each has. The episode constitutes a Level 1 shared experience because of its quality of strongly individual expression in which each looked straight ahead rather than at the other. Katy and Denia free associated in a kind of "parallel play," wherein each girl's cataloging of what she owned sparked a kindred reaction, rather than genuine interest, from the other.

Katy started the "list-making" process of sharing and Denia followed, but otherwise neither seemed to accommodate to the other very much as the interaction unfolded. This Level 1 example raises the question of whether there needs to be a complementarity of interpersonal orientation in ongoing shared experience or whether two assertive-expressive actors can have "successful" (lower-level) shared experiences:

KATY: "Do you know what I have? Surf and Tub." She smiles as she names the toy.
DENIA: "I have this." She points at something in the Barbie catalog. "This kind. I have these kinds, and the pool."
KATY: "I like the Surf and Tub. It's really neato. It has flippers. It has a mask thing. It even comes with its own separate tub. It's for California Barbie."
DENIA: "Oh, that's nice. I have the ice cream one."
KATY: "My sister does."
DENIA, rubbing stomach: "Mmmm, I love ice cream."
KATY: "I have Barbie News." She stands up. "I have Barbie Kitchen."

DENIA: "I have, yah, me too." She reaches for the catalog.
KATY: "I have Barbie McDonald's. . . ."
DENIA, showing catalog to Katy: "I have this, see. . . ." (She names something.) "I have it. And I have a pony."
KATY: "I have. . . ."
DENIA: "And I have this one, I have the rockers, too."
KATY, as both look at catalog: "Let's see, I have this one."
DENIA: "I have her. I have her and I have the . . . . I have her. I have a lot of cars."
KATY: "I have cars."
DENIA: "I have, I have a bed and her. And I have a house."
KATY: "I have—I have, Linda has this one."
DENIA: "I have the house, too, and a bed. Ohhh, they're kind of pretty, all those Barbies. I wish I could have them *all.*"

Level 2. The following discussion about Garbage Pail Kids between two fourth-grade boys (age nine) in their third session bears a superficial resemblance to the previous Barbie discussion. But despite the similar content (what each child has acquired of a specific collectible toy), the tone and level of engagement were quite different. The boys' talk was much more a reciprocal conversation, in which mere cataloguing was supplanted by genuine interest in the other and the sharing of useful information about how to store one's toy collection. Nonverbal cues confirm the Level 2 "diagnosis": whereas the girls in the previous example sat parallel and never looked at one other, the two boys sat facing each other and made frequent eye contact, their body postures reflecting a more intimate connection.

Jefferey was generally the more leading of the two participants in this interaction, having initiated the topic and then giving strong advice on how to store the toys. The balance of power in the conversation was rather fluid, however, with Michael asserting himself, helping direct the flow, and interrupting Jefferey:

JEFFEREY: "That's a Garbage Pail Kid, you know, One Chop Scott."
MICHAEL: "This?"
JEFFEREY: "Yeah."
MICHAEL: "It is?"
JEFFEREY: "Yeah. The one with the eyeballs going into the head."
MICHAEL: "Oh yeah, and the wheelbarrel [sic]?"
JEFFEREY: "Yeah."
MICHAEL: "I have that. I have that complete set." He makes a plane noise.

JEFFEREY: "I have a hundred and fifty something of them. How many do you have?"
MICHAEL: "I have two thousand. I have too much."
JEFFEREY (inaudible)
MICHAEL: "They can't, they can't hardly fit in the bag, so I put them in a garbage bag."
JEFFEREY: "Whoa!!! You mean they're all mixed up, all over the place. Oh, my god! I keep mine in a neat pile."
MICHAEL: "Mine doesn't stay in a pile. The elastic won't hold them. It's bigger than the elastics."
JEFFEREY: "I know, so you know what you do? You take all the elastics—"
MICHAEL, interrupting Jefferey: 'It won't fit in a plastic, it won't fit in a bag like this." He reaches for a plastic bag that's nearby.
JEFFEREY: "Take a ton and fit them all in different groups."
MICHAEL: "It won't fit in a bag like this. It won't."
JEFFEREY: "I know."
MICHAEL: "It fits in a trash bag."

From Level 2 to Level 3. Children naturally fluctuate across levels of shared experience, just as they do across levels of interpersonal negotiation, as social interaction unfolds in a particular interpersonal context. Just minutes after the two fifth-grade girls engaged in the silly Level 0 shared experience described above, they had the following (more serious but still somewhat silly) Level 2 shared experience. Here Margo, though generally the more self-transforming one, brings up the subject and goes on to ask Connie her opinion on who the strongest girl is. Connie seems in control of the second part of the discussion, but the subject is *Margo's* brother:

MARGO: "Kathy called me on the phone once and she said 'Margo, who do you think is the strongest girl in the class?' And I go, 'I don't know,' and she says, 'I probably am.'"
CONNIE: "Oh my *God!!* She really said that? Was she joking?"
MARGO: "No!"
CONNIE: "Oh, she is *stupid!!!*"
MARGO, smiling: "She's the class wimp, O.K." Both look at the trainer, seemingly self-conscious about their gossiping. Margo taps nervously on table.
TRAINER: "What?"
CONNIE: "Nothing." She giggles.
MARGO: "Who do you think is the strongest girl in the class?"

CONNIE: "You and Lisa."
MARGO: "Which one?" [There are two Lisa's in their class.]
CONNIE: "No, actually you. Because you're sort of the strongest in the class because. . . ."
MARGO: "Because my brother beats on me all the time and I can take it."
CONNIE: "Her brother is 15 and he is six foot . . ."
MARGO: "Six feet four."
CONNIE: "Four."
TRAINER: "Wow."
CONNIE: "And he has feet this big." She spreads her hands about eighteen inches apart.
MARGO: Nods.
TRAINER: "That *is* tall for that age."
CONNIE: "And feet this big. I mean I saw his shoes, and I thought they were clowns' shoes."
MARGO: Giggles.

Margo's and Connie's Level 2 shared gossip about "stupid" Kathy, speculation about the strongest girl in class, and knowledge about Margo's brother had a different tone than Jefferey's and Michael's Level 2 sharing. The boys conversed about each other's interests, whereas the girls discussed in-common topics. Although both episodes were on a reciprocal level, the form of the boys' sharing—a direct focus on the other's interests as they related to those of the self—is closer to the kind of support and affirmation of self and other that is characteristic of Level 3 mutuality and collaborative sharing.

There were no episodes of Level 3 sharing in the many hours of free play that we videotaped in our elementary school intervention. Nor would we expect there to be—the children were too young. Though we cannot provide an example of Level 3 shared experience from these data, we can nevertheless describe what Margo and Connie's discussion would look like at Level 3.

First, the topic would have to change from who the strongest girl in the class was to the subject of leadership. If Margo and Connie compared their feelings about being a leader in class and discussed what kind of leadership would be optimal, the conversation might turn to the dynamics of their own relationship. Indeed, the girls' relationship was not always as harmonious as the two episodes of shared experience from the fourth session suggest. Margo complained that Connie bossed her around too much and she clearly resented it. Indeed, this represented not only the greatest source of conflict in their relationship but also its growing point—as the sessions went on Margo was able to become more assertive and Connie was able to tolerate Margo's new strength in their relationship. The Level 3 capacity to stand outside the interpersonal system and initiate a frank exploration of how each felt about self and other and their relationship was at least several years away for these two ten-year-olds, however.

One critical factor in the significance of collaborative (Level 3) shared experience appears to be the length of time the two persons have spent together. Shared experiences at this level are not simply immediate, short-term reactions. Rather they are transactions based on a common history in a dyad, a history that allows each partner to reveal, in a variety of ways, some characteristics of the self to the other, to lower defensive postures, and to permit the self to be vulnerable. That a "history together" is needed before these advanced forms of shared experience can develop is part of the reason why autonomy processes often seem to be more central than intimacy processes in the early phases of relationship building in pair therapy, as we argue later in this chapter.

Precocious and Primitive Shared Experience

The reader may not have noticed much difference between the foregoing examples of shared experience at each level drawn from our videotapes of normal children in a public school social problem-solving intervention and those of troubled children in pair therapy presented in the previous section. These examples showed only subtle differences at the lower levels. For example, Korey and David's Level 0 motoric imitation was rigidly repetitive, whereas Connie and Margo's (also Level 0 but more conscious) imitation reflected the one-of-a-kind spontaneity of a silly moment of hilarity. The examples at the higher levels, such as the Level 2 gossiping of Jane and Harriet on the one hand and Connie and Margo on the other, were strikingly similar in tone and form.

This *apparent* equivalence derives from their decontextualized form. Once we put shared experience episodes into their interactive context, it becomes quite evident that there are marked differences in the *meaning* of the sharing for normal and troubled children. The comparison of the decontextualized shared experiences demonstrates that level cannot automatically be equated with pathology or health—low-level sharing is not necessarily pathological, and instances of high-level sharing do not always represent generally healthy functioning. To a greater or lesser extent, all children are capable of functioning at a range of levels.

In the three in-depth case studies presented in chapters 8 to 10, episodes of shared experience will be positioned in their elaborated pair therapy context. The two examples that follow will describe a less detailed setting to show the power of even some contextual information in interpreting the meaning of episodes of shared experience. In the first example, context will help differentiate "crazy" Level 0 sharing from Connie and Margo's "silly" Level 0 sharing. The supportive setting of the second example shows how context can elicit rarely glimpsed cutting-edge development.

Holly and Jessica are early adolescents in pair therapy together. Here is a glimpse of experiences they shared in their thirty-seventh session. Their pair therapist had withdrawn to the observation booth next to the pair therapy room at the pair's request because they wanted to talk about a boy in Jessica's class with whom Holly is infatuated. In fact, Davy barely knows that Holly exists, although the two girls' discussion, part of which is reported below, may seem to indicate otherwise:

> HOLLY: "What else did Davy do today?"
> JESSICA: "He threw a book at the teacher."
> HOLLY: "What did he say?"
> JESSICA: "'I hate algebra,' and threw it at the teacher."
> HOLLY: "All right, Davy. Yeah, that a boy. I love him. He's my boyfriend." Gently, "He's sooo cute."
> JESSICA: "He opened the window of the class and the wet rain came in."
> HOLLY: "All over the teacher?"
> JESSICA: "No, all over a kid. It fell on a fat kid named Barry. You know what he [Barry] does? Whenever it's lunchtime, he walks in front of me. He gets his food. He says, 'Hold it,' even if it's a long line. I say, 'Move it!'" [This is dubious indeed—Jessica is very passive.]
> HOLLY: "All right!"
> JESSICA: "This is how he blows farts in class."

At this point Jessica blows air through her pursed lips onto her arm. It seems like Jessica reported that Barry displays this behavior simply to justify her own desire to indulge in the same act. In fact, it is hard for Holly to resist joining in, and she begins to do so. Soon the twosome are having a shared experience, although it has a contestlike quality to it. Each seems to try to make more noise, longer than the other; at the same time they both laugh and giggle. Eventually, after about a minute and a half, Holly returns the pair to her own preoccupation:

HOLLY: "What did Davy say?" Holly is obsessed with Davy. She connects all reports to him, and assumes that he is involved in all interactions.
JESSICA: "He smiled and burped like this." Jessica demonstrates.
HOLLY: "Big or little?"
JESSICA: "The size of this room."

At this point, Holly, giggling, initiates a second sequence in which for at least a minute both girls burp in each other's face, in what we consider another example of shared experience, albeit at a low level.

Although the common activity we call a shared experience was at a very primitive level in this interaction, we will suggest in chapter 8 that it played a significant role in the restructuring of Holly and Jessica's interaction to a higher developmental level. There this interchange will be put into a broader context when we describe the entire course of the girls' pair therapy in detail. But for the moment consider the striking contrast that the following example of "precocious" shared experience provides to the glimpse of the "primitive" and "regressive" episode between Holly and Jessica.

Benjy and Ezra are both bright, articulate, and four-and-a-half. Both are somewhat short for their age, but Benjy is a stocky, droll blond, already a "character," and Ezra a slim, quieter child with a mop of dark curly hair. They have been good friends since each was a year old, when they started in a play group together. Since age two, they have been together daily in nursery school, for the last year and a half until two o'clock. Each is well liked, with many friends, but each also clearly regards the other as his best friend. They play together frequently after school and on weekends, started having sleep-overs at age three, and spend a good deal of time together in the summer.

Over the past several months, both boys have been increasingly involved with Superheroes in their play. The theme has appeared in drawings, elaborate role-playing, costumes at Halloween, and fantasy play with blocks, Legos, and small Superhero figures. Along with issues of aggression, power, and mastery, their super-hero play has raised issues of mortality and the first struggles to come to grips with the (lifelong) frightening idea of death.

It is mid-winter, and Ezra has come back to Benjy's house after school. They are in Benjy's room settling down with a snack of milk and pretzels. They chat in a desultory way about school, and then turn to a sleep-over planned for the weekend. A discussion of what

Benjy should bring to Ezra's house brings them to the subject of falling asleep at night:

> BENJY: "I can never go to sleep when I'm alone. I'm
> bringing my blankey. And my Snoopy."
> EZRA: "Me, too. I always have to have my Snoopy. I talk to
> him to stay awake sometimes. I get scared to go to sleep."
> Ezra looks troubled at this point, his face clouded as he
> looks at his friend.
> BENJY: "Yeah, I know." He also seems to feel concerned.
> "When my mom turns off the light, I use my Little
> Professor [an electronic calculator-type toy with a lighted
> numerical display] for four hours." Silence reigns for a
> moment or two.
> EZRA: "Sometimes I dream I'm gonna die. I don't like to go
> to sleep." Both children are clearly expressing fear, and
> each is increasingly focused on the other as well as on
> himself.
> BENJY (heartfelt): "Yeah." Then, "You know what I do,
> Ezra?" He looks directly into his friend's eyes.
> EZRA (intently): "What?" He is equally focused on Benjy.
> BENJY: "I keep my milk right here [he indicates his bedside
> table] and I always drink it down just halfway, right to
> here." He demonstrates on his milk glass.
> EZRA (thunderstruck, after a pause): "I do, too! Just half
> way. Then if I wake up . . ."
> BENJY (intensely finishing Ezra's thought): ". . . it's right
> there!"
> EZRA nods emphatically and, after another pause,
> continues: "Know what I'm gonna do? I'm not gonna eat
> too much, and I'm never gonna get any taller. That way, I'll
> never have to die."
> BENJY: "Me, too. Just stay this size."

And a thoughtful silence reigns. Both boys are visibly relieved and exchange smiles, then continue the discussion of the upcoming sleep-over.

The boys, by the looks on their faces and the intensity of their tones of voice, have evidently experienced and shared quite powerful concerns. The charm and naivety of their solution notwithstanding, they experience the airing and sharing of these concerns, in the context of trust and intimacy, as providing both comfort and validation of their fears (if not verification of the strategies used to deal with them). Interestingly, neither child's mother, until overhearing this conversation, had been aware of these particular concerns, although each had noticed some "stalling" around bedtime.

In chapter 2 we presented dyadic social interaction episodes between two younger "normal" boys and between two older troubled girls to demonstrate the three analytic steps in our interpretive/empirical approach to studying interpersonal negotiation. We use the same three steps—identifying appropriate interactions, "diagnosing" their level, and interpreting the interactions in context—to study shared experience. To illustrate how the three steps work in the analysis of shared experience, we have again presented two examples. By chance—not by design—the shared experience episodes also take place between two younger normal or "well-adjusted" boys and between two older troubled girls. Note that we do not wish to imply anything about gender differences in comparing normal males and atypical females on two occasions—they were simply the best examples we had to make our points.

Identifying the Shared Experience. Both episodes fit the earlier definition of shared experience. Benjy and Ezra see eye to eye and engage, with rapt joint attention, in an expressive conversation, with a shared affect of solemnity and under-control fearfulness. The interaction between Jessica and Holly is equally expressive and harmonious, but the affect and meaning they share is entirely different—hysterical playfulness and silliness. We have identified both these interactions as relatively intense shared experience, as falling at one extreme end of the continuum of social regulation. This identification is based on an accumulation of significant indicators of shared affect centered in a preoccupying theme identical for both participants, with their consequent sense of fully engaging themselves in the sharing of that theme. The difference in the kind of affect expressed in these two shared experience episodes is the most obvious difference between them, but they also differ in form, or, in our structural-developmental terms, in level.

Diagnosing the Shared Experience by Level. The rapid escalation of Jessica and Holly's "fake farting" and "fake burping" is classic Level 0 impulsive contagion. Their "contagious" interest in Davy is a more atypical example of primitive Level 0 shared experience, a long-running, slightly demented infatuation that Holly invents but in which Jessica gets caught up and shares the excitement. In contrast, as young as they are, Benjy and Ezra seem to be engaged in a Level 2 process of sharing in-common and profound concerns in a reciprocal and heart-felt discussion that soothes and comforts them both. Both dyads express strong feelings, but in Holly and Jessica's lower-level sharing, the arousal produced by the Davy fantasy is expressed through burps and farts rather than words; their feelings are neither identified nor connected to the idea of being infatuated. In contrast, Benjy and Ezra work through rather than merely express their deep feelings, which are more socially regulated and verbal, and hence under better control. Demonstrating Sullivan's notion of the value of the development of communicative competence, the boys connect their feelings to words and connect their feelings through words to each other.

Interpreting the Shared Experience. What do we make of these two examples of shared experience in relation to each other? Frequent observations of the two boys indicate that they deal with issues of autonomy and agency quite effectively for their age, using primarily Level 0 and 1 strategies and a balance of self-transforming and other-transforming orientations. What may surprise us, at first blush, even for children with such a long-standing and close friendship, is the level of trust, intimacy, and articulateness that enables them to share experiences of this nature (at what we have identified as Level 2). Even as adults, reading this description we can identify with the power of their concerns, and with the unique satisfaction and relief provided by this kind of sharing. Thus, all that is surprising really is that Benjy and Ezra are only four-and-a-half. (And given what we know about the range of ages at which social developmental achievements can occur, this example should be regarded as typical, even if occurring at a tender age.) What we can learn from an observation like this is how pervasive and powerfully need-fulfilling such intimacy is for us all, and how much of a handicap the inability to achieve this connection could be. For children like Holly and Jessica, already some eight years older, this level of articulateness and ability may eventually be achieved, depending in part on the fortuity of their future experiences (e.g., the opportunities they will have for corrective therapeutic interactions), but it is certainly not possible now.

The differences between Holly and Jessica's sharing of experience in the opening scene and that of Benjy and Ezra give us some clues about the ways in which close relationships "work." The shared experiences in the two dyads are somewhat similar in that they both clearly constitute experiences of closeness for the respective pairs. However, they are dramatically different in tone and immediate outcome. Benjy and Ezra are focused, satisfied, and soothed, whereas Jessica and Holly become overstimulated, close to losing control at times. Moreover, the boys focus on the concerns of both, the girls only on the concerns of Holly.

The contrast poignantly illustrates Werner's point that low-level functioning in older children is qualitatively different than low-level functioning that may have a similar surface form in younger children. This comparison for these examples is somewhat imperfect, however, because Benjy and Ezra are "functioning" (here, sharing) at a developmentally "older" (more complex) level than we would expect, given their chronological age and their more age-typical negotiating and cognitive abilities. Their case would perhaps better illustrate Werner's point if we cast them as sharing less precociously, perhaps dissolving into complete hilarity over a burping contest and building simple connection and intimacy at a four-year-old level. But in the case of Holly and Jessica, the illustration of Werner's point is perfect. They are not ages four or six, but twelve and fourteen, and their primitive sharing has different meaning and consequences, for several reasons, because they are older.

First, certain developmental lines have changed for them, although others have not. One change is in the focus of much of the shared experience. The lustful preoccupations of Holly and Jessica, despite their primitive forms, constitute typical early adolescent content.

Second, even if we had described the shared experience of these two dyads as similar in form (i.e., developmental level) by inventing an episode of more age-typical sharing for Benjy and Ezra, the sharing would not have the same results, because the developmental requirements of preschool and early adolescent functioning are very different. There would be a developmental match between Benjy and Ezra's low-level sharing and the simple connection functions it serves for four-year-olds. But low-level functioning in "higher-order organisms" of twelve and fourteen is atypical, a distortion of normal development, and does not meet their early adolescent needs for more mature forms of intimacy.

Like the troubled pair of Tania and Janine that we presented in chapter 2 in relation to the more normally functioning dyad of Brian and Jeremy (although here the focus is on shared experience rather than negotiation), Holly and Jessica's social regulation is pathological for two reasons. First, there is a gap between their (lower-level) social behavior and their (higher-level) social-cognitive capacity (we will present evidence that their social-cognitive ability probably *is* age-typical in the later chapter).

Second, the social milieu and tasks of preadolescence require higher-level functioning. Hence, their shared experience, though an important beginning, does not completely meet their developmental needs—it does not quite "work."

From a more strictly cognitive view, Werner's point is clearly made as well. In the example of Benjy and Ezra as it really occurred, their cognitive "behavior" is at a developmentally appropriate level, even if their affective "behavior" is well above it. The "fantasy solution" (drink half the milk only, then don't grow taller) to their struggle with profound issues of life and death reflect the age-appropriate level of their cognitive abilities, which do not include the concept of reversibility. Benjy and Ezra lack a reciprocal level of knowledge about their world and *fill in* this cognitive/conceptual gap with an understandable fantasy, which serves their developmental needs.

In contrast, the nature of the fantasy/reality boundaries in the interactions of Holly and Jessica do not fulfill their developmental needs as adequately. Despite having more complete knowledge, they still fail to hold on to the distinction between what they "imagine" and what they "can know" of real events, and so they allow each other to *distort* perceived reality with their fantasy and function well below their cognitive level. There is consensual validation, though not external verification, in Benjy and Ezra's separately created and then touchingly shared fantasy of "limited growth." Holly and Jessica consensually validate each other in a weaker sense—neither can easily differentiate fantasy and play (Davy burped; I say "Move it") from reality, and so they get caught up in each other's wish-fulfilling distortions.

Benjy and Ezra cognize and negotiate age-typically and, at least in this case, share precociously. They meet—or more than meet—the challenges of their chronological life stage. Jessica and Holly cognize age-appropriately, but negotiate and share at a level that is about eight to ten years behind their chronological life stage, and hence cannot meet the challenges of early adolescence. If they continue to distort their perceived reality, the outlook for their continued growth is not good. But their case study in chapter 8 will demonstrate that the sharing and validation seem to provide crucial positive functions, even at this low level, and may be the beginning of real growth.

Our observation of Benjy and Ezra also sheds some light on the theoretical paradox of thought and action we discussed at the end of chapter 1. Despite their precocity, these children are not yet five, and their thinking is only beginning to encompass the notion that some life processes are reversible and some are not. Yet they share experience—"interpenetrate"—at Level 2. This can only be described as a compelling (and rarely glimpsed) example of the actual, earliest construction, through active attempts to master and work through powerfully felt disequilibrium, of new cutting-edge kinds of mental structures, structures that may not be touched upon or further developed again for months or even years to come. And certainly this is not yet reflective "conceptual knowledge" we could hope to measure or prove at this point. Rather it is a rare illustration of development in action.

Social Regulation during the Course of Pair Therapy

In making a transition from this section on the theoretical foundations of pair therapy to the next section on practical techniques, a number of issues confront us. The first set focuses on individual development. To what extent do children develop the capacities for intimacy and autonomy in some degree of synchrony? By this we mean the extent to which the cutting-edge development of a given level of maturity in the capacity to implement one social regulation process is mirrored in the same achieved level in the other. If there is not a general developmental movement across processes for individual children, does one process tend to lead and the other to follow, or is progressive movement more idiosyncratic than that?

A second set of issues revolves around the processes of relationship-building rather than individual development. One interesting question is whether one social regulation process takes priority at particular phases when a close relationship is forming. We will argue that in pair therapy issues of autonomy, manifest in processes of interpersonal negotiation, appear in most cases to be primary at the start (the notion of "honeymoon period" notwithstanding), and that intimacy concerns become more ascendant later on. But this is hardly the case for all developing relationships (nor is it *always* the pattern in pair therapy). For example, in romantic coupling it seems self-evident that initial interactions are based on powerful attractions, so that intimacy issues are experienced initially, only later to be displaced to some degree by boundary issues. Truly close relationships between equals seem to involve a balance of intimacy and autonomy issues.

Finally, we think it is important to raise a set of issues regarding therapeutic techniques and theories—how we translate the dual track theoretical model described in this section into tools for the therapist to foster intimacy and autonomy. What aspects of intimacy and autonomy, for example, should be considered when matching children for pair therapy? Is interpersonal negotiation restructured largely through the therapist's subtle attempts to foster closeness and connection, which "soften" the boundary of the autonomy processes in individual and dyadic functioning? (There certainly seems to be greater fluidity across orientations in the dyads we have observed when they are engaged in sharing experiences than when they are engaged in negotiating conflicts.) Or is shared experience restructured when autonomy skills are fostered and the individuals feel under control? Perhaps it works both ways. It is to these practical and research questions that we now turn.

Part Two

Therapeutic Techniques in Pair Therapy

CHAPTER FIVE

Goals and Matching in Pair Therapy

The aim of pair therapy is to foster the personality development and social relationship skills of very troubled children during the crucial preadolescent and early adolescent period when, as Harry Stack Sullivan noted and we have reemphasized, chumships normally develop. It is sometime during this period that troubled children's lack of ability to make and maintain friendships begins to become clearly evident and painful, not only to the other people in their world, but also to the children themselves. They are helpless in the face of interactions that lead either to destructive clashes of will or withdrawal, and they lack the emotional strength and communicative competence that would enable them to reach out and explore another's feelings and thoughts, and to reach in and articulate their own. Pair therapy attempts to provide a safe forum for these children to confront and successfully resolve differences in each other's perspectives and to reveal themselves and inquire about their peers, so that they finally experience positive peer interactions.

The pool of latency-age and early adolescent youngsters whom we treat with pair therapy exhibit a wide range of pathologies, including personality disturbances, affective disorders, developmental delays, psychosomatic illnesses, conduct disorders, and learning disabilities. Some have been victims of abuse or neglect, and many have grown up in multiproblem families with pathogenic structures. All the children share common areas of difficulty, particularly in school conduct and academic achievement, although few lack the intellectual capacity to function adequately in school settings. But almost without exception, the referrals seen by our intake committee note severe difficulties in the ability of these children to form and maintain peer relationships, to make and keep friends.

That our pool of children and young adolescents comprises a relatively disturbed and isolated group of course influences the specific form our treatment takes. Nevertheless, as troubled as these children are, it has been our observation that they share with better functioning peers a strong, though often more confused and perhaps more primitive, desire to combat loneliness and isolation through meaningful contact with other children their age. Like all children, they want to express themselves, share positive experiences, and be liked. What they seem to lack to an extreme are the normal developmental skills and inner controls that better functioning children use, without much conscious reflection, to maintain ongoing play and other forms of connection with peers.

Although these youngsters have other psychological difficulties and problems in their families, these are not the primary focus of pair therapy. The treatment is oriented toward the here-and-now relationship of the pair, with the hope that gains there will prove generalizable, at least to a certain extent, to both partners' future "here-and-nows." It is a long-term treatment that uses the experiences and history of the developing relationship between the two children, and between each child and the therapist, to facilitate their social and emotional growth.

The joint research and clinical project of pair therapy began in the fall of 1979, motivated by both practical desires and theoretical interests. With regard to practice, we wanted to help children for whom traditional forms of treatment, including individual psychotherapy, did not seem to be enough. Theoretically, we were motivated by interest in the role of peer interaction and friendship in social development and the role of peer conflict resolution in the growth of the capacity to coordinate social perspectives.

Coincidentally, several clinicians in the early 1970s had independently introduced treatments of socially impaired children in peer dyads, variously termed "duo-therapy" (Bender, 1976; Fuller, 1977a, 1977b; Mitchell, 1976) and "peer pair psychotherapy" (Birnbaum, 1975). Just as we will do in this section of the book, each of these clinical innovators concern themselves with a set of basic issues. What are the goals of a therapy whose structure is two unrelated peers and an adult? How does one develop guidelines for selecting individuals to be matched? How are the processes of treatment best characterized? How do we evaluate the effectiveness of the treatment? Inevitably, differences in approaches will arise on the basis of differing theoretical perspectives and perceived expectations. For example, with respect to the question of matching the children, Birnbaum (1975) recommends selection based on similar diagnoses, whereas

Bender (1976) places a higher priority on specific interactional problems.

Pair therapy differs markedly from these other approaches in the pervasive influence on the treatment of both the developmental model of social regulation processes (informed by levels in the coordination of social perspectives) and the connection that we assume exists between normality and pathology. Our theoretical model frames not only the general goals but also the specific tactics of pair therapy, including the selection and matching of the two children, the use of play activities, and the role of the pair therapist in developmental terms.

Goals of Pair Therapy

In line with our developmental model, we have articulated the theoretically derived goals of pair therapy in the language of a hierarchical repertoire of strategies of intimacy and autonomy. Our goal is to encourage children who, despite a typically strong resistance to change, *are* motivated by their lack of friends, to develop and test out various new strategies in the safety of the therapeutic context. We hope they can then transfer these strategies to their dealings with the outside world.

The ongoing clinical goals and research questions of pair therapy come directly from our developmental model. We hope to expand children's repertoire of strategies for interpersonal negotiation and shared experience so that they will learn to interact and connect with peers at age-appropriate levels. To move toward greater flexibility and a balance of orientations at higher levels, the children must learn to use negotiation strategies appropriately drawn from different levels and both orientations. This will help them become sensitive to the contexts in which certain actions are best used and more resilient and resistant to the maladaptive use of regressive negotiating and sharing. In short, we want the children to learn how to make friends and maintain close relationships.

The concepts of negotiation strategies and shared experience can be misread as focusing on behavior alone, as surface forms of social skill. Yet the model maintains that each action level is based on a particular form of construal of self and other (the cognitive component), on identifying or locating affective disequilibrium and finding a way to deal with feelings (the affective component), and on what the primary purpose is (the intent component). Thus, to evaluate the child's ability to act maturely is to assess the level of affective, motivational, and cognitive functioning underlying the "surface behavior." Social actions involve both "deep" personality structure and "deep" cognitive competence on the one hand, and surface skills and behavior on the other. Because actions embody an underlying structure, mature negotiating and sharing of experience constitute more than simple, learned tactics, such as always initiating a request with "please." The path to maturity involves structural reorganization of the way a person relates to others. To be sincere and meaningful, words must reflect that underlying personality structure, not be "just words."

In short, pair therapy is not simply a social skills training program to teach children specific tactics for getting what they want at the same time as they learn to "get along." It is meant to be a deeper approach that fosters the reorganization of personality and understanding in the development of mutuality. The treatment is designed to restructure long-standing cognitive and affective aspects of social relations that have crystalized in primitive, and hence maladaptive, forms and made it difficult, if not impossible, for the children to "get along." It is therefore a dynamic, personality therapy as well as a psychoeducational, cognitive therapy.

The case of a pair named Andy and Paul will illustrate how we use the theoretical framework of negotiation strategies to identify specific developmental goals for particular children, beyond the general goal of fostering a child's flexible use of a repertoire of strategies. When these boys entered pair therapy at age eight, each operated consistently at a low level (Level 1) and in one orientation. Andy acted repeatedly in an other-transforming manner, ordering Paul to play the games he wanted to play, taking materials from Paul if he wanted them, controlling who got the food and soda that was available for both. Paul, on the other hand, seemed always to follow Andy's lead, doing what Andy wanted without sticking up for himself and his ideas. He acted consistently in a self-transforming way at a low level.

Andy and Paul both needed to learn the higher-level strategies that take into account the needs of both self and other. From a cognitive standpoint, then, our goals for them were the same: that they would move to construe relationships in a more reciprocal way and consider the wishes of both parties involved instead of operating with a construal of relationships in one-way, "I (you) lead and you (I) follow" terms. Affectively, too, there was a common goal: that they would experience and deal with feelings in a more reflective and balanced way, so immediate feelings would no longer rule their actions.

Although our long-term goals for them were the same, the different orientations of their behavior indicated that their immediate tasks were different. Andy had to learn to give more credit to another's needs, and Paul to give more credit to his own. For Andy this meant not only considering the wishes of others (cognitively), but also feeling safe and having trust in giving up some of his control (affectively). For Paul this meant allowing himself to be aware of and express his own wishes, with the faith that taking initiative and control would not be disastrous.

One real barrier to the development toward these goals by children like Andy and Paul is their own *defensive* resistance. Andy and Paul are, at some level, quite comfortable, or at least on familiar ground, in this complementary relationship. The therapist will likely meet with resistance from both children as he tries to pursue the identified goals. Andy will feel threatened by losing any of his control over Paul's initiative. Likewise, it will be frightening for Paul to assert his own wishes, thereby risking Andy's anger or the loss of the security of Andy's direction. Thus it may be asked, why should we try to change the ways Andy and Paul deal with each other, if the children are comfortable with this relationship? We have said that relationships at higher levels are more equilibrated. Yet is there not balance in this complementary relationship?

Yes, Andy and Paul's relationship at age eight is clearly "balanced," but it is a precarious form of balance we would call a "rigid (im)balance," both asymmetrical and low-level. Although stable, it is rigid and limiting, does not incorporate the flexibility and sensitivity required for adaptation to the more open, unprogrammed interactions of real life, and therefore does not work well, to the detriment of both boys' lives. For it to "work," each boy needs to achieve higher-level, equilibrated balance in his interactions.

An incident in a pair therapy session with Andy and Paul provides a concrete metaphor for these ideas about maladaptive imbalance in peer relationships. Andy told Paul he wanted to ride the seesaw on the playground, so they each took an end. Andy brought his end of the seesaw down to the ground. Paul was lifted into the air. Thereafter the seesaw did not move. Andy sat with his end on the ground smiling up at Paul, while Paul sat in the air with his legs dangling frantically. There was stability, a *type* of balance, but not a reciprocal one. It was a rigid form of balance, a stable imbalance.

This is the type of balance that exists in relationships directed by low-level strategies in which the actors play only one role and function in only one orientation. Andy is down, Paul is up. Andy gives the orders, Paul follows. The problem with this kind of relationship is that the individuals cannot move and grow. This lack of flexibility causes no difficulty as long as two children choose to maintain these unchanging roles, and as long as nothing else changes. But difficulties immediately arise when someone who will only sit at the bottom tries to seesaw with someone else who will only sit at the bottom, or when someone who will sit *only* up or down tries to seesaw with someone who wants to go up *and* down—that is, to use it "normally." The seesaw will rock spasmodically or it will break. Two children who can function only with unilateral control, whether control by themselves or another, will be unable to establish a relationship that is mutually satisfying. Furthermore, a relationship such as Andy's and Paul's will lose its balance when put in a different, unisolated context, such as the school playground. What if Paul is made captain of a team and has to direct Andy? What if a third child, who is more controlling than Andy, is protective of Paul and bullies Andy whenever he approaches Paul? This is only a sampling of potential problems.

The more flexible, equilibrated balance of higher-level interactions is like that of a seesaw holding two people of equal weight and equal inclination to shift. When they are in balance the two sitters are at equal levels, and each can move up or down in synchronous response to the movement of the other. In high-level interactions, each person is able to both assert his or her own desires and act with respect toward the desires of the other. This flexibility gives a person the ability to adapt to a variety of situations with a variety of people. The person can act as both a captain and a follower, to direct and be directed as the context requires.

One person can use a combination of self-transforming and other-transforming stances even within one negotiation sequence. The ability to take on different roles in different situations reflects a trust of both self and other, a willingness to take responsibility and also to be vulnerable. Responsibility and vulnerability are no longer seen as positions of winning or losing, but positions for sharing with others and positions that "work better" for getting your needs met without undue interpersonal stress. This is a long-term goal of the treatment process for both members of the pair. Part of the therapist's role is to provide enough safety and continuity that the children themselves will begin to be less invested in rigidity and experience the inadequacy of their behaviors themselves.

In fact, one of the strongest values of the model in guiding our intervention is that it helps to identify the specific next step for a child or pair. The researcher as well as the practitioner can readily put forth the long-term goal of having the capacity for mutual relationships wherein the individual can be both responsible and vulnerable. But how do we help a child like Andy or Paul to this point? The theoretical model acts as a conceptual map that allows us to identify where the child is now and where we should encourage him to go next. With Andy, for example, we find that he is acting primarily at Level 1 in an other-transforming manner. He needs alternative ways of construing the self-other relationship, or experiencing and dealing with affect, and of acting to change the self or other. Thus, for this child, our next step is to establish a context that encourages his experimentation with self-transforming strategies and his use of more reciprocal, Level 2 forms of interacting. In chapter 7 we will return to the story of Andy and Paul to illustrate three tactics with which the therapist can implement the developmental goals for a pair.

With respect to the relation of theory, research, and practice, the psychological model that we have so far described can function in two ways in pair therapy. At the molecular level it can be used to scan the pair therapy sessions to identify specific instances, those when conflict is imminent or when negotiation or shared experience are ongoing, and describe the level and orientation of the children's actions. When the model is used this way, its applicability is clinically limited, for dyadic negotiation and shared experience in their pure forms between the pair are only a part (though a significant one) of the triadic interaction in each session. The model can also be used at a relatively molar level in a general description of the way each child typically relates to the other, as distinct from how each interacts in specific instances. In this latter sense the model acts less precisely and more metaphorically, as a way to organize a wide range of interchanges involving social regulation processes observed across sessions. Summarizing these discrete instances of interaction in this way (some of which may not fit our strict definitions of negotiation and shared experience) constitutes a way to view the central tendencies of each child in terms of both developmental characteristics (levels) and styles (orientations) of interpersonal relating.

For empirical research purposes, we tend to use the model in a molecular approach to try to reliably identify contexts for interpersonal negotiation and shared experience in the stream of the triadic interaction and then to code them either within each particular therapy session, from negotiation to negotiation and shared experience to shared experience. For clinical purposes, we tend to use the model more loosely, across sessions, from week to week and month to month. From many observed social interactions, we inductively abstract an overall characterization of each member of a pair in the language of levels and orientations, and set our sights on the facilitation of the growth of each child's repertoire to a more advanced level and greater balance between orientations. Of course, we wish to integrate the clinical and the empirical approaches for theoretical purposes to begin to understand how specific interactions build into long-term relationships and what precisely it means to say that individually, a youngster is capable of forming a close relationship, and that interactively, a relationship has formed.

Although we attempt to improve the children's ability to develop and flexibly use effective strategies for negotiating and sharing experience with their pair-mates from a repertoire of possible alternatives, the treatment is not limited to one circumscribed aspect of social development. We also pay attention to a related set of more general cognitive, behavioral, and affective goals for the therapy.

"Cognitive" goals at an individual level include the improvement of the children's ability for self-reflection. In the actual sessions this means being able to help a child stop his or her action for a moment to examine the thoughts, feelings, and motivations underlying it. A second, and related, goal is to improve communicative competence, the children's ability to express to their pair partners (or therapist), either in words or through symbolic gestures, their personal thoughts, feelings, and motivations about actions taking place in (or outside) the pair therapy sessions. This often entails learning that their partners (in particular) and others (in general) cannot read their minds. At the same time, it means learning that their partners are affected by behavior caused by a mood that is brought into a session but not directly reported. For example, it took fourteen-year-old Brenda quite a long time to realize that if she came to pair therapy in a bad mood, and did not acknowledge and explain the cause of her mood to her partner, Donna, then Donna would often think that Brenda was either angry at her or did not like being with her, even if in fact the mood was unrelated to pairs or to Donna.

Included among the cognitive goals for the pair as a unit is the capacity for joint planning. If the "pair" decides to put on a puppet show or use walkie-talkies to play out a jungle patrol fantasy, they must be able to plan it and lay out basic ground rules. Often the pair will act impulsively together on an idea for an activity without planning adequately for its successful implementation. When

Janine and Barney decided to do a puppet show, they wanted an audience, but made no coordinated plans for letting others know when the show would be performed, let alone that it was open to the public. The therapist's role here was to help the children learn how to plan. He asked questions about the plan rather than making the plan for them, or even with them. For instance, the therapist asked Barney and Janine to explain to him where the audience would sit, what time the show would begin, where it would take place, and how they would announce it.

We also pursue "behavioral" goals, consisting of interpersonal and social skills, for each child and the pair as a unit. Some are general social skills like learning to take turns, ask for information, listen, state feelings rather than bark orders, compromise, and give and take. However, for children who feel the constant need to use threats and coercion in order to meet their needs and secure their ends, it is not enough to suggest, for solely pragmatic reasons, that they try politeness to achieve their needs. It is crucial that these surface behaviors be linked in the child's mind and heart to some understanding of why they work, in relation to a consideration of both the perspectives of others and what it takes to move others. Behavior has a social logic that needs to be understood *and* felt.

Considering the pair as a unit, it is a long-range behavioral goal that they be able to interact together for the length of a session without the continuous, in-the-room presence of the therapist. It should be stressed, however, that pair therapy is not peer therapy. Our aim is not for each child or adolescent to function primarily "as if" a therapist to each other, but rather "as if" a friend.

What is the difference? We believe there are important differences. Foremost, the role of the therapist to each of the children, as in individual therapy, is to provide a special type of objectivity and impartiality. It is an involvement without an overinvestment, a kind of distance and perspective, even with the provision of caring and empathy. This distanced yet personal involvement distinguishes therapist from friend. We expect the adult to adopt this therapeutic posture, but not the children. As a therapist, you do not get angry personally when a child arbitrarily calls you "a fat slob" or "a bitch." As a friend, you do. Pair therapy is essentially a dyadic relationship mediated by the adult therapist. This role will be spelled out in more detail in chapter 7.

Regarding "affective" goals, there is a dual focus in pair therapy on trust and control. Each child must trust the other child and the therapist in increasingly mature ways (see chapter 1). The child needs to know that his or her actions will be viewed accurately, fairly, impartially, and consistently by the therapist. The child also needs to trust in a *basic* way that the therapist will keep each child safe, and will help them both cross rough waters without falling apart or causing serious damage. Trust of the pair partner means having the strength to risk being vulnerable to attack without fear of being permanently damaged. Vulnerability may be expressed by taking the chance to get angry at a partner who is bossy, or by taking the chance to give in and let the partner have first choice. Hopefully, through pair therapy the child can become better able to deal with painful, but natural, feelings arising out of interpersonal contexts, feelings inherent in all personal and meaningful social relations.

Control is as central an issue in pair therapy as is trust. The children referred to us tend to be either out of control or over-controlled, and need to find a better balance, a way to feel in control and to feel safe. The therapist provides control as well as trust and support—indeed, these are intertwined. The children also need to deal with their own need for control vis-à-vis the pair-mate. One primary affective goal of pair therapy is to help the children understand how to deal with the control of the self and other peers and adults when their interaction is in momentary disequilibrium.

From a practical perspective, pair therapy provides a chance for two children to interact directly with each other over issues that are real and meaningful to each of them. These interactions generate positive feelings, sharing and communication, self-expression, and the feeling of being understood by someone whose interests are close to your own, as in Sullivan's notion of consensual validation. Also generated are negative feelings around issues of possession and control, jealousy, and conflict of interest. From a therapeutic perspective what is important is that the pair therapy interactions allow these feelings to be put out on the table, and to be put there without disastrous results. There is a third party, the pair therapist, who holds a relatively objective perspective on the interaction. All interactions generate interpersonal feelings, and reflection provides a means for dealing with them. In sum, one general goal of pair therapy is to help each child integrate feelings and actions through empowerment, communication, and shared reflection.

Matching Children for Pair Therapy

We do not think of pair therapy as an effort at matchmaking between two selected children. It is not our aim to take two associates, classmates, strangers, or even enemies and make them into friends, at least not initially or necessarily ever. Rather, the aim is to give each participating child—usually rejected or isolated in part as a function of his or her own immature, inappropriate, aggressive, or withdrawn social behavior—the experience of and internalized capacity for getting along with peers and understanding what is in disarray when he or she cannot.

Of course, we have found that some children who are paired do, in fact, come to associate more with one another in school or elsewhere, even to the point of becoming friends and getting together with each other at home on weekends. However, others establish no greater or significantly different contact outside of pairs than they had before. Some come to get along quite well within the pair to the point of clearly becoming emotionally dependent upon each other, but due to powerful external factors, such as their perceived status by other peers, they associate hardly at all with one another at other times during the school day.

Given our theoretical perspective, we believe in pairing children according to their relative developmental levels and interpersonal orientations. The pool of potential candidates is in school from 8:30 until 4:00 each weekday, so we have the opportunity to observe the full repertoire of interpersonal negotiation strategies each child uses. Clinical material and case histories that provide insight into conduct are also accessible. In matching children we consider not only which developmental level and interpersonal orientation each typically uses, but also the consistency of the modal actions.

With respect to level, children referred to the pair therapy project tend to exhibit one of two usual initial patterns: they are either fixated at functionally low levels (rigid rather than flexible), or they oscillate recklessly and unpredictably from higher to lower levels without the apparent capacity to weather rough situations with stability at higher levels (labile as opposed to stable). With respect to orientation, we also tend to see similarly extreme patterns: either a child is capable of functioning in only one orientation regardless of context, or the child fluctuates wildly from one orientation to the other.

It needs to be stressed here that these troubled children tend to function in a predominant orientation to a much greater extent than "normal" children. We frequently characterize children as other-transforming or self-transforming in this book. Our clinical observations suggest that these characterizations can at times be valid for this population, and we see them as a function of, and a part of, their severe difficulties. The reader should be cautioned, however, against attempting to make this kind of characterization outside this population. It can be risky and unwarranted, as we have warned earlier, to attempt to characterize anything beyond a strategy itself as self-transforming or other-transforming.

Whether looking at level or orientation, these children's interpersonal behavior tends to be rigidified into patterns whereby they either become swept away by aspects of the immediate context (e.g., grabbing for all the new games on a table without regard to whether they require a partner or whether the partner is interested in playing) or refuse to accommodate to any aspect of it (e.g., clinging to an empty soda can and ignoring additional snacks, new games, partner, and therapist). In either case, there is no assimilation of the context to a stable, organized self. To provide a context for the development of at least the beginnings of a stable self is one goal of pair therapy.

Our work with pairs suggests that the most efficacious match is usually of two children who are capable of using the *same level* social actions, but who use predominantly *different orientations*. If the children have the same range of action levels, the therapist can encourage, and the level of the partner's actions can promote, the same or next higher level of behavior and reflection in each child. If they have the opposite orientation, they may learn from each other's opposite mode, and may feel safe enough to try out actions in unfamiliar orientations. In fact, we suspect that this trying out of the other orientation may be an initial step in the process of movement to the next higher developmental level, a level that invariably embodies a more balanced representation of the self's and other's needs than the lower developmental level.

Although matching children with the same developmental range of social actions has been most effective, pairing children who use predominantly the same orientation appears to be somewhat problematic. Two children who both have other-transforming orientations often literally repel each other, like two positive (or negative) poles of a magnet. Two self-transforming children may tend to leave a vacuum and fail, on their own, to interact or make contact. Still it should be noted that pair therapy is itself a dynamic process. Regardless of the predominant orientations two children bring to a pair, this dynamism begins from the first session as the pair seek to find a balanced relation between their respective orientations. Usually, an initial dominance hierarchy is established quickly. As we shall see in the next chapter, it is the therapist's role to restructure the balance and elevate the interaction to a higher level of social competence.

The following two examples illustrate selection along the theoretical lines just described. Cindy is an eleven-year-old who is isolated in her classroom and has no playmates at home. During recess and lunch she usually sits in a removed part of the room reading as she nibbles on food. When outside for recess she usually watches others playing, hovering on the outskirts of a group. She will occasionally make a comment that indicates her interest, such as "That looks like a fun game," but she does not directly ask to play. When Cindy is engaged in play, it is usually only if another child has approached her. When another child tells Cindy to push her in the sled, toss the ball, or ride on the seesaw with her, she complies.

Cindy's predominant strategies are Level 1, self-transforming. She acts as if her "will" is secondary to the will of others, complying with directions of others without asserting her own wants. Even when expressing her interest in a game, she does not ask to play directly. Cindy adapts her own wants to the expressed or perceived wants of others, and her orientation is clearly consistently self-transforming.

Kate, at ten years old, has very sporadic relationships with her peers. At times she is seen with another child who appears to be loyally following Kate's plans and playing the games Kate decides to play. Kate flatters the playmate: "Hey, let's play kickball now—you're so good at it." Later, we see an argument sparking up between Kate and the other child. Kate orders the child to give her the ball, and the other adamantly refuses. Kate's face turns red with frustration and her words sputter and finally stop. Kate suddenly runs over to the playmate, grabs the ball out of her hands, and runs across the field with a fiery look.

Kate uses a variety of levels in her strategies for dealing with others. She manipulates a playmate (in a Level 2 way), pursuing her own wish to play kickball by flattering the playmate so she will want to play. But when Kate's wishes come into conflict with those of the other child, she uses orders (a Level 1 strategy) to try to get her way. And then we see Kate "drop" to an impulsive, physically forceful action (grabbing, at Level 0) when she is frustrated by her lack of success with ordering. Thus, although we may identify Kate's usual level of negotiation as Level 1, we see that she is able to use, and does use, a variety of levels. However, her orientation is consistently other-transforming.

Cindy and Kate were chosen to be a pair primarily on the basis of observations of the two in school. The pairing was very successful. By successful, we mean that we saw developmental movement by each child in the pair context in their two-year period together.

They moved steadily toward using higher levels of negotiation, and using them more consistently. As their pair therapy progressed, each demonstrated both a more balanced consideration of the needs of self and other, and a more balanced identification and control of feelings. In short, they developed a closer peer relationship than either was capable of before.

We feel that one reason why this pair worked so well was that it involved one child who was predominantly self-transforming and one who was other-transforming. Kate served as a model for Cindy, who could observe that these strategies got Kate what she wanted. Cindy was able to see other-transforming strategies could be used without costing her the other person's association—Kate did not end up rejecting Cindy when Cindy attempted to be more assertive. Conversely, Cindy was a model for Kate, showing her that self-transforming strategies were safe to use. Kate was able to see that she would be neither lost nor engulfed. Of course, the therapist played a crucial role in keeping the pair together as each child experimented with alternative strategies.

Another reason for the positive development of this pair was that they were equally matched in the strategy level they most frequently used (Level 1). This meant that our immediate goals for their developmental movement and learning of alternative strategies were similar. As we mentioned, one hypothesis we have developed regarding the children who are strongly and consistently of one interpersonal orientation, and concurrently at a low level in that orientation, is that they may need to try out the opposite orientation in order to move up in level and toward balance between orientations. Children such as Cindy and Kate are acting with strongly polar orientations at Level 1. Because lower-level strategies have more polarized orientations, in order for Cindy to feel comfortable using higher-level strategies, she first needs to feel comfortable using other-transforming strategies at Level 1 (e.g., orders or commands). Once she has broken this form of rigidity and feels comfortable with the new orientation, as well as her usual orientation of accommodating, she can come to use higher-level strategies that attend to both her own wants and the wants of others. These children must first feel comfortable using the opposite orientation at a familiar level (their modal level or even a lower level) before they are able to work toward a balance of orientations in moving up to a higher level of strategy use.

This hypothesis supports the value of matching a pair that employ polar orientations, and it is supported empirically by the interpersonal growth observed in pairs like Cindy and Kate. However, there is also a counterargument that children in a pair using predominantly low-level strategies from opposite orientations might model the lowest and "least appropriate" use of the opposite orientation for each other. This situation has the potential to stimulate the other child to use equally low-level strategies that are of the opposite orientation, thus promoting movement only across orientations rather than toward a balance of orientations at higher levels. Or, with only the low and more drastic form of the other orientation modeled, the other child might be "scared away" from it.

Our reply to these arguments is that within our population of pairs, we have found instead that with therapeutic guidance the children are more likely to develop toward an integration of orientations and toward higher-level strategies when paired with a child of opposite orientation. They seem to become less frightened of making use of the opposite orientation, rather than more so. The sensitive guidance of the pair therapist is one reason for this. He or she uses the very real safety and trust established in the therapy setting, which is often quite new to these children, in combination with judiciously applied "restructuring" techniques, to stimulate the children's natural growth tendencies, tendencies that their past experiences have largely thwarted and stifled.

A related reason we feel that similarly low-level strategies are not simply "modeled" in the opposite orientation by such a pair has to do with the fundamental tenets of our theoretical orientation. Although we see modeling as a powerful force in social development, we do not consider it the primary means by which growth occurs. Instead we view the "modeling" of the other child as one of many stimulating, challenging, and conflict-producing experiences that a growing person encounters and acts upon, and to which he or she reacts, in an active and continuous attempt to make sense of his or her world and to learn to live in it. It is a natural, active, and fundamental human drive to do this. To assume that a person who is exposed to a certain behavior will adopt it simply ignores the active, discriminating, and self-generating nature of development. More systematic research is needed to clarify how the complexity of such polarity and the way the members of the pair identify with each other's orientation influence their movement in pair therapy.

There is one final note of possible difficulty in matching a polar-orientation pair: the children may find their complementary roles very comfortable and stable, and so resist further growth. This concern may be valid, but it is the role of the therapist to help the children overcome such entrenched forces of regression or fixation. Pair therapists try to assist the natural process of discovering, or reacting to, the inadequacy of these rigid forms of relating. We will address in chapter 7 how the therapist can accomplish this.

Consider for now, however, an alternative type of match: two children who tend to use different levels of strategies, but the same orientation. Alex and Jeff met together for pair therapy. Alex was identified as a child who used primarily Level 0 and 1 strategies. He seldom, if ever, used Level 2. Jeff, on the other hand, oscillated from Level 0 to Level 2 strategy use, frequently interacting with Level 2 strategies. This discrepancy in the level of their strategy use was a point of difficulty throughout their pair therapy, as was their use of the same (other-transforming) orientation. Jeff's Level 2 strategies were often misunderstood by Alex, and therefore were usually ineffectual. As a result, Jeff often resorted to lower-level strategies. One day when they went outside to play kickball, the beginning of the game was held up because Alex stood clutching the ball, refusing to pitch it. He wrapped his arms around the ball, skipping a few steps away from Jeff with every step Jeff took toward him, as if trying to initiate a game of chase. Jeff looked at him with exasperation. "Come on," he urged Alex, "we both wanted to play kickball. Why don't you throw it?" Alex only clutched the ball even tighter, shaking his head "No." "Why don't you throw it?" Jeff asked again. Alex continued to sidestep Jeff at every move. When finally Jeff threatened, "I'm just leaving if you don't cut it out and pitch the ball," Alex angrily threw it.

The difficulty here for Jeff was that his Level 2 strategies were evidently too high for Alex to appreciate and learn from. Having no success in his use of higher-level influencing strategies, Jeff was rewarded only for lower-level strategies such as threats. As a result, the pair's interaction tended to take on a Level 1 mode, lower than Jeff was capable of. It is, of course, valuable for a person to learn that low-level strategies are at times effective and may even be appropriate in particular contexts with certain people. This knowledge is part of an interpersonal flexibility and sensitivity necessary to deal appropriately with various situations. However, it is more important for these children to know the value of higher-level strategies, to be capable of using them, and, further, to recognize the difference between "appropriateness" and "effectiveness" in their motivation to use lower-level strategies.

To complicate the nature of their interaction even more, both boys tended to use the same, other-transforming orientation with peers. Alex was usually bossy or physically forceful in pursuing his own wants. Jeff was frequently manipulative, using flattery or bribery, yet he could also be bossy and forceful. After a year of therapy the boys had not worked through the early phase of establishing roles for power and control in the pair. Each child continued to insist exclusively on his own desires, and this stubbornness frequently caused the emotional tenor of their negotiations to deteriorate. As a result, the boys' strategy levels often declined over the sequence of an interaction, until one grabbed the pencil he wanted or chased the other around the room in anger. The rare times the children worked together toward any goals were when they "ganged up" to control the therapist. It was very difficult for this pair to move beyond initial phases of challenging each other and the therapist. As for Alex, the defensive, control-oriented, and possessive rigidity with which he functioned at a low level and in an other-transforming orientation prevented him from being stimulated by Jeff's use of higher-level strategies. Going head-to-head with Jeff when both were persisting in other-transforming behavior only served to maintain this rigidity, blocking opportunities and reinforcement for change that Alex needed.

However, two self-transforming children may prove a valuable match if the therapist can play an active role in encouraging self-assertion. Although each child tends to be hesitant to take initiative, each does not have to struggle against a forceful other. There is no apparent threat that the other will discredit the self's wants, as would be the case with an other-transforming peer. Rather, in this context the self-transforming child may, with encouragement, be willing to try out ways of dealing with another that assert his own wants. As we have said earlier, we feel that this step toward the opposite orientation is a movement toward a more balanced consideration of the needs of both self and other. Like nature, a pair of children abhors a vacuum, and two self-transforming children generate a vacuum that may be filled by one or the other child trying out a more dominant role. Once again, it is the therapist's role to provide a structure for growth in this situation, and to bear in mind that the new orientation is likely to be implemented at first at a relatively low level.

As important as we believe similarity in developmental level and complementarity in interpersonal orientation to be in matching children for pair therapy, there are other practical factors to consider to insure a good match. Pairing children of roughly the same age seems to help the children identify with one another, thus facilitating their interaction. We have also found that if the children are fairly equal in intellectual ability and communicative competence, there is a greater chance the match will be a success.

Other factors we pay attention to include whether the children are similar or different in their respective interests and ethnic, socio-cultural, or social-class backgrounds. Although some differences in background and interests can be valuable in nurturing each child's learning about differences and strengthening an understanding of others' perspectives, if the children have only differences in these areas, the task of establishing some bond and mutual interest will be a far more difficult one. Therefore we try to balance the commonalities and the contrasts in these areas.

At times we may also consider diagnostic classifications as a factor for matching. For instance, we matched two twelve-year-olds who both met the *Diagnostic and Statistical Manual of Mental Disorders: Third Edition* (American Psychiatric Association, 1980) criteria for the diagnosis of "Autism, Residual State." Both children had an earlier history of severe interpersonal and communicative impairment. Each had markedly improved, but both demonstrated behavior characterized by poor communication skills and somewhat inappropriate or bizarre social behavior. The match proved to be propitious. Both children felt secure enough in each other's presence to practice verbal interactions and to reflect together on their odd social mannerisms. Any group larger than two proved too overwhelming for both of these children. Their fragile communicative competence was not up to the functional requirements of the competition and confusion of a group. But in the dyad, with the therapist's help, they were able to improve their communication skills in relative privacy and security. The pair also provided the opportunity for these children to begin to identify with a person outside themselves, which is a healing benefit of the therapy for all pairs, but especially for these troubled girls.

Of course, another major issue in matching the children is whether the pair should be of the same gender. Most latency-age children in our culture tend to gravitate toward peers of the same sex in both casual play and close friendships, feeling a closer identification based not only upon gender per se, but also upon their gender-related similar interests and concerns (Pitcher and Schultz, 1983). This is less often a prevailing factor, though, for the children of this age with whom we work. For one thing, our children often do not have a wide pool of potential friends from which to choose. Also, in some ways, they may find being matched with a child of the opposite sex to be less threatening and less challenging.

As children approach adolescence and puberty, however, matching an opposite-sex pair is a potentially volatile decision and should be considered with great caution. Certainly such a match will greatly influence the nature of the interaction within the pair, perhaps in ways neither the therapist nor the children will be totally prepared to deal with, and in ways that will detract from the optimal focus of the treatment. Although we would not like to make a blanket rule against opposite-sex adolescent pairs, we would say that the positive reasons for matching a boy and a girl at this age should be very strong.

Another dimension to consider when matching pairs lies in the nature of the children's personal or family problems and difficulties. Two children may be a potentially good match by virtue of a common problem—for example, obesity or the loss of a parent—but it should be realized that these issues may not be shared or dealt with in the pair for quite some time. In fact, if two children are a poor match by virtue of the nature of their particular psychological needs or styles, this can offset the advantages of their having a common problem.

For example, we matched two eleven-year-old boys, both of whose fathers were alcoholics. Tom enjoyed structured, organized activities such as board games. He continually sought structure in all activities, even imposing devices such as counting out loud when he felt that he was losing control. Mark, on the other hand, balked at any structure, and was strongly drawn to athletic activities as a medium to play creatively, try out different roles, and work through issues of concern. But Tom was frequently frightened and confused by Mark's introduction of any physical activity, feeling utterly unable to compete with his more aggressive and better-coordinated partner, and unable to deal with the open-endedness of such play. As a result, this pairing was particularly difficult from the outset. To the extent that Tom and Mark were unable to establish mutually enjoyable play and a shared medium for working through concerns, pair therapy was frustrating and conflictual. It required some ingenuity and perseverance on the part of the therapist to help these two boys find some common ground or be willing to explore the turf upon which the other felt more comfortable.

Inevitably, matching must involve a consideration of any actual relationship that already exists between two identified children.

Do the two want to be paired? Do they have grudges? How has their relationship developed so far? Does one embarrass or humiliate the other by his behavior, or does one use the other as a scapegoat? Finally, we consider the more basic issue of whether the child wants to be in a pair—whether he or she wishes to develop socially and escape from feelings of isolation and alienation.

CHAPTER SIX

Ground Rules of Pair Therapy

Getting Started

Initial encounters between the therapist and the paired children are critical in setting a tone that will carry through the treatment. These first meetings present a set of subtle and intricate problems for the therapist, who must "set the stage" to create specific opportunities for both shared communication and negotiation between the pair. The therapist sets the stage by creating an atmosphere of acceptance and safety in which the children are free to express themselves, share their thoughts, feelings, and fantasies, and try out new ways of resolving conflicts. The environment must be personal, warm, exciting, and inviting, yet also objective, firm, fair, and, to some extent, impersonal. Establishing openness and limits at the same time is particularly tricky with children, because they tend to interpret the actions of others in their own developmental terms. For very troubled children, firmness, which is in some sense an acknowledgment of interdependence, may be seen, at least at first, as severe control. And they may view permissiveness, which can be considered an acknowledgment of autonomy, as no control or limits at all.

It is especially important for these children initially to experience pair therapy as a place where they are going to have fun as well as work. Creating positive interpersonal experiences early on, when the children are becoming invested in the pair, helps tremendously later on in guiding them through the inevitable rough spots. This initial period is critical in part because the children often come to pair therapy with very unrealistic expectations. Regardless of what their therapist has initially said about "pairs" as a place to do hard work at building friendship skills, the rumors of trips, toys with which to play, and almost individual attention from an adult tend to obscure the constraint-oriented aspects of the process.

When the children are initially chosen for pairs, they feel important and favored in getting something that not everyone gets. Remember, however, as a backdrop to these initial surface optimistic feelings, that troubled children also come with long-standing, underlying feelings of pessimism or confusion about social relations. The repeated failures and frustrations of their past relationships have left them with generally low expectations of social interactions. With these failures come a strong sense of neediness, a desperate, almost panicky, wish for friends, and a fear that friendships never really work. Will I make it? Will I get a lot? Will I get along with my pair-mate? What if he doesn't like me, or I don't like him? Maybe we'll end up fighting. Will I be safe? Do I really want to have friends?

Most of the selected youngsters do not acknowledge the potential pitfalls at first. They see pair therapy as a special activity and usually want to be a part of it. But pair therapy is a therapy. It is meant to deal with psychic pain and social dysfunction as well as have curative and positive effects. Growth and repair occur in the interaction, and we consider the pair therapy context to be curative even when it may be temporarily distressful. The context itself serves as a healing environment, an interpersonally corrective experience, in which play and conversation and attempts to frame them become forms of psychic rehabilitation.

The high but often ambivalent expectations of pairs are rudely confronted after a short "honeymoon period." Not surprisingly, early on, often within the first two or three meetings, the children usually discover that their partners may have views or interests that differ from their own, sometimes dramatically. Each child finds out relatively quickly that the pair partner will repeatedly get in the way of his or her own wishes. For example, the need to share one item, share the floor, or share the therapist's support and attention can evoke feelings of neediness and deprivation, whereby each child's view is simply that the more the other gets, the less there is for the self. Decisions about which activities to pursue highlight differences in the children's interests and skills, and accentuate strong feelings about control. Individual frustrations that are not related to the peer are often brought to sessions and spill over to affect the other child. It is not uncommon for one or the other pair member to decide that choosing still another partner, or just stopping the pair, is a ready solution to these unexpected but powerfully felt interpersonal difficulties.

The therapist can take steps to prepare the children not to fall into their usual desperate patterns when encountering these inevitable difficulties in relating. The children need to have the opportunity to work through these differences in a safe and supportive context. This context, in both its physical and psychological character, is established by the therapist, who insures (to some degree and within certain limits) the continuity necessary to ride out the rough spots. These children do not have the ego strength or the psychological or social skills and regulation processes to do this for themselves. Early on, the therapist should establish a productive tenor for pairs, one that will abide for its duration. He or she needs to reinforce this tenor repeatedly, for the children will test the mettle of any therapist and will need repeated experience of any tone or structure before they can begin to hear and then assimilate it.

When establishing the triadic system, the therapist must provide a sense of limits as well as possibilities. Certain institutional rules enforced by the pair therapist help establish a climate of firm control. We say "institutional rules" to emphasize that the rules are not to be viewed as the whim of a particular therapist, but instead as consistently applied by all therapists to all pairs. These initial programmatic pair therapy rules may be drawn up on a chart or written on a blackboard. They are essentially safety, boundary, and therapeutic implementation rules that provide initial parameters for the therapy. The ground rules are all based on perspective coordination and respect for oneself and one's partner.

Rule 1. No violent fighting or abuse is allowed. It is important when setting up this rule to repeatedly articulate the difference between disagreement, arguing, and being angry, and physical or verbal violence. The former three are as much a part of the process of relationship building as sharing, playing, or collaborating. The latter two are not. This rule acts to help insure the physical and emotional safety of everyone involved. For the overaggressive or "acting-out" child, this rule acts as an external control to help channel the child's expression of affective disequilibrium into appropriate forms and block inappropriate expression. For the withdrawn child, this rule provides the confidence that this is a safe place to interact and to express feelings and ideas without losing control or fearing reprisal.

Rule 2. The property in the pair therapy room must be respected. No throwing or destruction of objects or walking on, defacing, or wrecking furniture or other equipment is allowed. It is pointed out that this rule is made to protect property that not only others, but the self too, will want the opportunity to use. We discuss both the immediate effects of destructive actions (material or monetary damage) and the long-term consequences affecting users of the room (no one will be able to use the damaged item).

Rule 3. The pair must stick together. There will be many times in pair therapy when a potential and easy solution to a conflict is to split up. However, one of the purposes of pairs is to help the children work toward solutions, not just avoid problems or separate. This rule helps the therapist guide the children toward adaptation and compromise—for example, when they find that each wants to do a different activity. On trips out of the room or the school, there is often an impulse to run ahead, and this rule gives the therapist a rationale for stopping a child. It does not mean the pair partners always need to play together. Separate activities within the same space are acceptable. However, the therapist will eventually attempt to help each member of the pair express interest in each other's activities, and eventually become involved in them.

If the children challenge these rules, it gives the pair therapist the opportunity to justify them with social perspective-taking and appeals to social justice. The rule not to break chairs, for example, is not arbitrary but has a social basis—so others can use them. The children are also encouraged to designate their own rules as problems arise and the process proceeds. Self-initiated rules have special appeal and a special kind of power. Because the children have created and negotiated them, they feel the need to test them less often than rules externally imposed by adult or institutional authority.

The initial sessions are also a time for each child to get a reading of how the dynamics will be sorted out. Parallel play is sanctioned if that is what the children seem to need. There is no initial pressure toward collaborative interaction between the two. Instead, the therapist looks for and encourages the natural inclination of each child to interact, so that these inclinations can surface in a safe and promising context.

At times, one child will seek to interact almost exclusively with the therapist rather than the pair-mate. The therapist is then presented with the sensitive challenge of encouraging first dyadic interactions between the pair-mates, without rejecting the child's desire for connection with an adult and ultimately triadic relating among himself or herself and both children. Both need for adult support and reluctance to relate to peers are common among the children we see. Modeling an interest in the other child, demonstrating techniques for expressing that interest, and creating a safe atmosphere for a relationship to begin must be combined with great patience on the therapist's part.

The initial role and frame the therapist sets for himself or herself is of critical importance. It is important to keep in mind that being a pair therapist is not the same as being a friend. The therapist enters the therapy session with a particular interpersonal framework. This includes some perspective on the personalization that may occur in the session. For instance, early in the course of the pair whose case is presented in chapter 8, the more assertive child often bombarded their (overweight) therapist with insults, usually when the child was upset about losing a game or had been called on cheating. A barrage of invective such as "You fatso! You blimp! You're pregnant and going to have a whale for a baby! I'll stick a pin in you and deflate you! I hate you and I'll kill you!" was often accompanied by mock aggressive actions—flailing arms and threatening fists. At the same time, the child usually maintained a slight smile on her face, and did not overstep the physical boundaries, never actually striking the therapist. The therapist reacted to this invective consistently, with some acknowledgment of the reality of her obesity, but without anger. She ultimately focused on understanding the feelings or fears that lay behind the invective, not on teaching the girl "good manners." Often her pair-mate, the less assertive child, would imitate this girl's verbally assaultive behavior, in part as a way to make an alliance with her partner. Because the therapist did not designate herself as a friend, she did not take offense. Rather, as a therapist, she asked that each child treat each other as a friend, and refused to tolerate the same degree of verbal abuse within the pair, unless it was very clear that such activity was in fun, and not really a knock-down, drag-out battle.

The Pair Therapy Sessions

Typically, the children meet regularly, usually once a week (but this is quite arbitrary), for at least a year in sessions lasting approximately 45 minutes. The actual length of sessions is somewhat flexible, however, and is decided on a case-by-case basis. They can be as short as ten or fifteen minutes, or as long as an hour, depending in part on the length of time the pair can make use of and tolerate.

The selected children are told that they are being offered a time to meet with another child with whom we think they can work well in order to learn better skills for making, getting along with, and keeping friends. Of course, specific explanations will depend on a number of factors, not the least important of which is the age of the child. They are also told that pairs is a time to play and enjoy themselves as well as do the hard work of learning how to get along. The therapist's job will be to help make the sessions a fruitful place to do this, as we will discuss in detail in this and subsequent chapters.

The child's agreement to meet in pairs means contracting to keep the same partner and therapist for at least the length of one school year, so long as the therapist believes this is indicated. This commitment and continuity are absolutely critical to the therapeutic process. The pair is not required to do things together all the time, but they are required to stay together for the duration of the session, and shared play is encouraged. Toward the end of the contracted period, the continuation of the pair for some specified further length of time, usually another year, is discussed and renegotiated.

It is an informal convention that the first ten or fifteen minutes of pairs be spent in the pair therapy room. This "rule" can be bent, but it helps to facilitate the pair process because it provides a consistent sense of place and structure, especially for younger pairs. This transition from previous activities is a time for considering the day's activities and helps to provide the pair and the therapist with a sense of structure. Often the therapist will bring a snack to facilitate or even ritualize this transition. During this time plans and decisions are made for the day's meeting, which can be a difficult part of pairs. These include the planning of activities that have already been chosen (such as a previously agreed-upon trip to the store), the choices for the day, the resolution or examination of any difficulties from the previous session, or just the general "transition" into this often intense activity.

The pair therapy room is the size of a large home playroom, and is designed to be a comfortable place for children and early adolescents to meet. Although trips to the gym or out of the building do occur, generally the pair therapy room is used as a boundary. We assume, and communicate to the children, that there is enough to do in the room and that most sessions will be spent there. In addition to working with play materials available in the pair therapy room, occasional trips can be planned to nearby stores or, in good weather, sports activities can be undertaken on the clinic grounds. There is also an indoor gym available on occasion, although its use may require some sharing with others outside the pair. Despite the options available, space and facilities are by no means abundant, and learning to cope with limited resources in coordination with one's pair partner is a major aspect of the pair therapy process.

Types of Activities in Pair Therapy

As pair therapy is established, a sense of possibilities must be coupled with the limits outlined in the first section. The children need a supportive atmosphere in which rewarding and pleasurable activities are available. Preliminary planning should involve consideration of the kinds of activities that each child likes and dislikes, so that materials can be provided that will optimize the likelihood that each will feel good about the experience. In the early phases of the process of developing this treatment, we kept the pair therapy room richly stocked with play and game materials of interest to latency-age children and early adolescents. These included modeling clay, building blocks, and Lincoln Logs, drawing materials, hand puppets, plastic models, currently popular toys, and board games like Life, Monopoly, and Sorry that could be played by two or three people. However, this relatively lavish stocking of the room often amounted to an embarrassment of riches, sometimes providing too much stimulation and choice. Now we usually limit available materials to those agreed upon by each particular pair.

In our original approach we also set up sessions with interactive activities that would highlight the need for cooperation and sharing, encourage consideration of the other's perspective, and illustrate the usefulness of interpersonal communication as a tool. We found that this adult-initiated structure did not match well with the needs of the kinds of children we were treating. These children came into pair therapy with their own agendas, and our agenda, particularly our attempts to structure their activities in ways that felt "educative," was met with great resistance. We found that too much time was spent in battles between adults and children, when we wanted the focus to be on the interaction between the children themselves.

An alternative model suggested itself: to have enough attractive interactive materials available so that the therapist could step back and let the children work toward finding and agreeing on activities they wanted to pursue. We now have a backlog of experience about the types of activities that children find interesting, and we may bring in some materials, but we do not consciously plan a specific psychosocial or psychoeducational "curriculum" applicable to all pairs. We try to match available materials to the needs of each child and to the realities of the time and space in which the pair sessions occur. We do not specifically teach communication skills, perspective-taking abilities, friendship concepts, or negotiation strategies as a curriculum, but we look for opportunities to facilitate the children's growth in these processes.

When, for instance, a particular theme arises in a pair, the therapist may take the initiative to bring in materials or suggest topics designed to facilitate activities around that issue. If two eleven-year-olds begin to talk with each other about their homes, the therapist may bring in or suggest art materials so that the children can draw pictures of their houses as a way to encourage the pair to express themselves and share their thoughts and feelings about home life. If two early adolescents begin to talk about their difficulties in making friends, the therapist may suggest that they role play or view a videotape of friendship-making techniques, and follow it up with reflection on them. These actions on the therapist's part remain suggestions, but we have discovered that some activity is necessary. The children need to be doing something because pair therapy is not just talk.

The way in which the children choose and use the activities is as important as which activities are available. For example, some materials are likely to lead to solitary, parallel play, whereas others are more likely to involve interaction. Drawing materials, playdough, Legos, and two of anything, like models, are frequently used separately by the younger children. Puppets, a frisbee, checkers, other board games, or a kickball are materials that usually lead toward interactive play. In the early sessions, children may well opt for materials that do not demand interaction. However, if they want to, children can also use Legos or playdough interactively. Therefore, the children's approach to the available materials is as important in determining the developing play as the materials themselves.

The children's way of approaching their pair-mates when choosing an activity and deciding on roles and rules is also of great significance. This negotiation is a major source of the establishment of a balance of control in a relationship, in pair therapy as well as in real world contexts such as a playground. Attention should be paid to how an activity is chosen and pursued, specifically to the role that each child has in this decision. For example, does one child simply speak for the other? Who gets the first turn? How is it decided when the next turn starts? How are activities and rules changed or invented?

It is important, however, not to overfocus on the fairness of how decisions are made, overlooking the feelings motivating the children's method of deciding. Although the children may honestly feel they have a right to have a particular toy or choose a particular activity, these are sometimes signs or signals of other feelings that are difficult for them to express directly. The therapist must balance the role of "fairness moderator" with that of "feelings articulator." Consider the following example of this dual role.

Ten-year-olds David and Joey have each brought an activity to pairs. David has brought his trumpet so that he can practice for a talent show the next day. Joey, usually the more dominant member of this particular pair, has borrowed a tape recorder so that he can play a new cassette. Each boy is sincerely and highly invested in implementing his own activity. Unfortunately, trumpet playing and top-forty cassette listening are essentially incompatible activities, at least in the same room.

After quite a bit of hassling, wherein it becomes clear that neither boy is willing to give up his chosen activity, Joey suggests they flip a coin and the winner choose the day's activity. Although this is clearly a positive suggestion, past experience with Joey and coin flips leads the therapist to feel perhaps this solution should be modified. Joey has suggested coin flips in good faith in the past, but every time he lost, was utterly unable to abide by the outcome. Realizing it would be difficult for either child to give up his wishes entirely, the therapist suggests that the winner choose the first half hour's activity, and the loser then decide what to do with the remaining time. This idea is anathema to Joey, and he refuses to accept or even consider it. When the therapist tries to explain his rationale, Joey refuses even to listen. He clamps his hands down over his ears (Level 0).

At this point in the interaction, there are at least two potential explanations for Joey's adamant resistance. One is that Joey is so invested in doing his activity that he is unwilling to consider the therapist's compromise. If he accepted this compromise, he would be acknowledging a willingness to give up the activity he wants. This explanation does not make sense, however, if you consider that the essence of a coin flip, assuming one can abide by the result, is a willingness to chance giving up one's choice. If listening to his tape were uppermost in his mind, Joey would be wise to accept the compromise because it guarantees at least half a session of his choice. (Of course, it is possible he does not think about it this logically.) A second explanation for Joey's resistance is that the issue for him is not simply one of playing his tape but more one of who's going to have power and control—an issue of feelings more than fairness. *He* has decided upon the coin toss; therefore, whether he wins or loses, he has controlled the decision. When the therapist tries to modify the method, Joey feels he is taking this absolute power and control away from him.

The interchange continues with five more minutes of continued struggling resistance on Joey's part to the therapist's suggested modification. The therapist and David finally accede to Joey's idea, and he flips the coin for the all-or-nothing choice. Joey wins. Then, to the astonishment of both the therapist and David, Joey says, "I won! David, *I* choose you can play your trumpet." Joey's final response indicates that the issue of having control is of primary concern. As soon as Joey wins control over the choice of activity, he chooses to let David do what he wants. He is able to let David do his activity as long as it is he who controls what David does.

It is very hard to say to what extent this general motivation for control (as a separate issue from that of doing a specific activity) is conscious for Joey. It is also unclear to what extent he is aware of his probable unwillingness to give up his activity if he had lost the toss. Our goal is to work not only toward children's ability to negotiate equitable and reciprocal or even collaborative solutions, but also toward their ability to achieve greater awareness and control of their feelings. That is to say, for Joey, *that he feels* a need for control is something we will try to help him understand. *Why* Joey so powerfully feels the need for control may eventually require explanation as well.

We have found that the development of a pair's relationship is greatly enhanced if the pair, with their therapist's help, develops what we call a *home base activity*. The simplest description of such an activity is that the pair "is engaged in it" much or most of the time over a period of months or longer. The home base activity has several key properties. First, at minimum, through constant play or rehearsal, both members come to feel a high degree of comfort with and competence in the activity. Second, both children must enjoy it. Third, they do not quickly tire of it. Once these criteria are met, the simple doing of the habitual activity (for habitual activity is all it really is at this point) becomes the focus for the pair.

A typical example is two preadolescent children who repeatedly play a board game, like Sorry, until each knows all the strategies involved. In this sense it has a home-base or security-oriented function. It provides a safe and familiar ground against which the "real" interpersonal content of therapy is played out. And the pair can always refocus its attention on the game when the interpersonal situation, the reflection or conversation, becomes too stressful. Ideally, a home base activity repeatedly provides for the pair both contexts for serious negotiations and opportunities for meaningful shared experiences. As negotiations of various sorts are played out over time, and an activity begins to take on, or epitomize, the aspects that cause us to call it a home base activity, it becomes a fertile ground for a sharing of experience that is novel for these children. It becomes safe, predictable, dependable, and known. It is an activity through which the adult therapist can provide examples, mediation, and other facilitating stimulation to the pair that challenges their current level of functioning.

Meeting with a Child Individually

Although a stated pair therapy rule is that the children must stick together, when one child is absent the situation changes. The therapist generally meets alone with the remaining child, rather than cancelling altogether, so the child who was ready to meet does not feel deprived of the special time and possibly resentful toward the absent peer. However, the absent child may feel jealous or suspicious abut the pair-mate's having met alone with the therapist. In this case, the therapist can try to enlist the support of the child with whom he or she met to reassure the returning partner in the next session. Also, both children's feelings and ideas about the decision to meet without the absent child can be discussed at this time, providing an excellent opportunity for the children to attempt to put themselves in each other's shoes.

When one child is absent, the child who is present sometimes asks if another peer can substitute for the regular partner. We tend to discourage this, because it raises many difficult issues and complications. For one thing, it is unfair to the substitute because it suddenly exposes him or her to a special activity and then closes it off again just as quickly. Furthermore, with regard to the pair, a meeting with a different child raises issues that are tangential, and in fact contrary, to the focal work of pair therapy. A one-shot pair meeting with a different child is likely to be experienced as more positive than the problematic, continuing meetings of the regular pair. For the child who is present, it can feed an "it's the other's (the missing partner's) problem—it would be better with someone else" attitude toward any ongoing conflict in the pair. For the absent child, a substitution could raise painful feelings of jealously and inadequacy. In cases of absence, then, we encourage meeting with the remaining child alone.

The therapist can take advantage of an individual session to gain a sense of how the individual child perceives the pair sessions and his or her own interaction with the missing other. In one such individual session, Jessica was able to say that she was afraid to stand up to the more assertive (other-transforming) Holly, because "Friends are supposed to be nice, and not start fights." Asserting herself, Jessica thought, would displease not only Holly, but also the therapist, with whom she had begun to identify. The therapist gently pointed out in the individual meeting that sometimes one is doing a friend a disservice by not speaking up for oneself. Jessica was then not only able to realize that her assertiveness might be "helpful" for the pair but also was able to try out the implications of the discussion in subsequent sessions, knowing she had the therapist's support and approval.

There are also times when it may be appropriate deliberately to plan individual sessions with each of the pair partners. One particularly important time for this, even if only for a couple of minutes, is after a brutal or abrasive conflict between partners. If one child has treated the other in an abusive or rejecting way, repair may require individual attention. At these times, both children need reassurance. The victim needs to be able to sort out where the abuse was coming from, how much was actually related to what was going on immediately between the two, and feelings about having been a victim. The aggressor needs time to gain support for the process of making amends. He or she needs the therapist to help sort out the reality of the situation, and to prevent anger from extensively distorting the perception of either child's actual behavior beyond recognition. Even in a situation designed for two, one or both may need individual support from the therapist.

A separate and larger issue to be considered is whether the pair therapist should also meet separately with each of the two children in individual therapy. The implications of such a system of treatment are a fascinating subject, but one we cannot deal with in detail here. We will briefly note the advantages and disadvantages. One advantage is that a therapist who has the time to see a child in individual work, as well as in a pair, will be able to work through some of the more affectively charged issues that are too difficult, inappropriate, or personal to deal with during pair sessions. One drawback is that the sense a child has of "my therapist," the special person who listens to me, gets diluted if the child also has to share this individual therapist with a pair-mate, thus affecting both individual and pair therapy. We feel strongly that if pair therapists see one child individually, they must see both.

Terminating a Session (or the Pair)

There are times when a child or the pair may act in ways that contraindicate the continuation of a session. Pair therapists almost inevitably have to face this problem somewhere along the line. We have found that children who need pair therapy tend to have powerful needs for both nurturance and support from outside themselves, and these requirements make normal limits and controls problematic. There are many minor incidents (e.g., making a mess and refusing to clean it up, refusing to yield an unfairly grabbed snack, minor verbal abuse) that "normal" children would be able to solve that for these children provide the fuse for disintegration to explosive extremes of regressive behavior, behavior that can cause the disruption of the entire pair process. The pair therapist must be sensitive to whether the fuse has burned too close to a dangerous charge.

A straightforward, nonphysical fight between pair-mates is not an automatic signal to end a session. In fact, one of our goals is to help these children learn to "fight" at a higher level—that is, to be less rageful, less attacking, and less out of control in their resolutions of conflicts and felt needs. A valuable lesson for the children to learn in pairs is that they can fight, and that if they do so with some restraint, without pulling out all the stops, then the peer relationship may be in fact strengthened rather than torn asunder. These children are not unused to fights. They are unused to fights with constructive outcomes.

But when no constructive outcome seems imminent, it is time to end the session. Because the pair therapist must be concerned with two children, not one, the uncontrolled behavior of one child may require the discontinuation of the entire session. The decision to end the session for both children because of the behavior of one can be a painful one. It is extremely difficult to judge when this time has come. Beyond the specific rules set up at the beginning of pairs to aid in this decision, there are always those unclear cases where the therapist hopes that "if we can last a little bit longer," the kids will "get it together."

To stop a session in the interests of the *immediate* physical and emotional safety of both pair-mates is obviously important and necessary, even though the timing may be difficult to assess. But there is a further *long-range* value to both children in the termination of a session. Violent behavior in these children is not only a "bad pattern," difficult or impossible to control, it is also a testing of the therapist and the pair therapy setting. Termination of a session sends a clear message to both participants that their safety *will* be protected, that what has been promised is true. We have usually found the occasional necessary and well-timed termination of a session to be of long-term benefit for both children. Our experience suggests that although it may lead to loud protests of unfairness, ending a battle before it gets too drawn out or too brutal, establishes a basis for better dealings later on. If the children truly enjoy the attractive aspects of pairs, they will be motivated to control the kinds of behavior that cause further cancellations. The long-term nature of pair therapy, lasting over the course of one or more years, enables the cancellation of a session to function not as a punitive measure, but rather as both a caring action on the therapist's part and a time to take a break to establish real limits. Ideally, the cancellation of a session should be worked through with each child separately as well as with both together. Some consensus is needed on why the therapist took this action and what can be done to prevent his or her needing to take similar actions in the future.

More difficult is the evaluation that directs the therapist to the termination not just of the rest of a session, or a whole session, but the discontinuation of the pair itself. As already intimated at several points in these two chapters, there are some pairs, like some couples, whose connection and interactions do not seem to work in a way that is facilitating of the pair relationship or of the individuals involved. In fact, as is often the case with distressed couples, the dynamics of a certain pair may do more harm than good.

The most common instance and cause of this condition usually occurs when one child is so distressed, often due to circumstances related more to his or her life outside the pair, that the pain and discomfort is brought *into* the pair relationship and results in excessive abuse directed through displacement onto the pair partner. Ironically, but understandably, it is often more painful and difficult for pair therapists to observe (and deal with) this form of negative interaction than it is to be themselves the direct object of the abuse. Obviously the judgment call to be made relies on great clinical acumen, but strong measures must be taken to prohibit this form of interaction, a form that will ultimately feel bad to all concerned.

One alternative to complete discontinuation is to cancel one or several sessions, a suspension implemented so that the child in distress can get his or her "actions" together. If the cause of distress initially causing the detrimental social atmosphere ameliorates, then the pair can be reinstated. Strong efforts should be made to continue the pair through the end of the contracted period, usually the school year. Then if things seem to just be hobbling along, the contract for the next year need not be renegotiated. (Pair sessions need not arbitrarily be contracted only for a school year. Shorter term contracts are often indicated for a variety of reasons—uncertainty about the match, more specific short-term goals, etc.)

At other times a match may prove unpropitious, less as a function of situational factors, and more due to the conflicts of personality or irreconcilable differences. Or sometimes it is in the best interest of a pair to discontinue because one pair-mate has actually made gains much more rapidly than the other. We have already alluded to the potential danger of certain mismatches, such as two "other-transforming" children, but even the best diagnostic process may prove fallible. Obviously, a pair that is fixated or even regressing instead of progressing should not continue interminably. Regardless of the decision, the rationale for termination should be functional (a poor prognosis) rather than punitive. The pair needs to understand that it is discontinuing because it is not functioning well. Therefore the therapist should engage the children in a process of reflection on their actions and relationship as part of any premature termination of pair therapy.

CHAPTER SEVEN

The Evolving Role of the Therapist and Phases of Pair Therapy

The long-term treatment of pair therapy is analogous in some ways to fishing. After an initial flurry of excitement, it can go along session after session, like hour after hour sitting in a boat, and nothing seems to be happening. No bites, just waiting. Working with two children, many weeks can go by with "nothing" happening. Then in one session, or a series of sessions, a bullying child will display immense kindness, a fearful child will share deep fears, or a pair who have been battling for control will develop a means for sharing it and begin laughing happily together. Just as fishermen must be prepared with vigilance, patience, and a tolerance for uncertainty of outcome, pair therapists must be ready, too. They must set the scene, keep their patience and consistency constant, maintain their confidence in the face of no visible results, and if and when the time arrives that the work and waiting can pay off, their alertness, sensitivity, and skill should be at the ready to facilitate the children's growth at key moments.

The comparison of course breaks down eventually, because in pair therapy, as much like wary fish as troubled children can sometimes act, unlike fish they have a basic motivation, albeit deeply buried or distorted, to progress and succeed in making connections with others. The therapist's job is to help them develop tools to do this and facilitate opportunities to use those tools.

In the previous chapter we described a set of parameters for constructing a safe and stimulating therapeutic environment, one in which two children who would otherwise be unable to establish an extended interaction can begin to establish and be nurtured by the positive effects of such an interaction. We have used our theoretical model of social regulation processes to articulate a set of developmental functions of the therapist that, together with the general ground rules, comprise the pair therapy program.

The pair therapist's functions are "developmental" in two senses. First, the therapist's role changes according to which

160

phase the therapy is in, and these phases, as we detail below, are themselves developmental. The course of the therapy reflects predictable changes in the social interaction of the three members of the triadic therapeutic system. The development of the social interaction results from both natural growth in the pair's relationship (facilitated of course by the presence and support of the therapist) and the therapist's more active efforts to restructure the pair's relationship once it is established.

The second reason the therapist's tactics are developmental is because, in addition to being (at least to some extent) phase specific, they also depend on the developmental level of the two children involved. Pair therapy tries to effect developmental transitions in the maturity of the pair's interaction (and relationship), and pairs begin therapy at different levels. (Because we specifically match the pair by level, we can speak of *the level of the pair.*) The role the therapist plays in both support of already acquired levels of functioning and efforts to help the pair grow differs according to the type of transition he or she is trying to effect, which, depending on the developmental level of the pair, is either a Level "0 to 1," "1 to 2," or "2 to 3" transition.

Developmental Phases of Social Interaction in Pair Therapy

A developmental approach to the study of social behavior need not, and ought not, be limited to examination of the slow age-related growth of an individual's competence—that is, to ontogenesis alone. The developmental "attitude" is equally applicable to other processes of social growth, interaction, and organization, such as the orthogenetic processes identified by Werner. A developmental attitude provides a way to read the barometer of regressive as well as progressive movements that occur in the life of a social interaction process, such as the growth of an interpersonal relationship over time. So far we have used a developmental approach to assess the maturity of interpersonal negotiation strategies and shared experience, and to identify goals in pair therapy in terms of our developmental model. A developmental view is also useful to identify predictable *phases* across the "life span" of pair therapy as a social interaction process and to analyze how these phases relate to the children's individual and dyadic development and the therapist's role in facilitating it.

Development, which involves both differentiation and hierarchical integration, is not just general or cyclical movement that occurs across time. It is easy to identify chronological phases of pair therapy, such as "initiation," "maintenance," and "termination," yet without a developmental underpinning, this does little more than tell us that there is a beginning, a middle, and an end. Across a calendar year, temperature rises up the scale in summer and drops down again toward winter, but this is not development either, it is merely movement that occurs across time. Nor is the development of a social interaction process simply the characterization of a start to finish or a movement over time up and down a quantitative scale, as temperature moves in a year. In our view social development is a spiraling qualitative reorganization of individuals in relation to their social world, in terms of increasing differentiation and hierarchical integration of self in relation to other, or dedifferentiation and disintegration. Likewise, the course of social interactional processes involves qualitative reorganization. Progression is not just "more," as in degrees of temperature, and regression is not just "less."

By observing the course of over fifty pairs during the last ten years, we have identified five phases in the social interaction of the pair and the therapist that develop sequentially during the process of pair therapy. In the first two phases of the social-interactional process—"sizing each other up" and "establishing a dominance pattern"—the triadic system gets set up; that is, a relationship is established between each child and the therapist, and between the two children. Usually one child assumes a self-transforming (submissive) role and the other child assumes an other-transforming (dominant) role in their developing relationship. In the third "stable imbalance of power" phase the dominance pattern established in the previous phase becomes the status quo. In the fourth "restructuring" phase, the therapist's now more active role prods the pair's interaction to shift upward in predominant developmental level and become more balanced in interpersonal orientation. In the "consolidation" phase, the new level and style of interaction and a closer relationship among the triad consolidate. These phases appear to occur in the same sequence in all pairs, although not all pairs traverse them at the same rate, or achieve all later, subsequent phases.

Phase 1. Sizing Each Other Up: Who Is This Other Kid and What Does He Want? The earliest meetings of a pair generally represent a short period of sizing up what the roles, rules, and limits of the situation will be. Each child tries to ascertain whether it will be safe to be with the other person. Will I be bullied? Will I be in control? Each child tries to find out if the other is to be feared, envied, or liked. They both check out what the play will be like. Can I have my own way, and how often? In a more primitive, need-driven way, this phase resembles the way adults often size each other up, assessing relative power and status.

With most latency-age and some preadolescent children, this preaffiliative phase consists mostly of parallel play, or play directed to and through the adult, rather than direct interaction between the children. At any age, it is a period when straightforward negotiations between children seldom occur, or if they do, they occur in tentative and incomplete segments. Hence there is usually relatively little direct conflict (a "honeymoon" period) because each child is unsure of how to approach the other, or in fact, whether he or she even wants to. The length of this phase can vary from seconds to sessions. (In some pairs we have treated, the "honeymoon" was unusually long, so that a period of relative harmony and good will preceded the beginning of "sizing up.")

Phase 2. Establishing a Dominance Pattern: Who's in Charge Here? In the second phase, the focus becomes the division of materials, decision-making power, and the therapist's attention. When the children find they cannot both have the adult's attention at the same time, they may compete for it. The therapist encourages them to seek out each other for play, but this too raises issues for negotiation because the children are forced to arrange how they will play together. Who will be leader and who the follower? Who decides what games we play or what topics we discuss? Who gets to go first or use the one softball mitt? Although on the surface, many of the issues at this phase seem to revolve around competition for materials—for *what* is done—the issue of what specific materials are chosen is often a mask for underlying concerns: who is most liked, who wins, who is most powerful, who is in control, who makes the choices? The children sometimes gingerly, sometimes bullishly, try to work out these issues of control in their developing relationship.

Phase 3. Stable Imbalance of Power: Arriving at a Temporary Equilibrium. After the previous period of struggle for control, the children often arrive at an interim sort of balanced interaction and settle into it. The testing of the previous phase has been resolved into a predictable, more stable way of relating—a *kind* of balance. It is actually a stable *imbalance* of power, with the degree of asymmetry dependent on the developmental level of the two children. One child is established to a greater or lesser degree as the dominant controller and the other as the follower, or, in the language of our model, one is relatively other-transforming and the other is relatively self-transforming. This phase is characterized by a superficial calmness in accepted, relatively stable, forms of interaction.

Ordinarily, the structure of a dyad—that is, two children who both have their own feelings and wants—encourages natural movement toward ever greater balance and reciprocity. We saw an example of this at Level 1 with six-year-old Jeremy and Brian in chapter 2, and the average nine-year-old can establish an age-appropriate reciprocal (Level 2) balance. However, troubled children slip more readily into an entrenched and extremely asymmetrical balance. Therefore it is the task of the therapist to intervene actively upon this stable imbalance, leading to a "restructuring."

Phase 4. Restructuring to the Next Level. In this phase, the type of interaction initially established in the pair is restructured to the next level, facilitated by the therapist's intervention. The interaction shifts in two dimensions. First, there is a shift from relatively asymmetrical balance (one controller and one controllee) to less extremely polarized power relations. That is, the self-transforming child becomes more assertive and the other-transforming child becomes more willing to give in.

Second, there is a shift in the predominant developmental level at which the children interact. Many of the troubled children with whom we work come into pair therapy using predominantly unilateral (Level 1) strategies. For them, this phase represents a "1 to 2" shift, in which the therapist, using therapeutic tactics described in the next section, attempts to prompt a shift away from a "one wins—one loses" view to an attitude of reciprocity, a focus on acknowledging and acting on the views and wishes of both self and other. We also work with predominantly impulsive (Level 0) pairs and predominantly reciprocal (Level 2) pairs, in which case the restructuring of balance represents "0 to 1" and "2 to 3" shifts, respectively.

The progression of this phase represents forward movement in differentiation and integration of efficacy and control between self and other. The first phase of sizing each other up involves a first, tentative move to explore the differentiation of the self's and other's wants, with as yet no integration of these wants in interactions of mutual effect. The struggle for a dominance pattern "balance" represents a simple dichotomous differentiation and integration of control and efficacy. The restructuring phase aims for growth toward a (more balanced) form of interaction that is both more differentiated and more integrated than the previous balance, in discriminating and taking account of various feelings and capabilities for efficacy in both self and other.

Phase 5. Consolidation of the New Level of Interpersonal Functioning. The newly restructured level of social interaction is extremely unstable and vulnerable, fragile even within the relatively supportive pair therapy context. The fifth phase of the therapy gives the pair the opportunity for "horizontal" rather than "vertical" growth to consolidate their restructured functioning through practice across a range of contexts that include varying degrees of stress. Probably to a greater degree than the other phases, the period of consolidation is unpredictable—it can take a short time or a relatively long time. If and when the consolidating level becomes predominant—that is, applied relatively consistently across contexts—the phase 5 consolidation progresses to a new state of balance. This is in effect a new phase 3 (at a higher level than the original phase 3) that can then develop into a new phase 4 restructuring to the *next* level. In other words, if pair therapy lasts long enough (and the new level is consolidated for *both* members of the pair), the pair's relationship can cycle (actually spiral) through the five phases to a second round of phases 3, 4, and 5.

Theoretically-framed Functions of the Pair Therapist

There is a three-way interaction among the phase of the therapy (i.e., the stage of the triadic interaction), the developmental level of the pair, and the role of the therapist. Although each phase has a life of its own, the developmental levels of the two children interact with the phases to determine the form each phase takes—that is, the level at which it is played out. This interaction of phase and level establishes which type of therapist effort will be optimal to foster transition to the next highest level.

We have identified three particularly salient "therapeutic functions" of the therapist, each of which is important for facilitating a specific type of developmental gain in social maturity. We call these three tactical frameworks (1) "empowering," the facilitation of a sense of power, efficacy, and control; (2) "linking," the mediation of reciprocal problem-solving and communication; and (3) "enabling," the fostering of mutually shared reflection. All the therapist's functions are available and used in each phase of therapy at all developmental levels. Yet even though the therapeutic repertoire does not change, the therapeutic emphasis does.

The most level-specific phase of therapy is the *restructuring*. Each of the three functions of the therapist particularly characterize the therapeutic restructuring efforts in different developmental transitions. The empowering role is uniquely effective in "0 to 1" transitions, the linking role in "1 to 2" transitions, and the enabling role in "2 to 3" transitions.

In contrast, the therapist's role is more phase-specific and less level-related in the first phases of sizing up and establishing dominance, when the more general support and limit-setting role of the therapist in helping the pair's relationship "naturally evolve" places a somewhat greater reliance on all three functions at all developmental levels. In the consolidation phase, the pair's use of the newly acquired levels requires "bolstering" and "harnessing," and so the therapist relies more on level-specific functions, although probably to a lesser degree than in the restructuring phase. We will now describe how each of the three functions of the therapist are both generally used with pairs at any level and specifically used to restructure particular levels of interpersonal functioning.

"Empowering" a Sense of Power and Control: The "0 to 1" Restructuring

Themes of good and evil, strength and weakness, and power and control pervade our lives from infancy to old age, and thus in some ways transcend developmental levels. However, the form that these concerns take is very much influenced by a person's developmental status. In mature adulthood, concerns about interpersonal control center around the ability to establish a particular type of understanding and intimacy in a long-lasting close personal relationship. For most four- to six-year-olds, the issue of control among peers is appropriately experienced and expressed in the framework of Levels 0 and 1: in terms of physical power and direct psychological control over attention, activity choice, and the use of materials. For troubled children, the form of the control issues is closer to that of the four- to six-year-old than the adult.

The structure of pair therapy confronts the child with another whose wants and points of view will differ from one's own at times. The therapist encourages each pair-mate to acknowledge these differing wants and views in their relating, rather than to back-shelve their own wants or overwhelm the other's wants so that they seem to disappear. It is in working through these conflicts and differences that they can discover the use of higher-level strategies, strategies that show an increasing balance of control between self and other. Without any conflict, children would never need to develop these higher forms of strategy. And without consistency and safety, and the therapist's gentle push, they could remain fixed in the old limiting patterns of reacting and interacting, no matter how "bad" (i.e., dysfunctional) they were.

In a sense, our developmental model represents a theory of empowerment, and children are further empowered at each new level. Yet the transition from Level 0 to Level 1 empowers the developing person in a uniquely concrete way. In Level 0 impulsivity there is no perspective coordination at the moment of action. As a result, Level 0 strategies are extremely polarized in interpersonal orientation. These children either step on others (e.g., grabbing what they want) or allow themselves to be stepped on with absolutely no resistance. But if these children have at least developed the capacity to coordinate perspectives at Level 1 (differentiation of the self's perspective from that of other), even though they cannot apply it in their action, then the task of the therapist is to help the children recognize and be able to express their own needs and wants rather than just acting on them or totally abandoning them.

This (Level 1) ability to express what one wants with "I" statements instead of projection or impulsive action (e.g., "I want . . ." instead of grabbing or being grabbed from) necessarily involves some consideration of the other in Level 1 perspective coordination. To express the self's wants, to use one perspective, at least means that two perspectives are recognized as separate.

With children who easily regress to extremely disturbed behavior, the therapist needs to help them maintain control of their interactions by effectively distributing power and setting firm limits when they are getting out of hand. When the therapist uses concrete empowering tactics with a Level 0 pair to render implicit control issues explicit (though unilateral), the nature of power and control becomes more consciously available to the children. In the "0 to 1" case we describe in the next chapter, Holly and Jessica's pair therapist used empowering tactics to restructure their negotiations around the chocolate bars she gave them at the beginning of each session. The adult set limits on Holly's impulsive usurping and encouraged Jessica to assert herself, to the point that Jessica was eventually empowered to resist with Level 1 logic ("No, I don't want to give you my candy") and Holly was empowered to accept not getting any.

One particularly effective empowering tactic is to facilitate interactive fantasy play between the two children. Interactive fantasy play is not something that we came up with on theoretical grounds but something we have observed children engage in time and time again at a certain phase of pair therapy. We support and encourage it because the activity provides copious opportunities for self-mastery and shared experience. Although the adult therapist provides the facilitative atmosphere, the children provide a spontaneous pull to interactive fantasy play dealing with issues of power and control.

Typical preschoolers also learn to deal with these issues in their fantasy play with peers. Young children feel for and test the limits of the power and control they can assert over themselves and other children of approximately equal developmental status. Children are able to act out deep and frightening concerns in the presence of another, and to hear and feel that the other has shared these concerns in some way much more readily in fantasied than real-life relationships. It is not uncommon for the playmate to say "Oh, yes, I worry about that, too," but even without this direct acknowledgment, the other child indirectly acknowledges and shares in the importance of the theme through the enthusiasm and involvement with which he or she joins in the play.

Either the natural opportunities for this type of play or the ability to take advantage of chances for it tends to be markedly absent from the history of the Level 0 children seen in pair therapy. If these children who have not experienced the benefits of this kind of interaction somehow find the chance to "return" to this creative activity, they can manipulate and demystify these issues and thus learn to use their Level 1 perspective coordination ability in their peer interaction.

Interactive fantasy play, primarily used by pairs functioning at Level 0 (who tend to be the younger pairs, aged eight to twelve), is a way to try out roles for control over the self and other in a safe, "not-quite-real" context. In the real-life context of everyday social interactions, these children are usually quite rigidly aggressive or fearful. However, in the relative safety of fantasy play, they are able to work with different ways of controlling and orienting to self and other. In trying out various roles in the context of fantasy, the children can work through some of the fears and worries that contribute to the low-level imbalance of their interaction and limit their use of the opposite orientation. As those fears are shed, the pair can come to try out more equilibrated uses of control in real life. Dealing most commonly, as we said, with issues of physical power and either-or, all or none, psychological control, children not only deal with autonomy-related concerns but can also generate powerful intimacy-related shared experiences in fantasy play.

This type of interactive fantasy play, facilitated by the therapist, played a pivotal role in the first year of therapy for a pair named Andy and Paul. They were the pair we saw stuck on the seesaw in chapter 5. Andy and Paul spent three years together in pair therapy. When they began therapy together at age eight, they acted predominantly, yet not exclusively, at Level 0. Andy, who was dominant, controlling, and other-transforming, was capable of a range of strategies. If the interpersonal situation was just right, he was able to act at an age-appropriate reciprocal Level 2, but with the least amount of stress he quickly dropped to Level 0. Paul, who was submissive and self-transforming, sometimes interacted in a unilateral Level 1 way, but, like his pair therapy partner, he dropped much too easily to impulsive Level 0 actions when the interpersonal situation was even mildly stressful. Whereas Andy often managed his fearfulness with enraged temper tantrums, Paul often hid under tables.

The Level "0 to 1" transition in Andy and Paul's therapy differs in some respects from that of Holly and Jessica, which we describe in detail in the next chapter, because Andy and Paul had regressed to Level 0, whereas Holly and Jessica were developmentally delayed and had never displayed higher-level strategies. Whether the predominant level of a given pair is low-level because of regression or developmental delay, in either case the therapist's role is similar (here, an empowering role), but the potentiality for and timing of subsequent growth is probably quite different.

At different times over their first year of pair meetings, Andy and Paul used roles in fantasy play that symbolized their view of their actual roles in real life. One day, Andy initiated a fantasy in which he was the television/comic book character "The Hulk," a large, powerful, fearsome mutant who is good inside, but who cannot control his feelings to let the good direct him. Paul then took a part as "Mini-Man," a being of his own creation who is smaller than anyone else in the world and can hide in flowers. In choosing and playing out these parts, the children acted out the most extreme and primitive aspects of their own notions of themselves and were able to play through worries over power: Andy as The Hulk, having too much power, being out of control and destructive, and testing out the consequences of this destructiveness; Paul as Mini-Man, being powerless and overwhelmed, checking out and manipulating in play the results of this powerlessness.

At another time in their play, Andy picked up a harsh, metal robot model to instigate a fantasy fight with Paul. Paul grabbed a soft, malleable cloth puppet of a bumbly, pudgy brown dog for defense. Andy, disturbed by this inequity, picked up another robot model and pushed it toward Paul, saying, "Here, Paul. Use this." But Paul would not. He was not yet comfortable with trying a stronger force for himself or a force equal to his opponent, even in the context of play.

Yet the pair therapist picked up on Andy's tentative move, and using concrete empowering tactics, encouraged the boys to move from blind (Level 0) control to taking turns in control (Level 1). Although not yet ready to share control (Level 2), both boys made significant use of the play context to try out new roles for power and control as they learned to take turns at absolute, all-or-none control in a subsequent form of interactive fantasy that developed part way through the year and was repeatedly drawn upon in subsequent sessions.

The play was a fantasy in which one boy had the power to control the thoughts and will of the other by virtue of a psychological "force field." One boy would "zap" his partner with a line of invisible power emanating from his fingertips, and upon being zapped the other boy would be hypnotized to carry out the bidding of the zapper. It was an invisible science fiction version of marionette play, with human marionettes. It was usually Andy who initiated this fantasy, with himself as the controller. He would "zap" Paul to roll over on the mat, to kick the ball, to remain silent. Yet once Paul entered into the spirit of the fantasy, he was frequently able to take charge of redistributing the power, saying, "I have my blocking field up" to resist Andy's control. Then, he would spontaneously say "Now I have the power," and zap an uncharacteristically compliant Andy, who would topple to the floor.

The most fascinating aspect of this type of play lies in the fluidity and flexibility of its process, as the source of control changed from one to the other and back again. There were no formal rules for who should have the power, or for when and how it was switched. Rather, this ability to switch rested in the willfulness of one child to take the power away from the other, and in the willingness of the other to have the power taken and act in compliance to the peer. Paul could have simply continued in his submission to Andy's power; or when Paul said "Now I have the power," Andy could have said merely "No," refusing Paul's invisible and now impotent string of force. Instead, both Andy and Paul were actively drawn to try out these different roles for control within the safety of shared fantasy. Although at that point they still stuck steadily to their respective other-transforming and self-transforming modes in real-life relating, the readiness with which they tried out the opposite orientation in the fantasy was a remarkable step forward.

Theoretically speaking, we believe that this switching of roles in play is a key therapeutic process, in effect a way to *share experience*. Andy was able to relax his defenses and express the message that part of him was happy to be or even had a need to be controlled, taken care of, told what to do. He could abandon for the moment the tenderly held goals for which he generally fought so fiercely. Although such messages are often still too scary to express directly in real life, they can be allowed expression in a play context in which things are "not real" and have no actual consequence. And Paul, often too frightened to take the initiative in actual interactions, was able to take steps toward assuming the control that felt too risky in real life, despite its practical and emotional attractions. He could begin to use other-transforming methods in the context of interactive fantasy play without the risk that he would be held accountable for his methods or have to face real consequences. When it is just play, children can dress rehearse for changing roles on the stage of real-life interaction.

"Linking" Two Perspectives in Reciprocal Communication: The "1 to 2" Restructuring

The therapist's linking efforts are the second major type of therapeutic intervention in pair therapy. In this role the therapist works with the children as mediator, facilitating reciprocity in the children's communication with each other. Our model of interpersonal negotiation and shared experience gives the therapist tools to help the children communicate directly to one another, and, what is more, *understand* each other. In the linking role, the therapist tries to help the children not only stick together and work through their conflicts, but also consider the wishes of both self and other in their dealings and think through alternative strategies in the heat of stressful frustration of wishes. These particular tasks require functioning at Level 2, when one starts to consider the perspective of both self and other in interpersonal dealings and deal directly with the self's affective disequilibrium.

The adult acts as a link both verbally and through his or her physical presence, with the goal that this role as a structurer will become less and less necessary. Almost immediately in pair therapy, issues of fairness as well as power and control arise. The therapist persists in not tolerating strategies for avoiding tough issues, by gently pointing out incomplete resolutions and by raising the question of fairness when someone appears to be dissatisfied. The therapist draws withdrawn children into *explicitly* sharing their experiences or fantasies and helps to clarify their frequently personalized and idiosyncratic statements. With more aggressive children, the therapist may need to refine the focus for the pair, assisting them in articulating their points of view and defining what it is that they are negotiating.

Through these linking techniques, the partners are given the opportunity and motivation to experiment with new and more adaptive ways of negotiating conflicts and communicating with each other, ultimately without the therapist's help. Hence, when the pair feels secure enough, the therapist may step to the side of the room or the observation booth where he or she can maintain a psychological presence, providing support and monitoring safety. When the therapist is asked (rather than ordered) to leave, it often signals increased confidence and intimacy in the pair and indicates that progress is being made.

The linking role requires time to be established. To be effective in this role, therapists must have the trust of each of the pair partners. This means that they must be perceived as fair and impartial, and also as caring about each child. As therapeutic mediators, they must be sensitive not only to surface fairness, but also to underlying feelings, which do not always adapt to the logic of fairness. The following account illustrates the linking role of the therapist, and how the relationship he has established over twenty months allows him to function effectively in this role. Although the outcome is not perfect, it represents significant and ground-breaking forward progress for the children.

Andy and Paul are now almost ten, more than halfway through their second year of pair therapy. They have made "fast" gains since we last saw them switching roles in their fantasy play. They successfully navigated the restructuring from Level 0, and their Level 1 modes of functioning have consolidated in a new stable imbalance of power. Andy is still dominant and Paul is still submissive but these orientations are less extreme than the year before. Now the therapist's linking efforts have become more salient than his empowering efforts as he moves to restructure their interaction to an even higher level.

After starting their meeting in the pair therapy room one day,

Andy and Paul decide they want to play kickball in the gym. However, upon arriving at the gym, they discover that another boy is already there shooting baskets with his therapist. Both Andy and Paul are obviously disturbed by this hindrance to their plans:

> PAUL declares in a whine "Oh rats! Now we can't play. They're using it."
> ANDY immediately yells out "Hey" (to the boy shooting baskets) "What are you doing here? Hey, you can't use this gym. We're gonna play kickball here."

Immediately we can see two distinct ways of reacting to the situation. Paul appears to feel helpless, and he gives up, making no attempt to pursue his desires. He decides conclusively that they can't play rather than incur the risks incumbent on negotiation. Andy, on the other hand, reacts with indignation, as if the others have no right or fair claim to use the gym, as if his wishes were the world's command, failing even to acknowledge conflicting views or claims. Yet these two reactions represent the same Level 1, "all or none" definition of the situation. Whereas Paul accommodates completely (although he does not withdraw), Andy lays total claim (although he does not lose his temper):

> ANDY turns to the therapist and asks "Can't you get rid of the intruders?" Before the therapist can speak Andy turns again toward the "intruders" to yell "Hey you guys, this is our time. You can't use the gym now; we want to play kickball."
> PAUL appears to be in a humiliated rage. "Shut up, Andy," he screams. "Jeez, just shut up, will you! Jerk!"

At this point both boys appear to construe the situation quite egocentrically. Andy's desires appear to be so paramount for him that they define the situation to the exclusion of the consideration of the needs and feelings of any other, even Paul. His failure to consider the others' perspectives stems from the affective loading of the situation rather than the level of his capacity for understanding. Paul, too, reacts only on the basis of his own fear and humiliation. Standing back, Paul can recognize Andy's limited perspective on the situation, but his affective reaction to it predominates and he does not express his insight into Andy's feelings. Paul appears either to personalize Andy's childish behavior (as if it somehow reflects badly on him) or to see it as a strategy so blatantly inappropriate that it simply will not work. No longer completely self-transforming, Paul uses a unilateral command ("Shut up!") both to express his own feelings and to attempt to control Andy's behavior. He seems as desperate to stop Andy as Andy seems to be to seize the gym. It is at this point that the therapist intervenes:

> THERAPIST: "Wait a second, guys. Maybe we have some other options. Let's step over here for a second and talk about it. Let's work out some strategy." They withdraw to the side of the gym.

Having worked with them for twenty months, the therapist has gained a degree of respect and trust from both boys. Although they sometimes get angry at him, a three-way alliance has been established that allows him to have some influence over them, and when he suggests the possibility that an alternative strategy for success may be possible, they are willing at least to listen. The actual request the therapist makes is for both boys to step back from the immediacy of the situation and consider other courses of action. The therapist listens and construes the ongoing negotiation as two children who are enmeshed in a process of ordering others around. But the therapist does not ask them to reflect on the process quite yet. Instead, he focuses on alternative strategies for defining their wants and dealing with others in ways to try to achieve them.

There are, of course, other directions the therapist could take. For example, he could move in the direction of exploring the importance of having the whole court, or the feelings aroused by not getting what one expects, or the difficulties of dealing with a new or less familiar person. These issues are as salient to the situation as is the immediate process of dealing with others, but in the midst of the action, these sometimes subtle or painful insights are difficult to attend to, acknowledge, and deal with, and so are best saved for a time when the children are less stressed, perhaps even in individual sessions with each partner. For now, in the ongoing interaction, the therapist acts as a link to encourage productive problem-solving, with an awareness that these affective issues exist as motivating influences:

> PAUL, with prompting by the therapist, suddenly makes a suggestion. "We'll take half the court," he proclaims, and promptly moves to carry out this decision. "Here will be home plate," he announces as he sets down a base.

Paul acts as if his decisive action will ensure the success of the idea, an idea that, incidentally, avoids the need to confront the other users of the gym and avoids the step of jointly considering alternatives. The therapist realizes that although Paul has worked out a possible solution in his own mind, he has not worked out the means to implement that solution. Hypothetical solutions are a good first step, but implementation is far more difficult, involving, among other things, interaction with others:

> THERAPIST, prompting: "Paul, don't you think you might want to check out your idea with Andy, and with those guys there?"
> PAUL is visibly annoyed. "Let's play. Come on, move it!" he says.

This is said in a whiney, demanding, annoyed tone of voice. Paul rejects or actively denies the reality presented to him by the therapist. His solution, now assertive rather than withdrawing, does not deal adequately with the physical constraints of the play area or with the wishes or expectations of other significant actors in the current unfolding drama. But in typical Level 1 fashion he ignores this:

> THERAPIST: "Oh, I see. You want to go right ahead and play. No more discussion." The therapist, to help Paul deal with, rather than ignore, the real aspects of the situation, raises the realistic problem that the "outsiders" would then be playing basketball in the middle of their outfield. "I think the ball would go down there and it could hit them or get in their way."
> PAUL emphatically denies this: "It will not! It won't hit them!"
> ANDY, now dealing directly with Paul's idea: "We can't do this," he says. "The court's too short. I'm not playing that way."
> THERAPIST: "Well, then, is there something you can work out with them?:"
> ANDY answers, "Well, we can tell them it's our time."
> PAUL (disdainfully): "It is not!"
> ANDY: "It is. They were here for a long time before, so we should have it now."
> PAUL challenges with irritation, "How do you know that?"
> ANDY: "Well, they were here when we got here, so it's our turn."
> PAUL counters, "You don't know how long they were here before us, dummy."
> ANDY turns away and ignores Paul's last insulting remark, but yells out to the others once again, "Hey you guys, it's our turn to use the gym."
> PAUL now blurts out in a frantic, desperate whine, "Cut that out!" At this point he moves to the side of the gym,

drops down to sit on the floor, and hangs his head
between his knees in a display of what seems to be both
disgust and embarrassment.
THERAPIST, in a calm voice to Andy: "It seems that Paul
doesn't agree with you. Can you think of some way to work
this out?"
ANDY: "We could negotiate with them."
THERAPIST: "Paul, Andy has suggested that we try to
negotiate."
PAUL just waves this off with a hand gesture.
THERAPIST: "It seems that Paul would rather not try to deal
with them directly."
ANDY: "We could see if they would take turns using the
court, they could have it for five minutes, then we would
use it for five minutes."
PAUL: "They won't go for that."
ANDY: "Well, maybe we could ask them if they want to play."
THERAPIST: "Andy suggested asking them to play. What do
you think, Paul?"
PAUL: "I don't care. I just want to play."
ANDY immediately carries out his idea by asking the others
if they want to join in a game of kickball. As they accept,
Andy and Paul excitedly call out what the sides will be.

In the end the boys have decided to let the others "share their
experience." Throughout this exhausting interaction the therapist has attempted to keep the lines of communication open both
between the two boys in the pair and between the pair and the
"outsiders." He attends to the ways that the boys are negotiating,
to the underlying reasons for these ways of negotiating, and to
sources of possible aid in leading the children to more productive
ways of interaction, which consider both self and other.

Not only does the therapist know both boys are capable of higher-level understanding of others' perspectives than they are using,
he is also well acquainted with the powerful affective forces and
past experiences with similar interactions that interfere with the
boys' ability to apply their insight in action. He brokers the trust
he has built with the boys to help them link the perspectives of
self and other. Choosing to sidestep the heavier issues for the moment, he asks for reconsideration, points out practical issues of
implementation, interprets or reflects the boys' statements and
actions, indicates factual barriers, draws attention to others' perspectives, asks leading questions, and "translates" or transfers
each child's communications for the other, all the while maintaining a degree of impartiality and allowing as much active control

and substantive input for the boys as possible. He does not dictate a solution or control their behavior. As a result, unkind or inappropriate things may be said and done, and the solution arrived at may not be ideal. But strong feelings are vented, no disastrous results occur, and the boys *themselves* arrive at what is at least an adequate resolution, a success that has strongly gratifying and reinforcing effects for these two heretofore largely unsuccessful children.

Past observations suggest that on their own, without their therapist's mediation, Paul and Andy would not have been able to arrive at a mutual solution. They probably would have either given up on the game (and displaced their feelings of frustration onto each other), or bullied the others off the court, if they could have managed it. Any child's natural inclination is to care for his or her own wants. Learning to care about another's wants as well, even at the level of simple, self-oriented reciprocity, is a slow process. In the most optimal of conditions, most children naturally learn through interactions with parents and peers to do this on their own.

But the past experiences and inner limitations of the children we see in pairs have built up pathological structures of relating that forcefully oppose this movement to the discovery of higher-level negotiation and shared experience. The therapist in the linking role facilitates the pair's construction of strategies that consider both self and other in reciprocal (or even collaborative) fashion. This role is difficult at best, for it must be undertaken in the midst of fast-paced interaction in which feelings run high. The therapist as mediator must on the one hand have a good sense for tactics that establish reciprocity and fairness, and on the other be sensitive to the pathological nature of the psychological structures that get in the child's way of naturally learned reciprocity.

"Enabling" Mutually Shared Reflection: The "2 to 3" Restructuring

The third therapeutic tactic we use from the perspective of our developmental model is the "enabling" or facilitating of shared reflection between the pair partners. When the partners feel secure enough to look at their own behavior, they are encouraged to do so both in an in vivo, ongoing way, and in retrospective evaluation of past interactions.

The therapist stimulates ongoing peer feedback by seeking the partners' opinions of their own and each other's attempts at communicating and negotiating, and makes their reflections safe by counseling them on how to communicate in a supportive and con-structive way. If the interchange becomes too vituperative or the feedback is hurtful or distorted, the therapist intervenes by help-ing the partners to reflect on their own feedback, to test its ties with reality, and to think about how it may have been heard by the other partner. In later phases of treatment, the therapist can use the therapeutic alliance to train the partners to counsel one an-other about the adaptiveness of their behaviors or even the depths of their feelings. At lower developmental levels the therapist may also help the partners assess their communicative difficulties or maladaptive negotiation strategies through dramatic role enact-ment.

Retrospective reflection, which may in practice overlap with on-going reflection, means engaging the pair to develop a yardstick for evaluation and understanding their behavior together by stepping back from their interactions. In a wrap-up, for example, the nego-tiation strategies used in the course of a session can be evaluated, with the goal of developing a capacity for self-observation that can be useful to the children in future moments of disequilibrium. During spontaneous struggles, the pair may be asked to stop, step aside from the heat of battle, and, from the position of observers, reflect on the adaptiveness of their behaviors. Often, this cannot be done immediately. However, whenever they have had struggles that have not been resolved or the consequences of which have carried over from one hour to the next, the partners learn that these issues will be addressed in the next session.

As partners reflect on their own feelings and behavior, they can often see parallels between their partner's struggles and their own. They learn by experience with their peer that they are not alone in being so troubled. As Sullivan noted, consensual validation arises from each partner's capacity for seeing the other's problems in ac-tion and by sharing troublesome thoughts and feelings.

Of course, the development of the reflective process to a point of full effectiveness takes time. In lower-level pairs, and in higher-level pairs in the first months of therapy, retrospective reflection is often quite perfunctory. Both partners' responses to earlier inci-dents may remain unchanged, and despite their therapist's questions or insights, both may still actively resist really looking at what has occurred. But the goals of this technique are long-term. By establishing the habit of trying to reflect back on their interactions, the therapist lays the groundwork for the triad, and then the pair eventually, to be able to do so more productively.

By mutually shared reflection, which is the hallmark of Level 3 collaboration, we mean the sharing of feelings by two children about their relationship, or about those concerns external to it, that potentially lead to consensual validation of each one's experience by and for the other. Although this is surely a focus of intervention shared by many therapies, it represents an explicitly identified goal construed in Level 3 terms in our model. Essentially, this level of interaction requires both children to begin to conceive of friendship as involving mutual support and help in expressing feelings, ideas, and needs, which is a Level 3, mutual way of conceiving of and dealing with relationships.

Although we would like to see all pairs develop this kind of communication, we have found that it occurs rarely and briefly, is hard to attain, and is all but impossible to maintain regularly. These children are limited not only by their often ingrained, pathological ways of thinking about and dealing with relationships, but also by the effects of experiencing interpersonal stress and the emotional and psychological energy demands of carrying through with interactions that require Level 3 strategies. The children must be willing to take the risk of vulnerability that is required for such interaction. The therapist's role is to attempt to "enable" the pair to overcome these limits and risk this vulnerability by encouraging them to talk about things they want to talk about but hesitate, for many reasons, to do so.

In their third and last year of therapy together, Andy and Paul, now eleven, became much more self-reflective. At this point, their pair therapy had progressed through the "1 to 2" restructuring phase, although the boys' reciprocal functioning was still quite shaky. One sign that Level 2 was beginning to consolidate in Andy's and Paul's relationship, however, was a glimpse of cutting-edge mutually shared reflection in an interaction that occurred during one of their last pair therapy sessions. Their shared reflection was not fully Level 3 to the extent that it is not clear how much real sympathy and empathy Andy and Paul were sharing—Were they truly commiserating or merely bemoaning their fates in the presence of the other? In either case this was a special moment for this pair.

Andy and Paul are slated to leave the Manville School at the end of the year to return to public schools. Andy is particularly upset by and ambivalent about having to leave, and he has spent the last several weeks expressing a great deal of fear and anger. The therapist infers that he is in part angry because he feels rejected, as if being sent away. It is as if by freely showing this anger, and making his life and others' more difficult and painful at school, it will be easier to want to leave. In their last session, Andy and Paul are able to acknowledge some of the feelings of loss and rejection rather than deflecting them into anger.

For the first twenty minutes of the session, Paul sits alone in the meeting room. He comments at the start of the session that he thinks Andy is probably upset that he cannot go on an afterschool trip because it conflicts with pairs time. This indeed seems to be the starting point for Andy, who has been roaming the halls with building anger and frustration. The therapist leaves Paul in the meeting room to find Andy, whom he finally discovers in a fit of crying and yelling in a school corridor. When Andy finally arrives in the pairs room, his pain at missing an afterschool trip appears to be one of many feelings about his many losses:

> Andy's eyes are swollen and framed in red, his breath is short from crying. PAUL asks in a concerned tone, "Are you okay, Andy?"
> ANDY's response to Paul is to lash out "Shut up," and then shuffle to a table at the far side of the room.

Although two years before, Paul would have reacted to Andy's verbal repulsion with fear, perhaps even by withdrawing under a table, he now seems to have gained the sense of safety, and the distance and insight not to personalize Andy's rebuke, but rather to see it as an expression of pain. He simply pauses, motionless, watching Andy put his head down on the table and begin to cry again, with heavy sobs and full abandon:

> Pulling in words between his short breaths, ANDY talks confusedly about his mother. "She's coming in at 3:00, I think, and then she's leaving again, after, and maybe I could see her if I didn't do anything after school, but now I won't get to see her. . . ." Between his bouts of crying, Andy continues to talk of missing his mom. PAUL apparently wants to offer Andy some comfort, and as he watches ANDY closely he walks slowly, with uncertain steps, toward him, stopping after every few. He is tentative, perhaps because he is afraid Andy's anger may well up again toward him. Paul picks up a can of soda, and he offers it to Andy with an outstretched arm.
> ANDY says "I don't want any," but now his tone is sad rather than angry. Andy turns toward the adult and asks him to leave the room. It appears that he wants to be alone with Paul.
> PAUL still looks tentative and anxious, however. The idea of being alone with Andy in his frustration is probably for him a frightening one. Now Paul asks, "Mind if I leave you

alone, Andy?" wanting to withdraw.
ANDY stares openly at Paul for a few moments, looking
surprised and hurt, and then turns his head away. "Go
ahead, I don't care." He says this into his chest with a
muffled sniffle, his head bent down.

Paul's wish to offer support and caring has come out in uncertain
moves checked by his fear of Andy. He is not sure if Andy will get
angry again, and he is afraid of being physically hurt. The therapist airs this fear for Paul, trying to show Andy that it is fear that
makes Paul want to leave, not lack of caring:

ANDY talks again, his voice laced with thick sniffles: "They
probably won't let me go early, because they don't know
about what I'm missing. They don't know I'm missing my
mother."
PAUL spontaneously speaks to offer a kind of
understanding, "Hey listen, Andy, you miss your mother, I
miss my father. The only time I get to see him leave is
when I wake up pretty early. He comes home about
midnight and I'm fast asleep."
ANDY wipes his nose with his sleeve. His eyes are focused
on Paul as he listens to him talk.
PAUL talks on, "I hardly ever see my dad because he has to
work overtime."
ANDY offers, in a calmer voice, "My father works almost
every day. Matter of fact he works every night except
Saturday, Sunday, and Friday. So I'm usually left with the
babysitter. Tonight I'll be with the babysitter."

Both boys talk about important lacks in their lives, lacks that
they have seldom aired with their therapist. Their looks and tones
make it clear that the feeling is one of sharing this experience of
lacking, rather than what might on the surface seem like some
one-upmanship of who is worse off. Both boys are silent for a while,
looking at each other:

PAUL says, "Yeah, Dad misses us. We miss him."
ANDY's tone is low. "That's the problem—my mother
doesn't miss me." Suddenly Andy seems to become aware
of the intimacy and openness of his statement, and he
turns to the adult to say in a loud, irritated whine, "Why
don't you take a break and get outa here, huh?"

Apparently Andy feels that the adult is intruding on the intimacy
and sharing going on between Paul and himself. This step to ex-
clude the adult reveals an important and singular bond of trust

building between the boys. The therapist checks if it is all right
with Paul to leave the room and go next door behind the mirror:

> PAUL immediately says "Sure." Although his tone is one of
> ease, his body is stiff and he holds his breath.

It looks as if Paul is consciously trying to put a check on his fear
of Andy's potential harm for the sake of staying with Andy to be
helpful. This is something he could not do even a few minutes earlier. But now, by permitting the adult (who assures them he will be
close by) to leave the room, Paul further opens the way for building
trust between the boys:

> ANDY relates an incident from the past weekend, when he
> and his parents were going to go out together. As Andy
> tells it, he rode off on his bike telling his mother where
> he'd be, but his mother forgot to call him. He ends, "And
> when I came back my mom had gone to bed, and my dad
> had gone to sleep. And I was left alone." Andy talks about
> the facts of the incident as if his mother were at fault for
> not calling him, yet there is a sense that he feels himself to
> blame.
> PAUL says softly, "I'm sorry." After a brief pause, he adds,
> "By the way Andy, if you see any raffle tickets around, I've
> lost mine." Rather than being put off and hurt by this
> sudden change of subject on Paul's part, ANDY immediately
> picks up on the new topic. "Let's go look for them in the
> afterschool room," he says.

In a moment both boys are heading out of the room, leaving
behind them the reflective sharing about feelings of loneliness and
loss. Paul's sudden change of topic, and Andy's ready acceptance of
this diversion, illustrates the emotionally draining effect of "shared
reflection" interactions. There is a great deal of emotional energy
expended in interacting at this level of openness and intimacy. For
Andy this energy was invested in overcoming the fears of vulnerability and risk in exposing his feelings. For Paul, his energy
was challenged in fighting off, for the sake of showing support in
friendship, his fears of being left alone with Andy's unpredictable
behavior. The apparent ease of this transition probably also reflects
that the interaction served its purpose—sharing and trust provided comfort and relief.

Even six months earlier, this pair would not have been able to
attain this level of sharing or exhibit the self-reflective capacity
underlying it. Paul would have been too frightened of Andy's aggressive expression of feelings and the possibility that this

aggression would be directed toward him. And his concerns would have been well founded, for Andy would not have been able to reflectively identify the basis for his disequilibrated affect—that is, sadness within—and most likely would have expressed his feelings as anger without. Paul's capacity to withstand Andy's initial rejection ("Shut up!") helped Andy to feel that it was safe to use a more unfamiliar and thus, to him, frightening mode of coping with feelings—that is, admitting his vulnerability and sharing with a peer his feelings of both sadness and fear.

This level of interaction occurs only rarely with the pairs of troubled children we see, but it is a goal for the treatment process. This kind of relating cannot be forced or dictated, but it can be facilitated and enabled. When feelings are running high, the therapist can act to smooth over rough spots by clarifying or recasting what is said. At other times, the best way for the therapist to foster this level of relating and intimacy is just to be there and let the children be.

A Context for Relating Action and Reflection

We put forth as a goal of pair therapy, as determined by our model, a restructuring of long-standing cognitive, affective, and behavioral aspects of a child's maladaptive social behaviors. The type of intervention that we feel this model calls for in pursuing these goals is one directed toward both actual behavior and reflection about behavior.

In trying out more subjective, reciprocal, or collaborative ways of interacting, the child will acquire the concomitant structure of construing the self-other relationship that is embodied in the strategy, the corresponding experience and control of affect, and more balanced orientations to changing self or other when conflict arises. Likewise, through reflection that attends explicitly to the wishes of both self and other, the child will come to incorporate a consideration of both self and other in his or her construal, affect, and orientation in social interaction.

We do not expect these changes to occur quickly, simply, or directly. Rather, we expect a process of gradually filtered learning to occur through an interaction between behavioral and reflective experience. Our focus on both behavior and reflection on behavior is based on the belief that children's general understanding of thoughts and feelings about interpersonal relations are constructed by the processes of both experiencing and examining actual interpersonal interactions.

The socially maladjusted children seen in pair therapy have to a large extent grown up in environments in which only Level 0 and Level 1 strategies are perceived as "successful." Most of them feel they have little effect on their family or other social environments unless they resort to physical force or a stance of battling, "dig in the heels" control. Conversely, they often tend to feel overpowered by others in their home environments and learn to accommodate with a Level 0 or Level 1 way of experiencing and dealing with affective disequilibrium, often impulsive fight or flight. For children interacting consistently at a given level, our method of intervention is to encourage both successful experiences with the use of the next level of behavior and reflection on that experience. As they come to use the next level strategies successfully, they will learn to draw on these strategies more readily.

It is important to stress that this "learning" takes place not only on the planes of behavior and cognition, but also on the plane of affect. We have identified in the movement to higher-level strategies an increase in the ability to trust the self and other, to be vulnerable, to yield or gain control. Earlier, in describing the interaction of Andy and Paul, we noted that Andy was afraid to give up his position of control. His new movement to using higher-level strategies involves a greater willingness to allow a balance of direction between self and other. The ability to trust, to yield or share control, rests in part on the affective growth that comes from his unaccustomed experience of the safety and success of higher-level strategies. With this experience Andy can learn that he will not "lose it" when he gives up some control, nor will he be "destroyed" when Paul gains some control. In essence, the interpersonal growth that we seek to facilitate in these troubled children requires that they redefine what it means to be in control of the self (and other).

There is no great mystery to this process. The emphasis, in some sense, is on practice and exercise. The failure, for whatever reason, to confront disequilibrating experiences in a supportive setting in the past has deprived these children of the opportunity to struggle for new levels of equilibrium, and the concomitant opportunities for growth. Social skills, like physical skills, such as running long distances, require repeated, planned, organized, and structured practice. And like competing in a road race to better one's own best time, social development requires practice and involvement under real-life competition and stress, not just under conditions of only reflection or rehearsal.

One reason growth in social skills is so hard to achieve is that functioning in the context of conflict is seldom one for which the participant is well-prepared—strong feelings usually take us by surprise. Pair therapy provides a context in which conflict is likely, if not inevitable. But it also provides a context in which there is help and support for the participants when they find themselves in conflict intrapsychically as well as interpersonally. Although pair therapy should by no means be construed as simply a boxing match, the pair therapist, like a boxing coach alongside the ring, helps the pair-mates in the midst of stressful interactions to keep their heads. Unlike boxing, the adult coaches both participants.

That the children we see are "disturbed" by a conventional, lay person's definition, is something we do not dispute. We make no claim that pair therapy alone is going to "cure them" or that other therapeutic interventions will not be useful for them. What we do maintain however, is that the model gives the therapist a powerful developmentally-based set of tools, suggestions, and techniques to make sense of, sort out, set goals for, assess progress in, provide crucial appropriate corrective experience for, and facilitate growth in children's interpersonal behavior as it is and as it develops. It is our conviction that pair therapy can result in profound therapeutic gains for children that go beyond the mere strengthening of their social abilities to restructure their personalities.

PART THREE

Clinical Research

CHAPTER EIGHT

Establishing Boundaries and Borders

Holly and Jessica, two early adolescents, rush into the pair therapy room, leaving their slow-moving pair therapist several minutes and flights of stairs below. As soon as they enter the room, Holly, the dominant partner, directs Jessica to join her on the floor in a corner of the room in a safe little cozy area "protected" by chairs and a sofa to continue a conversation that has occupied the last several sessions. This private conversation is on a topic of intense interest to Holly: the thoughts, feelings, and actions of Davy, a boy in Jessica's class. Still trying to catch her breath from the run up the several flights of stairs, Holly begins. "I love Davy. What did Davy do mischievous today?" With equal excitement, Jessica, Holly's pair partner of a year and a half, responds in a secretive whisper, "He forgot his homework."

In a quizzical voice, as if to ask how forgetting one's homework is so mischievous, Holly pushes for something else, something more. "He forgot his homework? What *else* did he do mischievous?" Now both girls are beginning to catch their breath. But before Jessica can respond, Holly provides Jessica with an example of what she considers mischief. "Did he do this to the teacher?" she asks, as she raises her arm, makes a fist, and extends her middle finger upward toward Jessica in a gesture generally known throughout American culture to signify disrespect, contempt, or hostile feelings toward the person to whom it is directed. In response, Jessica begins to giggle, and then in a spirit of collusion, shared excitement, and escalation, builds upon the lead of her pair partner. "He did this!" she says, as she uses both hands to imitate and accentuate Holly's gesture. "He did doo, doo, doo, doo, doo, doo, doo," using both upright middle fingers in rapid succession. And then she adds for good measure, "He stuck two fingers up the teacher's nose."

In response to Jessica, Holly says with an approving

sigh, "Oh, Davy," as in "What a terrific guy." This reaction
has the effect of spurring Jessica on to even further
exaggerated claims. She says with a silly giggle, "He hit
the teacher in the stomach." Holly replies with real
approval, "Davy, he's sooo cute." Jessica then adds, "He
farted, too."

How are we to understand the meaning of this interaction? Does
Holly really expect that Davy would "give the finger" to his teacher?
What does Holly think it means if he does? What is motivating
Jessica's response? Is she kidding, serious, or something else?
Does she think Holly believes her reports? Can this interaction
possibly suggest some form of social development in relation to the
interactions of these two girls in earlier sessions, or is it just obnox-
ious behavior? Out of context, of course, it is difficult to say. In this
chapter we will put this initial piece of behavior, and the rest of the
behavior observed in this particular pair therapy session (including the glimpse you had in chapter 4), into a richer and more
meaningful context. The larger developmental context includes information about the individual histories of each of the children,
the history of their time together in the pair, and the knowledge we
have of sessions previous and subsequent to this one. Specifically,
we will describe the pair therapist's role in empowering Holly and
Jessica's transition from Level 0 to Level 1 social interaction.

The Match

Jessica and Holly were selected as partners for pair therapy in
part because they both exhibited behaviors and interpersonal orientations characteristic of a class of difficulties categorized as
borderline. In using the term "borderline" to describe these girls,
we are following a characterization similar to that of Fred Pine
(1985) in his book *Developmental Theory and Clinical Process.*
That is, we do not use this term as a unitary diagnostic category for
a single unifying mechanism, constellation, or syndrome, but
rather as a classification of an array of phenomena having some
larger developmental and pathological commonalities. These characteristics include broad levels of fluctuation in ego functioning,
inability to cope with anxiety with a resorting to both neurotic defenses and psychotic distortions, a real fear for the very integrity of
their minds and bodies, bizarre and peculiar thoughts, in part
based upon excessive fluidity and poor separation of fantasy from
reality, the controlling of excessive fear by keeping play mostly monotonous and conversation dull and superficial, and most critical

of all, poor and superficial relationships with others, despite frequent reliance on others to modulate and control their behavior.

Holly and Jessica at the time we began to work with them were by no means merely neurotic, but they were certainly not clearly psychotic either. In any case, each in her own way had severe problems in the way she related to others. And, not coincidentally, both strikingly lacked a stable personality organization.

Jessica is a slight, immature-looking fourteen-year-old with short, straight hair and glasses. She speaks in a whiny staccato, with a pressed anxious tone. Her awkward manner suggests a babyish self-image in a body that is growing and changing more rapidly than she can manage. She exhibits primitive physical behaviors such as grunting, burping, and lip-smacking, and has poor eye contact, either avoiding altogether or "staring through" another person. Her voice and body tremble easily in interpersonal contexts of even the slightest stress. Jessica appears to have a great deal of difficulty managing affect. At times she behaves in a bland, almost machinelike manner. At other times she appears to be flooded by feelings that cause her to giggle uncontrollably and inappropriately, and move her body in fits and starts. She tends to laugh at sad events and is easily frightened by actions or events that would not make most children her age feel fearful. She is quick to become painfully embarrassed, sometimes for reasons not apparent to others.

Conversation with Jessica, under calm conditions, suggests that she has intact reality testing, yet at the same time, an extensive involvement with a very vivid fantasy life. She appears to be particularly fearful about approaching womanhood. Interestingly, Jessica's difficulties in differentiating reality and fantasy and her preoccupations do not interfere with her performance on more academic tasks. Her anxieties appeared to interfere mostly with social functioning, the development of self-esteem and self-assurance, and the negotiation of normal early adolescent social developmental tasks.

In the two years at the school prior to the referral for pair therapy, the school staff had noticed that Jessica seemed to very much want to be involved in peer interaction and had made some minor progress in improving her social skills. Her behavior, however, still made her an easy scapegoat for her peers, especially the boys, and Jessica needed an adult's presence to continuously bring the effects of her own behavior on her classmates to her attention. For example, she ate with her mouth open and responded to the reasonable criticism of her peers by pouting or talking in a whiny, babyish voice. A referral for pair therapy was made because Jessica expressed a strong desire to relate positively to others and to be liked, and because highly structured settings and activities seemed to be one way to reduce the anxiety she was experiencing.

Holly is a thin twelve-year-old who is somewhat tomboyish in appearance. Conversations with her revealed that her dysphoric state appeared to be a function of feeling totally abandoned and alone in the world, rather than feeling badly about herself or guilty. In addition, she appeared to feel great disappointment about interpersonal losses. Unlike Jessica's family life, Holly's had been fairly turbulent, with a long history of family problems, in which there was some evidence of abuse, or at least neglect. Holly's problems appeared to be primarily due to severe inconsistencies in the parent child relationship that interfered with her ability to differentiate self and other. She was not, however, devoid of some developmental delays that appeared to be more constitutionally based.

Holly also had great difficulty interacting with peers. During school recess, she was silent and often alone. She enjoyed running around the playground by herself, galloping, neighing, prancing, and kicking like a horse. At lunch, she would sometimes imitate the way a horse eats. Her horselike behavior, which appeared to have a self-soothing function, diminished by the middle of her first year at the school. But during group lessons, Holly continued to occasionally attract the attention of her peers by shouting out answers, becoming silly, or insensitively criticizing the mistakes of another student.

Although fragile enough to regress to more psychotic forms of functioning under stress (for example, her horselike behavior during the first few months at the school), Holly showed some signs of strength. It was felt that her ability to take solace from self-soothing objects and activities signaled a potential for further growth, particularly if she could integrate this function into her relationships with others. Pair therapy, with a female therapist who would act consistently and a peer with whom Holly could interact in a safe atmosphere, offered this opportunity.

Jessica and Holly were matched as a pair because they had both important similarities and some significant differences in their observed behavior, background, and intrapsychic organization. In matching them we considered the fact that both girls were of roughly the same age and intellectual ability. They also shared some key diagnostic characteristics: disturbed interpersonal relationships, disturbances in the clear distinction between fantasy and reality, excessive and intense anxiety, and severely impulsive behavior. Both girls were isolated within their school classrooms and both tended to use fantasy to cope with the stress of unstructured, uncertain, or challenging situations. Their difficulties suggested that they needed a female therapist who had experience in dealing with children who on occasion regress to psychotic behavior and who could maintain control by using her own power effectively.

In pairing the two girls, special attention was given to important differences between them: family background, the degree to which constitutional and experiential factors appeared to have influenced their current status, and the specific fears, fantasies, and preoccupations that interfered with their social functioning. Most importantly, their typical orientation toward dealing with interpersonal conflict differed. When faced with a conflict between herself and a peer, Jessica tended to shift her own behavior, feelings, or interests to accommodate to what she perceived the other person's goals to be, rather than to challenge or try to change the other person in any direct way—she was self-transforming. Holly, on the other hand, although also "shy," typically dealt with here-and-now interpersonal conflict by trying to get the other person to do what she thought she wanted—she was other-transforming. Thus, this match fit the profile of similar developmental level and opposite interpersonal orientation that we have found to be optimal for fostering a pair's interpersonal growth.

Jessica and Holly met weekly with the same female therapist for 47 sessions over an 18-month period. The evolution of their relationship over the course of treatment is described below. The therapy is divided into two periods, marked by an abrupt shift in the pair's focus following the thirty-third session.

Treatment Period One: The Game of Life

Prior to their inaugural session, Holly and Jessica were introduced separately to their therapist and to some of the basic tenets of pair therapy. During the first session, Jessica and Holly were asked to decide together upon a game or activity from a list of available options, all of which were meant to encourage shared play (e.g., board games, crafts, etc.). In this initial session the two girls quickly established a dynamic interaction pattern that lasted through each of the thirty-three sessions of their first thirteen months in pair therapy, which we have called "period one."

From the first moments of this first session, Holly moved to dominate the interaction as she was to do in all the sessions that followed. She was more active in scanning the room and exploring the available materials, and she unilaterally chose Life for the pair to play, claiming some familiarity with this relatively challenging board game. Jessica, though completely unfamiliar with the game, accommodated to Holly's wishes immediately without suggesting an alternative activity for the pair's consideration or demonstrating any observable resistance.

Each session during the first period began with the two girls running ahead of the therapist to the pair therapy room and, at Holly's insistence, playing Life for the entire session. In this game, the players alternate taking a turn, which consists of spinning a wheel and then moving a token the designated number of spaces. Depending in part on chance and in part on skill, each player acquires a profession, a regular salary, a family, material possessions, and capital. As in real life, losses or gains are possible, depending on a combination of judgment and luck. The winner is the person who has earned the most money in traveling around the board.

Looking in on this pair from the vantage point of the observation room, we had the impression that for many sessions neither the competitive nor the cooperative aspects of the game had any "shared meaning" for either girl—they seemed to be playing two separate games. Holly appeared to be obsessed with attaining as much wealth as possible, independently of how well Jessica did. She expressed neither dismay nor excitement in reaction to Jessica's fortunes. Correspondingly, Jessica also seemed to be unconcerned with her own fortunes as well as totally disconnected from the competitive aspects of the game. When it was her turn, she spun the wheel and moved her token in a rote, almost affectless fashion, with little expression of feeling attached to either success or setback. Although indifferent to Holly's fortunes, Jessica did seem to be quite preoccupied with avoiding any possible confrontation with Holly. She was careful not to act in any way that would incur Holly's displeasure.

Activity choice was not the only way in which Holly asserted her dominance quickly and totally. And in all cases, Jessica complied immediately, doing nothing to challenge Holly. For example, Holly would spin the wheel and move her token, but then, impatient to get to her next turn, she would impulsively—without asking— spin the wheel and move Jessica's token for her. At other times, Holly would allow Jessica to spin the wheel for herself, but then would not wait for Jessica to move her token before spinning the wheel for her next turn. All this occurred without any visible objection on Jessica's part. Jessica appeared fearful, overcontrolled, timid, and submissive. Thus, Jessica, less overtly disruptive or aggressive but equally insecure and immature, colluded with Holly to produce a very rigid and primitive form of social interaction.

Characterized by Holly's impulsive, aggressive dominance and Jessica's fearful overcompliance, this pair's "negotiating" was predominantly at Level 0. The astounding primitiveness of their interactions, with Holly's total unconcern for Jessica's being and Jessica's total unconcern for her own participation (except to avoid Holly's wrath at all costs), was manifest in some unusual features in the course of their pair therapy. Because their interactions were so dramatically low-level, and their interpersonal orientations so extremely polarized, they went through the first two phases of pair therapy—sizing each other up and establishing a dominance pattern—within the first few minutes of the first session. Holly was so rigidly other-transforming and Jessica so rigidly self-transforming that the power relations between the two needed little *active* negotiation. Thus, the bulk of period one of Holly and Jessica's pair therapy corresponds to the third developmental phase of the therapeutic process of pairs, that of stable imbalance of power or temporary equilibrium. Although some pairs settle on a home base activity fairly quickly and others take much longer or never do it at all, Holly and Jessica established a fairly long-lasting joint activity within the first few minutes of their tenure as a pair.

Although this pair's therapy was atypical in the speed with which the balance of power was established, it was typical in revolving mostly around negotiation rather than sharing interactions in the first phases. The static and totally asymmetrical power relations between the two girls in their playing of Life were the most salient feature of the relationship. However, during this "stable imbalance" phase we were able to observe *some* progress in Holly and Jessica's negotiations around a snack that the therapist provided each week. She gave them each a chocolate bar at the beginning of every session. At first a pattern of negotiation similar to that in their playing of Life was observed when the two girls shared the snack. Holly would wolf hers down and then go through a predictable sequence of negotiations with Jessica in a blatant attempt to acquire whatever candy Jessica had not yet eaten. Holly would ask Jessica for part of her snack and, in the early sessions, Jessica would usually comply, saying that she did not like chocolate. In later sessions, though, Jessica began to show some resistance, and Holly would plead, then demand, and finally resort to grabbing Jessica's chocolate bar. At such junctures, the therapist would mediate the interpersonal problem-solving. She empowered and supported both girls by setting limits on Holly's low-level other-transforming actions and encouraging Jessica to take limit-setting (other-transforming) actions on her own behalf.

Almost never during this first period of treatment did either girl spontaneously engage in any direct conversation with the other. For instance, seldom, if ever, did either make any comment or venture any opinion on school life, much less reach out to connect with the other by inquiring about what life might be like for the other outside the sessions. Nor did either girl reveal why psychological reactions were taking place within herself. Neither shared any observations on their relationships with significant persons in their lives (e.g., parents, siblings, peers, or teachers), nor did they inquire into what these relationships were like for the other. In other words, there was virtually no spontaneous expression or psychological exploration between the two, even of the "random comment" variety.

This is not to say that there was not communication, connection, or shared experience evident between the two girls during period one, but like their negotiation, their connection-oriented interaction was at Level 0. Early on, each girl found that she could share experiences with the other through primitive (age-inappropriate) functions. The two girls engaged in competitions with each other to see who could scream, burp, or make fartlike sounds the loudest. Such contests evoked much mutual laughter, an important indicator of the occurrence of a "corrective interpersonal experience." However, these contests often escalated to an almost hysterical point, necessitating the therapist's intervention to help each child return to a less excited state. The need for the therapist's intervention at these "fun" times attests to the incredible paucity of the pair's social regulation abilities. But when the therapist "filled in the gaps" in these abilities, share they did. For these children to begin to share, even at a primitive level, constituted the start of forward movement, if their subsequent progress is any indication.

Treatment Period Two: "Life" Becomes Life

The hope that Holly and Jessica were making "invisible" progress in the seemingly monotonous months of playing Life was borne out by a dramatic shift to far more intense and risky interactions. At the beginning of the thirty-fourth session, Holly announced, "Jessica, I want to ask you a question about a boy in your class—Davy." With this question, the girls switched as suddenly to an entirely new track as they had initiated their endless game of Life. For the next fourteen sessions, until the end of the school year, the girls completely ignored their board game and, at Holly's insistence, spent all their time in a small fort in the corner of the room. There, surrounded by chairs and a sofa, they held a weekly dialogue. The primary topic of their weekly conversations was the activities and interests of Davy, the boy in Jessica's classroom.

Initially, Holly's inquiries were almost exclusively about how Davy felt toward her, a somewhat strange line of inquiry for, according to our own observations and discussion with the staff of the school, Davy was completely unaware of Holly's infatuation with him and showed no signs of even knowing she existed, much less having reciprocal feelings. Adding to the bizarre nature of the interaction between Holly and Jessica around this topic was the way Jessica, in her role as classroom reporter, provided a stream of romantic fantasies about how much Davy cared for Holly and fabricated stories about Davy's doings in the classroom. It was difficult, at times, to tell to what degree one or both of the girls entered completely into these fantasies and became so embedded in them as to be unable to clearly differentiate them from the "reality" of Davy's interests and activities.

Period two in Holly and Jessica's therapy represented a restructuring of balance in their interaction and a transition from their predominantly Level 0 functioning to more consistent, if fragile, Level 1 functioning. Following are excerpted verbatim transcriptions and summaries of the thirty-seventh session with running commentaries. This was the fourth session of period two, and the third session the girls spent largely "by themselves," with their therapist in the observation booth.

In presenting a microanalysis of this session, we hope to highlight some of the features of their interaction in this progressive period of therapy with a developmental analysis of the processes of shared experience and interpersonal negotiation. In particular, we will present three scenes from the session that chart the course of their transition. The first scene illustrates the starting point in quite primitive shared experience, the second shows progressive movement in the girls' negotiation and shared experience to at least some instances of solid Level 1 behavior, and the third scene illustrates a paradox that emerges with their shift to higher-level functioning: the gap between the relatively high social perspective coordination evident in their increasingly reality-based perception of Davy and their cutting-edge Level 2 actions, on the one hand, and their still age-inappropriate regressions, on the other.

Microanalysis of Session Thirty-Seven
Scene 1. Level 0 Shared Experience

We will now return to the scene that introduced this chapter. Recall that at our last glance, Holly, in a silly mood, has just asked Jessica if Davy, the boy with whom she is so powerfully infatuated, made an obscene gesture to the teacher whom he and Jessica share. Jessica immediately shares in the mood, imitating and amplifying the gesture as well as the fantasy by reporting or asserting that Davy "stuck two fingers up the teacher's nose." She then continues with more outrageous fabrications. Like much of the communication between the two girls (e.g., Holly's fantasy about how Davy feels about her and Jessica's reporting of Davy's activities in class), this report of Davy's actions is spurious, completely unverified by Jessica and Davy's teacher.

The conversation can continue because there is a complementarity between the primitive level of functioning of each of the two girls. Holly's need is to have her obsession with Davy fed. She has a crush on Davy, a fairly typical phenomenon for a girl of her age. However, unlike other girls her age, she is much less able to perceive, let alone acknowledge, the unrequited nature of her feelings. The more Holly is pleased by Jessica's reports, the more Jessica strives to report, regardless of how fantastic the reports might be. When Holly demands that Jessica tell her how Davy feels about her, there is really nothing to tell, for Davy, in fact, appears never to think about or even notice Holly. But Jessica's complementary need, at an equally primitive level, is to connect with and hold on to Holly's attention, no matter what the cost. This allows her to blot out the knowledge (at least partially, or at least at some level) that she is fabricating stories about Davy and Davy's feelings simply to please Holly. Jessica seldom generates any fantasy reportage based on a particularly high level of psychosocial or psychosexual knowledge. As judged by her reports, her thoughts and ideation seldom, if ever, rise far above preoccupations with bodily functions, and what makes her laugh is limited to scatological references and preposterous acts of naughtiness.

What makes us "diagnose" the shared experience here as Level 0, or primitive, is the lack of separation between the girls, the lack of awareness (in practice) of reality, the very low level of the ideation, and the almost unconscious-seeming slipping back and forth of ideas and fantasies and humor between the two. (Note further examples of this very contagious "unconscious" sharing in the screaming and giggling in the next passages, a sharing and connecting that for all its primitiveness would have been unimaginable to observers of Holly and Jessica several weeks earlier.) Although the shared experience is at a very low level, both girls show other signs of higher-level social perspective coordination, as we will discuss shortly:

> At this point, there is a knock on the door. Both girls realize that it is the pair therapist, who has just arrived from her slower walk up the several flights of stairs. Spontaneously, Holly, and then a split second later, Jessica, scream in reaction to the knock, an indication of how poorly each regulates affective arousal. Through a quick glance at each other they seem to decide together to ignore the knock, Holly by not moving to the door, and Jessica by watching to see exactly what Holly does. Instead, Holly acts as if there are a few more moments left to get in some crucial questions about Davy. There is another knock, and this time Holly responds, leaving the safety of their fort and moving to open the door. Jessica follows her.
> HOLLY: "Come in!" in a strident voice. (Somehow she manages to sound both angry and pleased at the same time.)
> Just as the pair therapist is about to pass through the doorway, Holly slams it in her face, laughing. The two girls giggle collusively. Then, in an excited state, both Holly and Jessica open the door together.
> HOLLY: "Come in," barking the order.

The pair therapist stands safely outside the doorway and tells the girls that she refuses to enter unless she can be sure the door will not be slammed in her face. Her tone is not angry, but sure and matter of fact. Each girl promises, but Jessica adds in a giggly, "bad girl" tone of voice, "Oh, shit." As the therapist enters the room Holly fakes a kick toward her:

> JESSICA: "We were talking about you."
> THERAPIST: "Oh, really? What did you say?"
> HOLLY: Interrupting, in an ordering tone of voice, "Where's those candy bars?"
> THERAPIST: "Is that why you let me in?"
> HOLLY: Assertively, "Yes!"
> The pair therapist hands each girl a single candy bar.

Each grabs greedily at her respective offering.

THERAPIST: "Do you want me to go back next door?"

[Behind the one-way mirror to the observation booth, a precedent set several sessions earlier.]

HOLLY: Wanting now to get back to her interrogation/discussion, shouts with great vehemence, "Yes!"

THERAPIST: "If you need me, just call."

HOLLY: "Shut up!"

JESSICA: Almost simultaneously, but just far enough behind to be imitating, "Shut up!"

THERAPIST: "I'll be right next door," and she leaves the room. Here she is responding more to the uncertainty each girl feels at being left without a source of direct and immediate adult control and limits, rather than to the salvo of rudeness.

Although primitive, the Level 0 shared experience with which this scene ends (Jessica's "unconscious," "contagious" imitation of Holly's "shut up") is a sign of progress. Jessica, who otherwise never displays this kind of assertiveness, appears to gain the courage to say outrageous things to the adult through her association with Holly. And the adult's imperturbable presence nearby sets the stage for better things to come.

Scene 2. Negotiation Moves to a Higher Level

As soon as the therapist leaves, Holly leads Jessica back to their corner of the room and returns the conversation to Davy with a question: "What did Davy do right after algebra?"

Jessica's reports range from the provocative ("He ripped up the book") to the scatological ("He farted") to the ridiculous ("He threw the teacher out the window"). When Holly changes tack somewhat and tests the limits of these reports ("Come on, did he really?"), Jessica does not recant, but simply changes the story line, as if this erases in some magical way her prior line of discourse. For Jessica, at least in practice, what one says does not need to have any consistency—she is quite willing to forego continuity.

Holly, who generally functions in relationships in either an unseparated or a one-way manner, asserts, with all seriousness, "He's *my* boyfriend," demonstrating no awareness or concern that she may not be his girlfriend. At this point Jessica surprises us, and Holly, by asking in a serious tone of voice, "Do you like him?" On the one hand, this is a strange question, as if Jessica had not been listening closely to the last three sessions of conversation between Holly and herself. On the other, it marks a shift in focus, away from reporting fantasized behavior to making a sincere inquiry into Holly's feelings. The question is grounded in affective reality. It takes a great deal of courage for Jessica to ask Holly a serious question about her feelings, and Holly responds in a gentle and uncharacteristically demure way, unable to provide a verbal response, but instead affirming her feelings with a gentle nod of her head. For these children, this is a remarkably "normal" and age-appropriate communication.

During this conversation, Holly has been systematically breaking up her chocolate bar into many small pieces, and eating each piece, one at a time, in a somewhat rapid and compulsive fashion. Jessica, on the other hand, has broken her candy bar into several large pieces, and has eaten a number of them without any particular attention. Down to her last several tiny pieces, and perhaps moved by the authenticity of the last moment's interaction, Holly makes her usual move for Jessica's candy with the following (untypical, for her, Level 2) proposition: "Jessica, I'll give you this magical piece for a bigger piece." In the past, Jessica has accommodated to Holly's requests or demands for a share of her candy, or if she resisted, it was either in a whiny, helpless tone of voice, or with an overreactive scream, "No!" Both the accommodation and resistance suggest how powerless she actually felt. This time, in an even tone of voice, Jessica responds, "Nope, I want my half," a straightforward, other-transforming, Level 1 response that is reminiscent of the easy self- and social regulation we saw between Brian and Jeremy in chapter 2. For Jessica to say, "Nope," and express her own needs, is, from a developmental perspective, a significant achievement, as normal and natural as it may sound out of this unique context. Not to be overlooked, of course, is the fact that Holly too is making gains. In this instance she neither puts undue pressure on Jessica, nor resorts to Level 0 grabbing.

Then Jessica switches the interaction back from this adaptive Level 1 negotiation to the sharing of experience with another fantasy gambit. "He threw his spelling book at the teacher." This initiation is also a somewhat new form of interaction—usually it is Holly who controls the flow of the interaction. After several more interchanges along these lines, Holly brings the interaction back to the negotiation around the distribution of the candy.

Holly says, "I'll give you these *two* magical [small] pieces for that [larger] piece" (Level 2). With a shake of her head, Jessica rejects the offer but softens the rejection by offering a smaller piece of her own chocolate to Holly. As she hands over this offering, Jessica verbally sets a limit. "That's all!" she says with real authority. Again we see the effective use of Level 1 and Level 2 negotiation strategies in the girls' social regulation.

> HOLLY returns the discussion back to Davy for a moment, but then in ground-breaking fashion, reaches out to make an inquiry about Jessica: "How many years have you been in this school?"
> JESSICA responds ("Four years"), but she cannot reciprocate by asking Holly the same question.
> HOLLY then goes on to inquire about how Davy interacts directly with Jessica. "Does Davy tease you?"
> JESSICA, with a hint of panic in her voice, responds, "He ignores me. He farts at girls."

As we noted earlier, when stressed, Jessica tends to regress to the scatological. Perhaps concerned that Holly will see her as a competitor for Davy's affection, Jessica quickly moves to refocus the discussion away from herself. "This is how he farts in school." At this point Jessica blows air through her pursed lips onto her arm, and Holly can't resist joining in. After Holly's two astounding forays into reality (Jessica's tenure at the school and whether Davy teases her), the girls regress to very primitive sharing, only to reach new heights of reality-based sharing a short time later.

Scene 3. The Gap between Social-Cognitive Capacity and Behavior

Once this interaction has run its course, Jessica picks up on her continuing theme, fabricating more silly reports of Davy's behavior. Then Holly requests, in fact demands, that Jessica become her messenger to Davy:

> HOLLY: "Say to him that I love him as a friend, even though he teased me over the year. Tell him that."
> JESSICA: "Alright." Jessica agrees readily and quickly. But then just as quickly, she moves on to another topic, as if by changing the subject, she can insure that Holly will not really remember to ask her to accomplish this mission. "You know what he did once. He wrote you."
> HOLLY: "Oh, Davy, I didn't know he liked me. What else?"
> JESSICA: "He wrote a love note today."
> HOLLY: "Really, where?"
> JESSICA: "On a piece of paper."
> HOLLY: "Tell him, say, 'Where are the notes that say I love you?' and then come up to my classroom, give the notes to

me, and I'll write him a note. But you have to get them
from him first. Ask him, 'Where are the notes that say I
love you?' "
JESSICA: Nervously, "Oh, he wrote them but he threw them
away."

Jessica here has created a potential smoking gun, but she thinks
quickly on her feet to do away with it. In fact, it is so important for
her to destroy this fabrication that she develops a relatively sophisticated line of reasoning to do so. In a teacherish-sounding voice,
she saves herself: "What are these? Davy, you pick them up this
minute and throw them in the trash." Hence Jessica suggests the
evidence once really existed but the teacher herself assured it
would be destroyed. Holly appears to accept this. All the while it is
very difficult to ascertain how seriously Jessica takes this invented
material, or whether either girl truly believes it, or just wishes it
were true, perhaps because it is so exciting:

HOLLY: "Does he really like me?" in a straightforward tone.
JESSICA: Sensing Holly's seriousness, "I think so," with
some tentativeness.
HOLLY: "Does he really? Has he said that he does?"

Holly has suddenly invited Jessica to leave fantasy and join her in
reality, and states that she will define reality to be what Davy says.
Jessica's shift in response to this is also noticeable. Truly responding to Holly's concern, Jessica abandons her former approach,
which has been to feed Holly exciting or positive information, saying "I don't know if he does." After all that has been said, this
admission takes some courage on Jessica's part.
    The girls continue to flirt with (hypothetical) reality, then retreat
back to fantasy—to make leaps forward, then regress. For example,
in response to Holly's later question, "Does he say that he loves
me?" Jessica finally admits, "I don't think so." Although she is risking Holly's disappointment, Jessica senses the need to be realistic,
and somehow has gained the strength to do so. Then, caught in the
web of her own need to keep Holly's attention, she resorts to saying,
"One time he said it under his breath, but he didn't know what he
was saying."
    Jessica is struggling for a way to please Holly while dealing with
something closer to reality, and she also is trying to account for
someone's having said something he or she does not mean. This
accounting is focused ostensibly on Davy, but she herself constantly says things she "doesn't mean." Davy is not portrayed as
lying here. Rather, if Davy (or Jessica) does not say something

clearly out loud, then he (or she) cannot be relied on to mean or be held responsible for what he (she) says. Jessica returns to the safety of fantasy communication, however ("He writes beautiful notes . . ."). And Holly also seems relieved to join her in this game once again ("Really," in a flip tone, "what do they say?").

A little later, however, Jessica emerges again from the fantasy frame to a reality frame, albeit a hypothetical one. "But what will you say if he bumps into you? What if he gives you a kiss? What if he walks by you and gives a kiss?" Here Jessica is entertaining the possible (if remotely so), which she has seldom done in interpersonal contexts. Now it is Holly who cannot deal with this "reality" and so she returns to pure fantasy, and—of course—Jessica is happy to follow:

> HOLLY: "Oh, gosh," in a gushy voice with a big smile. "Does he think about me a lot?"
> JESSICA: "No, but one time he thought about you and did not do his work at all."
> HOLLY: "What did his teacher do?"
> JESSICA: In a teacherish tone of voice, "Go out and do your work. Then come back."
> HOLLY: Pressing, "Did you ever hear him say he loves me?"
> JESSICA: "Yeah," said matter-of-factly.
> HOLLY: "Really?"
> JESSICA: "He tried to kiss the teacher once." Jessica makes a kissing sound.
> HOLLY: "What did she do? Pretend that you are the teacher or Davy."

This marks the first time in the course of their pair therapy that either girl has used role play explicitly and reflectively as a form of communication and problem-solving. The form in which they are using it here requires Level 2 perspective coordination abilities:

> JESSICA: Choosing to take the role of Davy, in a deep sotto voce, "Correct this, teach." She then pauses a second and makes a kissing sound.
> HOLLY: "What did she say?"
> JESSICA: "Go out of here for five years."
> HOLLY: Cheerfully, "Really? Come on."
> JESSICA: "No, five minutes. And do you know what? He never came back. He says now that he loves you. He can't be your friend anymore. He told me that."
> HOLLY: "Oh, come on. First you say he loves me. Then you say he doesn't."

Holly speaks to Jessica here in a natural way. She is dealing with the nature of Jessica's reportage as if she is suddenly now able to acknowledge real contradictions within the actuality of Jessica's reports that she earlier ignored by reverting to complete fantasy. In effect this is good practice, a way each girl can practice normal communication and reality-testing, even if the whole story is a fabrication. It is a context in which neither has ever been before. Neither has ever had a peer with whom she could work through issues of consensual validation, even if that which is being tested, evaluated, and considered is a house of cards.

Holly challenges Jessica in a matter-of-fact way, but it evidently makes Jessica anxious, judging from her next remark ("He went to the bathroom number two, and smudged it all over the teacher's face"). Is this Jessica's idea of humor? More likely she regresses in the face of Holly's direct confrontation, even though Holly did not sound particularly upset. Holly does not even *try* to "reality test" this last remark, but neither does she regress. Rather, she continues her earlier "reasonable" inquiry. Holly: In a firm and steady voice, "Does he love me or not?"

> JESSICA: Possibly as a function of Holly sounding so solid and steady, so serious, "No!"
> HOLLY: Testing the limits, or not being able to bear the definitiveness, "Really?"
> JESSICA: Sensing Holly's disappointment, "A little bit."
> HOLLY: Resolutely, providing her own interpretation, "He can't make up his mind whether he likes me or not."

This last bit of dialogue contains quite sophisticated interpersonal understanding (e.g., "He can't make up his mind"), a level of reciprocal reasoning that suggests that Holly and (perhaps) Jessica do have the social-cognitive capacity (Level 2) that is normative for their age. Holly refuses to return to the more pregenital fantasies, and so brings Jessica back up. Holly feels comfortable with the interpretation that Davy is ambivalent toward her, and can entertain the notion that she is not the only romantic interest in his life:

> HOLLY: "Ask Davy if he likes me as a friend."
> JESSICA: "Okay."
> HOLLY: "Does he think about other girls besides me?"

In this scene, we have seen the beginning of Holly's shift into realistic exploration of Davy's world beyond the fantasized relation to herself. In the weeks that followed, both Holly and Jessica found themselves increasingly able to function at this level. Jessica became a more accurate and observant reporter about Davy, and Holly was able to see him in a more realistic way, to accept that her feelings for him might not have been reciprocated. This development of more-typical early adolescent reality-grounded communication about boy-girl issues took a lot of work on the part of the two girls. At this point they were not yet ready to maintain it for very long.

Macroanalysis of Period Two: Restructuring the Relationship

Now we will place the three foregoing scenes from session thirty-seven into the larger context of the entire course of period two in their therapy. We will play out certain themes of each scene on a macroanalytic level of analysis, using the previous and subsequent history of the pair. This macroanalytic view of the movement of the two girls' interpersonal development will inform our understanding of both the microanalysis of session thirty-seven and the specific forms of Holly and Jessica's growth during this transition period.

Before proceeding with the macroanalysis of general themes in session thirty-seven, it is important to note that there is abundant evidence for at least Level 2 social perspective coordination abilities on the part of both girls. Jessica's ability to "read" Holly is almost uncanny at times. Again and again, she senses what kind of apocryphal information will succeed in pleasing Holly, when it is time to settle down and be more realistic or back off and retreat into fantasy, and in general how she can best meet her own powerful need not to antagonize Holly. (In this last area, her abilities were evident from the very beginning of pair therapy.) In period two she employs with consummate skill her understanding that Holly has a separate subjective reality that she, Jessica, can affect or manipulate. Holly, too, when free of her consuming need to dominate, or escape into fantasy, shows high-level understanding—for example, "He can't make up his mind." And together, they demonstrate Level 2 abilities on the rare occasions when they are able to do something like role play. This evidence of much higher-level capacity than they generally are able to apply is a significant factor in our interpretation of this case. The gap between their social-cognitive competence and their social behavior, which we discussed in chapter 4 when we compared this pair's shared experience to that of Benjy and Ezra, is also typically the case for most clinical pairs, and thus is often a theme in pair therapy and maladaptive social behavior in general.

To begin with scene 1, the principal general theme we observe is the fluid, multitype Level 0 sharing (unreflected upon fantasy, screaming, giggling, and imitation) that resulted in a sense of connection between the girls and, for Jessica, a brief foray into assertiveness toward the therapist. This is consistent with how we have come to expect or hope that the trust and safety established in pair therapy will function, despite the sometimes shocking content, the clearly low level of the sharing, and its maladaptiveness as a permanent way of relating.

Scene 1 also raises several interrelated questions. What was the role of the therapist in this Level 0 to Level 1 restructuring phase? Why was she literally expelled? Why did the girls abandon their home base activity? These questions are extremely important because the restructuring phase of this pair looks quite different than the restructuring phases of the higher-functioning pairs that we will subsequently present, in which the therapist played an extremely active role and the home base activity was a highly visible and ever-present jumping board to higher-level interpersonal negotiation and sharing of experience.

The girls' attitude toward the presence of the therapist in the therapy room changed dramatically with the onset of period two. In period one, the therapist had, on several occasions, offered to leave the therapy room, but the two girls had adamantly refused to allow her to go. Beginning with the second session of period two, the therapist's offer to leave was almost always eagerly accepted. Her physical presence had seemed necessary for the two girls to maintain control during the first treatment period, but during the second period, her psychological presence (and the ease with which she could be reached in the observation room) seemed sufficiently empowering and reassuring for the girls to take the risk of initiating direct and more intimate interactions with each other.

A careful look at the change in the therapist's role from period one to period two reveals something in these girls' dynamics that may or may not apply to other pairs as regressed as they had been. It was Holly, the tyrant, who made the decision that the therapist should leave. She was the one who always vehemently insisted that the therapist not leave before and the one who expelled her later (recall that she slammed the door in the therapist's face and faked a kick at her in scene 1 of session thirty-seven). Jessica merely followed Holly in this decision, sharing in the shutout of the therapist with (Level 0) imitation. From Holly's egocentric perspective, she needed the therapist in period one and Jessica did not count; in period two she needed Jessica and told the therapist to go away.

And recall that Jessica in this scene stated to the therapist, "We were talking about you," immediately switching her attention from Holly to the therapist, first "feeding" Holly when participating in getting the therapist out, then "feeding" the therapist with this lie. Both of these examples point out a dynamic characteristic of both girls: difficulty in dealing with more than one other person at a time—each had a hard enough time relating to one person, much less two.

Indeed, the transition from Level 0 to Level 1 functioning we are describing in this case may be viewed as a transition from externally controlled individual functioning to dyadic, unilateral functioning—that is, to be able to tolerate a genuine sustained interaction with another person, albeit one in which the members of the dyad implicitly agree that one will control and the other will obey in any given interaction. The girls, who could not at first really "relate" to anyone, finally internalized, or held onto, enough control, to set up a twosome they *were* finally able to manage. They needed to control their interaction, to "do it by themselves" (though the therapist really *was* there) because the 0 to 1 transition is a movement from the need for the outside control of impulsivity to more self-controlled, if unilateral, functioning, an empowerment in the most concrete sense.

Giving up the game of Life, which they could not play by themselves, Holly turned their focus instead to her obsession with Davy, which became a new home base activity they *could* share at that point. What is perhaps atypical for many pairs making this transition is the sudden expulsion of the therapist and dropping of the original home base activity. More basic are the common themes of the Level 0 to Level 1 transition implied by these sudden changes— the need for control and the use (and eventual internalization) of the therapist's control to establish safe limits.

Ironically, Holly's tyrannical, Level 1 decision to oust the therapist, so Jessica could feed her fantasies about Davy, stimulated the growth in their relationship in another way because it gave Jessica new status. Holly now needed her, and as Jessica began to feel this, it helped her to assert herself, strengthen her reality testing, and apply her higher-level abilities. Interestingly, the "structure" of Jessica's "We were talking about you" behavior that we cited to illustrate her inability to relate to more than one person at once focused her attention immediately onto the therapist, but the "content," colluding or ganging up with Holly against the therapist in a lie about her, is definitely focused on Holly, indicating the direction in which the relationship is heading.

In scene 2 we begin to see the shift in the girls' power relations as Jessica is able to resist Holly and Holly is able to defer to Jessica in unilateral—rather than impulsive—negotiations around the distribution of the candy bars. In subsequent sessions this negotiation even became reciprocal at times, as was hinted at by Holly's Level 2 "magical piece" gambit in this scene. Holly became able to ask for the candy in a playful and controlled manner. On one occasion, rather than using the more typical and familiar Level 1 threats, demands, or orders, Holly asked Jessica to "Do everything I do," raised her hands, and made a playful grab for Jessica's chocolate pieces.

Jessica was also able to react differently than before. Rather than reacting with either wild screeches or totally will-less abandonment of her claims to her own candy, as in period one, Jessica said, in a controlled and forceful voice, "Stop it, Holly" and pulled back her candy. Although Holly yielded, she proceeded in her playful manner, saying "I'll give you this magic piece of candy [a very small piece] for what you have left." Jessica responded in an other-transforming Level 2 manner that suggested that she understood that her own "force of reason" would be listened to and believed that it would have some effectiveness. She said, "Nope. I already gave you some before, and I want to finish what is left myself." That Holly abided by Jessica's reasoning, rather than responding only to the external control of the therapist or capitulating to her own felt needs, suggests that she also felt more in control and was able to barter and trade with her partner.

Scene 2 contains not only higher-level interpersonal negotiation, but higher-level shared experience as well, illustrating at least two general functions of shared experience. First of all, there seems to be a dialectical interplay between the negotiation and shared experience levels. Jessica's serious question about Holly's feelings ("Do you like him?") directly preceded the first round of Level 1 negotiation around the candy, after which Jessica uncharacteristically initiated more shared experience. After another round of comparatively high-level candy negotiation, Holly reached out to Jessica with her unprecedented question about the length of her tenure at the school. With the firming of the boundaries between the two girls evident in their Level 1 bartering over the chocolate, they were able to then "penetrate" these boundaries with Level 1 shared experience, or at least age-appropriate and open communication. However, Jessica's inability to reciprocate Holly's interest in her life signals that the "interpenetration" characteristic of Level 2 shared experience was beyond them at this point.

A close examination of the microanalytic sequence of interactions in scene 2—from higher-level (1) shared experience to higher-level (1) negotiation to higher-level (1) shared experience to lower-level (0) shared experience—fails to provide enough evidence to make macroanalytic generalizations about whether there is a lock-step process in which either sharing facilitates progress in negotiation or vice versa. However, it does amplify our earlier assertion, which intuitively makes a great deal of sense, that progress on one side of the social regulation continuum facilitates progress on the other.

The drop to primitive (Level 0) sharing at the end of this micro-analytic sequence also dramatically illustrates another function of shared experience, at least at its lower levels—namely, that it provides a pair under stress (here, the anxiety provoked by higher-level open and trusting communication) a safe place to which they can escape or regress.

The theme of scene 3 is one of great leaps forward and great leaps backward in the girls' sharing of experience. The girls were increasingly able to discuss hypothetical reality instead of fantasy in this scene and in subsequent sessions, but their forays into reality remained sandwiched between retreats back to total fantasy. As they began to move toward action in negotiating what kinds of actions Jessica might take on Holly's behalf, they brought things closer to reality, and closer to danger, which they were emotionally not ready to handle, despite their relatively sophisticated perspective coordination abilities.

That they did achieve new heights of sharing in scene 3, however, highlights the striking switch in the quality of the communicative interaction between the two girls from period one to period two. From a state of almost no direct communication between them, they turned exclusively to a setting for communication of shared experience. The communication often involved shared fantasy and seldom focused directly on the relationship between the two girls. Yet, toward the end of period two, the two girls began to share experiences through gossip and even some mutual joking.

For instance, at one point Jessica and Holly began exploring whether Davy was "really" interested in girls. Escaping from the fantasy mode, Jessica said to Holly, in a clearly sarcastic tone of voice, "If he does like girls and the teacher catches him thinking about them, she can get him a Barbie doll to hold." And Holly, building on this idea, responded, "Yeah, a life-size Barbie doll for his very own." There was real humor in this interaction, as confirmed by the girls' simultaneous spontaneous laughter in an all-too-rare moment of "normal," well-regulated (Level 2) affective cooperation. It was clear that they understood that "this is play" (Bateson, 1972) and were enjoying it together.

From time to time as we look at the corrective interpersonal experience that we try to provide to children in pair therapy, we are struck by the way in which some aspect of what is being corrected appears to tie in very closely to what we know from classic clinical theories and approaches. Looking at the Davy obsession from another perspective, we speculate that in addition to becoming the center around which the girls' relationship-building revolved (i.e., the focus of their interpersonal development), it also played an important function in the development of their respective selves, becoming the focus of concomitant intrapsychic development as well. The Davy obsession seemed to become for the girls a joint "transitional object" in Winnicott's (1971) sense, providing a pivot from their psychotic imaginings to the objective world of reality testing, and giving them access to the world of play.

Winnicott regards the transitional object as a key player at a certain stage of the development of the self. Normatively marking the transition from infancy to childhood, the transitional object (often a teddy bear or blanket) provides a developmental way station in a person's movement from a state of illusory omnipotence to a recognition of objective reality and from fusion with the mother to the beginnings of separation and autonomy. Solipsistic subjectivity, which characterized Holly and Jessica's state of being when playing the game of Life in period one, is the natural state of the infant, who feels in control of all the features of the world because of the mother's devotion. The child's relation with a transitional object bridges these two states, giving the child access for the first time to the realm of transitional experiencing, which remains an important realm of human experiencing throughout life. This is the realm of children's play and adults' creativity, an intermediate zone between subjective and objective reality, an extension of transitional phenomena into interaction with physical objects and other people.

Winnicott argues that the transitional object is paradoxical, at once real and symbolic. The child has a relationship to the object, which has an external existence but also an internal meaning insofar as it stands for the idealized mother and the child's relationship with her. The object represents the infant's transition from a state of being merged with the mother to a state of being in relation to the mother as something outside and separate. The transitional object acts as a pivot because, to the extent that it comes to symbolize aspects of the mother, its physical presence soothes the child.

The object is not only the child's first "not-me" possession, but also his or her first "creation": only the child can designate what object possesses the magic power that enables him or her to fall asleep holding it in the absence of the mother. Parents, who intuitively understand the paradox of the object, let the child control the object yet acknowledge its objective existence in the world of other people, thus allocating the object to neither the subjective realm (which is under magical control) nor the objective realm (which is often outside control). The agreement not to challenge the child's special rights and privileges with the object creates the transitional realm and opens up the world of play. When the child eventually internalizes those aspects of the mother that the transitional object symbolizes, then both reality testing and early autonomy become relatively solidly established and the object is given up. The transitional object is neither forgotten nor mourned; it simply loses meaning.

Benjy and Ezra's transitional objects (recall from chapter 4 that both had a "Snoopy" and Benjy also had a "blankey") served an age-appropriate symbolic function, allowing them to both go to sleep "alone" and have "someone" with whom to talk to stay awake. The two four-year-old boys appeared perfectly comfortable with the realm of transitional experiencing, and were capable of sophisticated fantasy play. Holly and Jessica, in contrast, totally lacked the ability to truly play throughout treatment period one and for much of period two. We believe that their ability to play and to perceive objective reality gradually developed because Davy, or rather the idea of Davy, developed into a shared transitional object, an object of their own creation that did everything they wanted it to (like a teddy bear would). It represented a temporary substitute for the therapist/ mother figure. The process of creating the idea of Davy and then recognizing it as "not-me" allowed the girls to internalize aspects of the therapist's role, in particular the rudimentary regulation that they lacked and that the therapist provided with her physical presence in period one. The therapist, in not challenging the girls' fabrications but instead providing a safe context for them to emerge, helped them create the transitional realm, the intermediate area of experiencing to which inner reality (Holly's infatuation with Davy in which Jessica participated) and external reality (Davy didn't know Holly existed) both contribute.

The Davy idea functioned like a typical transitional object in fundamental ways, but lacked one usual feature of age-normatively created ones: it was an idea rather than a physical object. This is because for young children who naturally create these objects, the transition entails both cognitive growth in symbol formation and emotional growth in object relating. Older children and adults with primitive emotional development, who like Holly and Jessica do have relatively age-appropriate cognitive development but who missed the object-relational, emotional side of the Level 0 to Level 1 transition, seem to be able to use fixed ideas rather than concrete "objects" as symbols of the anxiety-reducing aspects of the care-taker representative during the course of effective treatment. We speculate that in at least some Level 0 to Level 1 transitions in pair therapy, children must gain access to transitional experiencing through a created object.

Conclusion

With the case of Holly and Jessica, we have attempted to exemplify in very concrete terms how the study of psychopathology can lead to better understanding of normality. Certainly the case in general, and the session chosen for analysis in particular, are idiosyncratic ones. The choice was deliberate, not so much to shock the reader by the content of the material, but to show how complex any interpersonal relationship really is; to show what normal children and early adolescents have to suppress from their earlier stages; and, by extension, also, we hope, to show the extent to which coping and defending, ego strength and communicative competence, are developed and used by normal children growing up to deal with the powerful inner and interpersonal dynamics that are generated by the tasks of early adolescence.

Although the therapist is not directly involved, we feel the session taken in context shows what she has done to set the stage for and empower such dramatic growth. Also, the session provides a sense of what we consider to be one of the most therapeutic aspects of peer interaction, how peers in sustained interaction can help each other grow socially and emotionally. In trying to make the point that evidence for growth is to be found in this session, we also make the point that the session's meaning depends too on some knowledge of past and future sessions. The reader can, we hope, gain a concrete sense of the ladder of social development these two youngsters can potentially climb, realizing all the while how low on the ladder they are, and how fragile their foothold is.

Just how fragile were their gains? The progress Holly and Jessica made in the last twelve sessions of the year was fairly robust within the pair therapy sessions, but there was little generalization outside this extremely supportive context. Despite their age-appropriate Level 2 social-cognitive capacity, their Level 1 social regulation behaviors remained unconsolidated and, though Level 2 behaviors were in their repertoire at this point, they remained "cutting-edge," available for use only at rare moments in pair therapy sessions. Holly and Jessica rapidly became impulsive with little stress. This lability, the tendency to drop down rapidly and not be able to hang on the higher levels, is a common quality of most troubled children, particularly those with borderline characteristics.

Before concluding, we should attempt to put the issue of Holly and Jessica's "borderline diagnoses" into perspective. Many readers, especially those with extensive clinical experience, may balk at the idea that observations of such children can yield anything that is generalizable to "normal" or only "moderately disturbed" populations. To this skepticism, we would respond first by returning to our original "definition," that these children exhibit a cluster of characteristics, all of which are fluid and uneven in their manifestations, rather than a "hard" or "rigid" diagnostic syndrome, such as mongolism. As such, we regard their behaviors, abilities, and potential as part of a normal continuum or distribution, albeit at one end of the curve. Second, to the extent that any innate or immutable characteristics limit their potential growth, this reality of intrinsic equipment providing bounds for development applies to any and all individuals, and thus what we see they can do within their limits, and how they do it, has meaning that is enlightening for students of normal development. Third, we intuitively sense that the struggles Holly and Jessica go through to feel safe, connect, and grow up are only exaggerated versions of the universal aspects of these same issues for us all.

We have demonstrated, we think, how the microanalysis of two individuals in social interaction with one another can make the nature of the personalities and interpersonal development of each more vivid and clear. In typical clinical case studies, descriptions of individuals (children as well as adults) are often provided through the case write-ups of what these individuals tell to or do with therapists on a one-to-one basis. But these reports are filtered through the selective recall and interpretive processes of the therapist-narrator. Here, we have provided a window into the individual lives of two children through the observation of their *own* interaction. Though certainly not entirely, we to a greater degree let the actors speak for themselves. In essence, we believe that the observation of social interaction, using a case study approach, is a relatively un-cultivated but potentially very fruitful means for gaining an understanding of both the development and deviations of ego func-tioning. Such a method can lead to a set of categories of analysis that are ultimately useful for the description of persons in relationships and hence, as Sullivan would suggest, to individual personality development.

This chapter and the next two are companion pieces, with chil-dren of roughly the same age, but at different points on the developmental ladder. The youngsters in chapters 9 and 10 have an increasingly firmer foothold on social and emotional reality and maturity than Jessica and Holly, as we shall see.

CHAPTER NINE

Forming and Consolidating a Reciprocal Relationship

Arnie and Mitchell are the two friendless early adolescents we met at the very beginning of this book. Remember that as we described them, on the surface, Arnie appears to be obsessed with a desire for autonomy, and Mitchell with a need for intimacy. Prior to treatment each member of a pair often seems to have a primary problem with either intimacy or autonomy. But once in pair therapy the child's problems with both sides of social regulation tend to emerge. Like the rest of our pairs, Arnie and Mitchell had deficits in both developmental lines, functioning at immature levels when negotiating interpersonal conflicts and sharing experience.

Mitchell and Arnie were in pair therapy together for three years. Like Holly and Jessica, these boys progressed as a pair through the phases that we believe generally characterize this form of treatment—from sizing each other up, to establishing dominance and a stable imbalance, and then to restructuring at a higher developmental level. However, Arnie and Mitchell's therapy moved further along in its developmental course, beyond the restructuring to a fifth phase of consolidation.

Although the sequence of the phases is the same as in Holly and Jessica's case, the phases differ in content and form because Arnie and Mitchell are navigating the "1 to 2" rather than the "0 to 1" shift. When we left off their story in the last chapter, Holly and Jessica needed "horizontal" growth to consolidate their newly formed Level 1 social regulation processes, before more "vertical" growth (to a higher level) would have been possible for them. It is at this unilateral level (Level 1) toward which Holly and Jessica were working that Arnie and Mitchell are stuck when we begin their story.

Facilitating the shift from unilateral (Level 1) to reciprocal (Level 2) interpersonal relatability is a particularly common challenge for clinicians who work with preadolescents and early adolescents. Fixation at a unilateral level of functioning, which is characteristic not just of Arnie and Mitchell but of many troubled children, becomes dysfunctional in this age range. Most "normal" children slowly make this transition between ages 7 and 12, even though by early adolescence few have fully navigated it.

We use two new clinical and research techniques to describe the growth of reciprocal social regulation processes in Arnie and Mitchell's relationship during the course of their pair therapy. The first is a theoretical and methodological innovation: a set of "interaction indices" with which to describe changes within and between sessions in key aspects of the social interaction among the therapist and the two boys. A second innovation—one of therapeutic technique rather than empirical analysis—plays an integral role in the subsequent progression of Arnie and Mitchell's relationship beyond restructuring through the phase of consolidation. We call this innovative feature of our clinical practice the "developmental project," a refinement and advancement of the home base activity, discussed earlier in chapter 5.

Contextualizing Social Interaction

When we began to observe the course of Arnie and Mitchell's pair therapy, we wanted to describe the process—the social interactions—through which the pair achieved greater degrees of closeness and collaboration. However, the levels of shared experience and interpersonal negotiation shown in Table 1 failed to fully account for the complexity that every session presented, and seemed inadequate to fully illuminate the relationship-building process of pair therapy. Therefore, we further expanded our method in a hermeneutic direction to more adequately explicate the *meaning* of the social interaction and describe the rich interpersonal context of social interaction in which developmental change takes place (Mischler, 1979).

The weekly, approximately hour-long sessions of Arnie and Mitchell's pair therapy were recorded on videotape and simultaneously observed by two members of our research team through a one-way mirror in the pair therapy room. Each observer focused on one member of the pair, making note of his actions, mood, language, and interests during the session. The observers met with the pair therapist regularly after each session to discuss the interactions and see whether their perspectives matched, whether patterns seen from outside were also visible inside the room. The layout of the pair therapy room is shown in Figure 1. Note that "room" has two meanings in our analyses of social interaction, representing a

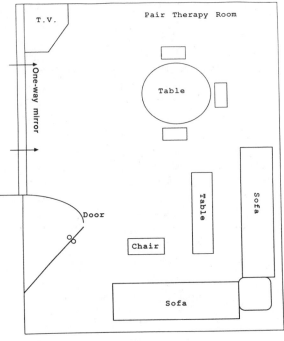

Figure 1

physical space (the room) and a psychological space (as in "room" to grow, or "room" between us, or not enough "room" in this town for both of us).

With this intensive, "triangulated" (three-person) method of observation, we identified a set of "interaction indices" that directed our attention to what seemed to be the most significant aspects of the social interaction in each session. By *interaction* we mean all the "things that are going on" in the pair therapy room, things that reveal persons' existing relation to, ongoing relating with, active creation of, and even intentions regarding their animate and inanimate environment. By *indices* we mean pointers to key aspects of that context, aspects that provide a variety of cues and clues for observers. The six "interaction indices" described below—spacing, pacing, mood, shared history, personal themes, and therapist's acts—point to key aspects of the physical and psychological interaction at a given point in time, and changes in the interaction over time. The interaction indices are not hard and fast categories, but signs or indicators of various aspects of the social environment. They are tools for contextualizing and amplifying a whole spectrum of social regulation, from the most conflict laden interpersonal negotiation to the most intimate shared experience.

Spacing. All three participants in a pair therapy session place themselves at chosen spots in the room and at chosen distances from and orientations toward one another. We believe the resulting physical geometry has a social meaning, on the assumption that changes indicate altered patterns of remoteness or intimacy. In other words, we regard "physical closeness" as not just a metaphor but a necessary (nonverbal) index of the degree of interpersonal comfort, trust, and collaboration in a given interpersonal situation. We have used this index to map a host of physical movements, including altered posture and dyadic and triadic repositionings.

Pacing. In addition to expressing meaning with speech, individuals act and talk in characteristic temporal patterns, including pace, response tempo, and degree of synchrony with others. By pacing we mean how the pair's speech patterns and the verbal content of speech manifest themselves, and the degree to which each actor is attuned to the communicative ability of the other actors. Pacing will vary, of course, depending on circumstances; factors such as social pressure, a dull but inescapable task, or a wish to impress others can alter the speed and harmony of a person's communicative actions. Nonetheless, there is usually a pattern and consistency to the pace or way we talk and act, and how we use feedback from others to modify or regulate the pace.

With the pacing index, we keep track of the distinctive pace set by each participant, as well as "what he said," of similarities and divergences in the boys' verbal orientation and level of comprehension, of discrepancies in communication that may indicate some greater problem, and the odd verbal note that may be a sign of some greater disharmony. In addition to providing a check on verbalized cognitive processes, attention to pacing allows the observer to develop a more refined social-psychological profile of each pair member. After all, words can be used to keep others at bay as well as to invite them toward shared meanings.

Mood. Friends influence each other's emotions. We adopted the index social mood to acknowledge the emotional range, variation, and relatedness of the expressed affect of a pair. In observing Arnie and Mitchell, for example, we wanted to be alert to any way that either boy's feelings modified the interpersonal context. Obviously, strong feelings can be expressed in any number of powerful or exaggerated ways. By the same token, feelings might not get expressed directly or articulated in revealing words: Arnie might show up feeling angry but indicate his mood only through body language or more-stinging-than-usual sarcasm; Mitchell, hurt at some perceived slight, might say nothing at all but withdraw and shut down instead of expressing his feelings.

Shared History. As a pair progresses through the course of treatment, the partners develop a common history and shared memories within the therapeutic context. Often some common background exists as a result of their in-common experiences in the general culture outside pair therapy. Arnie and Mitchell, for example, brought a similar awareness of and interest in G.I. Joe toys and various cartoons and movies to their therapy. However trivial this kind of common knowledge seems to adults, it is the stuff of which many early adolescent friendships are built—at least we believe many would not be initiated without this essential ingredient. Of course, at more sophisticated levels of development, friends evolve their own personal shared recollections. The shared history index was used to point out any instance—sophisticated or naive, stereotyped or idiosyncratic—of such mutual recollection. In particular, we were interested in understanding the extent to which these troubled children had more difficulty in recalling and using previously shared moments or meanings than less beleaguered children do.

Personal Themes. With this index, we looked for individual concerns, (unspoken) interests, or wishes that seemed to be shaping events. So we decided, in effect, to interpret each boy's ongoing preoccupations, sustained interests, fears, or desires. In Arnie's case, for example, much of his time had previously been devoted to elaborating a fantasy world of great destructive power. Occasionally, during the course of treatment, he let the therapist and Mitchell glimpse aspects of this world, where people can be torn apart limb by limb, and there are mutants and monsters and a "bomb of peace" so devastating it can destroy a galaxy. Mitchell, too, used pair therapy to disclose pressing concerns, including an increasingly intense curiosity about sexuality, a strong wish for a friend to pal around with, and, like Arnie, a fantasy life that threatened him with fearful forces. As in the case of mood, we were able to compare our interpretations of certain salient themes—Mitchell's expressed interest in having a friend, for example—to the observations of teachers, counselors, and individual therapists.

Therapist's Acts. This index enabled us to bring into focus what the therapist did to compensate for the boys' poorly developed social skills and regulation processes. There were countless moments in which Arnie and Mitchell clearly lacked the means for mutual social regulation or translation. At these critical moments, the therapist in the linking role provided bridging structures so that the boys' friendship could continue to develop, noting mutual interests or orchestrating otherwise parallel, exclusive discussions with the therapist into mutual conversations. (Note that "therapist's acts" is more of an "action" index than an "interaction" index because it does not describe the children's interaction, which is the primary focus of our developmental analysis. Therefore, in some contexts in this chapter we will refer to five rather than six interaction indices.)

Integrating the Three Analyses

The interaction indices are necessary but not by themselves sufficient to track the (developmental) trajectory of pair therapy. This analytic task is analogous to that of a navigator on a ship at sea trying to plot its course. The navigator is on a ship that is moving on an earth that is turning on its axis and revolving around the sun. Charting the ship's course involves plotting over time a series of positions representing an intersection of latitude and longitude, both of which are triangulated dimensions. Like plotting a ship's course in moving three-dimensional space, describing the trajectory of pair therapy requires triangulation in horizontal and vertical dimensions. There are simultaneous movements (potentially developmental) within and between all three individuals involved, including each boy's and the therapist's individual selves, the pair's relationship, and each boy's relationship with the therapist.

To more fully describe the path of the pair's relationship, we have integrated the interaction indices into our existing empirical methodology. The result is a research method that unites three complementary perspectives on the therapeutic process on successive planes of analysis—that of the individual, the dyad, and the triadic system (Bronfenbrenner, 1979). The first analysis (as briefly reviewed in chapter 1) is that of each child's individual *developmental level* of perspective coordination as manifest through interpersonal understanding. The second (chapters 2 to 4) is that of the relation between developmental level of perspective coordination and each of the two dyadic *social regulation processes*. With the case of Arnie and Mitchell, we integrate a third, hermeneutically informed "systems" perspective: that of *interaction indices*. This analysis addresses social interaction at a systems level, a triadic system comprised of three dyads (child 1-child 2, child 1-adult, child 2-adult).

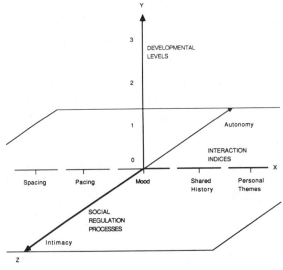

Figure 2

Figure 2 shows how we combined the interaction indices with our two previously developed analyses of developmental level and social regulation processes using a metaphor of "dimensions" of social interaction. We retained our developmental levels (0–3) as the Y axis of a graph and the continuum of social regulation as the Z axis (from autonomy at one extreme to intimacy at the other). We then added the five interaction indices along the horizontal X axis to provide a third dimension for charting the course of pair therapy. As we have arranged them along the X axis, the interaction indices allow for an articulation or specification of interpersonal messages or behaviors on two planes. One plane is formed with the Y (developmental) axis, where the relationships among the interaction indices range from the disconnected, alienated, and remote (low on the Y axis) to the proximate, integrated, and highly involved (high on the Y axis). A second plane is formed with the Z (social regulation) axis, where specific configurations of the interaction indices profile specific points on the social regulation continuum, ranging from extreme forms of intimacy (forward on the Z axis) to extreme manifestations of autonomy (backward on the Z axis).

The Match

Arnie and Mitchell were matched for pair therapy on the basis of a tendency to function at a similar developmental level in opposite orientations as well as other similarities. Both were thirteen and bright, and had interests in fantasy issues, brothers whom they felt functioned better than they themselves did, and tendencies toward suicidal ideation and withdrawal in the face of social "failures." When starting at our school, Arnie was wary and withdrawn while Mitchell was impassive and seemingly vacuous. With time Arnie showed himself capable of witty repartee and exuberant delight, and Mitchell eventually showed a warmth and zany playfulness that belied his apparent passivity. Despite these improvements, Arnie remained liable to devastating downward mood swings, when he would seal himself off with either a stream of verbal hostility or complete withdrawal. And Mitchell's mild manner could veer toward mean-tempered teasing or out-of-control tantruming if he felt deeply stung. Alternately, he would withdraw from contention, retreating to a sulky, walled-off state.

The narratives in the next three sections are selected from sessions across the three years of Arnie and Mitchell's therapy. Period one covers the first three months, from late September until just before Christmas vacation, when the trio—the pair and the therapist—got to know each other and the two boys demonstrated their habitual unilateral pattern of relating. In the first three sessions, the boys sized each other up and established a dominance pattern. Their interpersonal orientations were polarized (with Arnie as the other-transforming partner and Mitchell, the self-transforming one), yet less polarized and rigid than those of Holly and Jessica. A period of stable imbalance in power reigned until the middle of December. Period two marks a transition to greater reciprocity in the boys' interactions in a restructuring phase that lasted until almost the end of the first year. Period three captures a lengthy two years of consolidation.

During each of these periods, our three perspectives registered the therapist hard at work, providing links between Arnie and Mitchell. In fact, the *therapist's acts* was the one index we could count on to be consistently relevant to the ongoing social interaction throughout the course of their pair therapy.

Period One: Phases of "Sizing Up," "Establishing Dominance," and "Stable (Im)Balance of Power"

Arnie's and Mitchell's first session constituted the first developmental phase of pair therapy—getting to know each other in the context of the pair:

In the first meeting (10/22), the therapist acted to define the room in which they were meeting as a safe place. He offered lots of permission to both boys to decide on activities. At the same time, he placed clear limits on hurtful or dangerous possibilities: "I will make sure our time together is safe and that no one gets hurt." He actually provided a physical location for the pair by placing himself at a round table and asking them to join him.

By the middle of the session there was an activity going on, an explanation of "Dungeons and Dragons," carried out at the therapist's suggestion by Arnie, who had brought a tote (a paper bag) full of personal theme items with him. Notably, though, this was only superficially a shared activity. Mitchell's slumped body position, a wall of D and D books rising between the boys as Arnie lectured first from one and then from another, and the brisk unresponsive pace of his explanations, all showed that the boys were occupying the same table but not the same "space."

In this session the boys were in one place together but neither their speech—as shown by Arnie's obscure "Dungeons and Dragons" vocabulary—nor their timing were in any sort of synchrony. Arnie was talking *at* Mitchell, in a one-way (Level 1) fashion. Mitchell had the wilted appearance of someone who was being lectured; Arnie, in turn, looked like a boy who had little experience talking to peers, anxiously raising himself vertically in his chair or rocking back and forth as he dictated instructions.

In sessions two and three, which constituted the phase of "establishing a dominance pattern," there were signs of a different orientation in space, as the pair began to allow itself more of the room:

Mitchell started the 10/29 session by walking about the space. Arnie occupied the table and began building a card house of his own: a place "to live and have a family." The TV set, located in a corner cabinet in the pair therapy room and used for showing videotapes, became an object of Mitchell's interest. The therapist explained how the set operated and who got to use it—and also took the opportunity to say aloud that Arnie and Mitchell "are a pair."

The round table had been their initial spot, their point of introduction. Arnie went on to change the spatial balance of the triad by taking over a large area of this table to build his card house. And just as he affected the geographical balance by his physical position, so he also exerted an uncentering effect on the course of attempted conversation. His pacing was eccentric, fast-paced, jabbing—consisting of one-sided wordplay and quips. Invited by the therapist to join Mitchell in a game of "Sorry," he suggested playing "Unhappy" or "Apologize" instead. In this session, the pace was far too quick and the medium too wordy for Mitchell, who, with the therapist's encouragement, went about setting up a game board. Eventually, a shared game of "Sorry" began, but Arnie only agreed to play from a social and physical distance maintained by his move to the far sofa. Arnie's eccentricity, spatial and conceptual, ensured there would be no closeness.

Here Arnie, by distancing himself from, yet still playing, the board game was using space to help establish his other-transforming role.

The third session (11/5) continued this configuration. The therapist provided essential bridging and interpretive interventions. He had to, since neither the boys' placement nor the pacing of their activity showed much coordination:

Although the boys began this session at the TV together, they rapidly headed off in opposite directions. At the therapist's request, Mitchell dutifully turned off the set and joined him at the round table. Arnie reacted with exaggerated, playful anger to Mitchell's switching off the TV: "Touch it and you die!" Arnie then chose to settle in far across the room on the sofa, while at the table the therapist and Mitchell set up a game of Trivial Pursuit. Like a high-to-low current transformer, the therapist managed to absorb Arnie's fast-paced remarks and reissue them as communications of a sort that Mitchell could handle. Without the therapist's help, communication evidently would have been at a standstill because the boys' pacing was so dissimilar. When, for example, Arnie seemed ready to try a conversational gambit ("You seen 'The Terminator,' Mitchell?"), Mitchell failed to grasp the question rapidly enough and so, before he could respond, Arnie delivered the sarcastic follow-up, "Oh yes, you're too young."

Not in *pacing, spacing, mood,* or *personal themes* were these boys ready to address one another reciprocally. At all times they required the therapist to foster two-way communication. Arnie's spatial orientation (keeping himself at a distance yet making some conversational overtures to Mitchell) and his sarcastic unilateral negotiation style (ordering Mitchell not to touch the TV) suggest that, with his Level 1, *other-transforming role* well established, he was able to respond to the therapist's efforts to connect the boys. And Mitchell's dislike of Arnie's jibes and insults found a new voice through the therapist, as Mitchell turned to the therapist (with Arnie in hearing range) and said, "Tell him to shut up!" to which the therapist responded, "Mitchell, can you tell Arnie his insults hurt your feelings?" Here the therapist not only delivers a message to Arnie that Mitchell was unable to communicate directly, he translates Mitchell's unilateral (Level 1) order into a reciprocal and reflective (Level 2) communication.

Against this background, well into the session, there were signs that these two boys had gained (or perhaps were finally able to use) the capacity for coordinated interchange and sharing of experience when the therapist succeeded in linking them:

> First, Arnie was admiringly impressed by Mitchell's answering a "Trivial Pursuit" question about the location of the Galapagos Islands ("Oh, my God! How did he know that?"), then together the boys—along with the therapist—joined in a surreptitious giggle and shared banter over the meaning of the word "amazia" (a woman without breasts).

By the session of 11/19 Arnie and Mitchell's relationship was entering the "stable imbalance" phase. They began to be able to adopt more central positions instead of the previously described off-balance, wide-spaced configurations:

> Arnie began the hour by choosing his now familiar location, the far sofa, but Mitchell joined Arnie on the sofa, although at the opposite end. And while Arnie read a science fiction book from his omnipresent cache (now in a totebag), Mitchell looked in the bag, found a catalogue of practical joke items, and began to leaf through it.

Clearly, spatial barriers and distance were being tentatively reduced. However, it was still highly uncertain whether the boys would be able to coordinate their *pacing:*

> Directing his voice toward the therapist, Mitchell began to read aloud the one-liner gags from a series of joke buttons that could be ordered from the catalogue. As he read, his performance seemed divorced from an understanding of the words he pronounced. It was as though the process of reading to others felt pleasurable to him, but the meaning of the jokes themselves passed him by. They caught Arnie's attention, though, and therefore allowed all three participants a chance to share information. In fact, the

therapist took advantage of this opportunity to attune communicative competence by patiently explaining to Mitchell the meaning of the button, "I AM NOT GOING TO ARGUE WITH YOU. I WON'T HAVE A BATTLE OF WITS WITH AN UNARMED MAN."

The shared learning and the jokes themselves in this session would be recalled in a more consolidated reciprocal form of shared experience at a later date. But at this point, Mitchell's reading and Arnie's reaction had the feel of a tentative transition from unidirectional (Level 1) to reciprocal (Level 2) forms of connecting. As Mitchell sat on the sofa, facing outward and reading, Arnie did not seek a further distance. Instead, he continued to sit parallel to his pair partner, ostensibly reading his sci-fi book but actually tuned in and able to respond, or at least to editorialize.

A few weeks later (12/11), it was as if Mitchell had taken on some of Arnie's earlier eccentricity and other-transforming style of interacting. In turn, Arnie assumed the cooperative, task-oriented position Mitchell had held until now. This meeting shows both the highest level of social regulation achieved by the pair to that date—and the speed with which it disintegrated when the therapist was no longer available to bridge, modulate, and structure the boys' interaction:

> The session began with Mitchell at the TV. (It was also disrupted later on by the nearly irresistible draw that TV-watching had for him.) At the outset, though, while Arnie looked over a catalogue the therapist had begun a discussion individually with each boy that soon became an easy exchange of shopping lists. As Mitchell got more involved in the discussion, he moved from one side of the couch nearer to Arnie. The therapist, in turn, drew closer into a right-angled position vis-à-vis both boys. The three formed an intimate trio, aligned in space and matched in tempo throughout the length of their discussion.
>
> But then the therapist had reason to be out of the room for approximately five minutes, and he decided to risk leaving, in order to see what would unfold. The boys were charged with the responsibility of setting up a Monopoly game. It turned out to be a responsibility they could not yet handle cooperatively. Arnie, now more interested in social interaction, did begin to unpack the pieces and the board. Mitchell, however, raced immediately for the TV.
>
> When Mitchell charged for the TV set, Arnie was actually initiating a conversational gambit ("Do you play Monopoly at home?"). That interpersonal offering was lost on a

Mitchell intensely fixed on the isolating activity of TV watching. He tried to tune in a specific program and had trouble with the reception. At that point, he called upon Arnie for assistance. This was a purely functional request, however. It was followed by Arnie's making a quick feint at turning off the TV ("This is silly!") in an awkward attempt to indicate that he wanted Mitchell to come over and play Monopoly. He received in reply to this way of asking Mitchell to join him, a threatening, angry reaction ("Cut it out!"). When Arnie approached the TV again ("This is dumb!"), Mitchell spit out angrily, "No!" Don't change it, Arnie!" and under the force of his vehemence Arnie retreated.

Once again, their timing and use of space and language left each boy isolated (in Level 0 and 1 interaction). In what was for Arnie a significant move toward a higher form of intimacy, he offered Mitchell an opportunity to talk about their private lives away from school ("Do you play Monopoly at home?"). Had Mitchell been able to respond to it, or had Arnie been able to be a gentler persuader, this move might have brought the boys to a pattern of reciprocal interchange. Instead of continuing their Level 1 style of unilateral negotiation, they might have shared individual experiences of the same activity with one another. In other words, this was an opportunity for the kind of chumship that Harry Stack Sullivan identified as growth-enhancing. Their earlier coordinated use of *pacing* and *spacing* suggested they were heading in precisely this direction, but at this point it seems that reciprocity could only be achieved with the centralizing presence of the therapist.

Period Two: "Restructuring" from Unilateral to Reciprocal Interaction

In the second group of sessions (from 12/18 to 4/10), we saw the boys becoming more engaged with each other and with the therapist. In this restructuring phase of their therapy, Arnie and Mitchell's use of space became more settled as the right-angled sofas became the usual site for pair activities. Sometimes they shared the space; sometimes it was the site of their conflicts. But their predictable use of the furniture and their physical ease within this chosen corner of the room suggested that the space in some sense belonged to both of them rather than to one or the other. Apparently, Arnie no longer felt he had to protect himself from Mitchell and the therapist by peppering them from afar with unrelenting, rapid-paced verbal salvos that would both keep them at bay and keep the interaction under Arnie's control. Similarly, Mitchell no longer seemed trapped in an inflexible "good-boy" dependent position by the therapist's side. Because both boys widened their area of activity, the interaction indices of *spacing* and *pacing* began to show new, more coordinated patterns. But, of course, without the *therapist's acts* Arnie and Mitchell could not or would not have sustained a short conversation, much less an hour of unstructured companionship (see 12/11):

> The 2/13 session began with a lot of movement through the room. Eventually, the therapist and Arnie sat adjacent to one another, with Arnie on the sofa at the end of the room and the therapist in a side chair at a ninety degree angle to him. It required the therapist's repeated appeals to Mitchell, however, to get him to stop watching the TV and join the pair. Mitchell did join them, but not fully. He chose a seat facing the therapist across the coffee table, a position that put him at some distance from Arnie. Arnie, in turn, sat leafing through a fantasy horror book. In a visible demonstration of openness, his tote (now a wooden wine box strapped with rubberbands) was with him and in view. Mitchell proceeded to pick the Trivial Pursuit gamebook up from the coffee table and begin his own leafing-through. Although the pacing of the pair looked similar, it was in fact not congruent. Mitchell soon expressed this directly, complaining that Arnie never wanted to do what he wanted—say, to play basketball—but only "to sit and read that stuff." The therapist then posed questions about their differing interests in a way that suggested both boys might find compromise possible. At that point, the attention shifted to what Arnie was reading.
>
> Mitchell had changed his position. In effect, he moved into the trio, adopting a chair he placed in front of the side sofa as his perch. In the Trivial Pursuit game they were playing, the therapist supplied clues, cues, and prototypes for answers. He was, indeed, a storehouse of word resources. Mitchell then freely used this resource. As the therapist sounded out a hint, "Ma-chi . . . " (syllables in "International Business Machines"), Mitchell picked up the sound with delight, "Mushies!" When Arnie did not attend immediately to his joke, Mitchell, with heretofore unobserved force—active but controlled and legitimate—purposefully claimed Arnie's attention by calling his name and repeating the joke. Arnie then responded positively.
>
> Further along in the session, Mitchell offered another

sally ("Mr. Fried Egg Day" for "Friday"), and Arnie
hazarded a joke at the expense of the therapist ("If the
question is famous jerks, who played Dr. _____?").
Through his humorous put-down, which may have been
motivated by anger over the therapist's recent vacation,
the boys achieved a shared instant of fun and a moment of
verbal triumph over the relied-upon but dominant adult.

Mitchell's jokes were clearly presented with Arnie in mind.
Although at first Arnie was unresponsive, Mitchell neither wilted
nor raged. Instead, he proved persistent in a modulated way that
soon captured Arnie's attention and interest. Not only did Arnie attend, he actually wound up reciprocating with a form of humor
that matched him and Mitchell against the therapist, who willingly
served as a foil. As a result, the boys had comfortable grounds for
agreement, and Mitchell gained some equality in the relationship.

The session of 4/10 began with both boys in a bad mood and
moved to a crisis point when they got too close for comfort:

At the outset, the three participants took their usual
positions, with Arnie on the sofa that faced the door,
Mitchell joining him to his right, and the therapist across
the coffee table from them in an easy chair. Arnie placed
his tote on the table, lifted the lid, and left the contents
available. The therapist inquired about whether Arnie was
"feeling the effects" of his birthday, as Arnie's teacher had
reported earlier in the day. Mitchell reached into Arnie's
box and pulled out a hand-held miniature synthesizer,
apparently interested in it yet contemptuous in his
comments ("idiotic asshole organ"). Everyone's *pacing*
was off. When Arnie repossessed the synthesizer, Mitchell
turned again to Arnie's box and started rifling through its
contents, "looking for a movie." (Probably this was an
indirect way of saying that what he wanted to do that day
was watch a videomovie on the VCR.) Finally, he settled on
a pack of seeds. He jerked them from the box, yelling
"Watermelon!" in an attention-grabbing, annoying, almost
assaultive way.

Meanwhile, Arnie had started playing the synthesizer,
an instrument that not only has intriguing features (it
can mimic a violin, a flute, etc., and will play two
preprogramed tunes in a variety of ways), but also has
annoying, if not infuriating, features: in any of its modes
the synthesizer produces an edgy, harsh quality of sound.
Its volume can be pulsingly loud, and when one of its
automatic tunes is repeated again and again and again,
the effect on an unwilling listener is that of a faucet

constantly drip, drip, dripping through the night. Arnie's *timing* was syncopated to take full advantage of the irritating possibilities of the synthesizer. He used it to entertain himself in isolation, to drown out Mitchell and the therapist when he didn't want to listen to them, and to tease Mitchell with a provocative and unreachable toy.

As Mitchell went through Arnie's box looking for a movie and complaining there wasn't one, Arnie was playing away on the ever more attractive synthesizer. Then, with a "Let's see," Mitchell grabbed for it. The therapist responded by advising Mitchell to ask for what he wanted ("Try to use words"). But when Mitchell did indeed ask, Arnie blankly refused. Mitchell headed off for the TV in frustrated defeat, and the therapist acknowledged that "walking away" might feel like the only available option.

Clearly, in this situation words were not building an interpersonal system of exchange. At least for Arnie, they amounted to no more than tools to frustrate Mitchell's agenda. Like *spacing, pacing* was being used to act out angry feelings:

The boys continued a parallel struggle. Mitchell created noise with the TV while Arnie created noise with the synthesizer. Arnie engaged the therapist in a guessing game over what instrument the synthesizer was imitating; Mitchell tossed out a question about TV. The question, however, had no clearly intended target since Mitchell did not look at either of the two possible recipients. Only the therapist's efforts to recall Mitchell from the TV set brought the pair into its initial spatial relation again. Once settled in, their ostensible topic was Arnie's birthday. At that point, Mitchell unhelpfully elaborated on the idea of a birthday party in order to suggest that Arnie was the boyfriend of the most socially disparaged girl in their class: "Arnie invited Angela to a sleep-over," he teased.

Arnie largely ignored Mitchell and allowed the synthesizer to play automatically on and on. But the sexual theme Mitchell had initiated continued to play itself out in his actions. At one point he provocatively yelled out "Boner!" And when the therapist remarked that Mitchell seemed to have some thoughts about sex on his mind, Mitchell shouted loudly, "SEX!" All along Mitchell's pace seemed that of a much younger boy, with few attention-getting social gambits other than loud, abrupt moves and shock-value words. Certainly Arnie's unyielding combination of needling and ignoring thwarted Mitchell's quieter, more uncertain ploys. Although undoubtedly Mitchell was contending with both aggressive and sexual impulses, *personal themes* alone did not account for his behavior. His frustrations were clearly exacerbated by Arnie, who maintained focused attention just below or just beyond anywhere Mitchell appeared. When, for example, Mitchell tried to tie into the topic of the synthesizer ("My brother has a big one of those"), and thus take part in a conversation between Arnie and the therapist, Arnie ended the exchange with a quip at Mitchell's expense, the sort of fast-paced joking Mitchell could not sustain. In this exchange Arnie hazarded that Mitchell would only get to bring the synthesizer to school if he "threatened his brother." When the therapist asked, "He'd threaten him?" Arnie snapped back, "With his looks!"

It seems understandable, then, that Mitchell resorted (regressed) to the loud, slapstick style of teasing that was his baseline response. At the same level of indirect boisterous defense, he went on to imitate the sound of the unshared synthesizer. It was as if to say, if I can't *have* the synthesizer, I'll *be* the synthesizer. "He's got the sound down," noted the therapist. But Arnie feigned no interest, insisting on the therapist's continuing a separate conversation with him.

Again, Mitchell approached, asking if he could borrow the *Field and Stream* magazine he had drawn from Arnie's box ("If you're not going to use it, I want to show it to my mother"). Arnie, in response, took the magazine and held it in his hand, in clear sight but out of reach. The boys were still smiling, as if they were merely teasing one another. First Mitchell risked a grab, but Arnie pulled the magazine away, too quick for him. Still smiling, as if this was all just teasing, they began to feint blows with their fists and forearms. Then Arnie hit Mitchell in the eye, not hard, but hard enough to injure Mitchell's pride at least. For a moment neither moved, both boys taken aback and frightened by what had occurred. Then Mitchell kicked Arnie. Again, it was not so hard as to do serious damage, yet too hard to be a joke. At that point, the therapist separated the boys, and both withdrew.

Paradoxically, during this exchange most of the categories we use to track the interaction showed synchronous activity. The boys were coordinated and reciprocal in their *pacing, spacing,* and *mood.* However, the interaction was conflictual rather than harmonious: the jokes here were made at each other's expense. Even

so, to get to this point of overt conflict they had to show characteristics of a level above power-oriented control (Level 1), the kind of
acknowledgment of the other person we have called self-reflective
reciprocity (Level 2). In a kind of inspired pattern of mutual irrita-
tion, Arnie and Mitchell proceeded to rub and rasp on each other's
nerves. They worked on each other until too much closeness produced an overheated state and striking out. They soon reached a
point where, if allowed to proceed, they were likely to either hurt
one another or flee the situation entirely:

> Immediately after Mitchell was struck, the therapist
> moved to intervene. (But as we noted he was not quick
> enough to prevent Mitchell from achieving a retaliatory
> strike, so Arnie too got hurt.) After inflicting some mutual
> pain, both boys retreated. Arnie sat stooped over—almost
> into—his box of personal materials, whereas Mitchell
> headed off for the TV. (If the therapist had permitted it, he
> would have proceeded to tune in a program and tune out
> the situation.) The therapist, therefore, moved decisively,
> changing his own location within the room, shifting to a
> midpoint between the now far-spaced boys. He began a
> therapeutic attempt to convert angry and perhaps guilty
> affect into words.
>   "Mitchell, are you feeling upset now? Arnie, how are you
> feeling?" Notably, in their responses to the therapist's
> invitation to talk, Mitchell's answers were unelaborated
> and muted ("No"), whereas Arnie's were filigreed with
> sarcasm ("No, I'm having a rainbow day!"). These boys
> were locked into a counterpoint of struggle, and their
> *pacing* and chosen *spacing*, although parallel, remained
> identifiably characteristic in orientation.
>   Mitchell, as we have seen, could not ask clearly and
> persistently for what he wanted. Arnie was terrified by the
> movement of aggression from the inner world of fantasy to
> the interpersonal world of reality. At this critical moment,
> the therapist had to draw on eight months of therapeutic
> capital: he had the boys move closer together, at right
> angles on separate couches. Their arousal remained too
> high, however, for them to tolerate this spatial
> arrangement. Arnie took advantage of his clear view of
> Mitchell to target him and shoot off a rubber band. (This
> ambiguous action probably both meant "Let's get back to
> business as usual" and signaled the potential for
> reigniting highly flammable, disorganized feelings.)
>   The therapist physically rose to intervene: "I'm going to
> call this pair session to an end if we can't get back to

normal and figure out what happened." His tone was
neither angered nor panicked, but authoritative and
definite. In a sequence of moves that changed their
configuration in space and altered the trio's timing, the
therapist effectively insisted on becoming the center of
activity—the gravitational point around which conflict
continued, but in a diminishing, increasingly redefined
fashion.

First, he took a position by Arnie on the sofa, which
placed him between the feuding boys. Second, he did not
end the session posthaste, despite his uttered threat, and
he did not insist on an I'm-going-to-get-to-the-bottom-of-
this approach to resolving the situation. As the therapist
sat down, Arnie initiated banter with him in an
exaggerated, aggrieved tone: "Don't sit on my books!" The
therapist responded lightly, then proceeded to test each
boy's capacity to tolerate looking back at what had
happened: "This conflict started when Mitchell asked to
borrow Arnie's *Field and Stream.*" Mitchell interjected, "I
just wanted to show my mother an ad for an inflatable
boat."

At that moment, neither boy had sufficient emotional
flexibility to process the disagreement in depth—for each
it remained a (Level 1) matter of who started it, who
should be blamed, and who should feel guilty. "We do not
need to *blame* anyone," said the therapist, translating the
reasoning to Level 2. But he allowed the subject to simply
fade from view. Sensing tension and the need for an easier
transition, he picked up the disputed *Field and Stream*
and leafed through it, thus signaling his willingness to
drop the matter as long as he was in control. And indeed
he was the central figure at that moment. Things quieted
down, almost as if everyone had taken a time out.

When conversation resumed, it was on a different tack,
with the boys taking turns at grilling the therapist on
contemporary politics. (Neither of them was healed
enough to interact civilly with the other, but they were no
longer in such pain that they could not accept the
therapist's serving as intermediary.) Arnie asked, "Do you
think Clint Eastwood will become president?" And
Mitchell followed with, "Did you vote for President
Reagan?"

Gently but repeatedly throughout the remainder of the
session the therapist tried to help the boys negotiate their
differences. Although too powerful to be ignored, his
influence was gravitational rather than coercive. At one
point Mitchell began to take apart the intercom phone,

and the therapist considered whether to set limits on this behavior but decided, under the circumstances, not to intervene. While Mitchell was absorbed in that activity, the therapist, somewhat on his behalf, asked Arnie if it was possible for Mitchell to examine the *Field and Stream.* "No!" he replied.

"And what's your reason?" "Because he made me mad," Arnie explained. "So you feel like punishing him?" the therapist confirmed. "Is there any way you two could bargain or negotiate about Mitchell's desire to look at the magazine?" Mitchell then turned not to Arnie but to the therapist and asked, "Could I Xerox this advertisement?" "You need to ask Arnie," said the therapist, "but maybe the three of us could go downstairs to use the machine." Because Arnie also wanted to photocopy some material, a compromise began to get worked out. At this juncture, with compromise in the air, the therapist no longer needed to position himself between the boys. He shifted to a chair across from the sofa on which both Arnie and Mitchell were now seated—a move that signified the fight was over and "re-pair" had begun. Although the details of resolution remained to be worked out, the pair had experienced an intense conflict and experienced surviving it.

Because there was so much activity during this session, all the interaction indices, except *shared history* were in the foreground. Much of this activity, however, was conflictual in tone. The boys were using the medium of closeness, but not in ways that promoted mutuality. *Pacing* charted idiosyncrasies in each boy's verbal presentation, and throughout most of this session it was apparent that Arnie and Mitchell were widely separated in *personal themes,* even though they were sharing a negative desire to thwart one another. Although the interaction indices showed no regression back to the utterly unbridgeable private vocabularies of the fall sessions, neither seemed really interested in conversation. Words and timing were used to provoke, with the utterly oppositional boys alternately enticing, teasing, and ignoring each other.

Their *moods* were at a high intensity. Anger and frustration seemed to underlie most of their interactions, which generally had an abrupt, sharp-edged quality. Finally, the anger took direct form when Arnie struck and then was struck by Mitchell; at that point, the slow simmer of the session boiled over. The translation of angry feeling into action did not, however, get rid of it. Instead, the burner merely was turned down once again to simmer, and the boys continued to struggle and snipe. For boys like Mitchell and

Arnie—or any individuals for whom social regulation is so much unfamiliar, untuned machinery—there are bound to be times in the process of moving closer together when the mark is overshot and discomfort at a "too-closeness" for comfort is the outcome. Only the therapist's presence allowed Mitchell and Arnie to stay in the room with one another, and in the end to feel to some degree that they had come through together.

During the latter part of the spring, Mitchell and Arnie once again took up the search for a consistent activity to which they could comfortably turn session after session. After spending a number of sessions viewing VCR movies together, the therapist encouraged them to try something more active—a fantasy-superheroes board game—as their home base activity. Because they had begun their first session with Dungeons and Dragons, it was as if they had traveled full circle during the school year. In the session of 5/6 and in the weeks that followed, the therapist deliberately took on the function of educational facilitator, hoping the boys could increase their capacity for interaction and collaboration if they gained equality in their practical game-playing skills. In these sessions Arnie continually grew impatient with Mitchell's much slower pace of acquiring new information, and the boys' disparity in *pacing* led to conflicts and breakdowns in communication. Mitchell, however, was becoming noticeably more verbal and several times took the risk of expressing his desires and emotions, complaining, for example, that in pairs "We use only Arnie's toys." And Arnie's antagonism and disdain was becoming less hostile and demanding (Level 1) and more controlled and teasing (Level 2). Conflict now had a different outcome than in the session of their fight a month before:

> Again the accusatory words flew back and forth, even
> toward the therapist in the session of 5/6. But this time,
> the word play engendered laughter at one another, with
> both boys falling into silly states. Arnie started to rock
> back and forth, and Mitchell imitated Arnie. At that point,
> the therapist tried to redirect conversation, but Mitchell
> interrupted. He grabbed Arnie's box, flipped it open
> flamboyantly, and declared in talk-show style, "Okay, now
> for the Battle of Wits!"

This *shared history* contribution referred to the interchange far back in the winter, when the therapist had tried to explain the meaning of the joke button. Now Mitchell was reintroducing the phrase, enhanced by his sense of humor and control. The result was that what began as a personal memory became transformed into a social idiom; "battle of wits" became for the triad a symbolic and shared verbal indicator of their collective abilities and mutual history.

Mitchell showed the others he had come a long way. Apparently, Arnie agreed. When at the end of the session the therapist complimented the pair on the way they had played the game, Arnie added his own typically cynical version of mutual congratulations— "Yeah, better than usual." Was it the case, perhaps, that Arnie's retreat afforded Mitchell needed time and space to redefine his status in pairs? Although the session was fraught with discord between the boys, both left it having taken a necessary step toward a higher level of autonomy, a step also necessary for gaining a higher level of intimacy. At the end of period two, it looked as though, however uneven the process, reciprocal persistence was replacing unilateral insistence.

Period Three: Consolidation

In the next period of Arnie's and Mitchell's pair therapy, the role of the home base activity became far more important. Although Arnie and Mitchell did not settle on a home base activity during the first two periods of their therapy, they did try out various activities for one or more sessions, including board games and movies. Such activities focus the interaction, fixing the *spacing* and *pacing* of the pair and moving the rest of the space to the background in a figure/ground relationship. When the chosen activity takes on the qualities of a home base activity, it becomes an even more potent source of influence on the triad's interaction and the course of the therapy. Because the pair is repeatedly "engaged in" a home base activity, it focuses not only the *spacing* and *pacing* of a pair, but also focuses the *mood*, builds the *shared history*, and even brings *personal themes* into closer synchrony. When the role of the home base activity is spelled out in these terms, two arguments are given greater specificity and power: that the interaction indices analysis illuminates this role, showing better how it works, and that the home base activity increases the likelihood the pair will progress along developmental lines of both intimacy and autonomy.

The home base activity that Mitchell and Arnie finally settled on at the very end of their first year of therapy was one with special therapeutic properties. At that time the therapist introduced the pair to a computer game that appealed to each boy's particular preoccupations, and also met the requirements of a special case of the home base activity we have come to call a "developmental project."

The establishment of this developmental project marked a change in the developmental phase of their therapy, from the unstable and fragile restructuring to the consolidation of their newly reciprocal interactions. It also marked a concomitant change in the nature of the *therapist's role.* Just as we have noted that empowering, linking, or enabling seem to characterize the therapist's role in various level-to-level shifts, so too we saw a change in the adult's role as Arnie and Mitchell moved from one developmental phase to the next. His effort switched from the linking of (Level 2) restructuring to the bolstering or harnessing of consolidation.

The Developmental Project

A home base activity ideally provides the pair with repeated contexts for serious negotiations and repeated opportunities for meaningful shared experiences. It is an activity through which the adult therapist can provide challenges, examples, mediation, and other facilitating stimulation to the pair that is above their current level of functioning. That is, the activity needs to be complex enough that it can be "played" or approached at a number of levels. As a result, in a way that is similar to how Griffin and Cole (1984) describe what Vygotsky (1978) called "the zone of proximal development," there is always an area just above the typical level of functioning of the pair available to the therapist to target his efforts.

In some cases, a home base activity can be established that enables the pair members to take crucial steps on behalf of their own development. It then becomes a truly developmental activity— what we call a "developmental project"—in several senses. First, it becomes compelling enough for both partners over a significant period of time that it assumes the properties of a "quest." Second, this level of involvement creates a zone of proximal development between, by, and for the partners themselves. Third, and perhaps most significantly, the activity itself provides a series of developmental challenges of increasing complexity, both socio-emotional and intellectual, to both the pair and each partner. The activity itself has a developmental inner structure that unfolds over time. It challenges the participants increasingly as they become more involved. Such an activity, when the therapist can keep it safe and the partners are deeply drawn in, is an optimal context to foster the development and integration of intimacy and autonomy processes and movement toward a collaborative attitude. Toward the end of their first year in pair therapy together, Arnie and Mitchell became engaged in such an activity.

THE QUEST FOR THE AMULET

When the boys arrived at the pair therapy room, they found a Macintosh Plus computer and the fantasy adventure game Wizardry waiting for them. The boys were familiar with the computer from their classwork, but the software package was new to them. For the next several sessions the therapist functioned primarily as an instructor, acknowledging the necessity to teach the boys to interact with the computer and learn the rules of the game. At the same time he continued to facilitate their interactions with one another. And in Wizardry, interactions become intense. The game became a developmental project not only for the waning sessions of this first year of pair therapy, but consistently (although not during every session) through the second year, making a crucial contribution to this lengthy and necessary consolidation phase.

The interaction indices reflected a social context in period three that was very different than that of the first two periods of Mitchell and Arnie's pair therapy. In the seating arrangement, schematized in Figure 3, the two boys, the therapist, and the computer formed a diamond. Thus, the *spacing* was a very strong and stable configuration that could withstand tremendous stress. The boys' *pacing* was more synchronized, because in order to play this complex game together the boys had to negotiate many decisions and cooperate often, and so they became increasingly motivated to pay attention and listen to each other. The game also helped coordinate their *moods*, as they suffered together the elations, frustrations, and disasters inherent in the playing of the game. The game provided a context for elaborated *shared history* in two senses: they played it together over time, and the game itself had its own unfolding history. The preoccupations of the game displaced the boys' previous preoccupations to a great extent, so that their *personal themes* in these sessions were woven into the game and their inner and outer lives were more unified as they thought about the game together.

To describe how this activity provides a context where the development of both intimacy and autonomy processes can be facilitated for the pair and each of the boys, it is necessary to describe the game itself in some detail. The first step in the game is for the boys to create or develop, between them, six characters. The role of these characters is to master, as a party, a series of ten increasingly complex and hazard-ridden levels of mazes below their castle, going down deeper and deeper into a dungeon. The goal is to capture a magic amulet hidden somewhere in the maze at the tenth level. The forms of the mazes are unknown and invisible. The only part

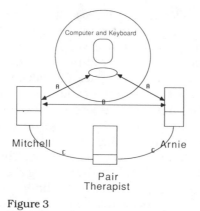

Figure 3

that can be seen on the screen at a given time is an area of several steps around the spot where the party is at the moment.

The various members of the search party have different innate characteristics and functions. Some are Fighters, with greater "degrees" of strength and endurance but lower "degrees" of luck and agility. Others are Mages, with more wisdom but less strength, or Priests, with greater piety, or Thieves, with more luck and agility (better to open booby-trapped treasure chests) but little strength or piety. Cooperatively, all these character traits can be put to good use in the party's quest for the amulet. The longer the team stays together and does not get lost in the mazes or defeated in battle with the antagonists they meet there, the more strength, endurance, piety, wisdom, and the like, their characters develop or acquire. Through successful encounters (battles) with the denizens of the mazes, Fighters get quantitatively stronger. Eventually, with the attainment of enough "experience points," they are qualitatively transformed into Samurai or Lords with greatly enhanced powers. Mages acquire greater wisdom and power, in the form of new spells, the better to befuddle or bewitch enemies or locate the coordinates of where the party is in the maze, should it lose its bearings. Priests may progress to the status of Bishops, with qualitatively greater healing powers (e.g., the power to restore life, rather than merely heal a member of the party injured during a battle). Each member of the team develops through experience.

From a developmental perspective, successfully reaching the deepest level of the maze requires a match between the level of character development of the members of the party (in terms of their developing levels of strength, intelligence, agility, etc.) and the level of complexity of the tasks they must accomplish at each subsequent level of the maze. Only when the players have "experientially acquired" wisdom, weapons, wealth, and strength for their party by winning many battles and mapping the maze at one level are they in a position to take the party to the next. And since each maze level is not simply "quantitatively more difficult" than the previous one, but also "qualitatively more complex," the players of the game must master each maze level completely—and in a "consolidated" manner—before members of the party are "developmentally" ready to go to the next maze level. Impulsive and premature attempts to master deeper levels of the maze, when the search party is not "developmentally ready" or the current maze level is not fully explored and mapped, will lead almost surely to disaster, in the form of battles with opponents with strengths and skills far beyond the abilities of the party or the specter of becoming hopelessly lost in the maze.

Exploring all aspects of a given level of the maze, and systematically mapping each level as the party walks through it, is important to avoid becoming lost, but it is also crucial because there are certain "keys" to success at later levels that must be found at the earlier ones. For example, without the key to the elevator found at level 4, the party will not easily reach level 5, whereas at the previous levels all that was needed to move to the next level was to find the stairs going down deeper into the maze.

One final bit of information is worth noting. Although the quest for the amulet itself lasts many hours (a conservative estimate would be 50), it is not one continuous journey. Multiple trips into and out of the mazes are made, and each trip takes its inevitable toll on the members of the party in injuries, poisonings, or even death. The party must return regularly to the starting point, the castle above the ten levels of mazes, in order to perform certain restorative and character developing functions. Essentially, the castle above the mazes becomes the home base for the party, and hence, symbolically, for the two players. For instance, the party needs to return to the castle hotel on occasion to receive the proper credits for the battles and other experiences they have had, and hence, to develop their party members further. (Indeed, development for each character on the team occurs only at these periods of rest and consolidation in this game—as it well may in the real game of life.) They also go to the castle trading post to spend the acquired gold on weapons and tools that will further protect or assist the characters at deeper levels of the maze. They may even need to go to the temple on the castle grounds to resurrect a poisoned, paralyzed, or incinerated character, a feat that will take much of the party's gold and perhaps even some of their experience points, engendering a possible regression in some characters' competence. Each time the party "comes up for air," to receive the new spells or move to the higher levels of functioning it has earned in a successful expedition, the previously assimilated levels of the maze, initially experienced by the players as perilous or challenging, become more mundane and routine.

As is obvious, the game has certain developmental features that parallel, or even symbolize, processes of socialization and maturation. First, there are hierarchically ordered and qualitatively distinct levels of complexity, for both the characters and the maze environment. Second, there is a need for characters to consolidate skills and achievements at one level before developing competence at the next. Third, in the course of the game, there naturally emerge periods that call for consolidation of the "cutting edge" level or even regression to a lower level of game play. These are features built into the game's internal "structure," whether it is played together or alone. Thus, in a less conscious, but no less meaningful way, the two boys seek character development of the members of their party (interactions A in Figure 3) just as the therapist seeks character development of the members of the pair (interaction C). In both instances the name of the game is the acquisition of new "inner" capabilities through the adaptive processing of "social" experiences. The function of these capabilities is to help the characters (the live ones as well as the electronic ones) to meet life's developmental tasks.

Although the game has a great deal more complexity than just described, we can begin to understand how well it fit with the dynamics of Mitchell and Arnie, both as individuals and as a pair. The rich detail of the fantasy world of the game, the inherent complexities of the techniques, and the excitement of the quest attracted and motivated them very powerfully. And as a "therapeutic task," it challenged them to cooperate and persist at the very least. In addition, now instead of a triadic system, with a pair and a therapist, it became a quartet, with two "game players," a therapist, and a computer with its own strict parameters and a great deal of patience. The therapist functioned for the two boys both as a guide (who had played the game to its completion before) and as a facilitator (who encouraged functioning in a "zone of proximal development"), but he did not lead them directly in their quest for the amulet.

For example, although he knew that carefully mapping each level of the maze was crucial, rather than directing the boys to do so, the therapist briefly modelled this activity and merely suggested that it would be helpful. However, initially neither boy wanted to map, because it took away from the impulsive excitement of the game and generated anxiety by causing them to acknowledge taking the game seriously. But when Arnie and Mitchell were allowed to co-discover through sometimes bitter experience the value of careful mapping, of alternating between mapping and exploring, and of doing both tasks together rather than alone, they experienced an enormous sense of mutual achievement in persistence and self-control.

From a therapeutic perspective, the ways the game fostered interaction between the pair members (interaction B in Figure 3) stimulated and motivated interpersonal development in each. Because the likelihood of success at this game is greatly enhanced if it is played by two (for example, it is difficult to simultaneously explore and map the maze by oneself), the motivation for Arnie and Mitchell to discover and use cooperative techniques was very high. Among the many contexts for negotiating their autonomy were conflicts over which player could use the computer's "mouse" to "walk" the party through the maze, how the gold acquired during a successful expedition would be spent, whether to fight or flee a battle with unfamiliar foes, which spells to cast, or when to return from the maze to the castle for rest, recuperation, and character development. Again and again, the characteristics of the developmental project and the therapist's support were such that Arnie and Mitchell persisted in reaching increasingly reciprocal solutions.

Beyond cooperation and higher-level negotiation, they began to develop something emotionally deeper as well, a sense of mutuality with a peer, fostered by the many hours facing danger, disappointments, decisions, and victories together. Although this game can be played alone, and would still provide many of the same "individual" developmental challenges, the sense of shared experience, consensual validation, and collaboration that was achieved by engaging in the quest as a pair, clearly valuable for most early adolescents, was critical for Arnie and Mitchell's interpersonal development.

During the game the pair often found itself in a situation where a tough decision needed to be made. For example, when the stairway to the next level of the maze was found, the party had to be ready to take the risk and explore the new territory. Also, serious anxiety and panic could be generated by the realization that the party was in a battle over its head or lost somewhere in the maze. At best, these tense decisions or moments of potential panic were situations in which the pair, with some assistance from the therapist, worked out the problem together, and at the same time learned to deal with their own very real feelings. Although panic can lead to the loss of the party and all that it has come to mean to the players, there are often subtle ways out of tough situations that can be perceived if one's mind is not clouded by fear. Over time, they found two heads really were better than one in slowing things down and not acting out of impulse or panic. Thus, on the "good days," an affective "zone of proximal development," as well as an intellectual one, was created.

However, boys like Arnie and Mitchell, who have not had much experience with cooperation, let alone collaboration, particularly in situations where affect is heightened, might not have made the best use of the opportunity to support each other in a positive spirit if left to their own devices. This is where the therapist played an important role, helping the two boys harness their until now fragile working knowledge that a friend can help out in a tough situation and by bolstering a context for their having the experience of a successful two-person endeavor, whether it was a single battle or an extended expedition into the maze.

There are many more general inherent opportunities for shared experience in this developmental project. Any successful expedition into the maze was successful for not just one but both players. Feelings of excitement occurred not alone, but together, and were often shared. On the other hand, there is also always the possibility—indeed for novices, the probability—that a party will become hopelessly lost in the maze or be completely defeated in battle. Thus, they had many occasions of the shared bitterness of defeat (and the subsequent possibility of guilt or blame). The therapist endeavored to help each boy work through these real-life feelings in the interaction, feelings that they had to learn to deal with if they were to achieve more mature levels of intimacy and closeness.

The therapist's goal was to work to help the pair become a partnership, to foster a tempo of mutual social regulation. The therapist was there to facilitate and mediate, both emotionally and intellectually, not to tell them how to win the game. By the same token, the therapist was there to support, provide boundaries for, and ease their interactions, not to solve their conflicts and upsets for them. Following is a summary of the year and a half of Arnie and Mitchell's pair therapy after Wizardry was introduced:

> Initially, Arnie was more proficient at the game than Mitchell. This was clearly evident at the period when the

activity was first being introduced. Mitchell was intimidated not only by the game's inherent complexity, but also by the demanding exactitude of the computer. He had difficulty with the keyboard, with the mouse, and with the general level of precision necessary for computer activities. Often he would allow his frustration to express itself as a rageful disparagement of the "stupid computer," the keyboard of which he would pound in frustration or flee from in dismay. On occasion, he would blame himself for being unable to master some of the basics immediately, for he desired instant proficiency without being willing to expend the personal effort or tolerate the anxiety necessary to obtain it. Arnie on the other hand, was more confident as well as more computer-literate, so he often took the lead. With some wisdom, Mitchell chose to step back on occasion and let Arnie run the game.

Mitchell gained a great deal through observation. At first, he would fall into old interpersonal patterns, barking intrusive orders to Arnie, then when not listened to immediately, withdrawing, pouting, and whining. By the halfway point of the second year, he was feeling comfortable enough with the dynamics of the trio as well as the technical aspects of the activity to use higher-level autonomy skills in his social interactions: to speak for his fair share of computer time and to be constructively involved in decisions and choices. Rather than yelling or screaming, or conversely, not expressing his interests at all, he would more persistently and steadily make his interests known, patiently but insistently repeating his desire to get "on line."

At first, Arnie also used his old interpersonal patterns, insisting that he do the game all alone, that he did not need any help from "a nerd like Mitchell." However, with time, he seemed to learn to feel comfortable working with Mitchell, and could even acknowledge the value of depending on his help. Occasionally, both boys resorted to lower-level forms of negotiation, grabbing or demanding, but most of the time the therapist was able to encourage due process and reciprocity as the medium of negotiation for computer time. This provided a powerful exercise in self-control as well as self-assertion, which by the end of the second year showed signs of being internalized by both boys.

There were, as noted before, setbacks and defeats. The pain and despair each boy suffered early in the beginning of the second year of pair therapy when a party whose quest for the amulet, begun four weeks earlier, was lost in

the maze, was so tangible that neither boy could return to
the game for almost a month, and then only with the
therapist's gentle prodding. But the inherent excitement
and powerful developmental lure of this activity won out,
and throughout the rest of the year, the boys, with greater
patience and wisdom, increased the strength of their new
characters and made progress in the game—and in the
way each dealt with the other. At times the boys
temporarily lost interest in the activity, or became
frustrated by setbacks or lack of obvious progress. At
times, they simply wanted some variety, to take a walk,
visit a store, or celebrate a birthday with a trip to the local
fast-food emporium. But in true home-base fashion, the
quest was always there to fall back on, and it waited
patiently in its floppy disk for them to call it out at the
point where they had left it.

Almost as patiently, the therapist waited. His linking efforts had
long since become less necessary. Harnessing and bolstering, his
primary therapeutic tactics during this consolidation phase, were
on call. Arnie and Mitchell had developed the basic tools of reciprocity, and the therapist was there to help them continue to use
and strengthen them, pulling them up when they started to slip.
Mediation rather than straight translation became his job, as he
facilitated cooperation in potentially competitive situations, helping to keep negotiation and sharing in relative balance.

Beyond Consolidation

It is late in the fall of the third year of pair therapy. As
Mitchell and Arnie walk into the pair therapy room,
Mitchell says, "I'd like to go first on the computer for 15
minutes, then you can have a turn. You can go first next
time if you want." Both boys have brought to the session
snacks of crackers, granola bars, and milk, even though
they know the rule is "no food near the computer." Tacitly,
Arnie agrees to Mitchell's evenly stated request/assertion
by sitting off to the side (on the sofa) eating his snack,
while Mitchell, also without resistance, puts his snack off
to one side (on the coffee table) to have later. As things
have worked out, Mitchell has become increasingly adept
at Wizardry, and concomitantly invested in it. In fact,
much of the therapist's work of the session seems directed
toward helping Mitchell control and look at his feelings of
frustration or anxiety when in a difficult or tense game
situation. "Can you act with more control, Mitchell, when

you get upset?" asks the therapist. Mitchell responds quite undefensively, "I'm just not cool."

At this point in time, Arnie seems less interested in the actual play of the game and more engaged in the camaraderie of the threesome. Over the past several sessions he has taken on the role of "kibitzer." However, after finishing his snack and for a while perusing a magazine left in the room (he no longer brings his cache to each session), Arnie casually begins to engage in the game with Mitchell, giving advice on what spells to cast in specific battles. Finally, after about twenty-five minutes, he asks for his turn on the computer, and though Mitchell is highly engaged, he relinquishes control with equanimity. Unlike Arnie, however, who called out advice from a sofa some distance away, Mitchell maintains his physical closeness, remaining at the round table and reading the "spell-casting manual," actively participating as "under-explorer."

In this session, as in most so far during this third year, processes of negotiation as well as connection function relatively smoothly. This pair has learned to "get along." What they can now do is to work together cooperatively, if not collaboratively, on an activity external to each but of interest to both. What they still do *not* do, as a pair, is turn their attention to their own processes and dynamics. They do little planning for the future or reminiscing about the past. They reveal little of their personal concerns in life. What we do see happening is that Mitchell does begin to look somewhat inside himself, and Arnie cooperates more by default, by not acting scornful or making sarcastic comments. But this pair does not seem ready or interested in moving beyond the consolidation of Level 2 "getting along" to exploring other, more intimate Level 3 issues such as how each feels about the other.

The consolidation phase of the last year—representing horizontal consistency rather than vertical development, consolidation over a range of everyday contexts, practice under the various "playing conditions" provided by the developmental project—is largely accomplished for Arnie and Mitchell. Their ability and inclination to use reciprocal forms of interacting in everyday interactions is not "in consolidation" but "consolidated." What does this look like?

For Arnie, who has returned to public school part-time, things seem to be pretty steady, despite the stresses of this change. For Mitchell, who is preparing for a move to a less restrictive and more challenging school setting at the end of the year, life also appears to be more manageable. They have accomplished a great deal in making a transition to reciprocal relating; and they are friends. They show little inclination at the moment to explore greater intimacy or to begin to test the waters of restructuring toward Level 3 collaborative forms of interaction. Their stability and consolidated state are of course subject to further developmental change, whether regression or progression, as the forthcoming termination comes closer to reality. Were they to remain together in pair therapy, it appears that perhaps natural divergences of interests or nonsynchrony of growth in physical, intellectual, or other areas might well take Arnie and Mitchell farther apart rather than closer together. But what is clear is that within the limitations each brought to pair therapy, significant growth has occurred, growth that these limitations would most likely have prevented them from accomplishing independently, without the support of a created context for this growth.

From a more general perspective, when a pair has accomplished a major transition such as Arnie and Mitchell's, we do not expect further major developmental change to occur very soon. In "natural development," years generally go by between such major transitions. In the case of a corrective interpersonal experience, it seems reasonable to expect some time to elapse before a significant change would begin to take place or before we would see cues that we should begin to attempt to stimulate it. In pair therapy, as in life, prolonged periods of lowered intensity, of rest as it were, would seem to be the norm.

Developmental Levels of Interaction

Before developing the interaction indices, we picked out specific social interactions fitting the definition of either interpersonal negotiation or shared experience, then coded and interpreted them by developmental level. We still omitted, however, much of the stream of social interaction, dichotomizing some of it (into the two extremes at each end of the intimacy/autonomy continuum from negotiation to shared experience) and ignoring the rest (behavior in the middle fitting neither definition).

Our current methodology, informed by all three perspectives (developmental level, type of social regulation, and interaction indices), seems more adequate for describing the social interaction between the members of the triad in the pair therapy sessions than relying solely on the analysis of developmental level and social regulation processes. It is our view that structural-developmental models of the sort we have employed through much of the pair therapy project are basic because they provide a sense of the increasing adequacy and complexity of social development. We are well aware, however, that they have drawbacks. It has been of concern to us, for example, that such models connote an overorderly and unidirectional picture of the growth of interpersonal maturity. Also there is a tendency when guided solely by hierarchical assumptions to see social interactions—which occur in a continuous stream of mutually influenced events—as discrete, individualized units (Gergen and Gergen, 1982; Packer, 1985). Long ago in our pair therapy project we reached the point where it was less helpful only to identify, classify, and aggregate instances of shared experience or interpersonal negotiation as though we were bird watchers compiling a life list ("See, there's a zero, and there's a two, and here's a couple of one's").

Our revised model maintains the traditional developmental vision of increasing psychological complexity without restricting the rich interplay of a therapeutic triad to a uniform, steplike progression. What we try to do, in effect, is to bring our previously established arrangement of levels into conjunction with a continuum of social regulation processes and a set of interaction indices. The result is a loosely worked matrix, an expanded model of development, with less clear-cut boundaries but, we believe, greater depth and texture. In this integration we can now combine levels of the structural approach with the five interaction indices in the following way that is respectful of both developmental and contextual factors.

Spacing. In primitive low-level (0) forms of spacing, persons act without cognizance of each other's physical boundaries or their own physical relations to others. At the next level (1), participants divide space into what's mine and what's yours. Arnie and Mitchell used space in this fashion at the beginning of their pair therapy, with the other-transforming Arnie using extreme distancing and the self-transforming Mitchell using extreme encroachment, not as overt intrusiveness, but simply an unaware "hovering," an unconscious equation of close physical proximity with psychological acceptance by the other. With further development (Level 2), space is not just divided but coordinated, and the orientation of the self in space is toward the other (face to face, or at least side by side), with a tacitly negotiated distance between persons. At the most advanced level (3) in our system, space is experienced as shared. It is an integrated unit (this is *our* room) the ownership and use of which is continually attended to and renegotiated by the pair.

Pacing. At the most primitive level (0), pacing is totally out of synchrony. There is a naive solipsism involving privatized speech on the one hand and an often nonmalicious nonattendance to the other's utterances on the other. At the next level (1), communication is one-way, be it an attempt to share the self's thoughts or negotiate the self's interests. The other is expected to get into synchrony (step) with the self. Little attention is paid to the other's timing or content or reactions. At a higher level (2) pacing involves processes of clarification and explanation in an attempt to make sure the other "gets it" or the self comprehends. Active self and other regulation is evident in the form of the communication (asking questions, clarifying, etc.), and pacing is modified in response to others. A still higher level (3) is manifest in conscious efforts to establish patterns of feedback and response to the other's concerns as well as asserting one's own needs. Fairly well elaborated synchrony is seen between patterns and paces of talking and acting as well as meanings of talking.

Mood. In charting development in social mood, we were looking for instances of consensual validation, self-revelation, and affect expressed unambiguously in words or gestures rather than in veiled, self-protective, ultimately isolating ways. Most primitive (Level 0) is indirect expression of affect or a lack of any reaction to the feelings of the other. Somewhat less isolating (Level 1) is the sense that only one mood is allowed in the room at one time, with no room for other or conflicting feelings. Acknowledgment of the other's feelings is viewed as higher-level (2), and even more advanced development (Level 3) is evident in the motivation to work directly on the feelings of the pair in the room, to see the feelings of one as related to and affecting the feelings of the other, and to see the emotions generated in the therapeutic context as processes that need "tending to."

Shared History. In a pair with a poorly developed (Level 0) shared history or with individuals who cannot use their history, actions take place in a "continual present." There is no historical reference to the past or future. Each session is not only a new interaction but virtually a new relationship. All is up for grabs, and negotiation begins again each session. At a more advanced but still time-bound level (1), we find continuity manifest as the reference to or repetition of past activities ("Can we play that again?" "He got to go first last time!"). This level is followed developmentally (Level 2) by a much more conscious relating of (pointing to) past and present in the service of the continuity of the pair. A sense that "we are a pair because we have done things together" is established. At the most advanced level (3) we see the pair weaving the past, present, and future together. Part of the actual activity of the pair *is* to be historical—to reminisce, recollect, and plan for the future.

Personal Themes. This index can be ranged along a developmental continuum from primitive fears about body integrity and the physical safety of the self (Level 0), to concerns for total power and control (Level 1), to concerns about simple social interactions (Level 2), to social relationship concerns (Level 3). Thus, the self moves developmentally from asking who can destroy or save whom; to who has the power to tell what to whom; to who is doing what to or with whom and who do we like or not like; to how are we getting along, perhaps voiced as, why am I the way I am, or why do I do what I do as compared to others?

In contrast to our previous "critical incident" method, which is analogous to looking for a certain kind of fish and pulling it out of a stream with a net (our definitions of incidents of social regulation), then classifying it within the zoological fish taxonomy (classifying by level), in our current method, we do not "catch" the fish. Instead, we look for shifting patterns of relationships among the fish as they swim past (leveling by interaction indices), at the same time as we make a note of what kind of fish they are (type of social regulation). Both methods then interpret the "fish's" place within the ecosystem of the stream (in our case, within the microgenetic and macrogenetic course of pair therapy). With the earlier "critical incident" method, despite our best hermeneutic intentions, we in a sense decontextualized (typed) an interaction in order to determine its developmental meaning (leveling it) before interpreting it in relation to previous and subsequent interactions (recontextualizing it temporally). With the current method, we come closer to fully contextualizing and including each moment of interaction, by attending to the three perspectives simultaneously. Then we contextualize each moment again in another (temporal) dimension, interpreting it in its microgenetic and macrogenetic context, to yield a *developmental* analysis of social regulation as process rather than product. In effect the interaction indices give us a way to look at the relation between the two types of social regulation that eliminates the false dichotomy between them, reflecting the nature of social regulation as a continuum, and of interpersonal relationships as a complex mixture of the two.

Phases in the Closeness of the Boys' Relationship

Let us look now at how the three perspectives of interaction indices, developmental levels, and social regulation processes can be used to make sense of Arnie and Mitchell's course of pair therapy. Because the interaction indices describe the continuous stream of the triad's interaction, it begins to include more of the whole continuum of social regulation. The perspective provided by the interaction indices illuminates the "middle" ground of social regulation, not just the extremes of negotiation (autonomy) and sharing (intimacy). In so doing, it reveals the progression of the boys' relationship along all three perspectives. As the pair therapy progressed through the phases outlined earlier, the way each boy related changed in *level* (from Level 1 to Level 2), the relative balance of *social regulation processes* in the pair's interaction shifted (from predominantly negotiation to predominantly shared experience to a fluidity in terms of how one type of social regulation fades into the other, i.e., fluidity of movement along the continuum), and the triadic system showed greater synchrony among the *interaction indices.*

Negotiation was the major theme of the early sessions of Arnie and Mitchell's therapy. Arnie assumed the dominant role in the dyad early on, partly because of his faster *pacing* and partly by virtue of the primitive power of his *personal themes,* embodied in his ever-present cache. Arnie was (over)controlling in the first session, dictating his fast-paced Dungeons and Dragons lecture without any apparent consideration of whether Mitchell was comprehending the instructions. Mitchell did not venture to communicate the degree of his (mis)understanding or interest in the game; he simply went along. In the next two sessions, Arnie used *spacing* to establish his dominance. By physically distancing himself from the Sorry, Life, and Trivial Pursuit game boards and the other two game players, he forced them to play the games on his terms, which meant having Mitchell and the therapist physically participate in the game for him (moving his piece, reading all the questions, etc.).

In the "stable imbalance of power" phase of their relationship (e.g., 11/19 of year 1), their unilateral interpersonal negotiations continued to be salient, either dictatorial, or flowing through the perceived authority of the therapist. However, shared experience, albeit at Level 1, began to emerge as a significant aspect of their interactions. These shared interactions were still focused on the present moment, on overt behavior rather than on thoughts or feelings, and originated in the expressions or interests of one of the parties. The physical distance between the boys was reduced in these sessions, and at times they formed an "intimate trio" with the therapist. But when the therapist left the room for a short time (12/11 of year 1), their interaction disintegrated from triadic sharing into low-level, hostile negotiation, showing that the therapist's involvement was necessary for the maintenance of a Level 2 structure.

During this phase Arnie slowly yielded some control, moving both physically and psychologically closer and tolerating occasions when Mitchell set the pace. As with many of the pairs with whom we have worked, once an initial dominance pattern was set (here, Arnie in the ascendant position) and a negotiation style established (mostly Level 1 orders and commands), the pair began to feel safe enough to explore the less familiar and hence more frightening waters of closeness and intimacy.

The next (restructuring) phase of the treatment (e.g., 2/13 of year 1) marked the emergence of shared experience as the major theme of the boys' relationship, as a new ease with reciprocity allowed a more sophisticated synchrony. Changes in both *spacing* and *pacing* brought greater opportunities for shared experience. The pair sat in closer proximity, in arrangements that made them more of a reciprocal unit. For instance, Arnie and Mitchell became able to occupy a single sofa, to read together, and to turn directly toward one another when making comments. As Mitchell felt more comfortable in the relationship, he speeded up his jokes and quips, while Arnie in turn slowed his down, showing greater patience with his partner and greater interest in having Mitchell understand what he had to say. With this new interest in exchange on Arnie's part and new skill in engaging someone else on Mitchell's part, interactions that previously would have veered toward conflict veered toward sharing instead. For example, we saw Mitchell's wordplay during a Trivial Pursuit game evoke Arnie's laughter, with the result that Arnie became engaged voluntarily and went on to make several puns of his own.

Negotiation and consensus still seemed difficult for the boys. Clashes during this period, however, had a more focused, detailed, and specific (less globally undifferentiated) quality than those of the introductory period. Then, defense or disguise of the whole self had seemed to be necessary. Now, in contrast, conflicts occurred when a particular desire or expectation was thwarted. For example, Mitchell became mad at Arnie because Arnie did not want to play Trivial Pursuit or basketball, rather than being outraged at an undifferentiated, oppressive environment of which Arnie was just a nearby feature or convenient symbol. In other words, during these pair sessions *mood* was less diffuse and had more immediacy, specificity, and situation-groundedness than in the preceding period. Emotionally, the boys were more fully present and more willingly self-revealing.

We could not help but notice the tentative nature of Arnie and Mitchell's growth toward friendship, and its oscillating, to-and-fro pattern of development. Although some sessions in this restructuring phase demonstrated to us how the boys came to try out new forms of ease, others reminded us how new and unconsolidated these interactions were.

The session of 4/10 (year 1) was a major crisis of the restructuring phase. The structure of the session was that of intense negotiation—a fight—but the content or theme of the session was that of (attempts at but thwarting of) intimacy and connection. The session ended in a physical configuration much like that at the beginning with both boys sitting close together on a sofa and the therapist facing them across the coffee table from an easy chair. The presumed meaning of their spatial set-up—that a degree of interpersonal comfort could be counted on by all three participants—was challenged in this session, as Mitchell and Arnie learned that the danger of intimacy and closeness is a too-closeness that can feel like intrusion. The boys arrived at blows after thwarted attempts at connection, and the physical pain each inflicted on the other came as somewhat of a surprise.

Until the boys' shocked reaction to the semi-unintentional physical blows, the essence of their teasing was the kind of horseplay that most children engage in all the time. However, these boys were too vulnerable to tolerate the semi-accidental physical conflict. Mitchell and Arnie showed themselves as virtually without options in their anger and frustration with one another. They alternated between passive-aggressive strategies (not listening, not responding, handing a requested article over in a way that caused it to break or tear) and outright aggressive maneuvers. They displaced their original conflict onto a new set of issues or tried forms of withdrawal.

However, through the therapist's careful and caring efforts to "repair" the relationship, both boys showed a willingness to stay and work it out even when enduring some inner turmoil. This was a far cry from those early sessions when Arnie set up physical and psychological barriers to any connection with others and Mitchell was too undifferentiated, disorganized, and diffident to risk venturing out of himself. The pair ended on a note of continuity—physically where it had begun but psychologically a bit beyond: knowing their relationship was close enough to tolerate direct conflict.

After experiencing the crisis of the fight, the pair was less vulnerable to the disorganizing effects of disharmony in a close peer relationship. Although their *pacing* was often still at odds, they were able to "play" with their discord, turning an exchange of accusatory words a month after the fight into an experience of laughter and sharing. An important sign of change for Arnie and

Mitchell was a newfound ability to recall fun they had had together in the past with reciprocal *shared history,* notably, Mitchell's recollection of the "battle of wits" joke. Not only did he recall it, he was able to elaborate the memory with a sophistication that gave the experience a new and deeper meaning. As a result of the boys' new (Level 2) sophistication in regulating their social interaction, the therapist no longer had to coordinate every meaning-laden interaction; the boys began to do this for themselves.

The case just recounted amplifies a thesis: that movement toward attaining methods of relating to others based upon the capacity for mutual collaboration requires the development of both autonomy and intimacy processes. Mitchell could not share experiences with Arnie at a higher level until he felt empowered to negotiate his participation in the developmental project with some sense of equality. He had to feel a strong enough sense of autonomy to be able to express and to defend his own needs and interests in order to feel safe enough to allow himself to get close to Arnie, to share the tragedies and triumphs of the activity. Arnie was not motivated to negotiate conflict at a higher level with Mitchell ("You go first this time, Mitchell; I did the last time," rather than, "Out of my way, nerd") until he could begin to feel some familiarity with Mitchell's perspective, to see Mitchell more fully and completely. To strive for that he needed to be convinced of the positive effects of social interaction. At first this was simply filtered through a defensive structure that could only acknowledge the need for a partner in a unilateral way, someone to assist in playing the game more successfully. But eventually the positive affect associated with this kind of peer interaction stimulated the desire to share experience at a more reciprocal level in a more consistent way.

The Critical Role of the Pair Therapist

By incorporating the continuous stream of interaction, the three-perspective approach also illuminates the transformatory role of the pair therapist in the construction of the boys' relationship. The therapeutic process of pair therapy reflects not only the natural course of the pair's relationship, but also the way this course is challenged and changed by the therapist's intervention—that is, how the relationship gets restructured. In picking out interactions of interpersonal negotiation and shared experience ("catching fish") with our previous "critical incident" method, as described in chapter 2, we focused our attention only on those interactions occurring between the two children; although we ac-

knowledged the therapist's crucial role, we did not explicitly analyze it. With the focus on the whole stream of interaction provided
by the interaction index approach, we need no longer separate out
the dyadic interactions between the boys from what is actually a
triadic relationship comprised of three separate dyadic
relationships.

The integration of the three perspectives provides a powerful
new perspective for both our clinical research and clinical practice.
Each of the three perspectives illuminates distinctive aspects of the
therapist's role and provides the means to specify concrete therapeutic goals.

The *interaction indices* reveal moment-to-moment aspects of
the therapist acts that are effective in facilitating the relationship
between the pair. In the case of Arnie and Mitchell the therapist introduced and shared in activities that provide a shared history. He
tried to modify, match, and clarify moods ("How do you feel
when . . . "). He acted as a pace-setter, slowing Arnie down to
Mitchell's less rapid pacing. He articulated and interpreted personal themes ("You seem to have some thoughts of sex on your mind").
He tried to maintain a communal spacing, at times asking one
partner to join the other, or placing himself between the boys or in a
triangle. By attending to these interaction indices, a therapist can
formulate *immediate goals*, mapping aspects of the social interaction to take advantage of moment-to-moment opportunities for
intervention.

The *social regulation process* perspective shows that the therapist often targeted his efforts at the extreme ends of the
continuum. He facilitated the boys' interpersonal negotiation by
interpreting and translating communications to make them more
understandable and appropriate, and taking control when conflict
became physical or verbally abusive. He similarly fostered shared
experience by linking, repairing, initiating, and managing the
three-way conversations and activities that are critical sources of
sharing. By focusing on the interaction between the regulation
processes, a pair therapist can generate the kind of interplay between them that consolidates functioning at a given level and
readies the pair for movement to the next level. In this way, the social regulation process perspective can provide the therapist with
short-term goals for a pair.

Finally, the third, *developmental level* perspective reveals how
the *long-term goal* of developmental change in the pair's interaction gets reflected in the therapist's acts. Arnie and Mitchell's pair

therapist serves as an interpreter for each of their Level 1 negotiations (Mitchell to therapist: "Tell him to shut up") but translates them to Level 2 communications (therapist to Mitchell: "Can you tell Arnie his insults hurt your feelings?").

It is somewhat artificial, however, to separate the three perspectives when describing the therapist's linking role. It is really the integration of the three perspectives that provides the power of our analysis of the therapist's role in the construction of Mitchell and Arnie's relationship. As the therapist continued to untangle the idiosyncratic twists of each boy's speech and interpret the strategies routed through him into higher-level communication, noticeable changes occurred in the capacity of the pair to pace itself and to choose a mutually recognizable vocabulary. For instance, in the middle of a situation Mitchell seemed to experience as an absolute, irremediable clash of wills (over who got to choose the next movie the boys would watch together), the therapist interpolated a buffering midpoint: "Do we always do what Arnie wants and never what you want? Should we always do what you want and never what he wants—or are there possibilities for compromise?" The therapist continued in this way to serve as translator and pace-setter, presenting opportunities for ease, synchrony, and maturity these boys had rarely if ever experienced. The three perspectives together index the shifting relationship among specific aspects of the triad's social interaction to help us understand what drives growth (maturity and closeness) in the boys' relationship: the development of a triadic system supported by an adult who develops too.

What have we learned from this enterprise, this narrative analysis of almost three year's worth of interactions among Arnie, Mitchell, and their pair therapist? When we began to study this case, we chafed at the limitations of our developmental language of levels of negotiation and shared experience. There is no doubt that a hierarchical arrangement of levels, however flexibly interpreted, tends to pull our thinking about relationships toward the vertical, toward the more adequate and complex but not necessarily the more intimate. Yet what we also wanted to record in the case of Arnie and Mitchell was the closeness dimension—the modifications and nuances of aspects of the physical and interpersonal context that make experience in retrospect solid, synchronous, and fully realized. Our interaction indices, we believe, serve this function, balancing out the abstracting tendency of a universal developmental schema with information that is irreducibly specific and particular. What the method captures, in integrating the interaction indices with developmental levels and social regulation processes, is both the specificity of the interactions emerging moment to moment and their developmental trajectory over time.

We have learned something, we believe, about closeness in interpersonal relationships with the new access to and developmental understanding of interaction along the whole continuum of social regulation provided by the interaction indices. Closeness at any level involves a balance of intimacy and autonomy processes. A relationship without intimacy would have no closeness, regardless of the developmental level of the autonomy processes. Conversely, a relationship, at any level, based on intimacy processes alone would be a kind of bizarre enmeshment. Closeness, marked by a balance of—or, more precisely, a fluidity of movement between—the two poles of social regulation in close relationships, is possible at any level.

We also hope that this now completed phase of the pair therapy project has a practical contribution to make. If, as we believe, our indexical system of interpretation provides a more complete language for discussing therapeutic processes in work with dyads, it may give clinicians a conscious and reflective perspective on their work. What we believe we have done here, in charting small-scale shifts and movements in various aspects of the therapeutic interaction, is to take the practical wisdom of the therapist ("know how") and make it explicit "knowing that," so that it can become a consciously available tool for the therapist. Of course, long before we finished our analysis, this pair therapist had moved "gravitationally" to resolve conflicts, paid attention to the mutual history of the pair to promote a shared identity, and functioned as a "transformer," reworking communications so both children could understand them. Our interaction index method of interpretation does not disclose some new, previously unknown, therapeutic ploy, but it does offer a new way of thinking about moves that may until now have been made intuitively, and therefore without the surety of self-reflection. With the interaction indices, developmental levels, and social regulation continuum in hand, the therapist can walk into subsequent therapeutic situations with a more detailed and powerful way of looking at and understanding what happens.

CHAPTER TEN

Toward Mutuality

The Match

Donna and Brenda were selected as pair partners because of both similarities and differences in their family and psychological histories. Both girls were early adolescents with female siblings currently living in single-parent households, and each had some contact with her father. They also seemed highly in need of maternal affection and support, and had difficulties in separations from their mothers. Both had experienced hospitalizations for their emotional difficulties and did school work that was below their average to above-average capabilities, largely due to the range of social and emotional difficulties they experienced. The strongest argument in favor of Brenda and Donna's entering pair therapy was their sincere desire to have successful peer relationships.

But the two girls also demonstrated striking psychological differences in the ways they related to others and dealt with their own negative or frightening feelings. Donna was almost universally withdrawn and constricted, whereas Brenda when distressed displayed a wide range of extremely volatile behaviors. Brenda liked to be in the limelight, whereas Donna found the smallest beam of attention much too bright. Brenda's predominant interpersonal style was other-transforming; Donna's was overwhelmingly self-transforming.

It was recommended that the therapist for this pair be female, given the girls' sibling issues and relationships with their mothers. In October of Brenda's first year at the school, Donna and Brenda, classmates with the same teacher, enthusiastically agreed to commit themselves to at least one year of pair therapy with each other, and the first session began. At this time, Brenda was just twelve and Donna was eleven and a half. By comparison with the children in the previous two chapters, Brenda and Donna, although they had serious problems, came to pair therapy with greater initial strengths and generally higher-level functioning.

Overview of Three Years of Pair Therapy
Year One: Phases One to Three

Brenda and Donna met together for roughly ninety sessions of pair therapy over three years. Their first year comprised the phases of sizing each other up, establishing a dominance hierarchy, and functioning in a stable imbalance of power. As is common with older or higher-functioning pairs, the first two phases were accomplished almost immediately. The girls knew each other from class, and thus each had a sense of what to expect from the other. Complemented by Donna's habitual submissiveness and Brenda's impulse to control, if possible, the "senses" of each other that they brought to their first session gelled quickly into a dominance pattern with Brenda clearly in complete ascendance.

Negotiations in the first year were primarily at Level 1. Brenda chose a game; Donna played it. Donna did not understand something; she and Brenda both ignored it. There were occasional oscillations to Level 0, largely as a function of Brenda's mood swings. Sharing of experience was not a particularly salient aspect of this year of balance, but clearly the rather tediously low-level tone (not without its stormy moments!) of this year was part of an important building of connection, trust, and safety in the setting and between the girls. The slow progress each was making in school and individual therapy was complemented by the growing dependability they both experienced and constructed in pair therapy. Tacit sharing was identified as an important feature of this year, despite the girls' "failure" to move to higher levels of interacting. One example was that Donna appeared to identify somewhat with Brenda. Brenda dressed in a notably fashionable and carefully coordinated way, and Donna, caring more about her appearance, also began to dress in more feminine attire, particularly stylish blouses.

Their pair therapist functioned in the role we would expect. She kept sessions safe, physically and emotionally, for both partners. Her linking efforts were primarily mediating of the power aspects of Level 1 negotiating, clarifying of unilateral communications, and empowering of both girls when their interactions slipped to Level 0. There was little opportunity for attempts to stimulate restructuring until near the end of this year because both girls seemed to need more than anything else a place where they could "just be," a place where week after week, through art activities, walks to the store, or "bored" games, they could depend on managing to be okay at being who they were, whether angry or withdrawn, assertive or passive.

Year Two: Phase Four Restructuring

Brenda and Donna's second year of pair therapy consisted of a steady restructuring from Level 1 to Level 2. Their therapist from the first year was no longer available, and they began with a new "mentor," again a woman, who had particularly strong skills and experience to bring to two girls who at this point, though functioning far better than they had been, were seen as capable of a great deal more.

As she had in their first year, Brenda began by assuming much of the control of pair therapy. In fact, she quickly began to become exasperated during the activity choice period and say things such as, "It's time for *Donna* to choose," signaling the readiness of one if not both girls for change.

Donna's interactional style this second year began as immediate deference to Brenda and passive compliance to her every suggestion. She seemed somewhat uneasy with Brenda's attempts to "draw her out," especially when playing games, apparently because she was beginning to be able to acknowledge her lack of experience or comprehension. At these times Brenda carefully instructed Donna and waived certain rules, saying "It's only a game."

As time went on and Donna became more proficient at games (and concerned with winning them) and more animated and verbal, Brenda started to "miscount," claim the games were boring, and show considerable ambivalence toward even coming to pair therapy. As Donna began to voice suggestions or requests, Brenda either hesitated to agree or actively ignored Donna.

In addition to controlling the activities during the beginning of this restructuring, Brenda also tended to control the mood of the sessions. Sometimes she would enter announcing, "I'm in a funny mood. I want to laugh." At other times, however, she would come into sessions feeling angry or dejected, deprecate the activities available, and refuse to be easily cajoled out of her dark moods.

But Donna began to be able to show her *own* displeasure, in nonverbal ways, by facial grimaces, silent withdrawal, or tone of voice as she acquiesced to suggestions. She was more easily able to voice disagreements or unwillingness with the adult therapist than with Brenda, but this, too, began to shift. Also, as she had during the first year, Donna seemed to identify with Brenda's difficulty in exerting emotional control. Although Donna would not openly disagree with Brenda, she appeared to be undisturbed by Brenda's volatile emotions. Perhaps Donna vicariously experienced some release of her own suppressed anger and frustration by witnessing

Brenda's emotional outbursts. However, Donna was still only rarely willing for much of this second year to discuss or express her own emotions, or even to ask simple questions stemming from curiosity or lack of comprehension. The stance underlying both these postures seemed to be expressed by a motto Donna mentioned several times that year. When faced with someone or something unpleasant or confusing, Donna claimed, "I just bear with it."

As the second year progressed, Brenda became an increasingly invested, cooperative pair partner. She overcame her initial reaction to Donna's somewhat increased "presence," and better adapted to her partner's still more inhibited manner, not especially expecting a vigorous response from Donna, but alternating among taking advantage, pushing greater decisiveness on Donna, and, as Donna became more assertive, moving over psychologically to make some room for Donna on center stage. Brenda clearly still felt very much in control, though. Even as she pressed Donna to make all the decisions during the hour, Brenda showed satisfaction in this role. During this second year, Brenda also shared more material from her life at home. For example, she clearly enjoyed both Donna's and the therapist's positive responses to her enthusiastic retelling of movies or shows.

Brenda did not display temper tantrums in pair therapy the second year, but did display, although with decreasing frequency, a stormy, grinding inner rage. Early in this second year, this seemed precipitated mostly by events outside the pair hour, but in the middle months it frequently was precipitated by events within the hour, most often by losing in a game. Brenda herself was very aware of these feelings and their impact on others. Once, when annoyed by something one of the school kitchen staff had done, she said she would give her her "face" and scare her to death.

By midway through the second year, a home base activity was established, a competitive board game called Sorry. Although Brenda made no attempt to hide her displeasure when the game did not go her way, she no longer let the disappointment and frustration convert into anger targeted at her game partner, as she had in the first year. This seemed to be partly because the shared activity had acquired a positive value for her that she was not readily willing to sacrifice, but also partly because when Donna won, she did so with what appeared to be a sweet matter-of-factness that turned away wrath and left Brenda room to learn to accept her lot with as much grace as she could muster.

Donna's manner also changed subtly over the second year, shifting from communication with Brenda or the therapist largely through a shrug of the shoulder or a one- or two-word phrase to the use by the year's end of an articulate paragraph, uttered with genuine affect, or a several-minute conversation characterized by mutual give and take. These last conversations occurred mostly when Donna and Brenda joined in a common front about a topic on which they shared the same feelings. In the absence of this naturally derived motivation and support, Donna did not attain such a level of expressiveness, but it was encouraging that with it, she did. As the year progressed, Donna also more consistently made her wishes clear, at first mainly stating what she did not want, but later being able to let the therapist and her partner know what she did want.

By the end of this second year, Donna showed a notable tendency to come into her own during the countless games of Sorry that the girls and the therapist played. At first she made many concessions to Brenda's greater assertiveness. As she became more confident, she began to play the game in a way guided more fully by her own interest. She directed competitive strategies not only at the benign therapist, but also at the potentially rageful Brenda.

By the end of their second year, Brenda and Donna had come a long way. Just as Arnie and Mitchell, aided by their therapist's linking efforts, "learned" to negotiate using Level 2 strategies with awareness of themselves and each other, Brenda and Donna made this transition, too. One difference for the girls was that the triadic relationship among the therapist and the pair partners was in some senses closer. At least, physically they were generally in close proximity to one another around the table, and in the case of this pair, the therapist was an integral part of the long-lived competition of Sorry. From this "closer" position, she played the linking, translating, and mediating roles that support pairs in transition, and in all phases of pair therapy, and "slipped back" to her empowering role when necessary.

As the year progressed, the level of animation, communication, and comfort was clearly higher between the two girls and among the three participants. It seemed clear that consolidation was beginning.

Year Three: Phase Five Consolidation and a New Phase Four Restructuring

Brenda and Donna's third year began on a note of continued familiarity and comfort with Level 2 social regulation. They showed a clear investment in their shared activity and in getting along.

Again and again, the motivation to maintain a tone of cooperation and connection, or perhaps more accurately not to let such a tone be destroyed, moved both Brenda and Donna not to "lose it"—to overcome impulsive anger or passive withdrawal and to work at "keeping it." This investment in pairs, which increasingly overrode the potential or inclination for regression, was manifest in a growing trust as well. Gossip and laughter became more common, as were instances of sharing personal experiences or feelings. Although it was by no means constant, there were clear instances of both girls reaching out to each other and sharing at what could be seen as Level 3, or at the least a readiness for it.

The therapist supported Brenda and Donna's consolidation by helping them to harness their newly found skills, and as time went on she moved to facilitate the beginnings of a restructuring to Level 3. For these girls, the phase five consolidation of Level 2 interaction during this year can be viewed at the same time as a new phase three balance prior to a new phase four restructuring that began toward the end of the year. The therapist's enabling efforts in this nascent transition repeatedly "set the stage" for new forms of conversation for these two socially motivated, if insecure and unstable, girls. "Did you see any good movies this weekend?" "How do you think Donna's feeling about that, Brenda?" "Donna, what finally happened with you and your sister?" "So, what's this story I hear about your class?" Sometimes these "stage-setting" facilitations would fall on deaf ears, as Brenda sulked or Donna hesitated, but with increasing frequency, both girls took advantage of the opportunity provided by these enabling tactics. They slowly began to increase their exploration of the edges of each others' lives, and cautiously reveal to each other some significant features of their own. The girls broke significant new ground with sometimes almost trivial but at other times powerfully moving Level 3 sharing of experience.

In the next section we present four scenes from a session in the spring of this third year. This session illustrates the heights to which two and a half years of building had brought two vulnerable and frightened young women and the role the therapist played in enabling the climb.

Session Seventy-Seven:
An In-depth Inspection

The session we have selected for in-depth analysis is by no means a typical one. It is unusual in both the amount and the quality of the conversation, and it is marked by a relatively great amount of openness, expression of feelings, and intensity, compared to both earlier and later sessions. Our research suggests that such openness is never easy to maintain continually. Yet viewed in a historical context that includes both seventy-six previous and thirteen subsequent sessions, the nature of this session is not particularly surprising—in many ways it was to be expected.

Scene 1

Donna, Brenda, and the therapist enter the room together. Without speaking, the therapist sets up the game, an action predicated on the decision made at the end of the previous session to continue to play Sorry today. Donna shoots a few glances at Brenda as if trying to determine her mood. Donna smiles at Brenda shyly and sits down in her usual seat. Taking her seat, a stone-faced Brenda reaches for the cards and begins to shuffle them:

> THERAPIST: "Who wants what color?"
> BRENDA: Appearing quiet and moody, "Red."
> DONNA: "Who's going first?"
> BRENDA: "Doesn't matter to me."
> DONNA: "I'll go first."

The pair therapist is also trying to determine Brenda's mood. As play begins, Brenda is doing well in the game:

> THERAPIST: To Brenda, "Did you stack that deck?" This is said in a clearly kidding tone. Brenda doesn't answer, and Donna appears tense.
> THERAPIST: Again to Brenda, "How was your weekend?"
> BRENDA: Curtly, with a tinge of annoyance, "Fine." She sends one of the therapist's game pieces back to start, a sometimes optional competitive move.
> BRENDA: With a slightly apologetic sigh, "Sorry." (This is both the name of the move Brenda has just executed on the therapist and a commonly-used expression of sometimes mock regret at executing it.)
> THERAPIST: Resignedly, actually more mock resignation, "I know. I wouldn't expect it any other way." Then to Donna, "How was your weekend?"
> BRENDA: Glumly, to Donna, "It's your move."
> DONNA: "Good. I saw a movie called *Desperately Seeking Susan.* The one with Madonna in it."
> BRENDA: Her mood seeming to change, "Oh! Was it good?"
> DONNA: "Yeah." She is leaning her head on her hand so

that she is facing the therapist and partially blocking out
Brenda.
THERAPIST: "*Desperately Seeking Susan?*" The therapist
repeats the name of the movie with an inquisitive tone.

A three-way discussion of movies continues for a while. When
Brenda asks Donna what the movie was about, Donna looks down
at the game board, making eye contact with neither Brenda nor the
therapist. "Oh, it was about Madonna. . . ." She laughs self-consciously, seemingly having a hard time remembering what the
movie was about. Brenda laughs with her, and Donna continues,
struggling to be articulate:

> DONNA: "Oh, God. Her boyfriend, right? He puts all these
> ads in, right, like 'Desperately seeking Susan'?"
> BRENDA: "Uh, oh."
> DONNA: "And so she goes around and she goes with men
> and then she kills them."

This is actually a misinterpretation of the movie. The Madonna
character does not kill anyone, but is wrongly suspected of the
murder of a man with whom she had been spending time:

> DONNA: "I don't know, but—she takes pictures and all this
> stuff—it's really good, though."
> BRENDA: Now looking at Donna and listening, becoming
> more receptive and responsive, "Oh, my God!"

Donna, as Brenda has become more responsive and animated
about the movie, is now making eye contact with Brenda. Finally,
the therapist asks for clarification:

> THERAPIST: "Who is this character? This main character
> who does these horrendous things?"
> DONNA: "Madonna."
> THERAPIST: "Who is Madonna?"
> DONNA: "She's a singer."

Brenda and Donna exchange glances, as if to say, "She doesn't
know who Madonna is. Incredible!" At this point, a break in the
conversation ensues for about five minutes, while all thee players
return their attention to the game of Sorry. The return to the home
base activity is broken by Donna:

> DONNA: "Let me think . . . what else happened?" (Donna
> uses this "What else?" several times during the session to
> keep a good conversation going or to distract attention
> from an uncomfortable moment in the game.)

BRENDA: "There was a lot of good stuff in *Friday the Thirteenth*, though. I mean, people got up and screamed. Can you believe that? People got up and screamed in the theater!"
Then, simultaneously:
DONNA: "Where did it take place? In a cabin?"
THERAPIST: "What did they scream at? I mean, for instance?"

Brenda looks at the therapist, then at Donna, and decides to answer Donna's question, which she has not heard:

BRENDA: To Donna, "Huh?"
DONNA: "Did it take place in a cabin or in the woods or something?"
BRENDA: "It took place in the woods."
DONNA: Laughing, "Like all of them."
BRENDA: Very animatedly, "I know. It started out with Timmy, the main guy who grew up to be [words unclear]. He was coming out of a dream, and this crazy man, he's digging at Jason's grave. You know that part where they come rushing on with a knife—he stabbed him here and then he stabbed him here [said with a kind of pseudo-revulsion]. It was *disgusting*. Then Jason got up and went to the little boy's face and said, 'Timmy.' It was pouring rain and then Jason went and stabbed him and then he woke up out of his dream sweating to death. That's how it started off."

This is only about one quarter of a long and gory description Brenda gives of the movie.

DONNA: Laughing off and on throughout Brenda's lengthy description, "Oh, God!"

Brenda, although she entered the session in a dark mood, has now, as noted, completely changed her mood and is telling with great enthusiasm and dramatic ability her experience watching *Friday the Thirteenth*. The easy way she talks continues to serve as a role model for Donna. This is one reason why we like to match individuals whose orientations toward interpersonal interaction are complementary. Brenda clearly benefits from this complementarity as well. If she, thriving on having center stage, felt she really had to compete with someone for it, she might find it much harder to come out of her powerful and controlling darker moods.

The videotape also reveals how vulnerable Donna still is. Just after our transcription of this scene ends, Donna is trying very hard to follow Brenda's narrative. She loses track of it and asks a question that reveals to Brenda that she has lost it. She seems to be very embarrassed, apparently ashamed to admit to being lost or confused, and thus demonstrating what it means to experience one's self-esteem as fragile. To repair this breach, the girls retreat once again to the safety of the home base activity. Only about five minutes later, and with the facilitation by the therapist, do they again build another shared experience, as seen in scene 2:

Scene 2

THERAPIST: "You spend a lot of time watching movies on TV, huh?"
DONNA: "Not really. Sometimes, cuz they are usually on late."
BRENDA: "Yeah, everything comes on late."
THERAPIST: "What time do you go to bed?"
DONNA: "I go to bed at 7:00, cuz I get up really early, I get up at 5:00. So I only get to watch movies on weekends. So I have to go to bed at 7:00, cuz I have to wake up so early."
THERAPIST: "Why do you have to wake up so early?"
DONNA: "Go to bed?"
THERAPIST: "No, you go to bed because you have to wake up so early."
DONNA: "Cuz my bus leaves. . . ."
BRENDA: "She lives all the way out in Needham."
DONNA: ". . . Needham."
THERAPIST: "What time does your bus come?"
DONNA: "It comes at 20 past 7:00. I get up at around 5:00."
THERAPIST: "So you have two and a half hours."
BRENDA: "Same time we get up, too. We get up around 5:40, set the alarm."
THERAPIST: "But it takes you over two hours to get ready?"
DONNA: "Not really. Sometimes, though."
THERAPIST: "Sometimes. I mean I wouldn't like that, having to go to bed so early and have to get up so early."
DONNA: "I wake my sister up, and my other sister, too."
THERAPIST: "The one who scratches you and the one who doesn't?"
DONNA: "Yeah."

Donna laughs somewhat nervously, and fidgets. She seems to experience some discomfort at having the therapist's attention focused on her, particularly about her sister's scratching her, an incident she had brought up several weeks earlier, but she manages to carry on. As background to this conversation, we should note that Donna has developed a fairly obsessive pattern of behavior in her daily preparations for school, arising much earlier than is probably necessary and fussing at length over being ready and on time. The therapist knows this and is gently probing in this area. By suggesting that it must be tough to get up so early, she is trying to engage Brenda in the conversation, thereby evoking other possible shared experiences. She turns to Brenda, and begins a discussion about her morning routine. During Brenda's long speech, Donna is looking down, possibly not listening, or possibly privately considering her own morning routine. Finally, Donna interrupts the therapist to become an active and interested partner in the conversation:

> DONNA: "What times does your bus come?"
> BRENDA: "Exactly 8:00 o'clock every morning. Exactly 8:00 o'clock every morning."
> THERAPIST: To Donna, "Yours comes before that?"
> DONNA: "Yeah."
> THERAPIST: "It's a nuisance to live very far away."
> BRENDA: "They changed the bus schedule now. They changed some of the kids on Somerville buses. Talinda is on my bus. Talinda is on my bus, Pamela is on my bus. UGH!"
> THERAPIST: "You don't like Pamela?"

Brenda then launches into a long monologue, standing up and imitating Pamela's walking and talking in a mocking and entertaining way ("She's doofy. I mean you can act doofy sometimes, but she overdo it, you know?"). Donna listens attentively and a two-way discussion ensues between the girls. As Brenda describes Pamela's fabrication about a boy wanting to marry her, Donna gets very involved with the story and interjects comments ("She's probably making up a lot of it." "Oh, my God!"). It is hard to be sure if Donna is just interested or also shocked, but in any case, she is clearly hearing stories here of a new sort for her. Not only does Brenda model more expressive and confident behavior, but she is less protected and more sophisticated, and so teaches Donna more about "life." Brenda continues to tell another story about Pamela:

> BRENDA: "I say, 'You overdoing it!' and she say, you know, last year, she paid fifty dollars just to go out with Lance. You know Lance?"

Here Brenda says something derogatory about Lance, which is inaudible. Brenda is clearly enjoying telling her story, and the therapist interjects several probing questions ("Where did she get fifty dollars?" "What's so wonderful about Lance?" "I don't know Lance at all. Doesn't he have a nice personality?"). The therapist continues:

> THERAPIST: "Well, I tell you. You got to watch out for guys like Lance who will take fifty dollars."
> BRENDA: "He got dukes in his pants. Ughhh!!! He got dukes in his pants."
> DONNA: "What's that?" Here Donna overcomes her shyness to say that she doesn't understand what Brenda means.
> BRENDA: "Doodoo." She laughs, and Donna throws back her head and laughs hard.
> THERAPIST: "Poor Lance. If he knew what was being said about him."
> BRENDA: "It's true. That's disgusting! He be sittin' on it. Eeewww!!"
> THERAPIST: "Let's hope he doesn't sit on it too long. Let's hope sometimes he goes and cleans it up."

Donna, during all this, is enjoying the story about Lance, and laughs, not nervously, but heartily, especially when Brenda screeches, somewhat gleefully, "That's disgusting!":

> BRENDA: "Somebody come up to him and say he got doodoo."
> THERAPIST: "You know there are some kids who can't control it."

Donna ignores the therapist's comment, and mentions Bobby, another classmate who soils. Talking about the kids in their class is a topic on which she and Brenda are together, and both she and Brenda want to keep it going. Brenda continues with a rendition of Talinda's reactions to Bobby's soiling and their teacher's handling of the situation. Donna joins Brenda in trying to explain how it is to an adult who does not understand, and she also gives a lively and cutting imitation of how the teacher deals with the problem:

> BRENDA: "I know, I mean, sometimes, you know, she [the teacher] wants to laugh, and she'll laugh like if you keep doing it. It gonna make her laugh. Keep on doing it, you know what I'm saying?"
> THERAPIST: "Well, laugh or no laugh, you could still send the kid up to change and clean up."
> DONNA: "No."
> BRENDA: "But the thing is, she don't want to 'hurt his feelings!'" Here she uses a mocking tone as she imitates the teacher's word and cadence, but then adds, more seriously, "You know, I mean, I can understand that. You

can't go up to a kid and say, 'Could you go upstairs and get
washed up, please?' I mean. . . ." Donna laughs.
THERAPIST: "Oh, yes you can." This is said authoritatively.
BRENDA: "No, you can't," Brenda interrupts.
THERAPIST: "You don't say it in front of the whole class. You
take him out and you. . . . "
BRENDA: "No."
THERAPIST: "Because if you don't, then the kids are going
to do what Talinda does."

Donna and Brenda ignore the therapist's comment. Donna goes
on, initiating the telling of a funny, hypothetical scene where
"You'd go up to a kid and go kksshhh," spraying Lysol. Brenda
laughs at this. Donna is now very loose—having a great time, really
"cracking up":

BRENDA: "Today we were playing basketball, right? So me
and Bobby [the boy who soils] had a basketball and we
both fell and rolled over, and I went 'Eww! Eww!' like this,
right, and Donald say, 'Time out, time out!' and I said,
'Oh, my God!' It was so funny, I went like this (scrunching
up her face to indicate how bad it smells), and like it was
gonna kill me, and I kept laughing. I kept laughing. I had
to stop for a little while. I am serious. I was like—oh my
God, what is going on?! And I was laughing and Donald—
I had to talk to Donald 'cuz Bobby felt bad, and everything.
And I was going 'Ewww! Time out, time out,' like that. Oh,
my God!!"

Brenda laughs while she tells the story, and at one point gets up
again, walking around in a circle. Donna laughs really hard at
Brenda's story. The more animated Brenda becomes, the more
Donna laughs. The more Donna laughs, the more animated Brenda becomes:

THERAPIST: Without putting a damper on the shared
hilarity, nor making the girls feel bad, the therapist
quietly sticks to her earlier point, clarifying in a kind and
supportive way. "So Bobby felt bad. I mean, that's why it's
better to send Bobby up very quietly than to let it happen
that the other kids are gonna make fun of him."

Eventually, the conversation dwindles and, again via therapist
intervention, a third scene begins:

Scene 3

THERAPIST: "Well, I have certainly learned more about some
of the kids in the Manville School than I knew before."

BRENDA: "Sure have." Implicit here is ". . . and we are the ones who told you."
THERAPIST: "And before this year, you had Miss A., right?"
BRENDA: Excited, "Oh, she was the best!" [This was a teacher to whom Brenda was very attached.]
DONNA: "I had her two years. She was nice."
BRENDA: "I love her."
DONNA: "In Miss M.'s class, you don't learn nothing."
THERAPIST: "I don't believe that."
BRENDA: Agreeing with Donna, "Oh, I know, I swear on my Bible! You know how much math I have learned this past year?" This is said in a tone of voice suggesting she has learned very little.
DONNA: "What did you learn?" The girls are banding together here again to educate the therapist about how it really is, to ostensibly criticize their present teacher, but more significantly to grieve the loss of the well-liked teacher from the year before.
BRENDA: "Division—everything. And you know something? Every time we're ready to review, I forget what to do."
THERAPIST: "This year?"
BRENDA: "I am not lying. Yes, everything she ever done or like reading or something or like [unintelligible], you know, like from before, she reviews it back to me like in a couple of months, and I forget."
DONNA: "It's so embarrassing telling people that you don't even know fractions."
THERAPIST: "But you know once you learn decimals, you can transfer them to fractions really easily. But the thing is, you've got to really know decimals."

As the three-way conversation continues, Donna and Brenda have both stuck their cups on the ends of their soda cans, most likely without being even aware that they are sharing experience at this level as well. Donna animatedly uses hers to emphasize her point:

DONNA: "When I go back to public school, right, I will have to stay back two years, because of my work. I'll be in sixth grade, because I was supposed to be in seventh grade this year and next year I'll be in eighth."
BRENDA: During Donna's speech, supportively, "Yeah," and then "Yup, it's true."
THERAPIST: To Donna, "Right. When you first came here, had you been in public school and came directly here?"
DONNA: "Yeah."

BRENDA: "Same with me."

DONNA: Pausing for a critical moment, and then adding, "I went on over to this other place, and they didn't have any schooling, and so I was there for two years." (This was the hospital psychiatric ward mentioned earlier.)

THERAPIST: "I see, so you missed out. I see."

DONNA: "It was like . . . how many years? I was there for two years, then I came over here for two years. This is my third year." (Donna's information is incorrect about the numbers and years, but not about what has happened to her.)

THERAPIST: "So when you came here you had two years to catch up? OK, now I understand."

DONNA: "But we had a tutor there."

BRENDA: "When I was in public school, right. . . ."

THERAPIST: "Did you come from public school?"

DONNA: "Did you come directly . . . "

BRENDA: "Yeah. See I was in public school, but because of my allergies I used to get sick, so I quit school almost for a whole year, and I had to have a tutor."

THERAPIST: "So you missed a year or two."

DONNA: "Yeah, I had a tutor, too."

BRENDA: "The tutor came to my house and gave me work, and after that I went back to school and I had a problem with my behavior. And I had a fight with one of my teachers and I actually—she pushed me on the ground and I bit her on the foot. I was really mad."

Donna laughs at "I bit her on the foot." She is resting her chin on the cup so as to be more at a level of eye contact with Brenda:

BRENDA: "I was really mad. I had to do something to get her back, so I bit her on the foot."

Donna laughs again at "I bit her on the foot," this time looking at the therapist, perhaps for her reaction. Every time Brenda mentions the foot-biting incident, Donna laughs, so Brenda keeps repeating "I bit her on the foot":

BRENDA: "Then I had to go see my doctor and get a shot for it, and I went back to school. Then I came here because of that. . . . No, I had therapy then, right, and after I bit my teacher on the foot." Both girls laugh.

THERAPIST: "Oh, you had therapy over it, right? Yeah, I know it's funny when you look back on it. It wasn't funny then."

BRENDA: "After I bit my teacher on the foot. . . ." Brenda pauses, as if to give Donna her cue to laugh, which she does, as Brenda herself does . ". . . they gave me therapy.

[Unintelligible sentence]. I never knew nothing about this place. And I was real mad and I was angry at myself, so I wanted to go for suicide, right? So they put me up here on a unit [an inpatient child/adolescent psychiatric unit], then they sent me back to public school for one more year. Then after that, they told me I was coming to this school."

Brenda talks about her suicidal feelings very matter-of-factly, like a story that has been frequently told. In fact, this is one of the first times she has ever spontaneously revealed this part of her life.

Almost immediately after this discussion, the fourth and last scene ensues in which the girls broach the often frightening and difficult subject of their futures.

Scene 4

DONNA: "You know, this [next] Wednesday I have to go like for an interview or something—not like a interview, but I have to get some testing done, so I won't be coming."
BRENDA: Expressing disappointment (for this means they will miss their next session), "Oh, my God!" It also indicates that Donna may actually leave the school in the near future.
DONNA: Laughing nervously in acknowledgment of Brenda's disappointment, "Yeah. Like you know, have you ever done testing where you look at these pictures and you say what they are about and things, and so I'm gonna talk to them about public school next year."
BRENDA: "Yeah. When I first came here to get an interview over the summer with Mr. B.—it was so stupid!! As soon as I came into his office, he just sitting there like that."

She is half imitating, half mocking the school principal, Mr. B. Donna and Brenda both describe their interview experiences with the principal, continuing to imitate him. During the following exchange Donna and Brenda talk directly to each other:

BRENDA: "Then you know, he just kept going like that and what else am I supposed to say? He just looked dead in my face after I finished my sentence, he's like—'So what is your problem?' You know, stuff like that. I'm like, 'What are you talkin' about?' "
DONNA: "I hope I'm not here next year in upper school." (Both girls are in the last year of middle school. Upper school is roughly equivalent to junior high school.)
THERAPIST: "Why?"
BRENDA: "I know about upper school next year."

DONNA: "I don't like the upper school."
BRENDA: "Jason is down there. Lance is down there."
(Down there refers to the fact that the upper school is on a lower floor than the girl's current classroom.)
DONNA: "He [Jason] likes me and I hate him. If he ever comes near me, I swear I'm gonna punch that boy right in the face."

She emphasizes this with the soda cans and cups. She is completely animated and unselfconscious, a far cry from the frozen, timid girl who in earlier sessions would not even make eye contact:

THERAPIST: "Who are you gonna punch in the face?" Then to Brenda, "Who did she say?"

Donna and Brenda look at each other in mutual understanding that neither will tell whom she said:

DONNA: "Don't worry."
THERAPIST: "I'm not worried. I'm just curious who you are gonna punch in the face."
DONNA: "Nobody, Forget it."
THERAPIST: "Oh, alright."
BRENDA: "[Unintelligible] is gonna be there."
DONNA: "I don't like him," comfortably asserting her opinion.
BRENDA: "Danny is gonna be there. Lance is gonna be there. Tony is gonna leave. Praise God almighty, he is gonna leave."
THERAPIST: "You don't know who is gonna be here and who is not gonna be here."
BRENDA: "Yessir, they told me already."
THERAPIST: "Some kids may not be here. They may be moving."
BRENDA: "[Inaudible sentence.] Two years, two years, and one [unintelligible]."
THERAPIST: "No way. No way."
BRENDA: Strongly asserting her point, that she is right, "Yessir, that's what Mr. B. told me."
THERAPIST: "What, at the upper school?"
BRENDA: "No, he said if you are here for two years, then you go right directly to the upper school."
THERAPIST: "Oh, you are going to the upper school. So you are going to the upper school next year. But you don't know which upper school kids are gonna still be there. That's what I'm saying."

Brenda starts whining, groaning, and walking around. The therapist thinks she is imitating someone:

> THERAPIST: "Who is that?"
> BRENDA: Indifferently, "Nobody."
> THERAPIST: "I thought it was an upper school kid. Anyway. . . ."
> DONNA: To Brenda looking at her sincerely, "I hope you're in my class, though."

Brenda looks at Donna, and nods affirmatively, seconding and reciprocating Donna's expression of friendship. Brenda starts imitating again, walking around like Abby:

> BRENDA: "Here's Abby."
> DONNA: Attempting to keep this going, "Who else? Who else? Do an imitation of. . . ."
> THERAPIST: Joining in thinking of someone for Brenda to imitate, "Upper school, upper school. . . ."
> BRENDA: "Pamela! Pamela!" Donna laughs.
> THERAPIST: "I'm gonna have to stop." She is indicating that the session time is up.
> BRENDA: Imitating Pamela, "She [Pamela] always comes up to me like 'Hi, Bren! What you doing now, Bren?'"
> DONNA: "She always does that."
> BRENDA: "Oh, shut up," this being what Brenda says, or would like to say, to Pamela. Donna laughs at this.
> THERAPIST: "Doug is in the upper school."
> BRENDA: "Eewww, he's a faggot! Ugh, ugh, ugh. . . ."
> THERAPIST: "Is there anybody who is. . . ."
> BRENDA: Interrupting, "Everybody's mental in that school."
> THERAPIST: "Everybody's mental? I don't think so."
> DONNA: "I wish I didn't have to go [to the upper school]."
> BRENDA: "I know."
> DONNA: "Probably will."
> BRENDA: "I know. No doubt about it."
> DONNA: Getting ready to leave the session, to the therapist, "You want the [soda] cans?"
> BRENDA: Annoyed, to the therapist who saves the cans after each session, "You always want the stupid cans."
> THERAPIST: "I'll see you next Monday. We'll go on with this conversation. It's fascinating."

Microanalysis of Session Seventy-Seven
The "2 to 3" Transition

Session seventy-seven is by no means a typical or representative one. Compared to most other sessions, it is uncommonly rich in instances of shared experience and somewhat uncharacteristically lacking in explicit instances of interpersonal negotiation. How are we to understand the relative lack of interpersonal negotiation in this session? In part it can be attributed to the phase of Donna and Brenda's pair therapy. To the extent that this period was still a part of a phase of consolidation of Level 2 interaction and a new phase of balance, we would have expected equal amounts of negotiation and sharing, intimacy and autonomy. However, this session was part of a period of sometimes dramatic, although not unexpected, initiation of a new restructuring, a phase often marked at all developmental levels by an ascendance of shared experience. Furthermore, the unusually large quantity of shared experience in this session seems related to a particular quality of the transition from reciprocal Level 2 to collaborative Level 3 interaction, which seems to require a much greater degree of intimacy than transitions at lower levels.

We believe that the qualitative "great leap forward" of Level 3 interaction is often first reached through intense *conversation*. Conversation falls on the intimacy side of the social regulation continuum. Usually, it is first manifest as reciprocal (Level 2) interchange about relatively objective experiences of the self and others. Much of Brenda and Donna's discussion of movies and gossip about classmates in this session and others represented this kind of Level 2 conversation. Collaborative (Level 3) conversation goes beyond this mere revelation of one's subjective experience in a relatively objective way to discussion of how one feels about the experience. We can infer *consolidated* collaborative sharing when we observe a subjective experience revealed, subjective feelings about the experience expressed, and validation of the experience and feelings about it through acknowledgement by the other ("I can understand how you feel").

The sustained conversation in session seventy-seven opens the door to collaboration for Brenda and Donna. Two features of their pair therapy provide this opportunity and help the girls "get their foot in the door" of Level 3. First, the home base activity is so well established that negotiation is pushed to the background, and second, the active enabling role of the pair therapist brings shared experience to the fore through the medium of conversation.

Interpersonal Negotiation and the Home Base Activity

The only interaction in session seventy-seven that fits the strict definition of a context for interpersonal negotiation occurred right at the beginning (and even here the conflict was potential rather than overt). In the opening scene, the therapist asks both members of the pair, "Who wants what color?" and, as is typical, Brenda assertively chooses first. What is less typical in this scene, but becoming comparatively more so, is Donna's (relative) assertiveness. Her statement "Who's going first?" is posed as an open question, not as a request that Brenda make the choice. Moreover, when Brenda abdicates the need to have first choice in the matter, Donna asserts her desire to go first. Although this is not a major feat for most early adolescents, for Donna this act of initiation represents an enormous achievement. In the earliest pair sessions, she literally could not make choices. Commonly she would self-consciously say, "I don't care." To say easily "I'll go first" symbolizes an investment of the self; for Donna, it is taking a chance, an act of agency.

On a microanalytic level, one factor stands out as particularly responsible for the seeming absence of negotiation: the role played by the home base activity. Pair therapy is not "just talk," as it might appear to be in therapy with adults, seen individually or in couples. Pair therapy, in essence, is very much linked to action and activity, even if the activity is not used much, as was the case for most of this session. The game of Sorry, known so well by the pair, was hardly used once the conversation got going. Yet, like the adult therapist, it was there if needed.

With the game Sorry solidly established as the home base activity, the negotiation among the threesome became "scripted" into a repetitive social situation with its own rules, understandings, and expectancies (Schank and Abelson, 1977). The pair no longer had to negotiate which activity to choose, or the rules and guidelines for performing it. When a particular activity becomes a home base, it becomes a mutually expected, and thus rarely negotiated, choice. Furthermore, the negotiation within the activity of the game of Sorry is itself scripted, unlike that within a developmental project, such as the Wizardry game that became Arnie and Mitchell's home base activity. Even though a serious three-way competition developed in the playing of the game of Sorry, the activity itself is driven mostly by chance (the luck of the draw from a deck of cards). Certainly, there are decisions to be made about which of the other players' pieces to bump and send back to home, but this is more an inner rather than an interpersonal negotiation. Moreover, the move has its own built-in apology ("Sorry"), which allows the player to soften its competitive character with compassion, although the ritual apology can also be tongue-in-cheek or even hostile.

At the end of the initial conversation in scene 1, there is a relatively long (five-minute) break in conversation when the girls reenter the psychological safety of the home base activity. This gap in the conversation, during which all three players returned to playing, exemplifies the "classic" role of the home base activity (as opposed to the more elaborated and active developmental role it plays when it becomes a developmental project). The classic home base is a jumping off place, a foundation that can serve as a springboard to higher levels of interaction—potentially conflictual negotiations, sharing that could engender great vulnerability, and greater affective connectedness in relative safety—a place to take a chance. The home base activity embodies the therapeutic atmosphere of pair therapy, providing a secure place to which to return after essays into higher, chancier territory. Watching the videotape of Brenda and Donna's seventy-seventh session dramatically demonstrates this function, not because they used it often (they were wholly engaged in it for only about five minutes in this session), but because they were able to leap so high from it into a conversation that included Level 3 shared experience.

Also embedded within the shared experience of session seventy-seven are interactions that are not, strictly speaking, interpersonal negotiation strategies, yet are on the negotiation side of the social regulation continuum. What is negotiative in these sharing interactions is the issue of who does the talking, who interrupts whom, whose topic of conversation reigns. In the first scene, for example, although Brenda understands to some degree that Donna intends to continue describing "her" movie, she decides to take her turn to complete the sharing of experience by narrating the movie she saw during the weekend. Perhaps because she is more loquacious and less self-conscious than Donna, Brenda presents a much more extensive narrative. Donna's reactions suggest that she greatly enjoys listening to her partner's animated discourse and appears happy to pass the conversational ball to her. Donna listens quite attentively, asking many more cogent questions than usual. Here Donna is still in her usual self-transforming role, but now that their interaction is at Level 2, hers is a slightly deferential rather than a totally submissive stance.

This experience also appears to facilitate thinking back for Donna—actively using her memory and beginning to reexamine her own past experience. Old movies are a safe place to begin this activity. In a segment of the transcript not recorded here, she actively continues the conversation, asking Brenda, "It was a long time ago, but did you ever see *One Dark Night?*" In the course of her involvement, she is so enthusiastic that for the moment she forgets about her painful self-consciousness and actually cuts Brenda off to tell her story. This is the first time in almost three years that Donna has interrupted Brenda, attesting to her growing assetiveness.

Donna's more assertive actions and Brenda's greater acquiescence have both clinical and theoretical import. Clinically, they suggest that both girls are developing a stronger and higher-level sense of self (particularly Donna) and of relationship (particularly Brenda). Theoretically, they suggest that Donna can now use other-transforming strategies in her interactions with Brenda, and Brenda is now secure enough to accept these strategies as part of their relationship. Although we interpret the fact that the orientations of both girls are becoming less polarized as development progresses, we do not seek to make the two girls alike. Our goals are that each feel enough power, control, and agency to achieve her own internal balance and the ability to experience her own behavior as chosen and within her control.

In its give-and-take and inquiry into Brenda's desires, Donna's behavior in this session is strongly and consistently Level 2, whereas her earlier, compliant, passive responses were usually strictly Level 0 or 1 and more extremely self-transforming. Similarly, Brenda's (Level 2) ability to share center stage and allow Donna to express herself also reflects a significant advance over her previous unilateral other-transforming style. To the extent that the two girls achieve Level 3 sharing in scenes three and four, the issue of who is talking is no longer negotiated. Rather, the interaction is collaborative, with an integration between the two interpersonal orientations. Moreover, in both scenes the self-transforming partner, Donna, initiates the courageous move to reveal a profoundly painful personal history.

Shared Experience and the Pair Therapist's Enabling Role

Probably the most crucial factor in sustaining the shared experience throughout the session and elevating it to Level 3 at certain moments of scenes three and four was the enabling role of the pair therapist. The session demonstrates how the therapist can serve a number of functions: facilitator of conversation, focuser on the affective aspects of interaction, educator, and even foil for the pair's social anxiety. Not only is she the safe adult against whom the children can play off their private adolescent world, but also she is a guide, model, and facilitator who has helped to establish the safety and consistency of pair therapy. The therapist also participates in their shared experience as a trusted adult partner in an important positive corrective interpersonal experience for these children.

Each of the first three scenes were initiated by a key stage-setting question to one of the girls from the therapist. The first scene was initiated by the therapist's question to each girl, "How was your weekend?" Donna went beyond her usual "Fine" or "Okay," and revealed that she saw a movie over the weekend. This engaged a heretofore moody Brenda, and the animated discussion that ensued, facilitated by the therapist's interest, set an intimate tone that carried through the session.

After the five-minute return to playing Sorry, Donna, again rather uncharacteristically, actively returned the conversation to the theme of movies by saying, somewhat enigmatically, "Let me think, what else happened?" This comment evidently refers to the movie Donna saw and was reporting earlier. However, this comment also seemed to be a deflecting move on Donna's part, related to her discomfort with the attention being focused on her during the immediately prior moments of the Sorry game. Just before her statement "Let me think, what else happened?" the therapist had declined to make an optional move because "If I go there, I'll knock Donna, so I won't do that." After glancing at Brenda, to see how she was reacting to this, Donna broached the movie topic again, perhaps in part out of feelings of embarrassment about being "protected."

The second scene of the session involves shared experience in a discussion of the school day and the people who populate it. Once again, the scene begins with the therapist's initial question regarding their nighttime and morning routines, which is designed to encourage each girl to talk a little more about herself. The therapist plays an interesting enabling role here. She attempts to facilitate a more in-depth examination of morning routines and transitions from home to school. However, when each girl seems satisfied with simple reporting or private reflection, and Brenda moves the conversation from getting ready for school to a discussion of transportation to school and their fellow students, the therapist flexibly shifts her own focus as well, asking questions that enable the girls to expand on this theme, which clearly interests both of them.

Throughout this interaction, the therapist functions as a facilitator, asking questions both for her own information and to help keep the conversation flowing. If left alone, the girls might ask each other only factual, objective questions. The therapist, in contrast, is more likely to ask and focus on subjective questions about reactions and feelings. For instance, she inquires whether the scary movies made it difficult for Donna or Brenda to sleep at night. In response, each girl lends the other mutual support and reassurance, Donna saying, "All you think of is that it's make believe. People make it up," and Brenda quickly following, "Right, it's just make believe. It's all an act," and adding, "But it *was* scary." And all three participants laugh. The laughter ties the shared experience together in an affective net meaningful to all three of them. This, we believe, is another example of the building of a corrective interpersonal experience and of the powerful positive potential of affective sharing.

Through a series of shifts from the earlier topic of fellow students, the therapist comes to gently asking each girl how long she has been enrolled, leading to the historical third scene about how each girl ended up in the Manville School. In the ensuing discussion, Donna reveals, "It's so embarrassing telling people that you don't even know fractions." At first, she suggests that the fault or blame for her difficulty lies with the teacher or school, and Brenda is quick to echo this complaint. Here we see cutting-edge Level 3 behavior, in which subjective experience is revealed, feelings about it expressed, and there is some validation expressed from the peer. However, the collaboration is transitional rather than consolidated because the feelings of the self and the validation from the other are implicit rather than explicit. If Donna had expressed herself in less objective terms ("I feel so humiliated and dumb, don't you?" versus "It's so embarrassing telling people. . . .") and Brenda had said, "Yeah, I know how you feel" rather than echoing Donna's complaint, this interaction would have been solidly and explicitly (rather than tentatively and implicitly) at Level 3.

The therapist uses this conversation as an opening for the exploration of possible other bases for their educational difficulties. She asks Donna a crucial question: "When you first came here, had you been in public school and came directly here?" She already knows the answer through participation in diagnostic and progress conferences and through Donna's record, but Donna is not aware that she does. Spontaneously, Donna says, "Yeah," and Brenda, "Same with me." However, after a critical pause, Donna makes a very brave and significant qualification. "I went over to this other place and they didn't have any schooling, and so I was there for two years." This "other place," as Donna calls it, was a day psychiatric hospital. Brenda, encouraged by this, reveals that she also had been out of school for an extended period of time and begins to tell her story. Once again, the two girls take turns sharing these painful experiences, Donna first, in a slow and tentative way, and then Brenda, in a more humorous mode that provides a kind of transparent cover for the pain of the original events.

This scene is a short one, taking only a few minutes, but it is nevertheless quite revealing. Notably, the girls provide each other great support, of the collaborative, Level 3 sort. For instance, each time Brenda tells the story of how she bit her public school teacher on the foot, it elicits from Donna an "it happens" kind of laughter. After the fourth iteration, she tells the most serious part: "I was really mad and I was angry at myself so I wanted to go for suicide." The story is told in a matter-of-fact way, divorced from its original affect, but nevertheless some of the facts are revealed, and the past is demystified through its association with a happier and healthier present. For a child with a painful, disturbing, and defeating history such as Donna's or Brenda's, to discuss it realistically and openly is extremely difficult. The cumulative effects of the pair therapy atmosphere, the developing relationship between the girls, and their relationship with the therapist combine to enable them to confront and share these stressful, usually hidden, and often humiliating experiences.

In the final scene, the shared theme is the future, which is as difficult to talk about as the past. Donna introduces the topic by revealing indirectly that she is being considered for a return to public school. This is done at some risk, for it may engender feelings of jealousy or loss in Brenda. The words, "So I'm gonna talk to them about public school next year," are easy enough to string together in and of themselves. The power of their meaning is only recognized in the context of the entire relationship, including each girl's individual history and their history together. This is an empirical and theoretical point as well as a therapeutic one. Therapeutically, history and context work for Donna (and for Brenda) by allowing such an expression to be revealed in a longstanding safe and positive environment that enables the actors to say and hear painful things when saying them is the best or bravest thing to do. Theoretically and empirically, observers can understand such statements to represent interpersonal development only when they are interpreted in the full context in which they occur.

Donna is the first to acknowledge her concern about moving from the middle school to the upper school. Brenda seems to share these concerns, expressing them by critically evaluating the students she knows there, not only verbally, but through a mocking kind of imitation and mimicry. Together the partners are able to admit their shared fear of the future. Now that each has the consensual validation that the other is also concerned, they can have a discussion of what it is about the upper school that bothers each of them. At this point, the time runs out, but the therapist throws a rope into the future by saying, "We'll go on with this conversation. It's fascinating." This insures the continuity that may be lacking in other aspects of each girl's life.

Consensual Validation in Peer Connectedness

Valuable corrective interpersonal experience—with its safety, consistency, and opportunity to generate in practice more positive and effective ways of interacting—takes place not only in the triadic interacting we have described, but, just as importantly, in a zone of proximal development between the two girls in which the adult is excluded. Whereas we see an adult and two peers as having particular potential to become a well-equilibrated system, with the adult ready to mediate, facilitate, regulate, and otherwise keep the system functioning, while always being ready to "let go," the session also suggests that one of the powerful aspects of this form of treatment may stem from the youngsters' willingness to try harder when asked to reflect upon and report difficult-to-communicate experiences if the request comes from a peer rather than from an adult. This "trying harder" itself, though, may be facilitated by the adult's quiet presence.

Perhaps an instructive contrast can be drawn with individual therapy. Certainly the effective individual therapist establishes an atmosphere of trust and safety, and may well, with a child, discover a secure and comfortable activity within which difficult issues can be broached, and may even experience shared laughter, affect, and understanding with a child. But he or she is still the therapist, still, both by definition and in fact, uniformly functioning appropriately and with control. This, for all its unquestioned importance, is in some senses "unreal." What we call a corrective interpersonal experience, occurring between two peers, certainly has its "unreal" or "created" aspects as well. However, what is more "real" is that the interactions between two peers—whether participating together in knowing who Madonna is or gaining the confidence to take or give away the first turn in Sorry or defusing the pain and menace of a frightening psychiatric history by using it to elicit laughter from a friend—belong to *them*. They create, guide, and control these interactions, for better or worse. Neither of them is a "safe adult," so their gains, failures, or achievements are as genuine and "normal" as they can be in a structured therapeutic setting. The negative interactions that so characterize these children's lives begin to be counteracted, replaced, or supplemented by positive interactions *of their own making.* What their lives have lacked, and other children's include, are just these normal, routine, positive experiences. When we look at these children in depth, we understand just how very significant, rare, and powerful such ordinary-looking moments are, whether it be retelling a movie, laughing self-consciously about past disasters, or worrying about next year in school.

In class Donna tended to remain unresponsive and constricted, and Brenda was often limited by anger and moodiness. Even in pair sessions, Brenda's frequent incoming anger was usually not mitigated by the therapist, but by her (growingly affectionate) interest and responsiveness to Donna. Donna for her part was motivated most strongly by Brenda. The positive corrective experience, as is the emotional sharing that is part of it, is most effective and intense between the members of the pair.

In scene 1 we see in the effort Donna puts into explaining the movie to Brenda (and in Brenda's beginning to pull out of her bad mood in response to Donna) how shared peer-cultural knowledge, not possessed by the adult, motivates the girls and helps to establish a further sense of connectedness between them. This occurs several times in the first scene (when Brenda chooses to answer Donna's question over the therapist's, when each girl gives a lengthy movie description spurred by her partner's responsiveness).

Donna is particularly responsive to Brenda's inquiry, "What was the movie about?" answering "Oh, it was about Madonna." Then a long pause ensues, in which Donna looks down at the game board, avoiding eye contact with either the therapist or Brenda. It appears that she is struggling to organize her thoughts. We should not underestimate how hard it is for Donna to pursue an impulse to express herself, to organize herself to tell a story, even one as seemingly simple as telling about a movie. Yet she appears to be highly motivated, because it is Brenda who asks her about the movie. If the adult therapist were to make this request, Donna might not be willing to try so hard, but for Brenda she uses all her resources to pull herself together to tell the story, perhaps also inspired by the example of Brenda's many animated and "successful" stories in previous sessions. The discussion about Madonna provides not only the beginning of a shared experience between the two girls, but in relation to the adult, an exclusive experience. The peers exchange amused, disbelieving glances when the therapist asks

"Who's Madonna?" This clearly puts the girls together and the therapist on the outside. Madonna fills the girls' world but does not even touch the adult's.

In scene 2, Brenda astutely analyzes classmates' strengths and weaknesses. She then discusses the trials and tribulations of being in a school where some students soil during the school day. At first Donna is a very willing and appreciative audience for this monologue, laughing from deep inside, as Brenda relates her stories, feelings, and opinions about these students. Donna then takes her turn in the comic routine, relating the funny fantasy scene of going up to Bobby and spraying him with Lysol. This therapeutic sharing is a public discussion of an experience that is never discussed in its immediate context, the classroom. And the quality of the sharing and the laughter is unique to the peer connection.

When the therapist remarks to the pair that it is in the best interest of a student who has soiled for the teacher to have him or her leave the class, both girls join together in consensual disagreement. Apparently each girl believes that such actions would be too humiliating. Although the therapist persists in stating her point of view, clarifying that it need not be done publicly, the pair continues to collude in a genuine, even if by our standards ill-informed, difference of opinion with her. In fact, Donna, who uses humor to express some of her own feelings (in relating the Lysol spraying fantasy), is very uncharacteristically loose and uninhibited. And the more Donna laughs, the more Brenda performs. It is a releasing shared experience for them both.

This particular incident is a good example of what Harry Stack Sullivan perceived to be the strengths and weaknesses of consensual validation. On the one hand, each girl's beliefs and attitudes about the situation are confirmed and validated by the other's. Each believes that it would be too humiliating for a student if a teacher were to confront or even acknowledge a student's problem with soiling. Even worse would be to direct that student to change clothes during class. But this consensus of two lacks verification— that is, a method by which the validity of the shared belief can be externally tested out rather than internally accepted. The therapist's attempt to educate, founded upon her own years of experience with this type of problem, is disregarded by the girls. Still, the value of the experience is undeniable. The laughter, embarrassment, and close connection between them look very much like what occurs between any two young adolescents. This is the zone of proximal development from which their Level 3 sharing springs.

This discussion of classmates provides an interesting contrast with Holly and Jessica's discussion about Davy. Although Brenda and Donna may seem somewhat ungenerous toward Bobby and his difficulties, even this unkindness reveals how much more firmly their dialogue is grounded in reality! Both girls are comparatively savvy about the interplay of others' feelings, the reality of the social situation, the teacher's reactions and position, and people's motivations and needs. This is quite a dramatic departure from the fantasy world Holly and Jessica created around Davy and their view of adults as (often authoritarian) unidimensional foils.

A Look at the Interaction Indices

At this point, it is no doubt abundantly clear how a thoroughgoing interaction index analysis of session seventy-seven would describe a solidly Level 2 social context that climbs to Level 3 at certain moments. Indeed, it might seem difficult to have come this far in our microanalysis *without* reference to the interaction indices. In this case, however, such an analysis is of necessity retrospective. We developed these six indices some time after Brenda and Donna's pair therapy. Still, even a retrospective and selective look at the context of session seventy-seven reveals both the power of these indices as analytic tools and the range of specific social regulation behaviors of developmental significance that occurred. In fact, the *therapist's acts* in her enabling role was explicitly analyzed, and the other five interaction indices were underlying and integral to the previous description of the social regulation processes in the triad's sustained conversation.

The girls' home base activity played a major role in orchestrating the gross *spacing* of the triad. Like Wizardry for Mitchell and Arnie, the Sorry game fixed the triad in space, here in an intimate triangle around the game board—stable, coordinated, and Level 2. The more subtle aspects of spacing provide additional clues about the course of the social interaction. For example, Brenda's initial moodiness is visible in such spatial factors as her body language and to whom she directs her eyes and posture. At times, particularly when Brenda is telling a story with fast-paced humor and enthusiasm, the intense connectedness of the conversation is evident in the way all three lean forward in their seats, trying to keep pace. At other times, the therapist leans back, giving the girls needed "space" to reveal painful memories. The triad's use of space is particularly dramatic when Brenda leaves her seat several times and paces around the room excitedly to make a point or imitate a classmate. Tacitly at least, the way in which all three, but particularly the girls, continually readjust posture, orientation, and eye contact in response to each other to maintain connection is a fluid and ongoing Level 3 "renegotiation" of *spacing.*

A fascinating example of how the subtle *spacing* cues reveal quick upward shifts in the developmental level of social regulation occurs early in scene 1. Donna glances questioningly at Brenda, and Brenda behaves as if Donna were not there: Level 0. Then when Brenda responds to the mention of "Desperately Seeking Susan" and looks intently at Donna, Donna responds, but does so by averting her gaze downward, yielding up the "air-eye-space" unilaterally to Brenda: Level 1. As Brenda becomes increasingly engaged, both girls sustain eye contact with each other, reciprocating and acknowledging each other's interest: Level 2. Moments later, the shared glance that contains a thousand words regarding their therapist's ignorance of Madonna brings them to a fluidity and mutuality in their use of space that, if not at Level 3, is certainly approaching it. This all occurs in a few minutes and we are looking only at eye contact, one aspect of *spacing,* but the indication of the level of the social regulation is clear.

The Sorry game also had an influence on the triad's *pacing.* In its role as a classic home base activity, rather than a developmental project, it "scripted" both the timing of moves and the talking related to the playing of the game. The coordinated, face-to-face orientation of the threesome and scripted talking that accompanies the players' moves functions as scaffolding, helping to keep the interaction at a reciprocal Level 2, both in this session and over the many long months they played the game.

Looking at the *pacing* variable is particularly illuminating in two areas, both of which we touched on earlier. First is the issue of negotiation, shared experience, and the spectrum of social regulation that falls between. Second is the issue of conversation, particularly as it pertains to intimacy and the 2 to 3 shift. We will look at them as one interconnected issue.

When we discussed this session in the context of the transition from Level 2 to Level 3, we pointed out that overt negotiation episodes were notably absent and stressed that although sharing was in ascendance, much of what went on was conversation, "on the intimacy side" of social regulation. Interaction indices, and here *pacing* in particular, pick up on developmental aspects of the spectrum of social regulation behaviors that are neither clear negotiations ("Who's going first?" "I'll go first") nor clear shared experiences ("I wish I didn't have to go." "I know"). Most salient about *pacing* for Brenda and Donna in all four scenes are the frequent, and sustained, episodes of highly synchronous, mutually responsive, elaborated, and balanced conversation. This is true of both timing and content. Fluidly responding and mutually attending, the girls, as a unit, converse in a clearly Level 3 mode. A great deal of their conversation is at Level 3 in all four scenes. It is perhaps here, between the extremes of negotiating real conflicts or explicitly acknowledging and sharing feelings, that cutting-edge Level 3 connection and mutuality first emerge.

Spacing and *pacing* give dramatic indications of the level of the interactions in this session. The other three contextual variables, although we will not go into such detail, give clear signs as well. Playing Sorry generated an atmosphere of very positive *mood*, because the girls were really having fun. Moreover, the potential negative feelings such competition can engender were mitigated over the many months they played the game as Brenda learned, partly from Donna's example, how to lose graciously. Shared laughter carried over from the game to the triad's conversation, but the latter provided opportunities for a much wider range of feelings to emerge, such as the poignant silence they shared when Brenda talked about "going for suicide," the girls' shared affection (perhaps somewhat idealized with time) for their past teacher, Miss A., their alleged current disaffection for Miss M., embarrassment and distaste over classmates' soiling, humiliation at being behind agemates in schoolwork, apprehension about the next school year, amusement at classmates' foibles, and direct affection for each other. The degree of acknowledgment and responsiveness with which these *moods* and feelings are expressed puts them variously at Levels 2 and 3 for the most part. Interestingly, with their frequent shared laughter, the girls also partially cover or mask a host of uncomfortable feelings. Although we suspect that if supportively queried, the girls could probably articulate these feelings more directly, this level of sharing as it in fact occurs is transitional rather than fully Level 3, because these strong feelings are not fully in their awareness and the laughter ("I bit her on the foot") is partially defensive.

Shared history is implicit in the long history of the threesome's Sorry competition, but it becomes explicit in, and indeed the basis for, the long engaged discussions of the past (reminiscing about movies and previous teachers and schools), the present (morning routines and classmates), and the future (what will happen next

PART FOUR

The Dynamics and Ethics of Change

CHAPTER ELEVEN

Coordinating Inner and Outer Experience

Thus far we have paid only modest attention to children's inner experience. Instead we have presented a model of interpersonal development derived to a significant degree from research and practice in the realm of social interaction. Our model examines intimacy and autonomy processes occurring in social interaction from a single theoretical perspective, describing levels (and, within them, styles) of interpersonal development. Early on, Table 1 provided a theoretical foundation and skeletal summary of the model, and chapters 2 through 4 described its contents. We hope the intervening chapters have filled out these theoretical formulations to some degree, giving the notion of levels of interpersonal development greater texture and meaning.

Sharing the widespread view that increasing inner complexity and sophistication develop as a function of the processes of social interaction (Baldwin, 1902; Mead, 1934; Sullivan, 1953), we tend to work from the outside to the inside, both clinically and theoretically. Yet the therapeutic process of pair therapy also works on the inside, aiming to produce change in the basic character structure of children's personality along with change in social behavior.

Our ideas about personality development, like our clinical goals to foster collaborative action and interpersonal maturity, derive from Sullivan's interpersonal theory of psychiatry and our own notions of interpersonal development. Sullivan contributes to our ideas about personality by conceptualizing it as a relatively enduring pattern of interpersonal relationships. In this view, personal maturity is viewed as the achieving and maintaining of a system of relatively durable and equitable relationships with other people. Therefore level of personality development is intimately related to the form of social interaction in which a person generally engages.

Using Sullivan's notion of personality as a starting point, we have applied our model of interpersonal development, based on the maturity of perspective coordination underlying ongoing social regulation processes, to evaluate the developmental maturity of personality as it is manifest in patterns of social interaction. A central theme in our understanding of interpersonal behavior in relation to personality development is that a person's interpersonal actions, as used at particular levels and orientations, have different meanings depending on the interaction of the *understanding level* (competence) of the person using them (a self-reflective process) and on the *social context* in which they are used (an interpersonal process). Thus our notion of personality focuses on the extent to which persons have been able to develop toward articulating a collaborative attitude or whether their level of social interaction has become fixated at or has regressed to a level lower than their level of reflective understanding. "Gaps" between (relatively higher) levels of interpersonal understanding and (relatively lower) levels of action represent failures to function consistently at a level of interaction (action) after the corresponding level of perspective coordination (thought) that underlies it has been achieved. Such gaps are particularly problematic when higher level behavior is adaptive in the particular interactive context.

Previous research has demonstrated that many troubled children tend also to have social-cognitive deficits (Chandler, 1973; Dodge, 1980; Selman, 1980; Shantz, 1983) and thus many of them exhibit a pattern of low-level understanding with low-level action. Yet the developmental differences between normal and troubled children are considerably greater in their social actions than in their social-cognitive capabilities (Beardslee, Schultz, and Selman, 1987). Although poor relationships and coping skills can impede the rate of social-cognitive growth, they do not necessarily stop it altogether. When children's cognitive abilities begin to become more reflective and less physical and action-based, usually in preadolescence and early adolescence, their social-cognitive understanding and insight about human relations can grow through any number of *indirect* experiences (e.g., through reading novels) despite the fact that their real relationships—and hence their interpersonal action—remains inadequate and unsatisfying. Therefore we consider the closing of the developmental gap between understanding (e.g., of friendship) and action (e.g., acting as a friend) to be a central clinical problem to treat in pair therapy.

Even the most "together" people sometimes show gaps between their most advanced reflective social thought and everyday action, particularly in early adolescence, a period when rapid social-cognitive growth often outpaces its consolidation in direct communication and social behavior. Such gaps or, put another way, lack of integration between interpersonal reasoning and relating, are a

CHAPTER ELEVEN

      Coordinating Inner and
Outer Experience

natural part of development for even the most emotionally mature and progressing adolescents, sometimes creating turmoil even for them. Yet, though most people show this gap to a greater or lesser extent at various times, and surely none of us acts as maturely as we are capable all the time, this problem is particularly severe in troubled children, whose gaps are habitual.

Sullivan's notion of personality as a pattern of interpersonal relationships helps us conceptualize why gaps between understanding and action become chronic. The interpersonal "thought/action gap" seems to be generated by distortions in feelings about the self, the other, or the relationship. When persons act below the levels of which they are capable, even—or especially—under what may appear to the outside observer as neutral or benign conditions, we believe they are reacting, at least in part, to inner, personal demands of historical importance rather than strictly the immediate interpersonal requirements of a situation or relationship. If (affective) reactions to others become fixated at a lower level, it is in part because of the connection between the present situation and the outcome of past interactions with significant others. Thus, chronic gaps between interpersonal thought and action, be the action expressive (as in silliness or other forms of emotionally immature relating) or negotiative (as in impulsive and unilateral conflict resolution), seem to derive from factors traditionally articulated within the province of psychodynamic rather than structural-developmental theory (cf. Noam, 1988).

In this respect, we have claimed that pair therapy is not merely a social skills training program, that it works on deeper personality levels as well. To back this claim and understand how children in pair therapy may change in depth, we need to draw on theories that use intrapsychic constructs. We speculate that the obverse side of the interpersonal self is an intrapsychic self with its own organizational sense of what constitutes close or intimate relationships (often termed "object relations") and its own set of conflict-resolving operations (mechanisms of defense) that parallel strategies for interpersonal negotiation and autonomy. We believe troubled children, especially those with interpersonal thought/action gaps, are powerfully influenced by their immature levels of intrapsychic development and their primitive defensive operations, and the larger the gap the more this is the case. More than just believing, we have begun to explore this issue empirically: two preliminary studies have supported the hypothesis that intrapsychic processes mediate between interpersonal thought and action (Fleischer, 1989; Schultz and Selman, 1989). These internal processes seem to inhibit normal developmental progression in interpersonal relating, often in reaction to real shortcomings in the children's experience of primary relationships. Common clinical experience suggests, however, that these internal processes continue to resist natural growth even after parts of the external world become more facilitating, as happens when children enter the therapeutic milieu of our school. This is due, in part, to the fact that *primary* relationships may not change significantly.

The children whose participation in pair therapy we described in the last three chapters had the cognitive capacity to coordinate social perspectives at a level equivalent to their age-mates, yet, as we have seen, their levels of interpersonal development, both with respect to intimacy and autonomy functions, were either uniformly low, or at best labile. In this chapter we will speculate about *why* some persons with higher-level interpersonal understanding fail to implement mature responses, even if they "want to," whereas others succeed. To do so we will consider how our developmental model of interpersonal growth might be related to intrapsychic development and how the inner and outer worlds interpenetrate in mechanisms of change. But first we will examine the patterns of change in our three cases to get a sense of the patterns of gaps and resistances to development we have encountered when conducting pair therapy.

Macroanalytic Comparison of Three Pair Therapy Cases

The pair therapy of Arnie and Mitchell was similar to that of Brenda and Donna in its tenure (three years) and initial developmental level (Level 1 pairs who transitioned and consolidated at Level 2), but the two cases differed in timing and developmental end point. Mitchell and Arnie remained in a long phase of consolidation, showing little inclination to go beyond the persuasive and cooperative interactions of Level 2 social regulation to share personal material more intimately and inquire about such issues for the other in a closer friendship. In contrast, Brenda and Donna showed signs of being ready to make further progress, and, indeed, began to enter a second restructuring phase toward a sense of "we can support each other" (Level 3) by the end of their third year.

Figure 4 compares the cases from the last three chapters using three graphs. In addition to showing the absence of any sign of a second restructuring to Level 3 in the case of Arnie and Mitchell, but the clear beginnings of one at the end of Brenda and Donna's

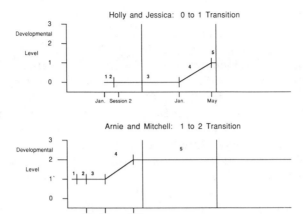

Holly and Jessica: 0 to 1 Transition

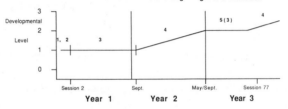

Brenda and Donna: 1 to 2 and Beginning 2 to 3 Transition

1 Sizing up; 2 Establishing dominance; 3 Balance; 4 Restructuring;
5 Consolidation

Figure 4. Timing of Developmental Phases in Three Pair Therapy Cases

third year, the graphs highlight differences in the timing of the
phases of the "1 to 2" shift in these two cases. The girls sized each
other up and established a dominance pattern in their first session
(though not, like Holly and Jessica, in the first few minutes), yet
the boys took a month to solidify their power relations. More
significantly, the "stable imbalance of power" phase of the boys'
therapy lasted only two months (October to December), whereas
the girls' Level 1 (im)balance lasted the entire first year (September
to September). Moreover, the boys' restructuring to Level 2 was
achieved in about four months (December to April of the first year),
but the girls' restructuring took the entire second year. Then, although the boys' interactions remained in consolidation at Level 2
for the next two years, the girls' consolidation rapidly progressed to
a new state of (im)balance, enabling a second restructuring (Level
2 to 3) to begin only six months after the previous restructuring
(Level 1 to 2) began to consolidate.

How can we account for the differences in these patterns? The different developmental trajectories of these two pair therapy cases may be related to differences in the history of the developmental competencies of the two pairs of children. Their clinical histories suggest that Brenda and Donna had regressed to lower levels (primarily Level 1 with oscillations to Level 0) from very shaky "1 to 2" preadolescent transitions that had occurred prior to their respective hospitalizations. At the beginning of their pair therapy, a mute and fearful Donna had little ego strength available to assert herself and a labile Brenda regressed dramatically in certain contexts—for example, she showed rapid decompensation at perceived signs of personal rejection. A long phase of balance and a slow restructuring were required while each rebuilt her shattered sense of self. Once the rebuilding had taken place, however, the consolidation at Level 2 was relatively brief, perhaps because it had been achieved before. In contrast, Mitchell and Arnie were well ensconced in Level 1 when they started pair therapy, and after a four-month period of balance made the shift to Level 2 relatively quickly. But, perhaps because they were breaking new ground instead of making up lost ground, they needed a long period of consolidation at the new level.

The pair therapy of the most primitively functioning of the three pairs, Holly and Jessica, lasted only eighteen months, half the length of time the other two pairs were together. Like Brenda and Donna, Holly and Jessica's stable imbalance phase (at Level 0 rather than Level 1) lasted an entire year. Like Arnie and Mitchell, their restructuring phase (to Level 1 rather than Level 2) occurred relatively quickly. Holly and Jessica's long period of stable imbalance at Level 0 before restructuring to Level 1 was needed, not to rebuild partially shattered selves, as was the case with Brenda and Donna, but to construct the basic core (a new level) of a self for the first time.[1] Once this was in place they quickly transitioned to Level 1 in the pair therapy context. The speed of this shift was probably due to both their competence in level of interpersonal understanding (reciprocal Level 2 perspective coordination) and the effectiveness of the peculiar vehicle with which they accomplished the shift (the Davy obsession, which functioned in their outer worlds as a highly unusual home base activity, and in their inner worlds, as we have argued, as a transitional object).

---

[1]As we mentioned in chapter 1, the child's capacity for relatedness emerges with the sense of core self (Stern, 1985), which is a necessary precondition for the capacity for self-reflective awareness of self and other that underlies social action at Level 1 and higher.

Intrapsychic Relational Processes:
Development of Inner (Object) Relations

What accounts for these differences in the timing of the phases of pair therapy, even when the level of the transition being navigated and the amount of gap appear to be the same? Why, for example, did Brenda and Donna begin a second restructuring after less than a year of Level 2 consolidation, when Mitchell and Arnie showed no signs of readiness for further vertical movement after two years of consolidation at this level? We think these differences are due in large part to the vagaries of each individual's inner psychodynamic development.

Throughout this book we have felt relatively comfortable building a descriptive developmental approach to interpersonal capacities. The interpersonal theory is meaningful to us and has remained close to our data, the interactions of peers in social contexts. But in characterizing the implications of a gap between levels of interpersonal understanding and action, we are always faced with a puzzling and recalcitrant problem: when there is a gap in developmental level of functioning between what one knows and what one does, why does our clinical experience continue to confront us with the tremendous difficulty all of us sometimes have, and some of us nearly always have, closing that gap?

The persistence of this problem compels us to look for explanations that go beyond both our theory and data. Although there are a number of places where we could conduct this search, the place that feels most productive is the neopsychoanalytic domain interpersonal theorists call "object relations." Although we prefer the term "inner sense of relations" or "inner sense of self," the phenomena that object relations theorists write about are familiar and seem relevant to the puzzle of the gap. Therefore we will speculate about how we can reconstruct these ideas about the development of a sense of an inner self, oriented to forming a sense of connection, within the bounds of our own approach.

Most object relations theorists propose that persons internalize deep into their psyches modes of interpersonal relating that stem from the quality of the earliest forming interpersonal relations they have with significant others, the caretakers of their early life (Greenberg and Mitchell, 1983). In this view pathological ways of relating to others in adulthood can be traced to inadequate development of these internalizations. In contrast to our own approach thus far, which has described contextually dependent variability in forms of relating based on the forces inherent in here-and-now interactions and relationships, object relations theory postulates that relatively crystalized internalized forms of relating pervade (or are brought to) current ways of interacting, and so understands psychopathology in terms of the relatively general and fixed forms of maladaptive past social experience and relationships.

From a methodological perspective, it is not surprising that such distinctions are made, for the data these clinical personality theorists usually draw on is material from projective tests (e.g., Urist, 1977) or intense introspection (e.g., of dreams and fantasy material representing the unconscious) from therapist-client interaction (transference and countertransference) that emerges in the context of long-term individual psychotherapy. Yet we feel that, insofar as such deeply internalized representations of interpersonal relations exist, our model can serve very well to describe them, or at least how they are manifest in actual social interaction, which is the most direct way to observe them.

To do this we must make a distinction between levels of interpersonal development that are forming and functioning in an age-normative way (as in the three-year-old in chapter 1 and the vignettes in chapters 3 and 4) and early levels that still function in a deeper, more pervasive way, once the person has gone beyond the age at which these particular modes of relating are normative, regardless of whether interpersonal understanding has progressed or not. In chapters 3 and 4 we described the lower levels of autonomy and intimacy in children, which are not to be viewed pejoratively as bad or pathological, even if they are "childish" or immature relative to what we expect eventually will develop. In contrast, in the following pages we will speculate on what persons who rigidly use low levels of interpersonal relating might look like when, for no other reason than, at their chronological age, they should "know better." Thus, unlike chapters 3 and 4, these descriptions are meant to depict the *personality structures* of persons who habitually relate to others immaturely in a puzzlingly consistent way, even when there is no obvious reason in the immediate social context for them to do so (i.e., when other people are treating them fairly and decently).

In essence, we are attempting to paint a picture of the types of distortions in interpersonal relating that occur when people consistently function rigidly at lower levels, either because they easily regress there or because their interpersonal growth and personalities were stunted in the course of the development of their primary relationships. We hypothesize that when interpersonal understanding is high, the fixated selves of low-level action are "driven" by the reaction of the actor to feelings of discomfort or distress in dealing with a significant other. The feeling states of the "gapped" actor appear to be very intense. We believe that when people act in relationships below capacity, they are impelled to do so by strong arousal, the historical, sociological, and psychodynamic antecedents of which are not always clear or easily susceptible to immediate observation or exploration of current circumstances.

As speculative as this work feels to us, it has a distinct advantage over traditional descriptions of personality development: it does not need to postulate hypothetical constructs such as the id, ego, or superego to account for people's social-emotional functioning (Kohlberg, 1969). Instead of positing reified personality *structure* it can account for calcified relationships in terms of personality *process*—that is, developmental patterns of interpersonal thought, action, and the gap between them.

Seven Selves-in-Relationship

There are many competing descriptions of the developmental sequence of object relations in the psychoanalytic literature. The ones most often referenced include those of Fairbairn (1957), Kernberg (1976), M. Klein (1975), Kohut (1977), and Winnicott (1971). We think our "selves-in-relationship" can serve as descriptions of different levels of object relations insofar as they are not mere action, but rather construals of self and other in action—how the self, with a chronic or temporary gap, acts in the face of an other, when no "real" other is there. Here we ask what the level of interpersonal *relatability*—of shared experience and negotiation, reflecting crystalized internal representations—would look like in persons who should "know better" but are fixated or regress easily interpersonally even though they have achieved more advanced levels of interpersonal understanding.

The following "selves-in-relationship," described at each level of applied social perspective coordination, suggest how the self is represented in our model by its action in relationships, how the inner self looks from its outer manifestation in a relationship context. With our interpersonal model, we can describe several "types" of "interpersonal selves" or "selves-in-relationship," in the Sullivanian sense of a person acting in an interpersonal context (relationship). These selves correspond to different general phases or levels of intrapsychic development and could be characterized in conventional object relations terms. But we choose instead to provide an alternative conceptualization of psychological growth that goes beyond more conventional "object relational" descriptions in characterizing not only the developmental level of the self acting in relation to others, but also the polar interpersonal orientations toward the significant other at each level as well. At each level qualitatively different selves act in self-transforming or other-transforming ways at each of the first three levels (impulsive, unilateral, reciprocal) and use an integrated orientation at the collaborative level.

Before describing the seven selves-in-relationship, we should clarify the nature of the Level 3 self-in-relationship. Unlike the other six selves-in-relationship, who, assuming Level 3 competence in the coordination of social perspectives, are chronically or temporarily gapped actors, the Level 3 collaborative self acts relatively maturely—that is, in a fluid rather than rigid way, reflecting its equilibrated coordination of high-level understanding and action. However, in our earlier work, briefly described in chapter 1, we defined and delineated a level of social perspective coordination (Level 4 in-depth and societal-symbolic perspective-taking) in older adolescents and adults that is higher than the Level 3 third-person and mutual perspective-taking underlying the collaborative process. Just as in chapter 1, where we noted that there are important developmental gains in social action before ("below") Level 0, in chapter 3 we made the similar point that, though Level 3 collaboration is a goal toward which to work with children and adolescents, it is neither a final nor necessarily optimal end point of interpersonal development. There we speculated what a Level 4 negotiation for intimacy in a relationship might look like in the context of adult development. Thus the Level 3 self-in-relationship described below represents an equilibrated and balanced self in the context of the optimal level of interpersonal maturity one might expect to be developed by early adolescence, but we expect to identify a more differentiated and integrated (Level 4) self-in-relationship in future research with later adolescents and adults. Nevertheless, as many before us have observed, many adults in all or some of their relationships are quite capable of acting in the following relatively immature ways:

The *Level 0 other-transforming self* is fused with action. In order to protect (defend) itself from the vicissitudes of conflict, this self attempts to dominate and control the interpersonal world by using a physical mode—either impulsive assertion or aggressive avoidance. This self's actions are unmediated by any communication with others or reflective counsel with the self (internal dialogue). Consequently, at this level the individual feels a powerful need to call all the shots. This self does not ask, it demands; it does not in-quire, it assumes. It grabs materials, intrudes into the interact-ions of others, and acts almost purely according to its own percep-tion of its personal wants and needs. In fact there is no construal of the social situation separate from the self's. Things must be done the self's way; there is no other way. Sharing means taking one's fill first before others even go to the well. Connecting with others means consuming or controlling them, or warding off being en-gulfed. Even helping others means doing for the other without asking if the doing is wanted, for self-esteem is tied to total control over events and other people. Holly in the first period of her rela-tionship with Jessica is a good example of the Level 0 other-transforming self. She intrusively moved Jessica's token, grabbed her chocolate and even her turn, and did not listen. Her impulsive activity choice of the game of Life in the first minutes of the therapy was emblematic of her need to control and her complete lack of awareness that the wishes and needs of Jessica and the pair thera-pist were not necessarily the same as her own.

If the other-transforming Level 0 self is a "tyrant," externalizing feelings through impulsive action, the *Level 0 self-transforming self* is a "tool," oblivious to others and fused with the world of inner fantasy. Mistrustful of the external world of other people, this self withdraws in defense. Passive and overfearful, its initial impulse in the face of conflict is to seclude itself from other people and seek solitary activities, often denying the existence of conflict. It does not intrude, but if approached by another with an interpersonal task that generates disequilibrium, it flails, flees, or stonewalls to ward off what is perceived as an intrusion by others. If involved in a more congruent interaction with another, the Level 0 self-transforming self appears mindlessly compliant—that is, he or she does not express an independent will or personal goal within the interaction. Connection with others means being carried away by the other, and cooperation at this level and orientation means let-ting the other carry out the task or do it for the self. Sharing with others means using magical thinking, hoping that satisfaction will come to the self without the self's communicating a want or need. With respect to the process of helping, when fixated at this level and orientation, the sense of agency is so impotent, nonefficacious, and weak that there is little feeling that the self can be of help, and being helped means having things done for one by others. Jessica is a case in point. In the first period of her relationship with Holly, her desperate need to be in control by being controlled (and cared for) seemed to match the intensity of Holly's need to control her. Jessica dealt with her diffuse, unbounded, undifferentiated, and all-encompassing feelings by panicky compliance to Holly's will.

Fixated in the mode of a *Level 1 other-transforming self*, persons have a weak sense of self but use a kind of compensatory domination of others in order to bolster it. Self-esteem is fragile, bolstered only when the self's weaknesses are denied or projected onto others. Domination of others is through verbal threats (rather than directly impulsive Level 0 actions). The self is dictatorial, but not tyrannical, as at Level 0. It bosses, insults, interrupts, and bullies, operating predominantly for personal power. Fairness to this self often means making sure of getting its needs and wants (still undifferentiated from each other) met first. Cooperation is interpreted as doing it your own way, for that is the best way. Sharing means taking what the self wants, but with a giving of what is left to others. However, rather than completely taking over, as at Level 0, there is some sense that helping means showing others *how* to do things. Arnie is a good example of this self in the first period of his relationship with Mitchell. His anxious overbearing lecturing to the bewildered Mitchell in their first session together had the effect of unilateral control over the interaction but also at least acknowledged that his partner's needs were separate from his. He maintained this one-way power throughout most of the first year with insults ("He'd threaten his brother—with his looks") and orders ("Touch it [the TV] and you die").

The fixated or regressed *Level 1 self-transforming self* acts in submission to others, with little confidence that he or she can affect their thoughts or actions. Attempts at initiations are passive (hovering rather than asking to join), with an all-too-ready willingness to give up and an underlying feeling of expected rejection. Thus the Level 1 self-transformer acts and feels victimized and powerless, and relies too readily on externalized authority for the resolution of conflicts that could otherwise be resolved by the contestants. Level 1 self-transforming selves-in-relationship do show some will, and a sense of rights or desires, but also seem to *feel* unworthy of having these wants or needs, as if their needy feelings were not "legitimate." They seldom exert themselves, instead taking an "I'll do whatever you say" stance. In situations that call for cooperation, this type of self-in-relationship often feels ineffectual in making a significant contribution. Mitchell exemplified this type of self early in his relationship with Arnie, with whom he submissively went along. Mitchell would, for example, let Arnie choose whatever game he wanted to play, though on occasion he let the therapist (and indirectly Arnie) know he did not want to play it.

The *Level 2 other-transforming self* is better equipped to tolerate feelings of personal inadequacy or weakness in the self, but attempts to maintain self-esteem and self-control through an influence- and power-oriented role. This can appear quite manipulative at times, but the line between manipulation and persuasion is not always clear. What is clear is that both manipulation and persuasion acknowledge the separateness of the other and the need to convince him or her by one means or another. Cooperation and sharing involve reciprocal give and take. Helping others includes the provision of emotional support. But in all these areas, there is still a need for interpersonal control to be experienced as located in the self. Brenda after the "1 to 2" restructuring was such a "self-in-relationship" with Donna. She controlled their interaction with masterful persuasion and storytelling, and her variable moods, but—at least when in a good mood—she was more than willing to listen to Donna.

On the other side, still somewhat anxious, timid, and a bit insecure, the *Level 2 self-transforming self* is more willing to stand up for itself and tentatively challenges the actions of others that do not coordinate with those of the self. Still a follower, there is nevertheless more confidence around the assessment of the self's strengths and weaknesses. This self is capable of give and take, with some active taking to offset the preponderant giving. Now we have a helper of others, or at least a self that has more confidence that it can learn new skills from others, and is willing to go out on a psychological limb to test the self. Donna after the "1 to 2" restructuring was this deferential self in her relationship with Brenda. Once Brenda started to talk, Donna tended to defer immediately, not only in her actions but also in literally forgetting her own thoughts. As her Level 2 self began to consolidate, though, she seemed able to assert herself to some extent, even to the point of finally interrupting Brenda, which was a major breakthrough for her.

The *Level 3 collaborative self* balances feelings of assertiveness and compliance, and with a firmer sense of the self, secure about where control of the self lies, this self is able to share power, attention, and materials more easily. This self can also put its desires into a long-term perspective. The Level 3 self-in-relationship is capable of integrating the self's personal needs with the needs of the relationship, of the self and other together, while simultaneously maintaining a sense of autonomy. Cooperation is based on the synchronous felt-understanding of the value of mutual fulfillment in the achievement of a common goal with an integrated feeling of mutuality. There is very much the sense of an autonomous self that is part of a collaborative relationship.

This higher-level self actively invests time and energy into the resolution of the problem, rather than expecting to be a passive participant in the process or to resolve it in one simple act of assertion. In this sense relating at a collaborative level is always a very active process, one in which initial goals may change. Almost invariably, it means a strong investment of the self in the relationship, a congruence between action and high-level interpersonal understanding.

What might an even higher level of intrapsychic and interpersonal development be about? We think this higher (Level 4) self would certainly be concerned with something that might best be called "interpersonal meaning." By interpersonal meaning in very close relationships we refer to the process of interpreting one another's thoughts and actions, an inner and interpersonal interpretation that is both negotiated and shared. From an object representational, as well as our own, point of view, what is important in a sense of relationship at any age or stage of development is the ability to count or depend on another person (cf. Bowlby, 1988; Bretherton, 1987). At the higher level it is understood that this sense that one person can depend on another requires they explicitly *share* and *negotiate* the meaning and interpretation of feelings and actions, not just the feelings and actions alone.

Most often when we speak of adolescent development we focus on the capacity for abstract or formal thought, the capacity to see larger world views (Piaget, 1965). However, the reflective understanding that the meaning of words and deeds must be negotiated between people is another salient, yet seldom acknowledged, dimension that develops significantly during this time. An example of negotiation of interpersonal meaning occurred in the following conversation in one of our older and most socially perceptive, albeit emotionally disturbed, pairs, a case study that is not reported elsewhere in this book:

> ADAM: "I'm not going to take your bullying any more, Barry."
> BARRY: "I'm not bullying you. I'm just kidding you. In the real world outside of here [the Manville school] they treat you a lot rougher than this."

ADAM: "Well, you might think you are only teasing or kidding around, but it doesn't feel that way to me. The way you treat me means to me you don't respect me very much."

Such a conversation is not atypical at all in the world of adult conversation and relationships, but is almost certainly nonexistent in the natural conversations of six- or eight-year-olds. Somewhere across the span of early adolescence, children become reflectively aware of the importance of meaning and recognize alternative interpretations of actions, their own and those of others. At this point they begin to both negotiate meaning and alter previously internalized meaning-making systems, which may be ordered along developmental dimensions (Kegan, 1982; Loevinger, 1976).

Personality Structure and Variation in the Gap

Most persons utilize different "selves-in-relationship" that are elaborated and articulated in different interpersonal contexts. We may have one interacting self with a spouse and another with a boss, but within each relationship context that self is usually either fairly consistent or any variation in level or orientation is predictable and explainable. As we have noted, one need not choose to function in all relationships at a collaborative level, because it is neither adaptive nor appropriate to collaborate mutually in some relationships. For example, buyers and sellers need not define their relationship this way. Nor should persons in naturally unequal relations (e.g., parents or teachers of young children) seek mutual understanding and collaboration in every instance, although in ongoing relationships this is something to strive for over the years. From a developmental perspective, however, it is important that people have the choice to collaborate in appropriate relationships and not be driven by the ghosts of those past relationships that were internalized at lower levels because of interpersonal inadequacies in their relationships with significant others.

Even when we compare selves-in-relationship that are consistent within a particular relationship context and are at the same level, they can have a different amount of gap between their understanding and the action they display. This difference makes them different "personality types," with different inner experiences, despite the superficial similarities in their outer actions. For example, if a person is enacting a self-in-relationship at Level 1, he or she may have achieved a range of levels of interpersonal understanding, and the size of the gap has a significant influence on the functioning of the personality and how we would characterize it.

Persons with a high understanding–low action gap may suffer more inner turmoil (affectively and cognitively) than persons low in both understanding and action, because once away from or out of the action situation, unless defenses set in, they will judge themselves more harshly. In other words, we might characterize a high understanding–low action self as *feeling* more "emotionally disturbed" in the sense of *being* more disequilibrated internally than a low understanding–low action self, even though the social behavior at the time of the action is likely to be somewhat similar. Low/low selves, whom we might traditionally diagnose as conduct disordered or sociopathic if they are older children or adults, may (or may not) be in misalignment with their social contexts (making them "socially disturbed"), but they are in a primitive or immature equilibrium of thought and action, and hence less "subjectively disturbed" than high/low selves.

In a familiar example, recall that Brenda acted as a Level 0 "self-in-relationship" with the new girl in class who "invaded her turf" and with whom she was in a constant battle in the period just before she returned to public school. This was after she had finished pair therapy with Donna and therefore after she had begun, though did not fully navigate, a "2 to 3" shift in the therapeutic context with Donna. Not only was Brenda's understanding at Level 3, she had achieved Level 3 interaction in her best moments with Donna, enabled by the pair therapist. Brenda's "momentary" 3–0 gap made her Level 0 relationship with the new girl in class much more internally conflictual for her than say the initial Level 0 other-transforming "self-in-relationship" was for Holly in her relationship with Jessica. The 3–0 gap colored Brenda's feelings about being suspended from school for her fighting: her affect seemed to represent a guilty form of humiliation rather than the rage or shame she probably would have felt at lower levels of interpersonal understanding.

Brenda's "interacting self" with the new girl was an example of the kinds of rigid or regressive selves-in-relationship we described earlier, which can become crystalized in one, more, or all relationship contexts below one's highest competence level. Because the pair therapy context is particularly supportive, the pair relationship there usually is among the highest achieved peer relationships that each child has experienced (e.g., Brenda's relationship with Donna). Despite the comparatively higher level of interaction that can be achieved in pair therapy, we see two forms of gaps in this context.

The first, chronic form of gap is a crystalization of actions consistently below a child's understanding level into a rigid "interacting self" with the pair partner. This type represents a lack of development of interpersonal action in the failure to either consolidate or ever apply an achieved understanding level. A less extreme example of this form of gap, when a cutting-edge level of action fails to become consolidated, was the case for Holly and Jessica at the end of their Level 1 restructuring, when Level 2 thoughts and actions were in their repertoire, but it was likely to take a lot more hard work before they could apply this level outside the highly structured and supported context of pair therapy. We see a more extreme example of this gap in the interaction of Arnie and Mitchell, who never applied the higher level (Level 3) understanding of which we believe they were capable toward the end of their tenure together, not even occasionally in the safe and facilitating pair therapy context. With respect to a desire for closeness or independence they did not seem motivated to move higher.

The second and more common kind of gap between thought and action seen in the pair relationship is one to which we are all susceptible to varying degrees: temporary regression in interpersonal action. This acting less maturely than usual can happen either because of emotional stress or because the interpersonal context does not invite it. Troubled children are especially prone to precipitous drops in the level of their social actions under perceived stress. Brenda, for example, often demonstrated this form of gap at the beginning of her pair therapy with Donna, when she was easily stressed in social situations. Like many other children in pair therapy, she could demonstrate a high level of interpersonal thinking in protected, structured environments. Yet despite this social-cognitive strength, with increasing anxiety (to which these children tend to be easily prey), their behavior deteriorates from coping to increasingly defensive behavior or, when their defenses completely fail, to impulsive behavior (Selman and Schultz, 1988). Although some regression is usual in the ongoing processes of everyday social interaction, troubled children's shift toward "emotionally disturbed" behavior with increasing stress is especially extreme.

Indeed, the major goal of the consolidation phase of pair therapy is to promote growth in the children's ability to maintain a newly restructured level of action across a variety of contexts, particularly those that are emotionally charged for them. In Holly and Jessica's case, the consolidation phase that was just beginning when their therapy ended was like that of Brenda and Donna's in containing cutting-edge behaviors a level above their predominant functioning (Level 2 for Holly and Jessica, Level 3 for Brenda and Donna). In contrast, Arnie and Mitchell showed no sign of cutting-edge (Level 3) interaction during the two years of their (Level 2) consolidation. We would speculate, however, that if Holly had not left the school and Holly and Jessica's therapy had continued, that they too would have needed a long consolidation period before further restructuring (to predominant Level 2 interaction) would have been possible. The psychological capacity to put one's most advanced level of interpersonal thought into action was still too underdeveloped in these two girls, despite their considerable gains. We think that Holly and Jessica would have needed a long consolidation before further restructuring if their pair therapy had continued, because requisite underlying psychological (ego or self) structures were not in place.

Managing Conflict in Defense and Negotiation

Thought/action gaps have different meanings and treatment implications when the level of action or interpersonal capacity is regressed (as with Donna and Brenda) rather than fixated (as with the other two pairs). In the case of regression, we can speculate that the person has multiple levels of inner relatability manifest when different levels of defense are operating. In the case of fixation, inner capacity and defense as well as interpersonal relating seem to be stuck at low levels. Thus, in regression, developmentally more advanced defenses seem to fail, whereas, in fixation, higher level defensive structures seem not to be in place.

The relation of intrapsychic experience to interpersonal experience is particularly salient in mechanisms of defense, a more specialized developmental line of inner psychological development than that of object relations. Defense mechanisms are habitual, often unconscious, and sometimes pathological mental processes that are employed to resolve conflict between internal needs, internalized prohibitions, and external reality (Vaillant, 1986). Whereas the kind of interpersonal gap we have emphasized is a discrepancy in developmental level between thought and action, the kinds of intrapsychic gaps engendered by defenses are between perceived awareness and underlying (unacceptable) feelings that otherwise would put the self in a state of ambivalent conflict, thus leaving awareness unconnected from action in a misinterpretation of the relation between inner and outer experience.

Intrapersonal conflict resolution is a central explanatory concept in psychoanalytic theory, in which it is typically assumed that anxiety-provoking unconscious wishes and motivations that provoke conflict as they strive for expression have an enormous influence on personality and behavior. Conflict, whether emotional or cognitive, is given a major role in theories of individual development because it provides dynamic opportunities for change (Shantz, 1987). The need to resolve inner conflict can be a motive for stagnation or regression if the psychic conflict is too overwhelming. However, defensive functions can have an integral and positive role in the development of the inner self if the degree of conflict is developmentally optimal.

Indeed, it has been suggested that the development of defensive functions is inextricably related to growth in levels of inner psychological structures to the extent that new levels of object relations are enabled by new defensive operations (e.g., Lerner and Lerner, 1982). The most well-known example of this is Freud's description of the consolidation of the "system Ego" when a "repression barrier" is erected. Another example of defensive operations resolving conflict and causing representational growth is Fairbairn's (1952) idea that the inner world of "good" and "bad" objects is created in a defensive reaction (introjection) to a bad object in order to master the bad object internally when such mastery cannot be achieved externally by the infant. The idea here is that some external protection is necessary for the inner self to *grow* to new levels of organization.

Defensive reactions to conflict more often serve conservative than progressive purposes, however. This conservative function of defense may be most adaptive during the period when psychological structures are initially forming. For example, once the infant achieves the initial cognitive differentiation between self and other, defenses protect the cohesion and integrity of poorly differentiated self-representations and object representations (M. Klein, 1975). Here defenses provide protection for the inner self to consolidate at a newly achieved level.

However, defensive reactions that become too conservative are maladaptive. In psychopathology, in particular, as defensive reactions to unresolvable conflict become entrenched in the personality, defenses impede rather than protect or enhance growth. The conservative function of defenses seems to win out in psychopathology and, we think, in interpersonal thought/action gaps.

What, then, is the relation between defense and interpersonal development? Defense mechanisms aim to resolve conflicts of the inner world; interpersonal negotiation strategies are used to resolve conflicts in the outer world of social interaction. Both are necessary ego functions, and each can be done more or less adequately. When we describe an observed behavior, such as the act of putting one's hands over one's ears, or over another's mouth, or throwing one's coat over one's head to block out unpleasant interpersonal stimuli, these observed behaviors may be a sign of an impulsive-physicalistic interpersonal negotiation strategy designed to deal with the other person and, simultaneously, a primitive defense mechanism designed to deal with internal stress. The action signifies both an unconscious attempt to block perception—a defense—and an at-the-moment unreflective strategy—a negotiation. Both constructs, defense and negotiation, are located at the interface between the intrapsychic and interpersonal worlds, and each process must necessarily deal with each side of the disequilibrium (i.e., both the interpersonal and the internal conflict).

But if both constructs deal with conflict, what are their separate and overlapping functions? Negotiation strategies are interpersonal actions and more often face outward toward relationships with others; defenses are intrapsychic perceptual mechanisms and more often orient inward toward the internal representations of others. There are negotiation strategies that are nondefensive (e.g., collaborative action) and defensive processes that operate outside specific or obvious interpersonal contexts (e.g., procrastination on a writing task).

One circumstance in which the functions of defense mechanisms and negotiation do seem to overlap considerably is in interpersonal thought/action gaps. Defense mechanisms resolve a conflict between an impulse and an ego demand (a socialization or reality demand) with either a defensively distorted perception (i.e., defense proper) or a perception that reconciles the impulse and the ego requirement—a high-level defense or what some (e.g., Haan, 1977) term "coping." Negotiation strategies are interpersonal actions based on a conception—that is, a certain level of perspective coordination. When individuals employ a lower level of negotiation than that of which they are capable (what we have referred to as the thought/action gap), there is a deviation of sorts taking place. That is, with regard to construal of self and other, and perception of emotional disequilibrium, the individual is, relatively speaking, employing a distorted view. It is distorted because he or she "knows better," not simply in the sense of greater accuracy of perception, but in being capable of a more mature form of understanding, one that is more coordinated with the understanding of others.

Thus, distortions in the perception and interpretation of social and emotional experiences inherent in defensive processes seem to play an active role when persons act interpersonally at a level below their level of social understanding. We hypothesize that when interpersonal conflict stirs up internal conflict that feels too overwhelming, the person's defensive warding off of the conflict prevents the application of higher-level interpersonal understanding in negotiating the social conflict. In defending the self from the vicissitudes of a direct confrontation with potential emotional conflict engendered by ambivalent feelings, defense mechanisms can distort the self's perception of either inner or outer experiences, sometimes to such a degree that an otherwise advanced ability to coordinate social perspectives is severely compromised, either momentarily or chronically.

Defenses seem to share a common basis with interpersonal negotiation in some of the developmental aspects of their organization. Although a number of theorists have suggested developmental schemes in which defenses are ranked from "archaic" or "primitive" to "higher-order" or "advanced" (e.g., A. Freud, 1936; Jacobson, 1971; Gedo and Goldberg, 1973; Kernberg, 1975), George Vaillant (1986) has provided the most workable developmental hierarchy of defenses. The qualitative hierarchy Vaillant identified in the development of defense mechanisms involves both changes in the perception of and operations on reality. Like the levels of interpersonal negotiation, movement up the ladder in the four Vaillant defense levels appears to be based in part on increasingly complicated operations and transformations, a "natural" developmental progression that is nevertheless subject to fixation and regression.

"Psychotic" defenses, which Vaillant notes are common in "healthy" individuals before the age of five (bear in mind Werner's distinction between ontogenesis and pathogenesis), include the mechanisms of delusional projection, distortion, and denial. This first developing line of defense, which is used naturally by very young children, is primitive in the sense that these defenses distort the transactions of the interpersonal world profoundly. Defense at the psychotic level often makes use of either fantasy as a complete substitute for interaction with other people (like Jessica and Holly's world of Davy) or massive distortion to avoid the conflict engendered by seeing another person's needs clearly, because acknowledgment of the other's needs threatens the self's perceived needs. We can see in the psychotic level of defense and the impulsive level of negotiation a kind of expulsiveness that disregards others' (and even one's own) needs or feelings rather completely. Holly and Jessica's pair therapy sessions were replete with examples of these primitive defenses.

"Immature" level defenses appear to involve one-step operations—for example, from having negative feelings in me to misperceiving them as in you. Level 1 negotiations are also one-step, or at least one-way or unilateral. Immature defenses include projection (attributing one's own unacknowledged feelings to others), passive-aggression, and acting out, all of which were often used by Arnie and Mitchell.

In contrast, "neurotic" defenses are inherently more complicated. More twists and turns are used to deal with conflictual feelings, and transformations of feelings in these defenses involve not only the locations of feelings but also their causes and sources. This level of defense shows certain parallels to the reciprocal operations involved in Level 2 negotiation strategies. Under the category neurotic defenses, Vaillant includes the mechanisms of repression, reaction formation, displacement, and intellectualization (isolating affective and cognitive aspects of an event or action). For example, if, as we believe, Donna and Brenda *really were* frightened, or perhaps excited—or both—by the violence in the scary movies, which if acknowledged would cause them some stress, then their frequent viewing of scary movies as "just a movie—more like a comedy" could be characterized as reaction formation.

"Mature" defenses, like Level 3 strategies, involve operations that integrate—rather than divorce—conflicting feelings, or feelings and ideas, or persons and their feelings. Mature defenses, which include humor, suppression, anticipation, and sublimation, do not "distort" the reality of conflict as much as they deal more directly with it, and attempt to transform the polarized feelings engendered by it. An example of mature defense from our cases (some would call it coping) is Brenda and Donna's shared anticipation of missing their current teacher when they knew they were moving to a new level in school the following year. This would be particularly the case if they had the insight that they were feeling angry that their teacher was abandoning *them*, at the same time they recognized that these feelings were "irrational" because this was not what was "really" happening.

We speculate that there is the following reciprocal relation between social-conceptual maturity or immaturity and level of defense. On the one hand, social-cognitive development level may play a necessary but not sufficient role in enabling a given level of defense to operate. At lower levels of social-cognitive maturity there will be limits on how "high-level" a defense can be used, and at higher levels of understanding, though higher levels of defenses are then possible, they may not be used. On the other hand, the repetitive use of lower-level defenses may impede further development of social understanding and maturity due to their greater proclivity to distort perceptions and feelings.

Two Examples: Projection and Passive Aggression

Defenses deal primarily with inner feelings, feelings associated with but often distinct from actions. Yet negotiation also deals with feelings. A focus on affective control and disequilibrium, one of three components of action that we use to make a developmental diagnosis of negotiative interactions (see chapters 2 and 3), helps show the coherence between developmental levels of interpersonal negotiation and defense mechanisms, how level of defense can be reconciled with level of negotiation.

Consider projection, an "immature" defense in Vaillant's scheme. Projection involves a transfer of an unacknowledged negative feeling or idea from its "actual" location (in the self) to a new location (in another) where it is incorrectly attributed to that other. After their fight in the session of 4/10, Mitchell and Arnie both blamed each other—"You started it." "No, you did." Arnie "forgot" he had been in a bad mood and had been alternately ignoring and teasing Mitchell; Mitchell "forgot" that he was upset by Arnie's mood and that he had teased Arnie about inviting an unpopular girl to a sleep-over. Because they did not recognize the "true" locus of their feelings, a distortion (an error or omission) can be said to be taking place. It seems particularly apt that projection, as an immature defense, is one of the defense mechanisms that parallels Level 1 negotiation, because at this level, feelings are seen as relatively separate distinct bits, not connected to the larger fabric of the emotional life of the self. The conceptual ground at this level is ripe to support the operation of "throwing" a feeling from its original locus (the self) to another. Level 1 conceptions of feelings clearly are logically compatible with this projective thrust.

Whereas feelings are seen only as objects at Level 1, and emotional disequilibrium is attributed in a unidirectional way to actions of others on the self, at Level 2, emotional disequilibrium is now owned, perceived as having a subjective component rather than due solely to factors external to the self. Feelings at this level have continuity with past and future emotional states. If persons have Level 2 understanding, then they have the "knowledge" that they can cause, and hence control, their own feelings. If on some occasion they say or do something implying that they attribute their feelings to another person, then this can be considered an instance of regression through projection, a form of distortion characterized not by immature development but by displacement from self onto other of responsibility for having, and having to deal with, certain feelings.

Passive aggressive behavior provides another illuminating example of the parallel relation between levels of defense and negotiation. In the use of passive aggression as a defense, an unacknowledged subjective feeling is made objective and put outside the self's control where it can be regarded as unarguable. In this way, the self avoids having to go along with the requests, wishes, or demands of others, and avoids acknowledging a conflict or hostility. Take the following as an example. Mitchell's "true" feeling is "I don't want to play basketball with Arnie because I don't like playing" (itself a low-level definition of a feeling that might be more "accurately" and completely stated or constructed as: "I don't want to play because I don't play as well as Arnie and he wants to play and I don't want to gratify him at my expense"). In his attempt to avoid Arnie's anger, Mitchell's defensive action allows h:m to reconceptualize this attitude as "I can't play basketball with you; I 'forgot' we were going to today so I 'forgot' to bring my sneakers," leaving him not responsible for choices. Or the attitude could come out as "We can't do it now—we have to finish this other game," leaving Mitchell with no other choice possible. Here Mitchell establishes a construal of the situation in which he *is* helpless (objective) rather than *feels* helpless (subjective). Therefore he is no longer responsible for his actions and cannot assume control, and so has no need to face his own anger or conflict, or Arnie's.

If Level 2 perceptions were operating, Mitchell would be in a better position to acknowledge his feelings and emotional reactions, because, at this level, feelings can be understood to reside within (are managed by) the self, and therefore can be controlled directly by the self. Mitchell would not feel the need to wait for events external to himself to change in order for emotional experience to be adjusted. Instead, by objectifying subjective experience, or by defining himself as helpless in the face of allegedly objective hurdles (both characteristics of Level 1), his self is "protected." Again, this form of action cannot be considered a developmental regression *or* a defense mechanism *unless* it is assumed that a higher minimal level (in this case Level 2) of conceptualization of self in relation to other has been achieved, as it was with Mitchell. If indeed this achievement has been demonstrated, then the less mature implementation of control is necessarily a function of "defensive distortion" away from one's optimal level of construal.

These examples demonstrate the mutually instructive relationship among social-cognitive level, use of defense mechanisms, and actual interpersonal relating. We see how a thought/action gap in a sense of autonomy can be conceptualized in terms of the mediation of defense mechanisms. When the sophistication with which individuals can perceive disturbing feelings threatens their emotional equilibrium, lower-level defensive mechanisms may kick in, effecting a regression to a less mature view of the emotional state that feels less threatening and easier to accept. In turn, this may lead to a lower level of action than otherwise might be possible if a higher-level defense was operating.

By considering the relation between these two "immature" defenses (projection and passive-aggression) and level of interpersonal development, we can see how the social perspective coordination model offers a "structural" basis for Vaillant's hierarchical grouping of the defense mechanisms. Just as both these "immature" defenses represent distortions of higher-level interpersonal understanding into Level 1 forms of affective perception and control, presumably psychotic defenses would correspond to regression to Level 0 affective perception and control, "neurotic" defenses would represent regression to Level 2 understanding from Level 3, and the "mature" defenses, which correspond to what some theorists call "coping," would reflect synchrony at Level 3. If so, then regardless of their specific content or dynamics, we have a foundation for arguing that defense mechanisms, two of them analyzed here in some detail, have a structural as well as a possible but as yet only partially tested (Schultz and Selman, 1989) empirical-correlational basis for their place in a developmental hierarchy.

This analysis provides a developmental account of natural progress in the way certain components of emotional turmoil are *identified* and hence *potentially* regulated by the self. We consider perceptual distortions (as in the more primitive mechanisms of defense) and lack of applied understanding (as in the conceptualization of feelings as objects rather than processes) as two separate but related factors that characterize immature emotional development. Realistic perception, comprising both the *general* capacity to understand emotional complexity (social-cognitive development) and the *specific* ability to identify particular inner conflicts accurately in specific situations or relationships (the development of mature defense and coping styles), is one aspect of emotional maturity. Dealing with or controlling feelings as processes in an interactive context (in interpersonal negotiation of conflict) provides another component of emotional development. Both are crucial for mature interpersonal relatability.

The "natural" use of primitive defenses in young children is undoubtedly to some extent a function of the limitations of their cognitive development. But for individuals who continue to use primitive defenses, even when progress in their social-cognitive development would allow for movement to higher-level ways of coping with conflict, the continuation of that progress is jeopardized and their ability to interact "age-normatively" is compromised. The use of higher-level mechanisms of defense allows a person more freedom to recognize inner conflict with less distortion, and hence enables the self to reach in and reach out in ways that permit the implementation of more mature interpersonal strategies. Because the distortions of reality that result from the lower-level defense mechanisms are massive, the person is less able to *perceive* relationships with others in an "accurate enough" way that enables higher-level interpersonal strategizing. These distortions limit the completeness of constructions of interpersonal interaction, impeding direct links between understanding and action.

Unrealistic or inaccurate perceptions resulting from the distorting nature of low-level defenses do not allow for, much less facilitate, the positive interpersonal and interactive experiences that provide the fertile ground for continued interpersonal and emotional development. Habitual use of lower-level mechanisms of defense can impede the growth of interpersonal maturity, in both basic social-cognitive understanding and interpersonal behavior, by blocking access to previously unacknowledged but very "real" feelings an individual needs to experience—and deal with—to be able to develop deeper, more mature concepts of reciprocity and act in a reciprocal or collaborative way with others.

Explaining the Gap: An Interim Summary

Our analyses thus far of two phenomena derived from ego psychology and neopsychoanalytic theory provide two ways to account for the often observed gap between level of interpersonal understanding and its implementation in relationships. The first explanation is a generalization about the individual's personality structure. It says that even though an individual may be capable of a higher level of understanding of relationships, there is a lack of full development of the deeper sense of the inner self—the way the self feels about the self-in-relationship—that inhibits or derails the person's ability to put understanding into action, in a full and consistent way.

The second explanation relies on the assumption that there are particular mechanisms of defense that get activated in particular situations—that is, situations involving inner as well as interpersonal conflict—and if these mechanisms of defense are at a relatively low level, they will impede the likelihood that higher-level capacity for interpersonal understanding will be put into action at an equally high level. Although the types of defenses a person uses may become habitual (as they do in "symptoms" of psychopathology), we do not regard these processes to be as pervasive across contexts and relationships as the inner selves-in-relationship.

This raises the question of how children change in pair therapy. If we aim to close the gap between interpersonal understanding and action, do we as pair therapists strengthen the children's defenses and enhance their inner sense of selves-in-relationship to enable higher-level social action to emerge? Or do we support higher-level peer interaction to enable the intrapsychic self to grow? In other words, does the therapeutic process of pair therapy work from the outside in or the inside out?

How Children Change in Pair Therapy

Throughout this book we have asserted that pair therapy operates in the outer world of social interaction in developing peer relationships as well as in the inner world of reflection on the interactive experience. Now we will make a further claim, clearly controversial, that this form of treatment can influence the development of the personality, the very essence of the self. Indeed, we have argued in this chapter that if each of the interpersonal transitions we have described in the developmental level of children's outer interaction (i.e., the "0 to 1," "1 to 2," and "2 to 3" shifts) is to be a change in the way of relating, it must go beyond growth in social knowledge and involve associated intrapsychic growth and reorganization as well, specifically in an inner sense of self and mechanisms of defense. What is not very clear is how this change occurs.

A common, though not universal, view of the therapeutic process is that it works primarily from the "inside out" through the interpretive activity of the therapist in a therapeutic alliance with the client (e.g., Barrett, 1983; Hartmann, 1956/64; Rapaport 1954/67; Strachey, 1934). Even in psychotherapy with children, interpretation is traditionally regarded as the primary mutative agent (e.g., Erikson, 1964). By "interpreting away" the maladaptive effect of what is distorted (that is, the feelings and experiences associated with the transference relationship), defensive resistances are removed and insight into the psychological truth about oneself leads to a restructuring of the essential character of the self. This view assumes that once there is insight, and only once there is insight, a new mode of action can be developed. The hope is that this understanding will be applied to the person's relationships in the "real" world.

A competing view of the therapeutic process is that it works primarily from the "outside in." The curative power of the "actual relationship" is recognized, for example, in Sullivan's belief that therapeutic transformations of the self always take place within and through a human relationship and in Alexander and French's (1946) notion, sometimes disdained, of a "corrective emotional experience." Even Freud (1915) emphasized the need for attachment between patient and analyst, and struggled with the role of the therapeutic relationship as a mutative factor in psychoanalysis, though he more often emphasized the mutative role of interpretation.

Instead of emphasizing one dimension of the therapeutic process over the other (the relationship or interpretive action), another perspective views them as inextricably intertwined and nonindependent (e.g., Zetzel, 1956). We share this perspective, which implies that basic structural change occurs in both directions, from the inside out as well as from the outside in. In pair therapy the therapeutic relationship *and* the therapist's interpretive activity *interact* to produce change in the children's social interaction and their psyches.

Although the two dimensions of therapeutic relationship and intervention can be differentiated, their integrative effect is more powerful than either alone. Indeed, it is well known that in individual therapy ill-timed interpretations (i.e., when the therapeutic relation is not firmly grounded) are often ineffective, if not counterproductive. Effective interpretations have an emotional impact precisely because of the status of the therapeutic relationship, which needs to be developed to the point at which defenses no longer impede the possibility for insight or new ways of acting.

Both dimensions of the therapeutic process function differently in pair therapy than in individual therapy and other forms of nonindividual treatment. The therapeutic relationship differs because of the uniqueness of the triadic system, and the therapist's interpretive activity differs insofar as it is guided by our model of interpersonal development.

Like couples and family therapy, pair therapy works within a system of "real-life" relationships in which transference between the therapist and each individual in the system becomes a background issue. But there is a major difference between the therapist's role in pair therapy and in other nonindividual therapies. Couples and family therapists join an established system in order to restructure it. In contrast, pair therapists create a new and nonpermanent system before restructuring the children's relationship. Instead of aiming primarily to help each person grow to repair their relationship, to establish a better (more developed) system and hopefully (but not necessarily) stay together, the pair therapist provides a facilitating context for a friendship relationship to grow so that the two children can grow individually. This "real" peer relationship provides a supportive context for the children to try out and consolidate what they learn.

The triadic relationship is a major vehicle of change in pair therapy. The therapist provides a supportive context in which a "here and now" relationship develops between the two children and provides a "corrective interpersonal experience." (We give a slight twist to Alexander's idea to emphasize the interactive nature of the corrective experience.) The essence of pair therapy is to provide a context where youngsters can have repeated positive interpersonal experiences that foster development of, or toward, mutually collaborative processes of interaction. For children who in the past have lacked these experiences, the context of shared interaction established by the therapist in pair therapy is as important as the specific techniques the therapist implements. The emphasis is on context, on atmosphere, on a healing experience for each of the two peers.

But the therapist's "being there" for the pair and management of their behavior is not enough to restructure the children's relating, to get each to relate to a peer in a more mature way than ever before. To *change* the pair's interpersonal thought and action, to promote growth in addition to repair, the therapist must actively intervene in their relationship as well as in each child's sense of relationship. Therefore pair therapists engage in insight-oriented interpretive activity geared toward autonomy and intimacy issues as well as facilitating the children's "natural" relating.

The insight-oriented function of pair therapy differs from that in other forms of treatment to the extent that it is informed by our model of interpersonal development. There are a number of consequences of its influence. First, the goal of interpretive activity differs. Instead of having an *adaptive* goal to remove symptoms, pair therapy has an explicit *developmental* goal to simulate an interpersonal process that was missed—namely, movement through the interpersonal levels of negotiation and shared experience. Because of this difference in where the therapy is headed, the nature of the interpretations pair therapists make differs from traditional interpretation.

Psychodynamic therapeutic techniques differ in the extent to which they emphasize the *present* relative to the *past*, the "here and now" (the working out of conflict in the present "real relationship" and "transference") relative to the recall or reconstruction of earlier experience. Even in those individual therapies that emphasize the here-and-now transference, the primary operational goal of interpretation always remains to integrate the person's past interpersonal experience into his or her current relating (e.g., Horney, 1939; Stone, 1981) or to explore the past for the light it throws on current ways of feeling and acting (Bowlby, 1988). In contrast, we believe that to produce structural personality change in children—to free the understanding of *present* relationships, even in neurosis or more severe psychopathology—it is not absolutely essential to interpret *past* relationship conflicts.

Indeed, our experience with pair therapy suggests that to foster personality change in children at the lower levels (0 through 2), one need not work with the children's past, but rather emphasize each child's development, as well as that of the pair's relationship, through the experience of structured interpersonal interaction. For Holly and Jessica, and for Mitchell and Arnie during most of their first year in pair therapy, their individual pasts pervaded their interactions but were neither commented nor reflected upon. When Mitchell and Arnie's interaction moved to Level 2, their relationship history began to be referenced occasionally but their individual histories remained subterranean. However, as children in pair therapy show competence at the higher levels, making connections between the past and the present takes on greater importance, and they begin to bring it up themselves. Indeed, the themes of sharing and understanding the past, present, and future are central to the Level 2 to 3 transition, as we saw in Brenda and Donna's pair therapy in chapter 10.

Though we recognize and try to understand the pervasive influence of earlier development (and the lack thereof) on the children's present relating in pair therapy, we rarely work with it (e.g., make interpretations in the analytic sense of linking historically determined current and recurrent feelings to early recall and reconstruction or, more common in child psychotherapy, to ongoing family relationships). Instead, we interpret the children's conflictual interactions within the sessions at a slightly higher developmental level to help the children reflect on their current way of relating. By linking higher-level understanding to lower-level action, the therapist reframes how the pair understands their interaction to make higher-level perspectives on self and other, and new alternative solutions available to them. Recall how the pair therapist in chapter 7 helped Andy and Paul work out a solution when they wanted to play kickball in the gym but found others already playing there. When the boys construed the situation without regard to the needs and feelings of anyone else, with an indignant Andy wanting to unilaterally seize the gym and a helpless Paul telling him to shut up, the therapist used linking tactics to encourage alternative strategies for defining their wants and dealing with others in more mature ways: "Wait a second, guys. Maybe we have some other options." "Oh, I see. You want to go right ahead and play. No more discussion." "I think the ball would go down there and it could hit them or get in their way." "It seems that Paul would rather not try to deal with them [the other occupants of the gym] directly."

Note that the pair therapist's techniques differ from those of the individual therapist in that what is clarified, interpreted, and worked through are *not* resistances against relating manifest in the transference with the therapist. Instead of focusing on the relationship between the adult and either member of the pair, the pair therapist focuses on the relationship between the two children. The children's approaches to conflict between each other can be demonstrated to have a certain unwanted effect and clarified precisely because they typically do not apply the highest-level interpersonal understanding that they have achieved to resolve the conflict.

For example, Mitchell's pair therapist might point out to him, "You seem to be ordering Arnie around a lot today." Then he could clarify—"You seem to be angry at Arnie. Why?" In this way the therapist encourages reflection on the mode of ongoing interaction between the pair, insight *that* children have a feeling or are acting a certain way. Insight about *why* the children have a feeling that may lead them to act a certain way can then more easily follow. It is the more immediate rather than distal, unconscious source of Mitchell's feeling that is clarified—what it is about the current interaction that makes him angry or who exactly he is angry at, rather than what was so depriving in past relationships that makes him vulnerable to such anger.

Often, disruptive affect is brought into pair therapy by one or both of the children. Troubled children lead troubled lives, and outside relationships and events, particularly those in the child's family, easily spill into the pair context. When this happens, as when anger is produced within the session, the short-term goal of the therapist is to get the child to identify and recognize his or her feelings in preparation for the longer-term goal of being able to identify what or whom is upsetting. Only occasionally, if the level of trust is high enough, the therapist may *broach* the latter subject (e.g., "You seem to be upset, but I haven't seen anything that's gone on here that seems so upsetting. I sense there is something else going on."). But the pair therapist would probably go no further than this on personal issues (and then it's up to the child to bring in the outside pain if he or she chooses).

Usually a pair therapist does not try to initiate a search for causal connections between the interpersonal present of the pair and the personal past and extra-pairs present of both members because he or she cannot put one of the pair on hold while exploring sensitive subjects with the other one. However, the triad holds an evocative power and safeness not found in one-to-one therapy between an adult and a child that enables, in its best and most therapeutic moments, the sharing of deep pain between the two children. We saw this in Brenda and Donna's disclosures of their respective hospitalizations and Andy and Paul's anguished loneliness and frustration at the unavailability of fathers who work nights and overtime, and a mother who was perceived not to care. Perhaps the most moving example of this unique potential in pairs was when one early adolescent girl disclosed her father's sexual abuse to her pair-mate, who in turn then found the courage to reveal her own experience of sexual abuse to a trusted teacher for the first time. (Neither the school staff nor each girl's individual therapist were aware of both girls' abuse when they were matched for pairs.)

Revelation in a triadic structure often feels safer than in a dyad. In each case, these pairs courageously risked the airing of deep concerns and fears, and admitted a rarely exposed vulnerability, exhibiting their highest but rarely used self-reflective capacities in the sharing of new levels of openness, intimacy, and support. This remarkable sharing reminds us of the power of "chumship" in promoting interpersonal development. As Sullivan (1953) noted:

All of you who have children are sure that your children love you; when you say that, you are expressing a pleasant illusion. But if you will look very closely at one of your children when he finally finds a chum—somewhere between eight-and-a-half and ten—you will discover something very different in the relationship—namely, that your child begins to develop a real sensitivity to what matters to another person. And this is not in the sense of "what should I do to get what I want," but instead "what should I do to contribute to the happiness or to support the prestige and feeling of worthwhileness of my chum." So far as I have ever been able to discover, nothing remotely like this appears before the age of, say, eight-and-a-half, and sometimes it appears decidedly later. [pp. 245–46]

Not only does our model of interpersonal development provide the developmental goal of moving the pair's interaction to a higher level, it provides the therapist with a guide to tailor his interpretive efforts to the developmental level of each child. Empowering, linking, and enabling actions represent "one level up" interpretations for children at Levels 0, 1, and 2, respectively. We link the children's reflection on the relation between ongoing feelings and the mode of their interactions not only by reframing interpersonal conflict at "one level up" but by offering "one level up" alternative solutions. Thus the pair therapist sometimes plays an explicitly educative and proactive role quite contrary to the analytic neutrality of traditional psychotherapy. Both the reframing of the identified problem and posing of alternatives at one level higher are basic interpretive mechanisms for closing interpersonal understanding/action gaps in pair therapy.

At different developmental levels, the therapist's interpretations differ in the extent to which they aim to engender insight or new levels of action. Empowering ("You can tell a friend you don't like them to grab") is inherently more action-based, whereas linking ("How can you two work together to solve this problem?") and, especially, enabling ("How does the idea of leaving this school and ending pairs make you feel?") make greater use of the children's insightfulness.

Across the phases of pair therapy there is a shifting balance between relationship- and insight-building, the two aspects of the therapeutic process. In the first phases, the corrective interpersonal experience aspect predominates as the initial triadic relationship forms. In the restructuring phase the therapist's more active interpretive activities—empowering, linking, and enabling—

facilitate a transition to the next developmental level. During consolidation both the corrective interpersonal experience and
reflection on it contribute relatively equally as the children learn to
first have insights into their mode of action, then insight into why
they are acting so, and then, ultimately, insight into how to act
differently.

However, insight without implementation is worth little, especially for children, who are less clearly motivated than adults to
form a therapeutic alliance. Children typically lack insight into the
fact that they have problems and rarely refer themselves for treatment (Shirk, 1988). Adults, in contrast, are self-motivated, and
those who seek treatment often struggle to find the courage to put
therapeutic insights into action. Indeed much of the "real work" of
adult individual therapy is done outside the sessions.

This translation of insight into action, implicit in the values we
hold, is facilitated by the triadic system, in which "real" interaction
is interpreted. In psychotherapy with children, especially young
children, the developmental limits of social-cognition interact with
their psychological problems to compound the complexity of treatment (Shirk, 1988). Clearly, children's conduct in psychotherapy is
mediated by their social-cognitive capacities. Although limitations
in children's cognitive development dictate a widely acknowledged
necessity for an experiential focus in their treatment, therapeutic
change for children no less than adults entails a reorganization of
meaning and the development of self-understanding. From a developmental perspective new patterns of relating are so fragile for
children that they must be strengthened in a therapeutic "holding
environment." This is why the consolidation phase of pair therapy,
analogous to—but going far beyond—classical "working through,"
requires a balance between the therapist's supporting and interpreting activities.

Psychological growth is often conceived of as a process of internalization (Meissner, 1981). Blatt and Behrends (1987), for
example, describe psychological growth as internalization in a
constantly evolving process of separation-individuation in an os-
cillation between union and separation. Therapeutic change
involves first the establishment of a "gratifying involvement," in
which gratification is provided in an appropriate form and at an
appropriate developmental level, enabling the person to function
with a degree of coherence and integrity that would not otherwise
be possible. The inevitable disruption of the relationship in "experienced incompatibilities" (Klein, 1976) then results in internalization of the lost functions of the relationship if (and only if) the

frustration is *optimal* (not too great). The major form of experienced incompatibility in a therapeutic context are the therapist's
interpretations. Thus psychological growth is viewed as occurring
when an established relationship with a more developmentally advanced person (e.g., the therapist) is disrupted (e.g., interpreted),
and the lost regulatory function of the therapist is internalized.

The process of psychological growth Blatt and Behrends describe
in individual psychotherapy works somewhat differently in pair
therapy. In the therapeutic process of pair therapy a "gratifying involvement" is set up between all three participants. The relationship between the two children forms at a higher level than would
have been possible without the therapist's regulatory involvement.
Then in the restructuring the therapist disrupts the triadic system
by "letting go" the form of his or her involvement (at lower levels,
control; at higher levels, support) with "one level up" tactics that
reframe the interpersonal context and pose alternative actions, enabling the children to internalize aspects of the adult's regulatory
function in a more autonomous and intimate peer relationship.
The corrective interpersonal experience in the beginning sets up a
pattern of object relating (selves-in-relationship) between the two
children that is then interpreted and becomes the mechanism
through which their defenses are reorganized. This is in contrast
to individual therapy in which it is the defenses (resistances) that
are usually more directly interpreted.

Shared positive experiences help the children build the ability to
participate in conflict-resolution processes with perspective and
without regression to less mature defensive postures. One aim of
pair therapy is to help children help themselves deal with conflictual feelings, to actively transform them so that they can feel in
control rather than having their feelings, recognized or not, control
them. One way to do this is to create an atmosphere in which the
locus and cause of negative or painful feelings associated with the
inevitable conflicts of dyadic relations can be accurately identified
and expressed, and then worked through and dealt with in the context of a continuing relationship.

For example, in the Level 1 to 2 transition, for the therapist to
establish a context wherein, if one child gives up an activity for the
sake of the other at one point in time, he or she can have the
positive experience of having his or her choice respected the next
time, is no mean feat, as simplistic as it sounds, particularly when
it is being established for children who have seldom if ever before
experienced this degree of stability and fairness. These seemingly
small, undramatic fairnesses that allow children to experience a

CHAPTER TWELVE

The Ethics of Mutual Collaboration

It is common to expect children, up to and even beyond age 11 or 12, to invoke the principle of fairness when often what is really at stake is not so much fairness but desires and feelings ("It's not fair that my brother stays up later than me." "It's not fair that I do the dishes because my sister has homework."). These misapplications of principles of fairness can be traced partly to certain natural conceptual limitations, such as the case of younger siblings who demand strict *equality* of treatment with older ones around issues of bedtime or allowance. At this age of concreteness, with its relatively objective notions of affect, complex notions of *equity* are simply conceptually beyond reach. Just as often, however, the difficulty can be traced to the lack of differentiation (and hence, integration) between the affective and cognitive aspects of social interaction, particularly the confusion, natural to some degree at this age, around the concept of fairness and the experience of (thwarted) desires or strong feelings. It is not necessarily "not fair" that an older sibling gets a larger allowance, but it certainly— and understandably—"feels bad." To be most (or equally) important to or most liked by someone else is not an issue that can be reduced to fairness. One cannot completely, if at all, make feelings of commitment logical, even though commitment, once articulated, entails basic principles of sincerity and reciprocity.

Or to consider another example, when one member of a pair has a previous engagement at the dentist causing the cancellation of a pair therapy session, although the dry-docked member may very well yell foul/unfair, the issue is not one of fairness—the cancellation rule is clear—but of feelings. The "jilted" pair member feels rejected or angry at the pair partner for disappointing him or her. These are all reasonable (in the sense of understandable) feelings, but technically the situation is not *unfair*. As parents, educators, or clinicians, we try to correct such logical confusion in a young child. But the continued confusion of feelings and fairness becomes a greater problem in later life when the social logic of fairness and the emotional logic of the way feelings work are expected to be better discriminated and coordinated. We all have either witnessed or enacted countless instances of situations in which the fair thing to do feels bad or frightening (so it often isn't done) and others in which it feels good or crucial to do what, if we think about it, is unfair (and so often it is done). Ethical development in a person is strongly tied to how these kinds of common conflicts are resolved, within the self and between the self and the other.

In the domain of ethical development, the idea of *felt understanding* is meant to speak to the integration of the intellectual understanding of fairness (e.g., negotiation), and the emotional power of feelings (e.g., shared experience, unfulfilled expectations, or strong conflictual emotions). Ethical development, to our way of thinking, requires more than just understanding on the one hand, or feelings on the other. It requires the capacity for *felt understanding*, emotional understanding in action, a differentiation and integration of the logical and affective aspects of an interpersonal conflict.

The more people can act as collaborative selves, the more they have the capacity for a higher level of autonomy and intimacy (and the integration of the cognitive with the affective), then the more they are likely to act in ways that are fair to both self and others, and thus to act maturely from an ethical as well as an interpersonal perspective. In one sense, we are saying that interpersonal maturity and ethical maturity are the same thing, at least when ethical behavior is considered to be the everyday respect for the self and others. But what we are really stressing is that consistent, holistic ethical behavior cannot be derived from social experiences using only the logical aspects of fairness as a means. Such a sense of fairness is inauthentic in the sense that it does not involve the whole actor. A complete ethical sense can be developed only in an individual in whom the positive affective and cognitive aspects of interpersonal development are integrated.

We hypothesize that the groundwork for that to happen requires not just the opportunity to resolve negative or problematic conflicts, but also positive shared experiences, either natural or "corrective," with others. Metaphorically, these positive shared experiences—with parents, peers, mentors, lovers—are like the charging of a battery, so that when the energy must be drawn to resolve conflict, it will be there. Reciprocally, as these conflicts are resolved successfully, they create new contexts for positive interpersonal experiences. Unresolved or poorly resolved conflicts, in contrast, continue to draw on the energy charge without replenishing it. The battery-charging metaphor applies over time in the developing individual as well, fueling the child intellectually and emotionally for growth to more mature interpersonal levels.

The Role of Values in the Attempt to Foster Interpersonal Collaboration

Throughout this book, in our articulation of the theoretical foundations of our model of interpersonal development (based as it is on the developing capacity to coordinate social perspectives), in our empirical and anecdotal descriptions of strategies for interpersonal negotiation (organized according to levels and orientations), in our consideration of forms of shared experience that facilitate closeness and intimacy (moving from a contagious kind of impulsivity toward mutually shared reflection), and in our clinical work with pairs of children and young adolescents whose capacity for deepened, stabilized, meaningful social relationships has been thwarted, truncated, limited, or impaired (for whatever reasons), we have suggested that when interpersonal development occurs, it is characterized by a dialectical movement through the interaction of the processes of autonomy and connection toward mutuality and collaboration.

Interpersonal collaboration based on the capacity for mutual coordination of social perspectives, as defined in this work, begins to reach its reco ;nizable form in preadolescence and early adolescence, when it requires hands-on practice to be strengthened. But the development of collaborative abilities and inclinations, once initiated, is a lifelong process. The wisdom of a collaborative attitude deepens as it is applied to the different tasks of human experience: to close friendships, marriage, raising children, close and collaborative work relationships, functioning as part of a couple or friendship across life's vicissitudes, including even separation or death.

As we have gleaned from research interspersed with everyday observation, collaborative abilities, even once developed, are by no means universally employed (nor need they be in all cases). The implementation of collaborative action is particularly vulnerable when people are under stress, stress based on the complexities of external life as well as the complexities of internal or interpersonal dynamics. But ultimately a collaborative attitude needs to be based on more than a psychosocial ability, it needs to be a free choice, a commitment.

We obviously value collaboration. We prescribe movement in this general direction in our clinical practice (e.g., for couples in long-term relationships as well as for children in pair therapy) as well as in our theoretical model. Still, we assert that not all interpersonal interaction *ought* to be at the collaborative level. This assertion requires that we sort out the prescription of this capacity (its value) from the description of its natural development and function. In other words, the articulation of collaborative action as some attainable goal or natural achievement, some telos in a developmental scheme, requires that we sort out the philosophical and moral stance of the researcher/clinician who advocates it from his or her scientific/therapeutic activity, describing or facilitating it. This clarification is necessary not because the stance and the activity are unrelated (in fact they are very much related), but because the two stances, the descriptive and the prescriptive, first need to be differentiated in order to be ultimately integrated.

Perhaps a good place to start this attempted clarification, this differentiation and integration, is with the joint empirical/theoretical suggestion that in dyadic interactions between individuals who have an ongoing relationship with one another, complex and balanced interactions between them are what we mean by collaborative relatability. Here the concept of collaboration encompasses the capacity for autonomy, self-reflection, and self/other differentiation on the one hand, and intimacy, the ability to consider the self as part of an ongoing relationship and to coordinate one's own goals with that of the significant other in mutual contexts, on the other.

But the trip over the bridge from theoretical formulation and empirical description to ethical prescription—that is, from the description of a developmental sequence or hierarchy leading toward collaboration as a capacity to the belief that interpersonal relationships should be collaborative, as we define it—is perilous indeed. That there is evidence that the capacity for framing contexts for interpersonal relating in collaborative terms follows in a developmental sequence on the heels of the framing of these interpersonal contexts in impulsive, unilateral, or reciprocal terms is not cause for asserting that all interpersonal interactions *should* be collaborative.

Instead, we take the position that *a call for* collaboration as a way of acting or a lifelong attitude is a basic value. Distinct from its empirical associations, it is a philosophical and ethical stance about what ultimately constitutes good or "ideal" interpersonal relationship processes. We believe that mature individuals invested in long-term mutual relationships will function better, both autonomously and intimately, if they define their individual needs and the needs of the dyad in terms of each other. Thus we claim that to define all needs in a relationship only individualistically—or only dually—is not functional (developmentally mature) for the relationship or for the individual in the long run, nor is it ethically mature for either party or the system.

Of course, research has a place in the clarification of questions of value, just as reflections on our values help to define the enterprise of research or clinical interventions in which we choose to engage. As an obvious example of an issue of value, whatever one values, it makes little sense to prescribe expectations of fully mutually collaborative behavior, as we have defined it, for a pair of five-year-old playmates who have neither the cognitive or emotional capacity for it. With respect to interventions, our strong belief in the value of collaboration as a critical ingredient of mature interpersonal relationships certainly has motivated us to develop the treatment of pair therapy as a means to foster this capacity. A developmental approach, starting as it does from the origins of a psychological process, from the beginning and working its way up, is one way of understanding the mature functioning of that process.

But research activity and philosophical assumptions are connected in less obvious ways as well. When we begin to focus on what constitutes mature forms of mutual collaboration—collaboration in intimate, long-term adult dyadic relationships, such as in a marriage—the need for the fullest integration of scientific and value analyses becomes more obvious. For instance, to see the dyad rather than the individual as the basic unit in close relationships is both a scientific assumption and a value presupposition. How does one (or is it two?) collaborate around decisions as seemingly mundane (at least on the surface, even if not at a symbolic level) as where to go on vacation, or as obviously basic as whether or not to have children or how to manage them? Are these decisions negotiable? Can they be made mutually? What does a collaborative process look like in friendships or couples who have lived and loved, felt and fought together, for twenty or thirty years? Answers to these questions require a constant interplay between empirical/descriptive and philosophical/ethical analyses.

One of the implications of our research is that it is inherent in the nature of the collaborative level of interpersonal development that each party take *action*, usually in the form of the transformation of initial goals or the redirection of energy and effort, to find a common ground with one's partner. This is the collaborative process in action, but more goes into it than that. An individual (or is it the dyad?) needs to decide, in the form of making a commitment, whether he, she, or they actually want(s) (or are able) to put energy to that purpose, energy that may be taken away from something else. The introduction of this term—commitment—reintroduces the idea of "will," the intentional or conative component of our model (see chapter 2), to be integrated with the affective and cognitive aspects that have been the focus of this final review. But the concept of commitment as a significant theme in research indicates a move toward the study of maturity in interpersonal relationships, of adults in their intimate interactions with one another, their social institutions, and their children. This is a topic that needs a forum of its own, not a tag-on to research focused on the problems of troubled children and the transitions to adolescence. Perhaps this is the road down which our research is heading.

We feel, even at this late juncture, that we ought to address, if only briefly, a very different cultural connotation or association of the term "collaboration." There is a use of the term in which the "collaborator" has often been seen as the evil turncoat or betrayer, the one who "collaborates" with the enemy. Perhaps a particularly salient example in recent memory is those French nationals who willingly worked with the Nazi German occupiers of France. Although this is still a powerful connotation in culture, perpetuated in countless postwar films and novels, the distinction between this notion and our use of the term is obvious. Collaborators in World War II were making a political, philosophical, and pragmatic choice "to collaborate," in the specific sense of "to work with" or to "go along with." This is obviously different from and independent of the "level" at which any given individual did so or our notion of collaboration. It is clearly a semantic distinction, though an important one.

However, beyond semantics, this subject raises another far more interesting idea. Is there such a phenomenon as collaborative thinking or behavior, in our sense of the word, that could be identified in, for example, the perpetrators of the Holocaust, those tried at Nuremberg? Can there be mutual (Level 3) perspective coordination applied in action that is not informed by prosocial values? The moral development (or lack thereof) of the perpetrators of evil on a grand scale is a topic far beyond and only tangential to the scope of this book. We will simply share one speculative train of thought.

Certainly in any powerful and successful group or social institution there will be numerous individuals who have achieved a (Level 3) third-person understanding and who can and do perform at Level 3 in social interactions. When these same people espouse and act upon values that are anathema to all cultures, can they be said to be behaving collaboratively in our sense of social interaction in which the needs of others or the relationship are felt and acted upon as being as important as one's own? Two answers suggest themselves. One is that the behavior is consciously false, insincere, and contrived, an assumption of the cloak of principled collaboration consciously manipulated to produce, in the case of the Holocaust, much lower-level ends. Alternatively, an individual or group of individuals could truly believe in the "rightness" of such actions.

In either case, we would make the following interpretation. Although Level 3 perspective coordination has been achieved, in terms of social-cognitive structures, something has gone profoundly awry in the corresponding affective social-experiential development. Truly psycho-pathological and sociopathological distortions of the ability to perceive and acknowledge in understanding and affect the humanness and being-ness of others has crystalized such that no genuine notion of respect for others can be integrated into the personality or its actions. This cut-off-ness from one's own link to humanity, from seeing the mutuality of how one's self is mirrored in and partakes of countless other selves can be expressed either in insincere manipulation coming from advanced cognitive capacity in the presence of atrophied socio-affective development or in both cognitive and socio-affective arrest. It can be seen not only in the massive cultural and political evils human history has witnessed, but also in smaller but no less deadly examples such as organized crime, street gang culture, schoolyard bullies, or the lone sniper who climbs a rooftop and massacres a neighborhood.

One powerful motivation for our research and therapy with some of the more disturbed children with whom we work is that we identify—without, we fear, being alarmist—the possibility that some children will "grow up" demonstrating adequate third-person perspective but profound deficits in socio-affective development that not only will deprive them of basic potential and fulfillment but also will render them capable of committing sociopathic or even violent acts. It is in this concern that our own value-bias, as clinicians and researchers, becomes most clear and explicit.

What Are the Prospects for Fostering Interpersonal Collaboration?

The prospects for fostering mutual collaboration are often viewed with cynicism (e.g., Sullivan, 1953). Although we acknowledge it is not easy to attain a collaborative attitude at a personal level in a world in which it appears to be so sadly lacking on an institutional level, we are cautiously optimistic about attempts to do so. The seeds of this optimism are planted in our ideas about human motivation, that aspect of our personality that causes us to act as we do. Like many others, we reject the early Freudian view that instincts alone motivate human behavior, and instead believe (like Sullivan, in particular) that human behavior and thought are primarily motivated by the pursuit of satisfactions and the maintenance of security. The interaction of security and satisfaction needs becomes elaborated into increasingly complex interpersonal needs, or motivational systems, as persons mature. The most powerful of these motivations, which lead us toward or away from others, is the need for balancing the processes of autonomy and intimacy in collaboration with at least one other person.

Sullivan (1940) notes that, circumstances not interfering, people live with the past, the present, and the neighboring future all clearly relevant in explaining their thought and action, but it is the influence of the near future (e.g., anticipations and expectations) that particularly distinguishes and determines human action. The patterns of motivation that get established in personality—and thus how interpersonal needs get transformed into action—depend on how much we act with foresight, the anticipation of the future, rather than with anxiety. When action is effectively satisfying, needs are differentiated, and foresight develops as the action is identified with both explanatory elements of the past and foreseen relief of emerging anxiety.

Foresight is disrupted by the disintegrating tendencies that the experience of anxiety calls out in particular interpersonal situations. In anxiety, there is no lever to begin the differentiation of needs because it is hard to get beyond the experience of anxiety derived from past dynamics to interpret present instances of it more adequately. With too much anxiety, foresight is transformed from a goal for action to a warning that calls out conservative defenses rather than constructive actions. Thus, intense anxiety interferes with progressive human action because it diminishes foresight and limits our choice of action appropriate to the needs we experience.

Not only is foresight, or the lack thereof, central in motivation, it is also relevant to therapeutic conceptions: people get better to the extent that they are able to develop adequate foresight. Events that alter people's anticipation of the future in interpersonal relationships either open up, or close, possibilities for further development of the personality and for mental health. In terms of our model of interpersonal development, Sullivan's ideas suggest that interpersonal collaboration will be fostered—and gaps between the interpersonal thought and action will be eliminated—to the extent that foresight replaces anxiety in people's interpersonal action.

These ideas also help us understand the course of the differentiation of feelings and fairness in children growing up. Since Freud, it has been commonly understood that one's interpersonal present is interpenetrated by one's interpersonal past. The past was an unbalanced time in which the logic of interpersonal security was by definition illogical. For the self's needs to be unmet meant by (low-level) developmental definition that the other was not caring about the self. All infants, experiencing life from moment to moment, feel abandoned or rejected at moments, whether or not they are. In fact, as mentioned earlier, it is small doses of frustration or "experienced incompatibilities" in established gratifying relationships that result in internalization and individuation in psychological growth (Blatt and Behrends, 1987). The reality of the natural developmental residue of illogical feelings of abandonment and rejection requires that we differentiate feelings from fairness, and recognize that our origins are in a past where feelings are not of necessity logical or fair, and that in the present we may be anxious, or insecure, even if the "reality" says there is no "real" need to be.

Biological needs regularly come and go but security needs must be constantly renegotiated at each new level of interpersonal development. The more secure one feels about the affection another has for one's self, the more equilibrated one is with oneself, and the more one seeks out others who are balanced in their own equilibration, resulting in an interactive spiral upward, a mobile equilibrium. There can also be a spiral downward if the self is not in balance with itself, because then it is less likely to attract on a long-term basis someone else who is balanced, and so the interpersonal system, the dyad, operates with more anxiety than foresight.

The human capacity to plan and think about the self and the other in the future comes relatively late, starting in preadolescence. But even once achieved this capacity is not by itself sufficient for collaborative action: more than just thinking about the "social" future, we must *feel* secure in future plans with our significant others. To *feel the future* we must integrate the logic of our present and past ways of achieving security and satisfaction. The reason Freud was pessimistic about human development is that he compared the self's satisfaction needs with what the society can yield to him or her, rather than recognizing the differentiation and integration of satisfactions (needs, instincts, drives) and securities (relationships) as a *developmental* task of the individual to be achieved not alone but in conjunction with specified significant others. A focus on the individual alone or on the individual's biological needs juxtaposed with societal constraints cannot illuminate by itself the problem of how to get along with others. To place the individual between biology and culture is to define a problem whose only resolution is compromise and pessimism. A focus on the intensely interpersonal nature of human needs, however, suggests we can work out our needs in collaboration rather than only in competition with others, achieving a *meaningful* compromise between persons rather than an uncomfortable compromise between biology and culture. Joint parenting work is a salient example of the need for a constant mobile equilibrium, a constant renegotiation between the adults in the best interests of the children as well as of the separate selves of the adult couple.

An interpersonal theory, whose basic unit is the interaction between members of the dyad, highlights the psychological potential of sharing and negotiating objective needs and subjective wants, and the philosophical value of achieving equilibrium by treating both self and others with respect. Our pair therapy treatment, which provides a context for two troubled children to begin to negotiate needs in a mutual, shared context, and thus with a freedom not possible in their past, is one attempt to develop interpersonal maturity and foresight, the *feeling* of the future. From our work thus far, we believe that the prospects for the child's quest for collaboration are promising if we adults value and attempt to foster it.

Conclusion to a Start

Ideas, theories, and programs of research, like people, nations, musical styles, and other organismic processes, are born, have an infancy, grow up (sometimes too rapidly), if lucky, have a relatively stable period to enjoy the perquisites of maturity, and then start their inevitable decline. If these programs of research prove to be useful, even as they fade they form the nutrients for later developing sets of ideas, theories, or proposals.

Scientific principles provide us with one set of tools or guidelines with which to evaluate where on this growth curve a particular approach stands. But it is up to the researchers working on the approach to decide when it is reasonable for the "coming out" of the ideas and data upon which they have been working. This is not always an easy or clear-cut decision. There are many audiences to consider, and each has its own particular criteria of when a public presentation, such as the one in this book, is warranted. One sign for the workers that a pulling together of ideas and evidence is ready for presentation is the feeling of being on some plateau—a place to pause before resuming the scientific journey, a place from which to look back to where one has been, and to look forward to where one thinks one ought to or wants to or is able to go. Although we feel there is quite a distance still to travel on the present journey, we hope it has been worthwhile for the reader to take the time to read this report to date. The effort to pause and pull together our evolving thoughts about interpersonal behavior and development has been worthwhile for us. We now see more clearly what needs to be done.

We believe that a developmental perspective on social conduct provides a unique but not exclusive perspective, a different and distinct way to hear and see some of the meaning embedded in the complex processes of interpersonal interaction. The model we have provided is broad and fluid enough to provide a number of variations and interpretations, and to augment or enrich other perspectives. It is also at a point of maturity where the future detail and precision work associated with empirical validation will be of great value. Our hope is that among our readers, there will be those who find enough interest and value in these proposals to integrate their own perspectives with ours and begin to undertake alongside us the further research necessary to connect with these ideas, propositions, and models, and thereby foster intellectual, affective, and philosophical collaboration in the larger scientific and humanistic community of which we are all a part.

References

Abrahami, A., Selman, R. L., and Stone, C. (1981) A developmental assessment of children's verbal strategies for social action resolution. *Journal of Applied Developmental Psychology,* 1981, *2,* 145–63.

Adalbjarnardottir, S., and Selman, R. L. (1989) How children propose to deal with the criticism of their teacher and classmates: Developmental and stylistic variations. *Child Development, 60,* 539–50.

Alexander, F., and French, T. M. (1946) *Psychoanalytic therapy.* New York: Ronald Press.

American Psychiatric Association. (1980) *Diagnostic and statistical manual of mental disorders* (3d ed.). Washington, D.C.: APA.

Baldwin, J. M. (1902) *Social and ethical interpretations in mental development; A study in social psychology.* New York: Macmillan.

Barrett, B. (1983) Preliminary notes on the epistemology of psychoanalytic transformation. *Psychoanalysis and Contemporary Thought, 6,* 483–508.

Bateson, G. (1972) *Steps to an ecology of mind.* New York: Ballantine.

Beardslee, W. R., Schultz, L. H., and Selman, R. L. (1987) Interpersonal negotiation strategies, adaptive functioning, and DSM-III diagnoses in adolescent offspring of parents with affective disorders: Implications for the development of mutuality in relationships. *Developmental Psychology, 23,* 807–15.

Bender, B. (1976) Duo-therapy: A method of casework treatment of children. *Child Welfare, 55,* 95–108.

Birnbaum, M. (1975) Peer-pair psychotherapy: A new approach to withdrawn children. *Journal of Clinical Child Psychology, 4,* 13–16.

Blatt, S. J. (1974) Levels of object representation in anaclitic and introjective depression. *The Psychoanalytic Study of the Child, 29,* 107–57. New Haven: Yale University Press.

Blatt, S. J., and Behrends, R. S. (1987) Internalization, separation-individuation, and the nature of therapeutic action. *International Journal of Psychoanalysis, 68,* 279–97.

Blatt, S. J., and Shichman, S. (1983) Two primary configurations of psychopathology. *Psychoanalysis and contemporary thought, 6,* 187–254.

Bowlby, J. (1988) *A secure base: Parent-child attachment and healthy human development.* New York: Basic Books.

341

Brenner, J., and Mueller, E. (1982) Shared meaning in boy toddler's peer relations. *Child Development, 53,* 380–91.

Bretherton, I. (1987) New perspectives on attachment relations: Security, communication, and internal working models. In J. D. Osofsky, ed., *Handbook of infant development* (2d ed., pp. 1061–1100). New York: Wiley.

Brion-Meisels, S., and Selman, R. L. (1984) Early adolescent development of new interpersonal strategies: Understanding and intervention. *School Psychology Review, 13,* 278–91.

Bronfenbrenner, U. (1979) *The ecology of human development: Experiments by nature and design.* Cambridge, Mass.: Harvard University Press.

Chandler, M. J. (1973) Egocentrism and anti-social behavior: The assessment and training of social perspective-taking skills. *Developmental Psychology, 9,* 326–32.

Cooley, C. H. (1902) *Human nature and the social order.* New York: Scribner.

Damon, W. (1977) *The social world of the child.* San Francisco: Jossey-Bass.

Dodge, K. A. (1980) Social cognition and children's aggressive behavior. *Child Development, 51,* 162–70.

Eckensberger, L. H., and Meacham, J. A. (1984) The essentials of action theory: A framework for discussion. *Human Development, 27,* 166–72.

Erikson, E. (1963) *Childhood and society.* New York: Norton.

———. (1964) Clinical observation of play disruption in young children. In M. Haworth, ed., *Child psychotherapy* (pp. 264–76). New York: Basic Books.

———. (1968) *Identity, youth and crisis.* New York: Norton.

Fairbairn, W. R. D. (1952) *An object relations theory of the personality.* New York: Basic Books.

———. (1957) *Psychoanalytic studies of the personality.* Boston: Routledge and Kegan Paul.

Flavell, J. H., Abrahans, B., Croft, K., and Flavell, E. R. (1981) Young children's knowledge about visual perception: Further evidence for the level 1–level 2 distinction. *Developmental Psychology, 17,* 99–103.

Fleischer, L. (1989) Intrapsychic process, interpersonal reasoning, and the development of mutuality in preadolescent friendship. Ed.D. diss., Harvard University.

Freud, A. (1936) *The ego and the mechanisms of defense.* New York: International Universities Press.

Freud, S. (1915) Observations on transference love (Further recommendations on the technique of psychoanalysis III). *Standard Edition, 12.*

Fuller, J. S. (1977a) Duo-therapy: A potential treatment of choice for latency children. *Journal of American Academy of Child Psychiatry, 26,* 469–77.

————. (1977b) Duo-therapy case studies: Processes and techniques. *Social Casework, 58,* 84–91.

Gedo, J., and Goldberg, A. (1973) *Models of the mind: A psychoanalytic theory.* Chicago: University of Chicago Press.

Gergen, K. J. (1985) The social constructionist movement in modern psychology. *American Psychologist, 40,* 266–75.

Gergen, K. J., and Gergen, M. M. (1982) Explaining human conduct: Form and function. In P. F. Secord, ed., *Explaining human behavior: Consciousness, human action and social structure* (pp. 127–54). Beverly Hills, Calif.: Sage.

Gilligan, C. (1982) *In a different voice: Psychological theory and women's development.* Cambridge, Mass.: Harvard University Press.

Gottman, J. M. (1983) How children become friends. *Society for Research in Child Development Monograph, 48*(3), 1–86.

Greenberg, J. R., and Mitchell, S. A. (1983) *Object relations in psychoanalytic theory.* Cambridge, Mass.: Harvard University Press.

Griffin, P. and Cole, M. (1984) Current activity for the future: The zo-ped. In B. Rogoff and J. V. Wertsch, eds., Children's learning in the "Zone of Proximal Development." *New directions for child development,* (no. 23, pp. 45–64). San Francisco: Jossey-Bass, 1982.

Grotevant, H. D., and Cooper, C. R. (1986) Individuation in family relationships: A perspective on individual differences in the development of identity and role-taking in adolescence. *Human Development, 29,* 82–100.

Gurucharri, C., Phelps, E., and Selman, R. L. (1984) The development of interpersonal understanding: A longitudinal-comparative study of normal and disturbed youths. *Journal of Clinical and Consulting Psychology, 52,* 26–36.

Haan, N. (1977) *Coping and defending: Processes of self-environment organization.* New York: Academic Press.

Hartmann, H. (1964) Notes on the reality principle (1956). In *Essays on ego psychology: Selected problems in psychoanalytic theory.* New York: International Universities Press.

Hinde, R. (1979) *Toward understanding relationships.* London: Academic Press.

Horney, K. (1939) *New ways in psychoanalysis.* New York: Norton.

Jacobson, E. (1971) *Depression.* New York: International Universities Press.

Jaquette, D. S. (1980) A case study of social-cognitive development in a naturalistic setting. In R. L. Selman, *The growth of interpersonal understanding: Developmental and clinical analyses* (pp. 215–41). New York: Academic Press.

Kegan, R. (1982) *The evolving self: Problem and process in human development.* Cambridge, Mass.: Harvard University Press.

Kernberg, O. (1975) *Borderline conditions and pathological narcissism.* New York: Aronson.

————. (1976) *Object relations theory and clinical psychoanalysis.* New York: Aronson.

Klein, G. S. (1976) *Psychoanalytic theory: An explanation of essentials.* New York: International Universities Press.

Klein, M. (1975) *Love, guilt and reparation & other works 1921–1945.* New York: Delta.

Kohlberg, L. (1969) Stage and sequence: The cognitive-developmental approach to socialization. In D. Goslin, ed., *Handbook of socialization theory and research* (pp. 347–480). Chicago: Rand McNally.

————. (1973) The claim to moral adequacy of a highest stage of moral judgment. *Journal of Philosophy, 7.*

Kohut, H. (1977) *The restoration of the self.* New York: International Universities Press.

Lerner, H. D., and Lerner, P. M. (1982) A comparative study of defensive structure in neurotic, borderline, and schizophrenic patients. *Psychoanalysis and Contemporary Thought, 5*(1), 77–115.

Loevinger, J. (1976) *Ego development: Conceptions and theories.* San Francisco: Jossey-Bass.

Lyman, D. R., and Selman, R. L. (1985) Peer conflict in pair therapy: Clinical and developmental analyses. In M. W. Berkowitz, ed., *Peer conflict and psychological growth.* New Directions for Child Development (no. 29, pp. 85–102). San Francisco: Jossey-Bass.

Mead, G. H. (1934) *Mind, self, and society.* Chicago: University of Chicago Press.

Meissner, W. W. (1981) *Internalization of psychoanalysis.* New York: International Universities Press.

Mishler, E. G. (1979) Meaning in context: Is there any other kind? *Harvard Educational Review, 49*(1), 1–19.

Mitchell, C. A. (1976) Duo-therapy: An innovative approach to the treatment of children. *Smith College Studies in Social Work, 45*(3), 236–47.

Modell, A. H. (1984) *Psychoanalysis in a new context.* New York: International Universities Press.

Mueller, E., and Lucas, T. (1975). A developmental analysis of peer interaction among toddlers. In M. Lewis and L. A. Rosenblum, eds., *Friendship and peer relations.* New York: Wiley.

Noam, G. G. (1988) The theory of biography and transformation: Foundation for clinical-developmental therapy (pp. 273–317). In S. R. Shirk, ed., *Cognitive development and child psychotherapy.* New York: Plenum.

Packer, M. (1985) Hermeneutic inquiry in the study of human conduct. *American Psychologist, 40,* 1081–93.

Piaget, J. (1954) *The construction of reality in the child.* New York: Basic Books (original work published 1937).

————. (1965) *The moral judgment of the child* (M. Gabain, trans.). New York: Free Press (original work published 1932).

Pine, F. (1985) *Developmental theory and clinical practice.* New Haven: Yale University Press.

Pitcher, E. G., and Schultz, L. H. (1983) *Boys and girls at play: The development of sex roles.* New York: Praeger.

Rapaport, D. (1967) The scientific methodology of psychoanalysis (1954). In M. M. Gill, ed., *The collected papers of David Rapaport* (pp. 165–220). New York: Basic Books.

Rutter, M., and Garmezy, N. (1983) Developmental psychopathology. In E. M. Hetherington, ed., *Handbook of child psychology,* vol. 4: *Socialization, personality, and social development* (pp. 775–911). New York: Wiley.

Scarr, S. (1985) Constructing psychology: Making facts and fables for our times. *American Psychologist, 40,* 499–512.

Schafer, R. (1983) *The analytic attitude.* New York: Basic Books.

Schank, R. C., and Abelson, R. P. (1977) *Scripts, plans, goals, and understanding.* Hillsdale, N.J.: Erlbaum.

Schultz, L. H., and Selman, R. L. (1989) Bridging the gap between interpersonal thought and action in early adolescence: The role of psychodynamic processes. *Development and Psychopathology, 1,* 133–52.

Selman, R. L. (1976) Toward a structural-developmental analysis of interpersonal relationship concepts: Research with normal and disturbed preadolescent boys. In A. Pick, ed., *Tenth annual Minnesota symposium on child psychology* (pp. 156–200). Minneapolis: University of Minnesota Press.

———. (1980) *The growth of interpersonal understanding: Developmental and clinical analyses.* New York: Academic Press.

———. (1981) The development of interpersonal competence: The role of understanding in conduct. *Developmental Review, 1,* 401–22.

———. (1989) Fostering intimacy and autonomy. In W. Damon, ed., *Child development today and tomorrow* (pp. 409–35). San Francisco: Jossey-Bass.

Selman, R. L., and Arboleda, C. (1986) Pair therapy with two troubled early adolescents. *McLean Hospital Journal, 10*(2), 84–111.

Selman, R. L., Beardslee, W. R., Schultz, L. H., Krupa, M., and Podorefsky, D. (1986) Assessing adolescent interpersonal negotiation strategies: Toward the integration of structural and functional models. *Developmental Psychology, 22,* 450–59.

Selman, R. L., and Demorest, A. (1984) Observing troubled children's interpersonal negotiation strategies: Implications for a developmental model. *Child Development, 55,* 288–304.

Selman, R. L., and Glidden, M. (1987) Negotiation strategies for youth. *School Safety,* Fall, 18–21.

Selman, R. L., Lavin, D., and Brion-Meisels, S. (1982) Troubled children's use of self-reflection. In F. Serafica, ed., *Social cognition in context* (pp. 62–99). New York: Guilford.

Selman, R. L., Schorin, M. Z., Stone, C., and Phelps, E. (1983) A naturalistic study of children's social understanding. *Developmental Psychology, 19,* 82–102.

Selman, R. L., and Schultz, L. H. (1988) Interpersonal thought and action in the case of a trouble early adolescent: Toward a developmental model of the gap. In S. Shirk, ed., *Cognitive development and child psychotherapy* (pp. 207–46). New York: Plenum.

Selman, R. L., and Yeates, K. O. (1987) Childhood social regulation of intimacy and autonomy: A developmental-constructionist perspective. In W. M. Kurtines and J. L. Gewirtz, eds., *Moral development through social interaction* (pp. 43–101). New York: Wiley.

Shantz, C. U. (1983) Social cognition. In P. H. Mussen, J. H. Flavell, and E. M. Markman, eds., *Handbook of child psychology*, vol. 3, *Cognitive development* (pp. 495–555). New York: Wiley.

———. (1987) Conflicts between children. *Child Development, 58,* 283–305.

Shirk, S. R. (1988) Introduction: A cognitive-developmental perspective on child psychotherapy (pp. 1–16). In S. R. Shirk, ed., *Cognitive development and child psychotherapy.* New York: Plenum.

Sroufe, L. A., and Fleeson, J. (1986) Attachment and the construction of relationships. In W. W. Hartup and Z. Rubin, eds., *Relationships and development* (pp. 51–72). Hillsdale, N.J.: Erlbaum.

Stern, D. (1985). *The interpersonal world of the infant: a view from psychoanalysis and developmental psychology.* New York: Basic Books.

Stone, L. (1981) Some thoughts on the "here and now" in psychoanalytic technique and process. *Psychoanalytic Quarterly, 50,* 709–33.

Strachey, J. (1934) The nature of the therapeutic action of psychoanalysis. *International Journal of Psychoanalysis, 15,* 127–59.

Sullivan, H. S. (1940) *Conceptions of modern psychiatry.* New York: Norton.

———. (1953) *The interpersonal theory of psychiatry.* New York: Norton.

Trevarthan, C. (1980) The foundations of intersubjectivity: Development of interpersonal and cooperative understanding in infants. In D. R. Olson, ed., *The social foundation of language and thought: Essays in honor of Jerome Bruner.* New York: Norton.

Turiel, E. (1983) *The development and social knowledge, morality, and convention.* Cambridge: Cambridge University Press.

Urist, J. (1977) The Rorschach test and the assessment of object relations. *Journal of Personality Assessment, 41,* 3–9.

Vaillant, G. E. (1977) *Adaptation to life.* Boston: Little, Brown.

———. (1986) Introduction: A brief history of empirical assessment of defense mechanisms. In G. E. Vaillant, ed., *Empirical studies of ego mechanisms of defense.* Washington, D.C.: American Psychiatric Press.

Vygotsky, L. S. (1978) *Mind in society: The development of higher psychological processes.* Cambridge, Mass.: Harvard University Press.

Walker, L. J., de Vries, B., and Trevethan, S. D. (1987) Moral stages and moral orientations in real-life and hypothetical dilemmas. *Child Development, 58,* 842–58.

Werner, H. (1948) *The comparative psychology of mental development.* New York: International Universities Press.

———. (1957) The concept of development from a comparative and organismic point of view. In D. B. Harris, ed., *The concept of development:*

An issue in the study of human behavior (pp. 125–48). Minneapolis: University of Minnesota Press.

White, K. M., Speisman, J. C., and Costos, D. (1983) Young adults and their parents: From individuation to mutuality. In H. D. Grotevant and C. R. Cooper, eds., *Adolescent development in the family.* New Directions for Child Development, no. 22. San Francisco: Jossey-Bass.

Winnicott, D. W. (1971) *Playing and reality.* New York: Basic Books.

Yeates, K. O., and Selman, R. L. (1989) Social competence in the schools: Toward an integrative developmental model for intervention. *Developmental Review, 9,* 64–100.

Zetzel, E. (1956) Current concepts of transference. *International Journal of Psycho-Analysis, 37,* 369–76.

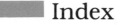 Index